D1279958

DATE DUE

	SEP 30 1994		

DEMCO NO. 38-298

POLITICS AND NATIONALIST
AWAKENING IN SOUTH INDIA
1852–1891

MONOGRAPHS OF THE ASSOCIATION FOR ASIAN STUDIES

Published by and available from: The University of Arizona Press
Box 3398, Tucson, Arizona 85722

The Association for Asian Studies: Monographs and Papers, No. XXVII

Edgar Wickberg, *Editor*

POLITICS AND NATIONALIST AWAKENING IN SOUTH INDIA, 1852-1891

R. Suntharalingam

Published for the Association for Asian Studies by
THE UNIVERSITY OF ARIZONA PRESS
Tucson, Arizona

About the Author . . .

R. SUNTHARALINGAM focused his Ph.D. research in South Indian history on the areas of social change resulting from the imposition of colonial rule. As a doctoral candidate in the School of Oriental and African Studies, University of London, he explored new social groups at some length in the hope of providing a comprehensive account of how this part of the South Asian subcontinent was brought to the threshold of nationalism. At the conclusion of his investigations, the author joined the history faculty at the University of Singapore, advancing to the position of senior lecturer.

Publication of this volume has been made possible by a generous grant to The Association for Asian Studies by the Ford Foundation

THE UNIVERSITY OF ARIZONA PRESS

ISBN-0-8165-0447-4 cloth
ISBN-0-8165-0468-7 paper
L. C. No. 73-93408

In Memory of My Father
and
To My Mother

Contents

TABLES

MAPS

CHART

ABBREVIATIONS

ARGMU   Annual Report from the Governors of Madras
         University

GOI   Government of India

GOM   Government of Madras

IHP   India Home Proceedings

JPP   Judicial and Public Proceedings

MEP   Madras Educational Proceedings

MJP   Madras Judicial Proceedings

MLP   Madras Legislative Proceedings

MNA   Madras Native Association

MNNR   Madras Native Newspaper Reports

MPP   Madras Public Proceedings

MRP   Madras Revenue Proceedings

PPHC   Parliamentary Papers House of Commons

PPHL   Parliamentary Papers House of Lords

PSC   Public Service Commission

RAMP   Report on the Administration of the Madras
         Presidency

RINC   Report of the Indian National Congress

RPIMP   Report on Public Instruction in the Madras
         Presidency

Preface

This book is an interpretive account of the origins of nationalism in South India during the second half of the nineteenth century. While recent historical studies have done much to enrich our understanding of the early and formative phases of Indian nationalism, especially in illuminating the events which led to the founding of the Indian National Congress, there is still considerable ignorance about South India's involvement in what is without doubt one of the most important chapters in the recent history of the subcontinent. Studies devoted exclusively to nationalist beginnings in the Madras Presidency are entirely absent; those which have an all-India focus have, by and large, glossed over the role of this province and to an extent created the impression that this part of the subcontinent was a political backwater, contributing little to the rising nationalist tide in the country. Even Anil Seal's otherwise excellent study on *The Emergence of Indian Nationalism* (Cambridge, 1968) has not quite effaced this impression. Although Seal sets out with the intention of exploring the role of Bengal, Bombay, and Madras presidencies in the birth of the Congress, the very paucity of material that is eventually presented on Madras does less than justice to this Presidency's part in the grand drama that he unfolds with such lucidity and liveliness. In this study, I hope to provide a more comprehensive portrayal of the way in which the southern Presidency was brought to the threshold of nationalist politics during the late nineteenth century.

While the rise of nationalism is the principal theme that runs through this work, I have borne in mind the fact that this movement in South India was preceded by demands for political and civil rights some decades earlier. Attention has been given to these earlier manifestations of political activity, although in so doing I have limited the scope of my inquiry to those movements which operated within what has been termed "the language of modern politics." In South India, experiments with modern forms of political activity began on an organized scale with the establishment of the Madras Native Association in 1852. The founders of this body did not see themselves as nationalists explicitly asserting the rights of a subject people: their concern was with specific political and economic grievances stemming from British policies and actions in South India. Nonetheless, these early activities can be seen as the gentle murmurs of protest which were to culminate later in the more overt formulation of Indian nationalism. This transition towards nationalism became manifest with the formation of voluntary associations in South India and elsewhere during the 1880s. It was these associations which first spoke the language of nationalism, formulated demands on behalf of the Indian people, and emphasized the dichotomy of interests between the alien rulers and the subject peoples. Equally important, these associations took the decisive step of creating an all-India organization.

In this study the changing patterns of political life in South India have been viewed primarily in terms of the new social groups which the Western impact brought into existence. British colonial rule, through innovations in the economic, educational, and administrative sectors of society, created the conditions for the rise of new groups. The importance of such groups lay as much in their

ability to establish claims for leadership in their
societies as in the sophisticated political methods
they employed in challenging the policies and assumptions on which the British Raj functioned in
India. I have focused attention on the formation
of these new groups in an effort to elicit a deeper
understanding of the dynamics of nationalism in
South India.

I have delineated three new elites which
played a seminal role in the political and social
movements of South India during the period under
study: the Hindu commercial elite, with its locale
at Madras, which was dominant during the 1850s and
expressed its power through the Madras Native Association; the administrative elite, recruited from
the products of the Madras High School, which spearheaded social reform movements during the 1860s and
after; and the professional elite, composed mainly
of lawyers, journalists, and teachers, which asserted its political influence during the 1880s by
establishing the Madras Mahajana Sabha and assuming
virtual control of the Congress organization in the
Presidency. The origins of these elites, their
political orientations, and their relationship with
the British rulers have been depicted in some detail. It is shown that each elite had its own perception of the needs and aspirations of its society,
and this perception conditioned, in turn, its demands and methods of political action. In the case
of the professional elite, it is obvious that its
position outside the British Indian administration
had invested it with enough independence to embark
upon nationalist ventures. As it is the activities
of this elite which bear directly on South India's
enrolment in the Congress, I have dwelt at some
length on the precise mechanisms that it employed
to build up links at provincial and all-India
levels.

A word of explanation about the concept of
elite. In my usage of this concept I have been
guided by the following definition of T. B. Botto-
more: "The term 'elite(s)' is now generally applied,

in fact, to functional, mainly occupational, groups which have high status (for whatever reason) in a society" (*Elites and Society*, London, 1964, p. 8). In this study of South Indian politics, I have perceived elite formation in functional terms. Looked at in this sense, there are not one but several elites. The three elites that I have identified are in effect occupational categories. Some may argue that two of these elites, namely, the administrative and professional, should be regarded as part of a single elite because of their common social and educational origins. Though this argument has some force, I believe that their occupational differences should be accorded recognition because it is this fact which was crucial in socializing these elites and conditioning their respective orientations. To some extent the generational difference reinforced the cleavages that developed between the two. It is also worth noting that prominent members of these elites saw themselves as belonging to different groups, endowed with different qualities, and playing different roles.

Some readers may be puzzled that this work has so little to say about the role of caste or language in nationalist politics in South India. Admittedly, such primary solidarities were important in regulating social and economic behavior. In this study it was found that responses to the Western impact varied from caste to caste and from region to region. These differing responses in turn affected elite formation, with certain castes and certain linguistic groups more numerously represented than others. Having said as much, it must be conceded that neither caste nor language became effective vehicles for political mobilization during the period under study. In fact, caste associations and linguistic movements were twentieth-century phenomena, and their rise has to be attributed to the failure of the professional elite to resolve tensions generated by the uneven rate of the Western impact in South India. It is beyond

the scope of this book to probe into these aspects
of South India politics.

This work is based almost entirely on primary
source material--notably, newspapers, records of
political organizations, and official records. Of
the newspapers consulted, the *Hindu* provided the
best insights into political developments in South
India. However, some of its early files are mis-
sing, and I have tried to fill such gaps by drawing
generously on the other newspapers published in
Madras, especially the *Madras Times, Madras Mail,
Madras Standard,* and *Athenaeum and Daily News.* The
records of political organizations relevant to this
study are not as complete as one might wish.
Though most of the petitions and published reports
of the Madras Native Association, Madras Mahajana
Sabha, and Madras Standing Congress Committee have
been traced, the unpublished minutes and proceedings of these bodies have not survived. More dis-
heartening have been attempts to locate the private
papers of the Indian personalities who feature
prominently in these pages. In my three trips to
India, inquiries among families of these leaders
only yielded press clippings, speeches, tracts, and
photographs. In cases where some correspondence
has survived, like the Kesava Pillay, Krishnaswamy
Iyer, and V. S. Srinivasa Sastri papers, such
materials deal with events beyond the scope of this
work. Government records, both published and unpublished, have been extensively used, partly to
gauge official reactions to political movements and
partly to collate statistical data concerning the
growth of liberal and professional education.
Tamil material, however, makes up only a small part
of the total reference data used in this work.
While some biographical works in Tamil exist, pamphlets touching on the political events in the
nineteenth century are scarce. However, I have
tried to make good this deficiency by utilizing the
*Reports on Native Newspapers in the Madras Presi-
dency,* a weekly digest of news and comments from
the various regional language newspapers published

in South India. This source is an invaluable guide
to understanding the political mind of literate
groups largely untouched by Western learning.

This study was originally conceived as a Ph.D.
dissertation for the School of Oriental and African
Studies, University of London. I owe a large debt
of gratitude to my supervisor Professor H. R.
Tinker, currently of the Institute of Commonwealth
Studies, who not only suggested the subject but
also guided me through the various stages of research and writing. His advice, unfailing courtesy,
and encouragement will always be warmly remembered.
I must also express my considerable intellectual
debt to Dr. R. S. Mehrotra whose influence on this
work is not easily expressed in words. It is rare
these days to find within the ranks of the professional historians a scholar so willing and eager to
share his knowledge of the subject. I also wish to
thank Professor R. E. Frykenberg of the University
of Wisconsin and Professor E. Thio of the University of Singapore for kindly reading sections of
this work and giving me their frank comments.
Though it is not possible to list here my numerous
friends in India who have assisted me in various
ways, I must single out for mention Mr. Emmanuel
Divien and Mr. V. Subrahmanyan, both of whom have
so readily and ungrudgingly responded to my calls
for help.

Special thanks are due to the various librar-
ies, institutions of higher learning, and foundations without whose help this study could hardly
have been completed. In India, I enjoyed access to
the *Hindu* library, the Madras Mahajana Sabha
Library, the Madras Record Office, the National
Archives of India, and the Nehru Memorial Museum
and Library. In England, I worked mainly in the
India Office Library, the British Museum, and the
Church Missionary Society library. To the librar-
ians and staff of these institutions I remain
deeply grateful. I must also thank the following
bodies for financing my research: the United Kingdom Commonwealth Scholarship Commission for

supporting me as a research scholar during the years 1963-66; the Lee Foundation, Singapore, for meeting part of my travel expenses to India in 1967; and the University of Singapore whose generous study-leave facilities enabled me to spend long spells in India and England in the pursuit of research and writing.

It remains for me to acknowledge my appreciation to Miss Irene Ee for typing the various drafts of this manuscript with patience and care. Finally, I am grateful to Professor E. Wickberg, editor of the Monographs Series of the Association for Asian Studies, for all the assistance he has given me in preparing this work for publication, and the University of Arizona Press for effecting publication.

R. Suntharalingam

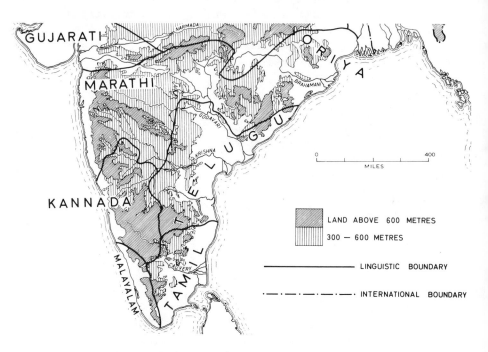

South India: Physical structure and linguistic divisions

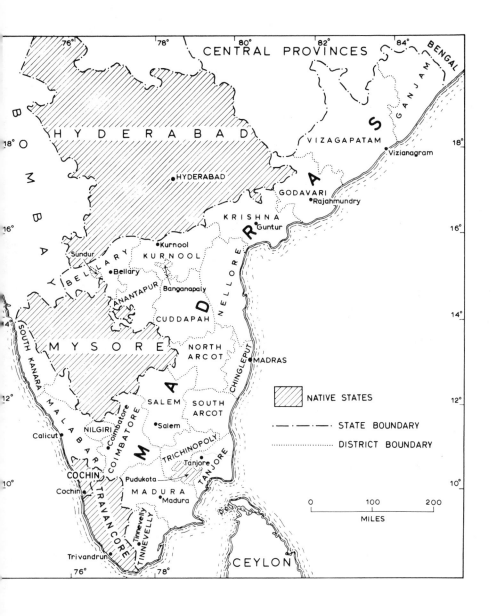

South India: Indian states and districts of Madras Presidency, 1886

Introduction

The part of India that lies to the south of
the Vindhya mountains embraces an area of considerable environmental complexity. In its physical
structure, it has been described as "a vast shield
area, comparable in a host of ways to the Lauren-
tian Shield of North America."[1] Its landscape is
dominated by the two major mountain systems called
the Western and Eastern Ghats. The Western Ghats,
extending from Tapti valley to Cape Comorin in the
deep south, consist of a steep and rugged mass of
hills clothed by some of the heaviest forests found
in the entire subcontinent. Enclosed between the
Western Ghats and the Arabian Sea is a narrow
coastal tract which constitutes the core of the
Kerala region and the littoral part of the Kannada
country. The Eastern Ghats, by comparison, are of
much lower elevation and are breached at a number
of points by the great rivers of South India, especially the Godavary, Krishna, and Kaveri. It is
precisely at these points that the coastal plain
attains its greatest width, forming delta basins
which have always been the most fertile and popu-
lous areas of South India. While the delta basins
of the Godavary and Krishna formed the center for
traditional Telugu culture, the Kaveri delta and
the littoral plain to the north constituted the

- 1 -

nucleus of the ancient Tamil civilization. Situated between the coastal plains on either side of the peninsula is the Deccan, a rolling plateau country studded with hills and intersected by narrow valleys.[2]

The regions of South India derive their unity from linguistic and historical evolution. Kerala is, perhaps, the most distinctive of the regions of peninsular India. Lying in the extreme southwest corner of the subcontinent, Kerala owed its identity to language: Malayalam. This language evolved from a slow fusion of Tamil and Sanskritic elements, occurring simultaneously with the Aryan cultural penetration into the region. A distinct Malayalam alphabet came into existence about the eleventh century, and, subsequently, a rich literature developed as well. The growth of an autonomous literary tradition was in some measure encouraged by Kerala's physical separation from the eastern regions of the peninsula, a separation imposed by the towering peaks of the western Ghats. Though this isolation was never absolute, there were nonetheless severe restrictions on the free movement of peoples and ideas. Cultural contacts remained minimal, and Kerala was largely insulated from the political encroachments of ambitious powers based on the eastern regions. In fact, for more than a millennium the people of Kerala were left free to develop and nurture an ethos all their own, the uniqueness of which was reflected in their caste and matrilineal arrangements.

However, the rigors of landward isolation were mitigated to some extent by Kerala's exposure to maritime influences. With its deep and sheltered harbors, Kerala had long been the focal point of traders from distant parts of the world. Arabs, Greeks, Romans, and Persians had frequented these ports since the beginnings of the Christian era, and their demands had popularized such crops as pepper and spices. Indeed, it was these products which brought Vasco da Gama to Kerala in 1498, thereby inaugurating the era of Western imperialism

which was eventually to engulf much of Asia and
Africa. The impact of the maritime influence was
not confined to trade and politics alone. It also
introduced new religious elements which gave
Kerala's population a distinctively polyglot character. Among the important non-Hindu communities
found in this region are Muslims, Syrian Christians,
Catholics, and Protestants, who together constituted almost two-fifths of Kerala's population by
the 1960s.[3]

Tamilnadu, Kerala's eastern neighbor, derived
its unity as much from its historical past as from
its present language. In the development of
Tamilnadu's history, literature, and sacred traditions, it is possible to discern some of the processes of Tamil regionalism functioning as far back
as the beginnings of the Christian era. By A.D.
third century, during the Sangam period, this extreme, southeastern corner of the Indian subcontinent had come to inherit an advanced Tamil culture
when society had broken away from its tribal
moorings, when monarchial rule became the prevalent
form of government, when academies were founded to
promote Tamil literature and the arts, and when
Tamil language was becoming the standardized medium
of communication among a people lacking political
or geographical unity. In subsequent centuries,
although Tamil language came to feel the impact of
Sanskrit and many Sanskrit words entered the language, it did not surrender its autonomy in structure, script, or speech patterns. What occurred in
the sphere of language was true of other aspects of
Tamil cultural life. Though there was selective
borrowing and adaptation from a variegated Aryan
culture, the Tamils continued to retain much of
their regional myths and symbols.[4]

Tamilnadu, however, had always concealed important internal contrasts which stemmed mainly from
physical and climatic factors. The basic contrast
was between the dry interior plateau country and
the wet coastal plain. The former, bounded by the
districts of Salem and Coimbatore, is a rainshadow

area where neither the southwest nor the northeast
monsoon is able to penetrate. The nature of the
terrain and the low rainfall ruled out wet rice
cultivation in this area. Emphasis was on dry
grains, especially millet, which was the staple
food. The coastal plain, embracing the districts
of Chingelput, North Arcot, South Arcot, Trichinopoly, Tanjore, Madura, and Tinnevelly, was on the
whole better endowed in terms of soil fertility
and rainfall. Wet rice cultivation here was sup-
plemented with cash crops like indigo, cotton,
sugarcane, and groundnuts. Not surprisingly, the
bulk of Tamilnadu's inhabitants lived in this
favored coastal tract, notably, in the Kaveri
delta, where fertile alluvial soils and elaborate
irrigational works had long permitted intensive
cultivation.[5]

Andhra, the land of the Telugus, is the third
linguistic region of importance in South India.
It is territorially more extensive than the neighboring regions and embraces both the coastal plain
stretching from Nellore to Ganjam as well as the
large tracts of interior plateau country containing the districts of Cuddapah, Kurnool, Anantapur,
and the eastern parts of Hyderabad State. Despite
these environmental differences, the existence of
a single written script has given a sense of unity
to the entire region. Telugu language is without
doubt Dravidian in origin, although in the course
of its evolution it was heavily impregnated by
Sanskritic elements. In all probability, the language originated in the deltaic basins of the
Godavary and Krishna and from here it was carried
into the interior plateau country by migrating,
cultivating castes in search of arable land. In
the fourteenth century, when Vijayanagar reigned
politically supreme over much of the peninsula,
Telugu literature enjoyed its golden age under
royal patronage. Since then, Telugu language became an important focus of community identification, overriding differences caused by physical
and economic phenomena.[6]

Although regional contrasts loom large in any
discussion of the ecology and linguistic traditions
of South India, it must, nonetheless, be recognized
that there are countervailing forces contributing
towards the unity of the peninsula. In a real
sense, unity and diversity are overlapping categories whose interplay, according to Selig Harrison,
"is the grand pattern of Indian history."[7] The
elements of unity in South India are to be traced
principally to Hinduism and its social institution,
the caste system, both of which have posited a
common body of religious and social values that
have transcended geographical and linguistic boun-
daries.

Hinduism is so perplexingly amorphous, if
pluralistic, that writers despair in their efforts
to describe it. "No religion," writes Drekmeier,
"is more protean, more resistant to description."[8]
Evidence of its pluralistic nature might be found
in its heterodox doctrines, its complex rites and
practices, and its belief in many paths to salva-
tion.

One aspect of Hindu pluralism is manifested in
its sectarian groupings. In South India, the principal Hindu sects were the Vaishnavites and
Saivites, the former predominant in Andhra and the
latter in Tamilnadu and Kerala. These sects had in
turn splintered into numerous, smaller groupings.
The Vaishnavites, for instance, were divided into
a number of schools, of which the most important
were the Sri Vaishnavas and Madhvas.

Though there were differences in ceremony and
doctrine between these two subsects, they, nonetheless, sprang from a single, great, devotional movement which began to sweep the Indian subcontinent
after the eighth century A.D. Originating in
Tamilnadu and drawing inspiration from numerous
saints and such Dravidian Vaishnavite theologians
as Ramanuja and Madhva, the devotional movement demanded a total surrender to God, denied the importance of rituals, mitigated some of the harsh
inequalities of the caste system, and invested

Hinduism with a framework of organization modelled
on Buddhism. Its long-term significance lay as
much in stimulating religious enthusiasm among the
masses through preaching in the regional languages
as in enlisting recognition among the rival sectarian orders of the essential unity of Hinduism.[9]

Although the influences which shaped the devotional movement were largely Vaishnavite, the
contribution of Saivism should not be underestimated. Among the various Saivite groups in South
India, that which was least affected by the bhakti
movement was the Smartha sect, the followers of the
monistic teachings of Sankaracharya. A Nambudiri
Brahmin from Kerala, Sankaracharya was among the
earliest to recognize the importance of the devotional school and in fact had reputedly composed
devotional poems in Sanskrit. His major achievement, however, was his exposition of the Vedanta,
which he produced by reworking the contradictory
doctrines contained in the Upanishads.[10] Sankaracharya's intellectual rigorousness and brilliance
won admiration among Brahmins who saw in the
Vedanta a philosophical system superior to anything
that rival Hindu schools could offer. Preoccupation with logic and philosophical speculation,
however, evoked little enthusiasm among the non-
Brahmin Saivites who found in Saiva Siddhanta and
Vira Saivism a more congenial home. Both these
sects had enriched the quality of the devotional
movement in South India, especially by their concern with developing the spiritual and ethical aspects of religion. They denied the importance
attached to rituals and caste distinctions, disowned polytheism, and advocated the true love of
the Supreme God, Siva. Vira Saivism, however, carried the revolt against the sacerdotal tradition
much further by questioning the sanctity of the
Vedas and challenging the primacy of the Brahmins
in the ritual order. That Vira Saivism was frankly
anti-Brahmin cannot be seriously doubted, and this
view is confirmed by the fact that it found a re-
ceptive hearing principally among the non-Brahmin

cultivating and trading castes of the Kannada region.[11]

It is not intended to suggest that sectarian groupings in South India were essentially a function of underlying social conflicts generated by the caste system. Little conclusive evidence is forthcoming to suggest such an assertion. Nonetheless, it is a characteristic of Hindu society that sectarian groupings, to some extent, developed along fissures created by caste. That this is not entirely fortuitous is suggested by the wide disparities that existed in status, roles, and wealth between the elite Brahmin castes and the rest of Hindu society.

Hindu society in South India, despite linguistic and sectarian cleavages, shared one feature, namely, that the ritually dominant group everywhere was drawn from the Brahmin caste. Richard Temple, writing in 1882, asserted that: in Bengal, Brahmin influence was moderated by the trading and literary castes; in the North-Western Provinces by the Rajputs and Muslims; and in Bombay, by the Parsis and Jains; in Maharashtra and South India, Brahmin influence was absolute, with the other castes in a position of almost total subservience.[12] A recent study on Maharashtra by Kumar affirms the validity of Temple's remark. Kumar depicts Chitpavan Brahmins exercising decisive influence over the other castes through their control of "the significant concentrations of power in society, namely, the institutions of religion, the administration and the ownership of land."[13]

In South India, the influence of the Brahmins was no less decisive. Despite their division into a number of endogamous groups, which were unevenly distributed over the peninsula, the Brahmins asserted their supremacy on account of their high ritual status, their ownership of land, and their control of some of the key administrative positions in rural society. In the Andhra region, for example, the most important groups were the Niyogi Brahmins, settled predominantly in the Northern

Circars. Through occupation of the best arable
land in the area and their exclusive control of
the key position of the *karnam* (village accountant),
the Niyogis were able to sustain their power over
many centuries during which they provided continu-
ous local leadership in the Northern Circars.[14] In
Tamilnadu, the Smartha and Sri Vaishnava Brahmins
enjoyed a comparable status, especially along the
coastal tracts and in localities where the great
Hindu temples were situated. In particular, they
were important in the Kaveri delta, which had been
the recipient of successive waves of Brahmin colo-
nists of different regional extraction, including,
Telugu, Desastha, Konkanese, Gujerati, and Kanarese.
The most numerous were the Tamil Brahmins, divided
into three categories: the Vedic Brahmins, domestic
priests, and temple priests. The Vedic Brahmins
enjoyed the highest status and they were drawn exclusively from Smarthas and Sri Vaishnavas. Traditionally associated with learning and cultural
activities, the Vedic Brahmins sustained themselves
from revenues of landed endowments granted by
ruling princes and other Hindu patrons.[15] In
Kerala, the Nambudiri Brahmins formed the dominant
caste, having an unchallenged primacy in the
ritual, literary, and economic life of the region.
Believed to be the descendants of the Aryan set-
tlers who colonized Kerala during the early centuries of the Christian era, the Nambudiris owed
their influence as much to their retention of Aryan
cultural traditions as to their economic independence vis-a-vis other social groups.[16]

The fact that the Brahmins were the dominant
and privileged elite of South India did not earn
them immunity from certain social constraints imposed by the caste system. One constraint which
distinguished them from the rest of Hindu society
was their abstention from any kind of manual work.
Ritual taboos, while allowing Brahmins to own land
and, indeed, conferring high prestige for it, pro-
scribed them from cultivating the lands themselves.
As a consequence, their lands were leased out to

non-Brahmin tenants or cultivated by hired laborers
belonging to the Harijan castes. Prohibitions
against involvement in trade and business were less
severe, although Brahmins who turned to such vocations were heartily despised by their fellow brethren and relegated to an inferior social position.
In view of these social constraints, Brahmins without landed property or assured priestly incomes
increasingly turned to secular vocations, especially in the service of the state.

The stereotype of the Brahmin engrossed in
the pursuit of knowledge and living in seclusion
from the secular world and its temptations is so
far removed from reality that it has often obscured
the real bases of Brahmin power in South India.
Among the earliest European writers to gain an
accurate insight into the true sources of Brahmin
influence was a French missionary, Abbe Dubois,
whose study, *Hindu Manners, Customs and Ceremonies,*
made its appearance in the early years of the nineteenth century. While highlighting the importance
of religion and land as sources of Brahmin affluence, Dubois also explains how this caste group had
successfully infiltrated the key positions in the
princely states of South India. According to
Dubois, the Brahmins' "main object, upon which they
expend the greatest ingenuity, [was] to gain access
to the courts of princes or other people of high
rank." Once they had secured a foothold, Brahmins
quickly gained the confidence of their masters and
maneuvred themselves into "the best and most lucrative posts" from where they proceeded to enrich
themselves "by carrying on unchecked a system of
injustice, fraud, dishonesty, and oppression."
Even Muslim and European rulers, argues Dubois,
were almost totally dependent upon Brahmins to run
their administration.[17]

While Dubois pinpoints some of the essential
qualities which elevated the Brahmins so far above
the rest of Hindu society, he has not sufficiently
emphasized their role in providing coherence and
stability to Hindu society. As guardians of the

Hindu tradition, the Brahmin elite not only formulated a moral and social code to regulate the behavior of society as a whole but also ensured that that code was stringently observed. In the latter task, the Brahmins drew upon the support of the various caste assemblies, which debated questions relating to social propriety and punished those who departed from the accepted rules of conduct. It was a system in which no group, irrespective of its position in the caste hierarchy, ever challenged the major premises which ordered the overall social framework. This consensus can largely be attributed to the pervasive influence of the idea of karma which stressed that individual character was determined by actions of earlier lives of the soul, and that improvement in status could only be achieved through diligent performance of ritual obligations. Hence, Hinduism and the caste system provided a body of common beliefs and values which offset the lack of a single literary tradition or a unified political system in South India.

EARLY BRITISH RULE IN SOUTH INDIA

Although Western imperialism reached India's shores as early as 1498, it was not until three centuries later that British colonial rule was established over large parts of South India. The elimination of the French threat, the annihilation of the power of Mysore, and the appropriation of the territories of Hyderabad, Tanjore, and Arcot left the British politically dominant in the peninsula, exercising direct authority over much of Tamilnadu and Andhra, as well as the Malayalam-speaking district of Malabar and the Kannada-speaking district of South Kanara, all of which came to form the so-called Madras Presidency.

The imposition of British rule in South India had been preceded by an era of considerable political turmoil and violence which can only be explained in terms of the fragmented nature of

political power in the peninsula and the perennial
ambitions of the competing regional states to dominate each other. As the eighteenth century drew to
a close, sieges and battles raged in an ever-
rising crescendo, bringing in their wake chaos and
devastation unprecedented even in the war-torn
history of South India. The regions worst affected
were Tamilnadu and Andhra. In Tamilnadu, the rule
of Mysore and Arcot was characterized by instability, imposition of illegal levies, forced labor,
and the consequent impoverishment of the rural community. The situation in the coastal Andhra districts was little different. While the area became
a focal point of power conflicts after 1748, its
inhabitants were left to the mercy of grasping rent
collectors, local chieftains, and *zamindars*. In
the interior Andhra districts, conditions were decidedly worse. Here the impact of over a century
of incessant wars led to widespread depredation,
banditry, and depopulation of certain villages.
Despairing of ever finding protection from a central power, the inhabitants of this area armed
themselves and lived in fortified settlements where
they could withstand assaults by neighboring
chieftains and marauding gangs.[18]
     The change from Indian to British rule symbol-
ized, among other things, a change from anarchy to
order. It was as if the long decades of chaos and
depredation were arrested at one blow, and in their
place emerged the security and stability of the
British Raj. Though this is a gross oversimplifi-
cation of what actually occurred, this generaliza-
tion has a grain of truth insofar as British
intervention in South India eventually ended the
destructive interstate conflicts of the preceding
centuries. However, the more important heritage of
the new regime was the creation of a centralized
state authority where the decision-making process
was rationalized, administrative procedures system-
atized, the machinery of public accounting and
revenue collecting perfected, and uniform and im-
personal law replaced customary rules.

One result of the change of regimes in South
India was the virtual destruction of the traditional political elite. The absolute monarchy disappeared from view, except in the rump principali-
ties of Mysore, Hyderabad, Travancore, and Cochin,
where the elite continued to rule, albeit shorn of
much of its sovereign power. Also affected were
the motley array of lesser chieftains, hill rulers,
and revenue collectors who had assumed the mantle
of sovereignty when the authority of the regional
powers began to wane. In Rayalu Simas, for instance, local chieftains called *poligars* had carved
out autonomous fiefs which they ruled with the aid
of armed retainers. When this area passed under
British control in 1800, there were no less than
eighty *poligar* chieftains and 30,000 retainers exercising sway over the region. Though many of
these chieftains were finally destroyed, some of
them were, nonetheless, turned into a peaceful,
law-abiding class of landlords or *zamindars* through
coercion and monetary inducements.[19] Elsewhere in
South India, a broadly identical policy was pursued. Local chieftains were invariably recognized
as *zamindars* of their fiefs so long as they acknowledged allegiance to the British Raj and paid a
fixed annual assessment on their estates.

The establishment of a class of *zamindars,*
notwithstanding the early tensions that developed
between central authority and localizing forces,
answered a real British need in enlisting the support of powerful elite groups in South India.
Though the numerical strength of this class of
rentiers was very small--there were only 869
zamindari families in the Madras Presidency in
1891-2--their potential strength could be gauged
from the fact that they controlled a quarter of
the territorial area of this far-flung province.[20]
Indeed, so large was the size of some of these
zamindaries, notably, Vizianagram, Venkatagiri,
Ramnad, Shivagunga, and Pittapuram, that they came
to be regarded as minor, political kingdoms with
considerable manpower and financial resources.

However, as the nineteenth century wore on, these *zamindars* regarded themselves less and less as independent rulers capable of challenging the British Raj and increasingly became one of its bulwarks, even believing that their position depended upon the continued existence of the Raj.

A distinguishing characteristic of this class of landed aristocrats was their innate conservatism. They were strongly attached to their traditional beliefs, participated in all religious rites and festivities, and patronized cultural activities. Western education was by and large ignored, except in a few conspicuous instances. William Logan's description of "the Malabar Rajahs and nobility" in 1875 applied with equal force to the landed aristocracy of South India as a whole: "Wrapped up in the narrow exclusiveness of their family mansions, their intelligence has had no field for its exercise except in the management of the internal affairs of the family, and has therefore gone to sleep, or, turned in on itself, has wasted its energies in interminable disputes which, in some instances, have wrecked the prosperity of the families."[21] Without enlightenment and self-discipline, the landed aristocracy of South India failed to live up to its ascribed rule as "the natural leaders of the people," and instead squandered its energies and wealth on luxury, litigation, and hankering for official titles and honors.

The *zamindari* system represented only one form of land control in South India. Far more pervasive in influence was the *ryotwari* system which embraced almost three-fourths of the total area of the Madras Presidency. The advocates of this system of land tenure wished to create not only "a large body of independent Rayets," who would be shielded from the "corrupt & faithless Zemindar,"[22] but also ensure that "every ryot will, on his own estate, be at once proprietor, farmer, and labourer" at the same time.[23] In reality, however, the *ryotwari* system achieved the contrary result of strengthening the position of the elite castes, mostly

Brahmins, who had long enjoyed superior tenure
rights to the soil. With the exception of
mirasdars in certain Tamil districts, whose claims
to be sole proprietors of the land were not recognized, the other superior tenure holders, whether
kadims of Andhra, *janmis* of Malabar, or *mulawar-
gadars* of South Kanara, were all invariably elevated to the status of modern landlords. The
consequence of this policy was to deprive lower
tenurial groups, who were mostly non-Brahmins and
Harijans, of their customary rights to the soil and
expose them to the dangers of eviction by their new
landlords.

There is little doubt that the early British
officials had failed to grasp the communal quality
of land control in traditional South India. They
had failed to recognize that there were no true
landlords in the modern sense of the term with exclusive rights to the land. Traditional rural
society had a well-graded hierarchy of "superior"
and "inferior" tenure holders. Each group in this
hierarchy had its rights as well as responsibilities; each group discharged its specific role for
which it was entitled to a stipulated share of the
produce. In short, it was a corporate system with
customary law and ritual prohibitions reinforcing
the rights and status of each of these groups. The
superior tenure holders, being mostly Brahmins, because of proscriptions against manual work, had to
lease out the land or employ hired laborers.
Equally, Harijans were denied the right to own land
or lease it by strong ritual sanctions.[24]

The British decision to confer absolute pro-
prietary rights to superior tenure holders had important implications. Existing cleavages, especially between the elite Brahmin castes and the
rest of Hindu society, were further widened.
Whereas in the past Brahmin power had been tempered
by social and customary restraints, the new order
imposed no brakes on the exercise of their power.
Backed by British courts and unfettered by any
elaborate tenancy rights, Brahmin landlords

asserted their newfangled rights to their maximum
advantage.

Nowhere in South India was this change from
communal to individual ownership more pregnant with
social and political implications than in the district of Malabar. Here, the British recognized the
janmis as landlords in 1792. Being mainly Nambudiri Brahmins and some Nayar chieftains, these
janmis did not cultivate their land but leased it
to *kanamdars* and *pattamdars*. The *kanamdars*, usually Nayars or Mappillas, paid a lump sum or *kanam* to
get their lease, which was renewed periodically.
The Mysorean conquest of Malabar in 1776 disturbed
the stability of this corporate agrarian system by
imposing a heavy assessment which deprived the
janmis of their share of the produce. Many *janmis*
also took fright at Tipu's threat of forcible conversion and fled to Travancore, leaving the *kanamdars* in virtual control of their estates. When the
British annexed Malabar, the *janmis* returned and
staked their claim as landlords, which was recognized. For some years the *janmis* were too heavily
indebted to the *kanamdars* to flex their muscles,
but when their debts were paid off by the 1830s,
they began to increase their demands and evict
those *kanamdars* unable to meet them.* The seeds of
an agrarian conflict were thus sown, and, invariably, the conflict assumed a religious character
as some of the evicted *kanamdars* were Mappillas.
The so-called Mappilla "outrages" began in November
1836 and their persistence for much of the British
period turned Malabar into the most violence-ridden

---

*
During the second half of the nineteenth century, land evictions in Malabar sharply increased.
In the 1880s, 90 per cent of the cases before the
civil judges in the district were eviction cases.
Governor Connemara called Malabar "the Ireland of
the (Madras) Presidency." *Tours of His Excellency
the Right Honourable Lord Connemara*, No. 111
(November, 1887), p. 4.

district of South India.[25]

That the British were predisposed towards the interests of the strongly entrenched social groups was more glaringly apparent in their decision to confirm those elite castes in the key positions in the village and district administration of South India. Early British officials, in their search for stability and security of the Raj, saw in the traditional village system an important instrument for building an enduring, colonial framework. Convinced that in the preceding centuries of political instability it was the resilience of the village institutions which had provided for order and continuity, British administrators, like Thomas Munro, resisted efforts to circumscribe the powers and functions of the village headman,[26] while others expressed concern that the *ryotwari* system with its stress on individual ownership would eventually undermine the corporate fabric of village society.[27] These arguments not only served to keep intact the established institutions of power in the villages during the first half of the nineteenth century but also permitted entrenched elite groups to perpetuate their power in rural society.

Power in the villages of South India was vested in the hands of *patels* (headmen) and *karnams* (accountants). In Tamilnadu, *patels* had a long history of dominating village affairs and limiting the interference of any external authority. As a rule, they were chosen from the most powerful families in the village who were in most cases large *mirasdars* drawn from the higher Hindu castes. Acting more often than not as a collective group, *patels* mediated in disputes between the village and outside power and maintained the peace within the village.[28] In Andhra, on the other hand, village heads called Pedda Naidus, Pedda Kapus, and Pedda Reddis, had to share power with the *karnams*. While the village heads belonged to the influential non-Brahmin castes and were dominant in the villages of the interior Telugu districts, the *karnams* were almost always Niyogi Brahmins and were influential in the coastal areas.

A reflection of British anxiety to retain the
traditional institutions of village authority was
their enactment of Regulation XI of 1816. Concerned that the authority of the *patels* had been
undermined on account of their frequent removal,
this regulation attempted to shore up their position by investing them with the powers of the
munsif and placing the village police under their
control. Other village functionaries were also
confirmed in their former positions, with their
old powers restored to them as far as possible.
Forms of remuneration were also to be governed by
traditional practice: village officials were to be
paid in the form of rent free land, grain contributions by villagers, or the levying of fees on
specific items of sale.[29]

The extent to which British respect for established village institutions had permitted entrenched, elite groups to maintain their power was
revealed in a report which Walter Elliot, Commissioner of the Northern Circars, submitted to the
Madras Government in 1854. Elliot's portrayal of
village authority in this area showed that the real
source of local influence, despite over half a century of British rule, was still the *karnam*, a
position largely controlled by the Niyogi Brahmins.
While the head *ryots*, be they Pedda Naidus or Pedda
Kapus, by and large received only meagre allowances
for discharging their duties, the *karnams* almost
everywhere enjoyed substantial *inams*, that is,
claimed fees in the form of a share of the produce,
and were entitled to travelling allowances for
official duties. Moreover, Elliot found that the
practice of payment by fees was a fertile source of
corruption. *Karnams* used their power to extort
various kinds of contributions from the cultivators
for the ostensible purpose of supporting charities
and religious institutions. Not surprisingly, the
Niyogi Brahmins who dominated this office in the
Northern Circars were anxious to safeguard it as a
family preserve.[30]

The policy of conciliating powerful, elite groups in South India also dictated to a large extent the British decision to confirm the Mahratta Brahmins in the key positions of the district administration. The power that this elite group came to wield during the early decades of British rule was founded mainly on its almost exclusive control of the position of the *sheristadar*. This functionary, well versed in local history and conditions, exercised surveillance over the Indian establishment in the Collector's *katcheri* (office). As the European Collector was often overwhelmed with multifarious duties, it was the *sheristadar* who attended to the onerous details of revenue collection and accounts, settling the annual assessment and authorizing remissions. In the eyes of the rural community, the *sheristadar* was the "real administrator" who controlled the sole channel of access to the Collector.[31] The other position of importance in the district administration where the influence of the Mahratta Brahmins was evident was that of the *tahsildar*. As the chief executive officer of the taluk containing a few hundred villages, the *tahsildar* discharged revenue, judicial, and police duties under the supervision of the European Collector.

Table 1
Communal and Caste Groups Occupying Elite Positions *

Caste/Community	Head Sheristadars	Deputy Sheristadars	Tahsildars	Total
Mahratta Brahmins	17	20	117	154
Other Brahmins	2	13	68	83
Non-Brahmins	2	3	45	50
Indian Christians	0	2	3	5
Muslims	0	0	13	13
Eurasians	0	0	0	0
Total	21	38	246	305

---

*Ricketts, *Report*, p. 335. The Table describes the district administration of the Madras Presidency in January 1855.

That the Mahratta Brahmins, whose numbers in
South India barely exceeded a few thousands,* should
be preponderant in the district administration deserves some explanation. Part of the explanation
lies in the power they had acquired in Tamil and
Telugu areas during the period of Deccani, Mahratta,
Mughal, and Mysorean rule. Since the sixteenth
century, when the Deccani incursions into these
areas began to gain momentum, Mahratta Brahmins of
the Desastha subcaste were recruited into the revenue administration and gradually displaced local,
elite groups at the district level. By the time
the British established their power in South India,
these Desasthas virtually held the keys to fiscal
and administrative power in Tamilnadu and Andhra.
Early British officials, anxious to legitimize their
position by wooing the support of powerful elite
groups, decided to turn to the Desasthas and draw
on their experience in creating the framework of
district administration. Equally agile and adap-
tive, the Desasthas met their new masters halfway,
assiduously studied English, and won the confidence
of the British superiors by their loyalty to the
Raj and their deep knowledge of local administration.

But this is only half the story. The other
half of the explanation lies in the skill with
which the Desasthas manipulated power to ensure
their continued domination of the district administration. Being a small, tight-knit community, held
together by strong caste and matrimonial ties, the
Desasthas were masters in the game of political
manipulation. They filled all important positions
in the *huzur katcheri* on a preferential basis, kept
the secrets of their profession within their family
and caste, and were able to survive dynastic
changes and political turmoil.

---

*In 1891, there were 33,275 Mahratta Brahmins
in the Madras Presidency. See *Madras Census*, XIII
(1891), p. 261.

The closed system of recruitment continued during the early decades of British rule. The sons of Desastha officials entered the *huzur katcheri* at a young age, slowly acquired the skills of their calling, and ascended the ladder of administration by forging matrimonial alliances with families in influential positions. In Guntur, for example, Frykenberg claims that if the aspirant to office was a non-Brahmin or Muslim, he would be indeed fortunate to get into the *huzur katcheri* at all. If he was a Niyogi Brahmin, his chances were better because of the regional influence of this caste group. Invariably, it was the Desastha who had the edge over all other applicants, as his kinsmen were in control of the *huzur katcheri* and usually had the ear of the British Collector who controlled, in theory at least, recruitment of all personnel below the rank of the *sheristadar*.[32]

That these administrative elites of South India performed their official tasks in an atmosphere of widespread corruption during the early decades of British rule cannot be denied. To some extent, their formation and orientation rendered this inevitable. The recruitment of district and village officials exclusively from certain castes, the belief that revenue collection was an exercise in extracting as much as possible from the subject population to fill the coffers of the state, and the adherence to old administrative practices meant that some of the abuses of the traditional system would be carried over into the British period. To an equal extent, official corruption was also a product of British revenue policy. By their widespread adoption of the *ryotwari* system, the British in South India not only foisted on the people a burgeoning bureaucracy of largely underpaid officials but also created the basis for official interference at almost every stage of agricultural activity.[33] Moreover, the concentration of revenue, judicial, and police duties in the same set of functionaries meant that there were no built-in checks on the activities of officials, while the complicated nature of the judicial process lent immunity to officials from any kind of court sanctions.

Although the instincts of the early British administrators were basically conservative, insofar as they were concerned with the consolidation of their authority through an alliance with established elite groups in South India, it is nonetheless important to see British rule as more than simply a system of political domination seeking its indefinite prolongation. Indeed, for purposes of analyzing social and political change, it will be more meaningful to view British colonialism as a dynamic force possessing certain inherently revolutionary tendencies which were capable of altering a society long characterized by the stability of economic and social institutions and the tenacity of its religious beliefs. One revolutionary tendency associated with British rule in India was Western education whose importance in effecting social and political change has long been recognized by historians and others. Equally revolutionary was the growth of the market economy in India which the British consciously promoted ever since they established their ascendancy in the subcontinent.

It is a moot point whether the introduction of the market economy reflected the narrow economic interests of the colonizing power. Whatever the real motivation, British attachment to the ideals of a market society, where the production and distribution of goods and services would be regulated by the market mechanism, lay at the heart of their decision to recognize private property, including individual ownership of land. Under the *ryotwari* system, land was made freely alienable, and its value was to be determined by the free play of market forces. Landholders no longer viewed their estates as ancestral fiefs whose produce they ought to share with other tenurial groups. Instead, they saw their estates as potential sources of income which ought to be augmented, even if it meant displacement of groups which had long customary

rights to the soil. Those with wealth invested in
land and put it to the best economic use.

A consequence of this change was the emancipa-
tion of labor from hereditary and communal obligations. Labor, like land, became a factor of
production and was available to the highest bidder.
In the nineteenth century, the movement of labor
into new sectors of the economy was encouraged by
the growth of the plantation industry, the development of public works, and the demand by Europeans
for domestic help, all of which were met by lower
caste groups either displaced from the land or
attracted by more lucrative openings for their services. Mobility of labor on any appreciable scale
could not have been achieved without resort to the
system of wage payments. Indeed, one was the
necessary corollary of the other, and especially in
urban areas labor was increasingly bought and sold
by money payments. The impact of this change on
the monetization of the economy cannot be underestimated. Moreover, British insistence upon collecting revenue in cash encouraged trends towards
monetization.[34]

A feature of the emerging market economy of
India was the expansion of foreign and domestic
trade. Prior to the advent of the West, Indian
economy was characterized by self-sufficiency, although a limited but lucrative trade had always
been conducted in some luxury items. In the nineteenth century, improvements in the technology of
production and distribution of goods had resulted
in a tremendous expansion in the volume of trade,
especially in agricultural products like sugar,
tobacco, tea, coffee, and cotton. International
and domestic trade began to impinge on several aspects of the economic and social life of South
India, particularly in those urban centers which
had developed in response to expanding foreign
trade.

Of these urban centers in South India, Madras
was by far the most important, although it must be
stressed that its preeminence stemmed in part from

the fact that it was also the administrative capital of a far-flung British province. It was in
this southern metropolis that the modernizing colonial system created the conditions for the rise of
a new indigenous elite. This elite came to play a
seminal role in the civic life of Madras in the
mid-nineteenth century, especially in harnessing
western techniques of organization and propaganda
to express its discontent against specific British
policies and actions.

1. Ferment in the Metropolis

FORMATION OF AN ELITE

In 1800 Madras ranked among the major cities
of the world. With its estimated population of
250,000, it vied with Bombay and Calcutta to be the
first city of the Indian subcontinent. In peninsular India, Madras dwarfed all other towns, eclipsing such ancient, dynastic capitals as Madura and
Conjeeveram and supplanting more recent, commercial
centers such as Calicut and Masulipatam. Within
the space of less than two centuries of British
settlement, what had been no more than an obscure
fishing village situated at the mouth of a shallow
river had been transformed into a modern metropolis.
The rise of Madras, notwithstanding the deficiencies of its harbor and its oppressive climate,
has to be related to the role that it played in the
commercial and political life of the British imperial system. By the beginning of the nineteenth
century, the varied interests of trade, industry,
and government were drawn to this city. It was
through this entrepot that an ever-growing volume
of goods entered and left the Madras Presidency.
Madras also increasingly became the center of various handicrafts and trades which drew men and
capital from the surrounding regions and beyond.
Economic activity of a vastly, expanded scale generated, in turn, such supporting institutions as

agency houses, banks, and insurance companies. Besides its commercial role, Madras was also the
administrative headquarters of the southern Presidency, a province considerably extended as a result
of successive British annexations of neighboring
territories during the closing years of the eighteenth century. With such enlarged responsibilities of government came the inevitable burgeoning
of the administrative and military establishments,
most of which were located in Madras. The Council
house, the Corporation of Madras, the offices of
the Board of Revenue, Accountant-General and
Auditor-General, and the military barracks were
located within Fort St. George. Residential quarters, including Government House, hospitals,
churches, and schools were shifted to suburbs like
Triplicane, Egmore, Chintadripet, and Mylapore.[1]

Like many colonial cities which the British
helped to build in Asia, the population of Madras
was extremely heterogeneous in character. In part,
this can be attributed to the conscious British
policy of encouraging the settlement of Portuguese,
Armenian, and Jewish traders. If the aim was to
infuse vitality into the commercial life of the
city, its long-term effect was to impart a cosmopolitan character to the southern metropolis. The
Portuguese for some years had resisted migrating to
Madras, but the fall of San Thomé to the Muslim
power of Golconda in 1662 precipitated an exodus,
with many Portuguese traders taking residence in
Black Town.[2] They were soon followed by Armenians,
regarded in the seventeenth century as "the great
merchants and brokers in the eastern world," who
settled in Madras in steady numbers after 1680,
having secured trading privileges from the British
Company. Investments in local trade, profits from
transactions in precious stones with Persia and
Europe, and a near monopoly of the Manila trade
accounted for the affluence of the Armenian community.[3] Some of its wealthier members, wishing to
keep alive their cultural heritage, sponsored the
publication of works on classical Armenian

literature. In 1794, an Armenian priest started in
Madras the earliest known Armenian newspaper,
called the *Azdarar* (Intelligentser).[4]

One group which received scant welcome in
Madras for many years were the English free merchants. The English East India Company, fearful of
encroachment upon its monopoly trading rights, had
severely restricted the issue of licenses to
British free merchants seeking trade in Asia. In
1710 there were only twenty-nine free merchants residing in Madras. At the end of the century, the
number had probably trebled. For much of this period, the free merchants struggled to stay afloat,
battling against the Company's monopoly system.
However, their fortunes changed during the early
years of the nineteenth century owing to the Company's shedding its commercial role, and the expanded opportunities provided by the rise of the
British Raj. The free merchants spread themselves
out in various directions, appropriating an increasing share of the business of the Madras Presidency.
With this expansion came changes in business methods. Free merchants, trading as individuals, now
began to constitute themselves into corporate
bodies. In 1812 there were twelve agency houses in
Madras, all European, and among them were such well-
known names as Arbuthnot, De Moute & Co., Binny,
Dennison & Co., and Parry & Pugh.[5] The free merchants had come a long way. In 1836 they formed the
Madras Chamber of Commerce to institutionalize their
economic power.

European participation in the expanding commercial activity in South India could not have been
sustained without the cooperation of an indigenous
mercantile group. Hindu merchant castes, function-
ally differentiated from the rest of society, had
been traditionally bankers, moneylenders, and wholesale and retail traders. Traditional banking
systems had been well developed in South India,
especially in urban society, where they financed
lucrative branches of business as well as advanced
loans to needy governments. However, under Indian

regimes the merchant class found it difficult to accumulate wealth, troubled as it was by lack of security of property, arbitrary exactions of the ruling groups, and state intervention in the profitable sectors of industry and trade.[6] The advent of British rule removed many of these impediments, while the creation of a market economy provided the essential preconditions for the formation of an indigenous merchant class. In South India, such a class first emerged in Madras.

Since its foundation, Madras had exercised a strong attraction among the mercantile castes of neighboring Tamilnadu and Andhra. These castes were mainly Chettis and Vellalars of the Tamil districts and Komatis and Naidus of the Andhra region. They were enterprising and were prepared to migrate to areas with commercial potential. Especially mobile were the Chettis and Komatis, who were attracted to Madras in large numbers by security of life and property as well as extensive investment opportunities. Some invested in betel, indigo, and arrack farms; some financed weaving and artisan trades; some sponsored overseas trading ventures; some speculated in real property, including land; and some were retailers of imported articles. However, during the early decades of British settlement in Madras, many of these merchants acted as intermediaries between the British and Indian communities. As go-betweens, they were called *dubashes*.

The need for *dubashes* stemmed from European ignorance of the laws and habits of the country. The English East India Company had engaged the services of a *dubash* soon after its settlement in Madras. His main duty was to facilitate the purchase of cotton fabrics for export by the Company and dispose of imported goods from England. However, as occasion demanded, the *dubash* performed other tasks as well, which included supplying provisions to the British community, mediating in caste disputes, and acting as ambassadors to the courts of Indian rulers.[7] Indeed, the Company's

dubash became an all-purpose agent discharging
multifarious duties. The services of the *dubash*
were also at the disposal of the Company officials
who used him to transact their private business on
a regular or temporary basis. Similarly, when the
English free merchants arrived on the scene, they
found the *dubash* an essential appendage in their
business operations.

The extent to which these *dubashes* utilized
their opportunities to amass fortunes is illustrated by the example of Pachaiyappa Mudaliar.
Born in 1754 to a poor Vellalar family living not
far from Madras, Pachaiyappa was fortunate in finding a patron in a wealthy *dubash* who encouraged
him to study English and then cast him into the
role of an apprentice *dubash*. He started his business career as a purchasing and selling agent for
wholesale merchants in Madras. Some years later
his services were engaged by an English free merchant to assist in the buying of goods for export
to Europe. In this way, Pachaiyappa diligently acquired a small fortune. After 1776 he branched out
into more ambitious ventures: collecting taxes of
villages, disbursing salaries of the personnel of
the Nawab of Arcot, and supplying the Company's
needs for grain and cloth. The success that attended these ventures made Pachaiyappa the foremost
dubash in South India and drew him inevitably into
the vortex of local power politics. At different
times he became the financial agent or advisor of
the Nawab of Arcot, the Raja of Tanjore, and the
poligar chieftains of the southern Tamil districts.
When he died in 1794, he left behind a large fortune which became the subject of a celebrated court
case.[8]

As the eighteenth century drew to a close, and
as the British began to impose their will over much
of South India, the halcyon days of the *dubash* came
to an end. Men of the stamp of Pachaiyappa faded
away from the scene. Wealth of such proportions
could only be amassed at transient, if confused,
times when the country was in the grip of political

turbulence. Once order returned, opportunities for
acquiring quick fortunes almost vanished. The next
generation of *dubashes* had to earn their wealth in
more pedestrian ways. Servicing the needs of the
Company was still a lucrative business, but here
dubashes found themselves in an unequal competition
with European agency houses which were more efficient and possessed larger capital resources. The
ending of the privilege of private trade that had
been granted British civil and military officials
further restricted the opportunities of the *dubash*.
In 1834, according to one account, *dubashes* in
Madras were described as "needy adventurers" looking after the modest needs of ship captains and
European visitors to the city.[9]

If the role of the *dubash* declined in importance during the early years of the nineteenth
century, Indian merchants with initiative and enterprise found promising outlets elsewhere to make
their mark in the competitive world of Madras. The
rise of the British Raj saw vast tracts of the
countryside come under the single political authority through which goods and capital could flow
without serious impediment or harassment. For example, it was now possible for merchants to purchase essential commodities at their source of
production and transport them safely over long
distances to areas where they would fetch high
prices. Trade in grain had always been important
in South India, controlled by a numerous class of
small merchants. Munro claimed in 1805 that the
grain trade employed more men and bullocks than
all the other branches of trade taken together.[10]
Times of scarcity and glut brought windfalls to
these merchants, as they were adept in manipulating
prices to their advantage. In a country noted for
its capricious climate, such opportunities were not
infrequent.

Capital acquired in this way was invested in
different ventures in order to spread out the
risks. Some investments were channelled into cultivation of such cash crops as indigo, sugar,

coffee, and cotton, usually as joint ventures with
European capitalists. Also lucrative was speculation in landed property. In Madras demand for land
in the central urban area stimulated speculation in
which merchants with capital participated. Land
was useful as security for business loans, while
some merchants leased it out at exorbitant rates.
However, it ought not to be assumed that the other
lines of business were unprofitable: loans at
usurious rates to the ruling aristocracy, investment in local handicrafts, textiles, and arrack
farms, and retail trade in various kinds of imported articles continued to sustain many merchants in
Madras.

Among the Hindu merchants who reaped the benefits of widening economic horizons, there were some
who were prepared to experiment with the superior
Western methods of business organization. The prominent place occupied by European agency firms had
induced some wealthy Hindu merchants to invest
their excess capital in these firms. Some Hindu
merchants even purchased the position of *dubash* of
an agency house by depositing a large sum of money
and drawing commission on orders. Those with
greater enterprise and capital resources decided to
venture out by forming agency firms of their own.
In 1851, for example, the *Madras Almanac* listed
three Hindu agency houses operating in the city.[11]
These were essentially family partnerships, started
by wealthy Chettis, Komatis, and Naidus, to compete
with their European rivals for a share in the
import-export business, speculate in indigo, cotton,
and textile fabrics, and participate in the retail
trade. This class of Hindu merchants shared little
in common with the old *dubashes*, being neither dependent on government patronage nor tied to an
European clientele for its existence.

Although the impact of the new economic forces
was to modernize the forms and institutions through
which certain indigenous trading groups carried on
their business activities, it is nonetheless true
that the Hindu commercial elite, which became

important in Madras during the mid-nineteenth century, remained strongly rooted to its old social
and cultural values. Neither the exposure to the
modernizing influences of an urbanized society nor
the elite's smattering knowledge of the English
language had in any significant way undermined its
adherence to its inherited caste and ritual obligations. The laws of commensality and marriage were
faithfully observed, the various family festivals
meticulously celebrated, and pilgrimages to temples
and shrines regularly undertaken. But some compro-
mises with tradition had to be made in an urban
society: the laws of pollution, for one, could not
be strictly observed in Madras. It was not possible to divide the city into Brahmin, non-Brahmin,
and Harijan sectors.

     In adhering to its traditional social and cul-
tural values, the Hindu commercial elite was merely
conforming to what everyone else in urban society
was doing. But where it differed was in its vigorous promotion of temple building and its patronage
of the traditional arts and Sanskrit education.
Almost every Hindu merchant had some connection
with a temple in Madras or in its environs. Many
in fact spent considerable sums in building or
maintaining temples. Temple building among the
wealthy merchants became such a mania that the
British officials commented wryly in 1756 that "in
this Country, Men who are fond of shewing their
Wealthy and Grandueur have as yet found no better
means of displaying them than by the building of
Temples."[12] To the Hindu, however, temple building
was less a display of wealth than an act of piety.
Similar motives also prompted this Hindu commercial
elite to erect *choultries* (rest houses), subsidize
Sanskrit education, and patronize the traditional
arts. Pachaiyappa typified in many ways the Hindu
merchant of the time. He regularly entertained
countless pilgrims and learned men in his house,
fed thousands of mendicants daily, erected *choultries* along the routes to famous shrines, gave
jewels and money to temples, and bequeathed a large

legacy in his will for religious charities.[13]

Despite its innate conservatism, the Hindu
commercial elite evinced no hostility towards the
British rulers. Partly, this attitude was determined by considerations of self-interest. As its
rise was the result of conditions created by
British rule, it saw its continued prosperity in
the maintenance of that rule. Equally important
was the fact that the early policies of the British
in South India did not directly impinge on the fabric of religious and social life of the Hindus. By
proclaiming at the outset the policy of religious
neutrality, the Company's officials gave cover to
all established faiths in India, even to the extent
of tolerating some archaic social usages. Obstacles that lay in the way of the free exercise of
religious and cultural activities were largely removed. To an extent, the British even usurped the
role of earlier Indian regimes by assuming supervision of Indian religious institutions and by
keeping a tight rein on the entry and free movement
of Christian missionaries.

However, this policy was not destined to last.
Agitation from the missionary societies in India,
reinforced by pressures from their supporters in
England, led to perceptible changes in British religious policy in South India during the 1830s,
resulting in the removal of restrictions on the
entry of Christian missionaries into the country
and the withdrawal of the government from the management of Indian religious institutions. These
changes, together with the growing involvement of
European officials in the activities of Christian
missions in South India, drove a wedge between the
Hindu commercial elite and the British rulers.

CONFLICT WITH MISSIONARIES

Christian missionary activity in South India
has a long and checkered history. Francis Xavier,
a Roman Catholic, had made conversions among Hindus

in Tinnevelly district during the sixteenth century. In the following century, a Jesuit mission
registered some success among higher caste Hindus
at Madura. However, such efforts lacked permanence,
and the overall Christian impression on Indian
society was slight, except for the contributions of
such eminent missionaries as C. J. Beschi, B.
Ziegenbalg and C. F. Schwartz in the field of
Indian languages and literature. To the Indians,
these missionaries, as Ingham points out, "were
important as individuals [rather] than as representatives of any unified body."[14] A weak, organizational base, coupled with the capricious behavior
of Indian ruling groups, robbed missionary activity
of the chance to make any sustained impression.

A new era in Christian endeavor began in the
wake of the Evangelical Revival which was sweeping
the West during the closing years of the eighteenth
century. Under the impulse of this religious
awakening, new societies sprang up in Britain and
America, some of which were anxious to carry their
message to the distant parts of Africa and Asia.
In South India this new drive was spearheaded by
five societies, namely, the Society for the Propagation of the Gospel, London Missionary Society,
Church Missionary Society, Wesleyan Mission, and
the Free Church Mission of Scotland.[15] Possessing
a sound organization and considerable financial
resources, the missionaries soon established a wide
network of stations, seminaries, schools, and
printing houses in the various districts of South
India. Simultaneously, they launched a successful
agitation against the restrictions which the East
India Company had imposed on their work in India.

The missionaries, who arrived in increasing
numbers during the early decades of the nineteenth
century, were very different in temperament from
their predecessors. Stirred by the fervor of the
evangelical movement, and arriving in India at a
time when the British were consolidating their
political power, these missionaries adopted an aggressive approach in their task of conversion.

Dogmatic to the point of intolerance, they believed
that Christianity was the superior faith entrusted
with the task of civilizing the world. They showed,
in contrast to their predecessors, less deference
to Indian traditions or susceptibilities. They dismissed as worthless much of India's heritage or
achievements. Hinduism was singled out for severe
condemnation. Described as "a system which abounds
in the grossest absurdities and most evident contradictions," Hinduism was accused of sanctioning
"appalling cruelties and vices."[16] Its devotees
were depicted as "a depraved people," their conscience "seared, the will enslaved and palsied, and
the whole weight and influence of society ranged on
the side of evil."[17] But the Hindus were not abandoned as a lost cause. Christianity, the missionaries believed, would be the key to the regeneration of the Hindus, and in achieving this grand
design every weapon in the armory of Christian missions was to be used, including help from the
ruling Christian power in India.

The initial missionary thrust was directed
against British religious policy in South India.
Their main grievance here was the apparent support
which the Madras authorities were giving to Indian
religions under the so-called policy of religious
neutrality. The missionaries argued that the religious policy of the Madras Government was not
neutral, either in theory or in practice. Under
Regulation VII of 1817, the Board of Revenue was to
supervise the management of Indian religious institutions and their large endowments. In practice
official intervention extended to minute details,
from the superivision of festivals to scrutinizing
the finances of temples.[18] Also, it was "almost
universal practice" in South India for the officials to compel the Harijans and Christian converts
from the lower castes to assist in Hindu festivals,
while European soldiers were posted in attendance
"to give additional effect to the show."[19]

Missionary opposition to this policy began to
be clearly articulated during the 1830s. It was

argued that official involvement in religious affairs had "a very pernicious effect" on the Hindu
mind and that it "seriously obstructed the labour
of the Christian Missionary."[20] In August 1836 the
European residents in Madras, including some prominent civil and military officials, presented a
memorial to the governor urging an end to official
involvement in Indian religious affairs and the
discontinuance of forced attendance of Christians
at Indian festivals.[21] Official vacillations led
to the protest resignation of Sir Peregrine
Maitland, the Commander-in-Chief of Madras.[22]
Faced with this growing volume of protest, the
Court of Directors instructed in August 1838 the
immediate ending of official connection with
Indian religious institutions. The missionaries
in Madras were jubilant. One of their organs remarked: "The unholy alliance of a Heathen Church
with a Christian State has at length been repudiated."[23]

The other missionary assault on Hinduism was
to be directed through the agency of Western education. This strategy was based on the assumption
that Western education would attract students from
the higher caste Hindus, and that young minds were
most susceptible to the teachings of the Gospel.
The fact that the state had done little to promote
Western education in South India, coupled with the
failure of the Hindus to fill the void, left the
field open for the missionaries. The first to embark successfully in this venture was the Free
Church Mission of Scotland. Rejecting the old
methods of proselytization, such as the offering of
"earthy inducements," the Free Church Mission came
to rely on Western education as the means to
attract converts. In April 1837 is started the
General Assembly's Institution in Black Town, then
regarded by the missionaries as "the Sebastapol of
Southern India, the citadel of Satan, the centre of
caste, pride and Brahmanism."[24] No attempt was
made to veil their real intentions, but this did
not deter many Hindu families from sending their

children to the school. For a while nothing serious happened, but in 1841 three high caste Hindu
students embraced Christianity despite parental
protests. The conversions created "a panic in the
Native community" in Madras and led to the precipitate withdrawal of many students from the school.[25]

The event caused the first major breach between the missionaries and the articulate section
of the Hindu community in Madras. No doubt, there
had always been in the Hindu mind a feeling of
suspicion of the missionaries, but there had been
no open display of hostility, at least among the
Hindus in Madras. However, the student conversions
of 1841, coming so soon after the official withdrawal from the management of religious institutions, embittered relations between the Hindus and
missionaries and led to feverish demands by the
former for some positive steps to stem the tide of
missionary advance.

One step that was immediately taken was the
starting of schools to offset the danger of expos-
ing Hindu youths to missionary influences. Thus
far, the main stumbling block was the lack of adequate funds, but in 1841 the Supreme Court in
Madras ruled that part of Pachaiyappa's large be-
quest could be utilized for educational purposes.
The trustees of Pachaiyappa's Charities, who were
Hindus nominated by the government, decided to
start a school to impart instruction in English
and the regional languages. A building was rented
in Black Town, and the school, named after
Pachaiyappa, was formally opened in January 1842.[26]

One of the trustees instrumental in this move
was C. Srinivasa Pillay, a man who had inherited
considerable wealth and was prepared to spend it in
the cause of Indian advancement. Though he himself
had not "tasted the delights and benefits of
[Western] education,"[27] Srinivasa Pillay was discerning enough to realize that Western education
would be one of the keys to India's regeneration.
He found in George Norton, Advocate-General of
Madras, an active and sympathetic friend. Norton,

since his arrival in Madras in 1828, had consciously tried to cultivate the friendship of progressive-
minded Hindus in the metropolis. He started "a
sort of conversation once a week at his own house
for the better class of natives to meet and discuss
subjects of general interest and information."
Education featured prominently in these discussions,
and Norton succeeded gradually "in raising the zeal
and co-operation of the Native public mind for the
advancement of Education."[28] Also, Norton persuaded his Hindu friends, including Srinivasa Pillay,
to organize the Hindu Literary Society, which came
to function as a forum for enlightened Hindu
opinion in Madras. In September 1833 this body invited Norton to deliver a series of lectures on
"the plan of Government and the system of administration of Justice in India." In these lectures,
Norton stressed the importance of Western knowledge,
not only to qualify Indians for higher administrative posts, but also to secure them their "Political privileges."[29]

The Hindu Literary Society was stirred into
action and in 1834 it started an English school
which was attended by students from "respectable
families."[30] But such efforts were too modest to
meet the demand for Western education in Madras,
and increasingly hopes were pinned on the government. In 1839, when the Madras authorities were
maturing plans for establishing a high school, an
address carrying 70,000 signatures from the inhabitants of Madras was presented to the governor
strongly endorsing the plan. As Norton says, it
would be "too much to suppose that the original
composition [of the address] proceeded from any
Hindoo," but there was no mistaking the genuine-
ness of the Hindu demand for Western instruction,
or the depth of their opposition to any system of
education which interfered with "the religious
faith or sentiments of the people."[31] The latter
warning was heeded when the High School of the
Madras University was launched in April 1841.
Norton became the first chairman of the Board of

Governors, and Srinivasa Pillay was nominated a
member of the board.

Starting schools was one of the ideas which
Hindu leaders in Madras conceived in their efforts
to stem the tide of missionary advance. Another
idea that was tried out was the starting of newspapers to counter the propaganda of the missionary
organs, especially the *Native Herald*, which the
Free Church Mission of Scotland had launched in
October 1841 in the wake of the tumult caused by
the student conversions earlier in the year. Since
1840 the Hindu cause was espoused by the *Native
Interpreter*, founded by C. Narayanaswamy Naidu, a
partner in the agency firm of G. Sidhulu & Co. In
October 1844 this paper was purchased by Gajalu
Lakshmanarasu Chetty and issued under a new name,
the *Crescent*.[32] Placed under the editorship of
Edward Harley, an ex-naval officer and for many
years a teacher at a school in Vepery, Madras,[33]
the *Crescent* emerged as the outspoken advocate of
Hindu interests in South India, giving free expression to the fear which many Hindus entertained
about missionary activities and the possible effect
that they might have on official religious policy.

Although the literary style of the *Crescent*
was Harley's, there is no doubt that the content
and tone of the paper reflected the political beliefs of Lakshmanarasu Chetty. Born near Madras in
1806 into a Komati merchant family, Lakshmanarasu
Chetty studied in a local school where he acquired
a fair proficiency in English. Even as a student,
he was an active participant in debates and lectures which stimulated his interest in issues of
the day and made him conscious of his rights and
responsibilities. On leaving school, he joined
his father's firm, G. Sidhulu & Co., one of the few
agency houses in Madras. Here, he helped in building up the firm into one of the wealthiest in
Madras, mainly through skillful speculation in textile and indigo trade. At the death of his father,
Lakshmanarasu Chetty became the chief partner of
the firm, enjoying a position of considerable

affluence and social prestige among the Hindu community in Madras.[34]

Despite his involvement in the family business,
Lakshmanarasu Chetty did not neglect his public
duties. He continued to read widely in English
works, making up for the deficiencies in his formal
education. He corresponded with leaders in Bengal
during the early 1840s on questions of public importance.[35] However, it was the escalating nature
of missionary agitation in India and England that
brought him into active political life. Like many
members of the Hindu commercial elite in Madras,
Lakshmanarasu Chetty became increasingly alarmed by
the implications of such agitation on prevailing
religious policy. He had witnessed the Madras
Government's decision to withdraw from the management of Hindu temples and endowments, a step which
he and many of his Hindu friends regarded as a concession to missionary agitation.

Also, he discerned a change in the attitude of
local European officials towards religious questions. Some officials had been drawn into the
activities of missionary bodies, sitting on local
committees, making financial contributions, and
even criticizing some aspects of official religious
policy. Such behavior cast doubts in the minds of
many Hindus, including Lakshmanarasu Chetty, as to
the ability of such officials to be impartial
arbiters in religious disputes involving Hindus
and Christians. It was even feared that the policy
of religious neutrality might be eroded from within
by pro-missionary officials. This fear had become
fairly widespread in Madras since the arrival of
Tweeddale as governor in 1842. It was alleged that
a "missionary party," consisting of a loose coali-
tion of officials and missionaries, had begun to
wield influence over the actions of the local
government. Among the prominent officials closely
identified with the Christian societies were
Tweeddale, J. F. Thomas, Chief Secretary to the
Madras Government, and Captain C. A. Browne, Military Secretary to the Madras Government.[36]

To Lakshmanarasu Chetty, the real danger lay
not so much in the activities of the missionaries
as in the involvement of important European officials in Christian proselytization. He did not object to the legitimate missionary endeavor—which
in any case had gone on for many decades without
creating alarm—but he was firmly opposed to official patronage in any form being extended to such
activity. Consequently, his anger was directed
against the local government, and especially
against those European officials who made themselves conspicuous by their pro-missionary procli-
vities. In starting the *Crescent*, Lakshmanarasu
Chetty had recognized the need for an organ that
would truthfully depict the dangers facing the
Hindus in South India, while at the same time
countering the strategy of Christian missionaries
and their official allies wherever such strategy
was to harness the government in the cause of
Christian proselytization.

Lakshmanarasu Chetty did not have long to wait.
In January 1845 the Indian Government published the
Lex Loci Draft Act. It was not maneuverings of the
missionaries, as suspected by the Hindus, but
rather the need for a code of law applicable to
Europeans, Eurasians, and Armenians that lay behind
the original conception of the *Lex Loci* report,
drafted by the Indian Law Commission in 1840. But
missionary pressure did influence the eventual
drafting of this legislation when three clauses,
strictly unrelated to the measure,[37] were inserted
to neutralize those sections of Hindu and Muslim
law which inflicted forfeiture of rights to ancestral property upon anyone renouncing these religions. To Lakshmanarasu Chetty and his Hindu
friends, this legislation was confirmation of their
fears that the government was throwing its support
behind the missionaries in subverting Hinduism.

A public meeting was convened in Madras in
April 1845 to declare Hindu opposition to the proposed legislation. Attended by over 200 Hindus and
presided over by Lakshmanarasu Chetty, the meeting

approved a memorial to the Indian Government which charged the latter with "a breach of faith" in drafting this measure. Particular objection was taken to the three clauses which the memorialists alleged were "a palpable invasion of their ancient rights, a direct attack upon their religion, and a peremptory subversion of their ancestral and inalienable Law." They urged that these "obnoxious clauses" be "altogether expunged from the Act," or further action be deferred pending an appeal to be made to the Court of Directors.[38] This protest, reinforced by another from Hindus in Bengal, won a temporary respite when the proposed legislation was set aside.

Here was a Hindu meeting of a new kind. In contrast to caste gatherings, which had traditionally regulated the internal workings of the Hindus, this was an overtly political demonstration attended by Hindus of different caste and sectarian affiliations in which the wider implications of an act of public policy were debated. Moreover, this was the first known Hindu gathering in Madras which had all the trappings of a modern political protest meeting: the permission of the sheriff of Madras was secured; a chairman was elected to conduct the meeting; a number of resolutions were passed; and a memorial was approved and signed for submission to the government.

The credit for all this belonged to Lakshmanarasu Chetty, a new kind of Hindu leader who was perhaps the first to adopt the Western forms of political protest in South India. No doubt his European friends, especially Harley, helped him with advice and guidance, but the initiative and energy were essentially his. In the years that followed, Lakshmanarasu Chetty showed his readiness to apply this new style of political agitation whenever the interests of the Hindu community warranted it.

Hindus living in the rural areas of South India, however, showed little of the organizational sophistication of their counterparts in Madras in

mounting opposition to missionary activities. In
certain districts, relations between the Hindus and
the missionaries had become so strained as to result in sporadic incidents of violence. Tinnevelly
was the district most affected by such religious
conflicts. Since the beginning of the nineteenth
century, Tinnevelly and south Travancore had become
the center of intensive missionary activities, encouraged by the mass conversion of the Shanars, the
hereditary, toddy-drawing caste which inhabited the
sandy coastal terrain. Some Harijans also went
over to Christianity, and by 1850 the size of the
Indian Christian community in Tinnevelly district
had swollen to 40,000.[39]

The emergence of a sizable breakaway minority,
drawn exclusively from a few castes, was bound to
create some degree of social and economic disloca-
tion. Socially, the converts rebelled against the
ritual restrictions which the caste system had imposed on them. Economically, conversion loosened
the bonds which tied these agricultural castes to
the landowning higher castes. The latter, confronted by a less docile tenantry, attributed their
troubles to the missionaries. Believing that their
problems would be solved if the converts returned
to their Hindu fold, the landlords resorted first
to persuasion and, if it failed, to persecution.
If the convert was a palmyra climber, he was deprived of his trees; if he was a tenant, eviction
followed; if he had property, he was disposses-
sed.[40] Sometimes persecution assumed the character
of intimidation and violence, which in turn provoked retaliation from the Indian Christians.

In November 1845, disturbances flared up in
Tinnevelly when Hindu mobs attacked some Christian
villages, molesting inhabitants, plundering houses,
and destroying property. The missionaries claimed
that Hindu religious societies in the district in-
stigated the disturbances in order to stem the mass
drift of certain caste groups to Christianity.
Also implicated was the Sadur Veda Siddhanta Sabha
of Madras.[41] Little is known of those who

organized this body, although it was claimed to en-
joy support of some wealthy Hindus in Madras. Its
aim was to mount opposition to the missionaries by
adopting the latter's tactics: it published tracts
in defence of Hinduism and recruited agents to deliver lectures in the districts.[42] What direct
role it played in the Tinnevelly disturbances is
not clear. The local police charged about 100
Hindus in connection with the incidents, and many
were convicted by the district court.[43] However,
on appeal to the Court of Sadr and Foujdari Adalat,
many of the sentences were squashed. At this stage,
the Madras Government called upon the Sadr judges
to submit copies of evidence taken in these cases
and the sentences passed. This led to a conflict
between the judges and the executive and culminated
in the suspension, and later the dismissal, of one
of the judges, Malcolm Lewin.

The dispute between the Tweeddale Administration and the Sadr judges was closely followed by
the Hindu leaders in Madras. The decision to suspend Lewin prompted Lakshmanarasu Chetty and his
friends to convene a public meeting in October 1846
to adopt a memorial to the Court of Directors as
well as an address to Lewin for his efforts "to
maintain the independence" of the judiciary.
Amidst popular excitement, with the local authorities alerting the police and the military for fear
of possible disturbance, the meeting passed a number of resolutions protesting against the activities of the "missionary party."

The main grievances of the Hindus were set
forth in detail in a memorial to the Court of Directors. It was claimed that the "Civil and Religious
rights and privileges" of the Hindus were being
violated by the missionaries, abetted and encouraged by the European officials. The Tinnevelly
disturbance received due mention. This district,
the memorialists asserted, had become "the emporium
of Missionaryism" under the active patronage of the
Collector, E. B. Thomas, brother of the Chief Secretary. The intervention of the Madras Government in

the Sadr judgment was attributed to "a clandestine
petition" which a missionary deputation presented
to Tweeddale in March 1846.[44] Tweeddale denied
these allegations and attributed the Hindu agitation to "a small and vicious party" in the metropolis which was embittered by the student
conversions.[45]

Preoccupation with religious controversies
had come to dominate the actions of the articulate
sections of the Hindu community in Madras. Missionary activity had become a highly emotive issue,
raising strong passions on all sides and obscuring
other questions. The breach between the Hindus and
the European missionaries, caused by the student
conversions of 1841, remained unhealed. The *Native
Herald* commented in 1843: "The excitement (of 1841)
has passed away; but ever since that day the
heathen in the city have used their appropriate
weapons of ridicule, contempt, and blasphemy
against God and his Christ."[46] John Anderson, who
was mainly instrumental in the student conversions,
said in 1844 that the Hindu "enmity against the
light is hardening their hearts, and making them
more unapproachable. They seem to be smitten with
judicial blindness."[47] The *Crescent* made no attempt to disguise what the Hindus in Madras thought
about the missionaries and their official allies.
"The Hindus," it observed in 1846, "stand aloof
from the Europeans, the influential part of whom
i.e. the evangelicals, they look upon as their declared and implacable enemies."[48]

Far more significant was the steady deterioration in the relationship between the Hindus and the
British rulers. Though this was in part due to the
active involvement of individual European officials
in the cause of Christian advancement, there was no
doubt that the strains in the relationship were
largely caused by the Hindu suspicion that the
British authorities in India were antagonistic to
their cherished religious and social traditions.
The *Lex Loci* Draft Act was a case in point. In
April 1850 the Indian Government detached the three

controversial clauses relating to inheritance and
enacted them separately, under the title of the
Caste Disabilities Removal Act. The decision to
legislate, after seemingly abandoning it five years
previously, brought a fresh volley of Hindu protests. The *Crescent* gave expression to the Hindu
anger when it charged the Indian authorities of
having acted with "shameful duplicity, profound
stupidity, and insulting tyranny."[49]

MADRAS NATIVE ASSOCIATION

In mounting their agitation against the missionaries, the Hindus in Madras were not aided by a
political association. It should not be assumed,
however, that the instincts of corporate action
were absent among the Hindus, or that they were ignorant of the advantages of organized political
protest. Urban life in Madras, by its very complexity and competitiveness, was compelling many
Hindus to redefine their relationship to each
other. When the Hindus first migrated to the city,
caste bodies emerged to regulate the activities of
their members and protect their traditional rights
from encroachment by rival groups. However, the
rapid changes that overtook Madras following the
establishment of British power in the area, coupled
with the slow erosion of certain traditional institutions and habits, called for relationships other
than those based upon kinship and caste.

An early example of this new kind of relationship was the Hindu Literary Society. Founded during the 1830s, this body admitted members from
different Hindu castes and occupations. Within its
ranks were found Brahmins as well as non-Brahmins,
Hindu pundits as well as merchants. This society
held periodic meetings and lectures, delved into
the country's history and literature, and took an
informed interest in current issues. Though not
exactly a voluntary association, it was the nearest
to one to be found in Madras during the first half

of the nineteenth century.

The Hindu Literary Society became somewhat in-
active during the 1840s, at a time when the anti-
missionary agitation was reaching new heights.
This agitation, among other things, had resulted in
a heightened sense of Hindu, communal solidarity in
Madras.   There were appeals for a voluntary association to give effective direction to this new born
Hindu consciousness.   Some Hindu leaders, notably
Srinivasa Pillay and Lakshmanarsu Chetty, however,
favored the idea of reviving the Hindu Literary
Society, hoping thereby to instill new vigor and
purpose into its activities.   In March 1846 a meeting was held in Madras to revive the Society.
Srinivasa Pillay, while calling for unity among
the Hindus, argued that failure to achieve it would
be "a great bar to their political advancement."[50]

This attempt to breathe new life into the
Society failed, but failure only underlined the
need for a new political association which would
give expression to the growing Hindu solidarity in
Madras.

The initiative to form a political organization came not, however, from Madras but from Bengal,
where the British Indian Association was launched
in October 1851.   Formed for "a period of not less
than three years," the association's immediate aim
was to voice India's grievances during the coming
inquiry into the affairs of the English East India
Company.   Believing that its representations would
carry "great weight if they were made simultaneously by the natives of every part of British India,
or by a Society having just pretensions to represent them," the British Indian Association solicited the collaboration of other Indian centers.
Madras was among those invited to cooperate, either
by forming a branch body affiliated with the
British Indian Association or by having an independent association with broadly similar objectives.
This invitation was discussed in February 1852 at
"a large meeting of the Native Inhabitants of the
Presidency," and it was then decided to form a

Madras Branch of the British Indian Association.
The constitution of the parent body was adopted and
a Committee of Management was elected to discharge
the routine matters of the branch association.[51]

It is apparent that this association was
largely the creation of the Hindu caucus which had
spearheaded the opposition to the missionaries during the preceding decade. The caucus consisted
mainly of merchants belonging to the Tamil and
Telugu non-Brahmin castes. The dominant figure was
undoubtedly Lakshmanarasu Chetty. His popularity
among the Hindus of Madras stemmed partly from his
courageous fight against official involvement in
missionary operations and partly from his readiness
to sacrifice his wealth in the cause of Hindu interests. The *Crescent*, for example, was known to
be run at considerable loss to Lakshmanarasu
Chetty. He brought into the Committee of Management a number of Hindu merchants, notably, P.
Appasamy Pillay, a senior partner of the agency
firm of P. Appasamy Pillay & Co., P. Veeraperumal
Pillay, a partner in the same firm, and A. Alwar
Chetty, proprietor of a large provision firm in
Black Town.[52]

But it would be wrong to conclude that this
Association was exclusively a body of the Hindu
merchants. Other interests were also represented.
C. Yagambaram Mudaliar, its first president, was a
rich *mirasdar* with extensive landed property in the
mofussil. Representing the small Western-educated
class were V. Sadagopah Charlu and V. Ramanuja
Chari, both graduates of Madras High School. It
was Ramanuja Chari who filled the position of
Secretary of the Association. Indeed, as the Torture Commission reported in 1854, these leaders
constituted "a fair representation of the Hindu
wealth and influence of the Presidency."[53] Exercising influence from outside the Association was
Harley, editor of the *Crescent* and trusted aide of
Lakshmanarasu Chetty.

Relations between the British Indian Association and the Madras Branch ran into difficulties

from the start. The Madras leaders found their
freedom of action "unexpectedly impeded by the
union of the Madras Association with that of
Calcutta." More important, there were differences
over the question of reform proposals to be submitted to the British Parliament. These differences became evident when Bengal drafted a
petition which, according to Lakshmanarasu Chetty,
related "almost wholly to the plans and recommendations of the change of government and for the
exaltation of the higher classes of Hindu," while
ignoring the "grand object" for which the Association was founded, namely, "the plain representation of tangible grievances and asking remedies
thereto." What took the situation to the brink was
the decision of the Bengali leaders to circulate
the petition in England without securing prior ap-
proval of Madras. The leaders of Madras, resenting
this "want of proper respect for their opinion,"
and, in view of "the uncertainty of the expenditure
attending a connection with the Calcutta Association," decided to form an independent organization
to serve the interests of South India. The new
body, called the Madras Native Association (hereafter referred to as MNA), was inaugurated at a
meeting in July 1852.[54]

The immediate task before this association
was to present its case in a formal petition to the
British Parliament. Data were painstakingly collected, and an appeal was launched for funds to
cover expenses, estimated at Rs 50,000. By December 1852 the document was completed, with Harley
putting the finishing touches, and a public meeting
was convened to seek endorsement before dispatching
it to England. The MNA summarized at the beginning
of its very lengthy petition what it regarded as
"the main grievances and wants" of South India:

That the grievances of your Petitioners arise
principally from the excessive taxation, and
the vexations which accompany its collection;
and the insufficiency, delay, and expense of

the Company's Courts of Law; and their chief
wants are the construction of roads, bridges,
and works for the supply of irrigation; and a
better provision for the education of the
people; they also desire a reduction of the
public expenditure and a form of local government more generally conducive to the happiness of the subjects and the prosperity of
the country.

THE MNA was sharply critical of the Company's
rule and dealt in detail with the shortcomings of
the revenue and judicial system in the Madras Presidency. Some of its harshest criticisms, however,
were reserved for the religious policies of the
Indian authorities. The MNA objected strongly to
the Caste Disabilities Removal Act, and charged
that in its implementation it had been "stretched,
even beyond the principle on which it was profes-
sedly framed." It also took exception to the diver-
sion of state funds to missionary schools under the
grants-in-aid system, contending that such a policy
would tend to "distinctly identify" the state with
missionary work. The British Parliament was also
asked to legislate, disallowing the Indian authorities' enactment of laws which caused "insult and
outrage" to the Indians and their religions.[55]
    This criticism of the British authorities, and
particularly the strictures on their religious
policies, created a split within the ranks of the
MNA. One faction, led by Srinivasa Pillay, decided
to secede, aggrieved at the tone and much of the
content of the petition.
    It must however be pointed out that there had
always been an element of friction between
Srinivasa Pillay and Lakshmanarasu Chetty, stemming
principally from their conception of the role that
the British Raj should play in effecting social
change in India. Srinivasa Pillay, who visualized
an India free from the shackles of caste, superstition, and poverty, believed that the British rulers
had a part to play in bringing about this

transformation. He wanted the Indians to give whole-hearted support to their rulers in achieving this grand design. Srinivasa Pillay had a long record of service in various charity and other organizations, including the Monegar Choultry, the Pachaiyappa Charities, and the Madras Literary Society. In these bodies, he had endeavored to cultivate cordial ties with the Europeans, be they officials, merchants, or missionaries, as he believed that such ties would strengthen the bond of goodwill between India and the West and elicit European help in the regeneration of the Indian people.

Lakshmanarasu Chetty, on the other hand, did not share much of Srinivasa Pillay's zeal for rapid Westernization or for seeking British aid to bring about social change in India. He was not opposed to social change per se* but he believed that change must come from within the community rather than from without. He was strongly opposed to the missionaries or the state, albeit an alien one, meddling in the religious and social affairs of the Indian people. Religious neutrality, Lakshmanarasu Chetty believed, was the correct policy for the British rulers to adopt. Where they departed from this, he wanted the Indians to declare their opposition and appeal to the Court of Directors and the British Parliament for redress.

After the break with the MNA, Srinivasa Pillay and his supporters formed the Hindu Progressive Improvement Society in November 1852. The program of this body included the promotion of widow remarriage, the encouragement of female education, and

---

*In 1864, when Keshub Chandra Sen visited Madras, Lakshmanarasu Chetty vigorously protested against "the absurd and injurious institution of caste." He also declared that he was for "a long time a zealous admirer" of the Brahmo Samaj. See K. C. Sen, *Diary in Madras and Bombay* (Calcutta, 1887), p. 16.

the uplifting of the depressed castes.[56] Many of
Srinivasa Pillay's coadjutors in this venture were
his Hindu friends, long associated with him in the
management of charitable organizations, such as the
Monegar Choultry and Pachaiyappa Charities.

His closest ally was M. Venkataroylu Naidu, a
pleader in the Sadr court, who shared many of
Srinivasa Pillay's ideas on the regeneration of
India. Venkataroylu Naidu was born into a poor
family, and his education was largely financed by
charitable friends and relatives. When he entered
government service, promotions came rapidly, but he
was summarily dismissed by the Tweeddale Administration for allegedly transmitting official papers to
the *Crescent*. He resorted to the court to prove
his innocence but he never regained his post and he
decided to enter the legal profession. Despite
these misfortunes, Venkataroylu Naidu harbored no
hostility towards the British. He fervently believed that Indians could only advance "by approaching closer and closer to their rulers" and called
for "an entire identification of European and
Native interests" to bring about the regeneration
of India.[57] For many years he had been a vigorous
advocate of widow remarriage, and wrote often in
the columns of the local newspapers urging some
action.

In July 1853 Venkataroylu Naidu started his
own paper, the *Rising Sun,* mainly to focus discussion on the social problems affecting the Hindu
community. In the same year, with the death of
Srinivasa Pillay, he assumed charge of the Hindu
Progressive Improvement Society and continued to
support the causes his predecessor had championed.
Schools were established for children of the depressed castes; scholarships were given to needy
students; and support was obtained for social legislation, like the Widow Remarriage Act of 1856.[58]
Venkataroylu Naidu was also anxious to provide the
youth of Madras with the opportunity to read widely
and acquire the facility of public speaking. Two
societies, called the Hindu Reading Room and the

Hindu Debating Society, were founded and they attracted students from the various educational institutions in Madras. Government support was welcomed,
mainly to acquire official publications free of
charge, and prominent Europeans were invited to deliver lectures or conduct discussion groups.
Through such means, Venkataroylu Naidu hoped to
stimulate the spirit of inquiry which he believed
would effect "a mighty revolution in India."[59] But
such grandiose hopes were rather misplaced in the
conservative world of mid-nineteenth century Madras.
Hindu opinion was hardly prepared to accept the
radical ideas emanating from the leaders of the
Hindu Progressive Improvement Society. Venkataroylu
Naidu died in 1863, and with him died many of his
projects, including the *Rising Sun*.[60]

The MNA was not adversely affected by the
secession of Srinivasa Pillay and his friends. If
anything, their secession strengthened the hand of
the faction led by Lakshmanarasu Chetty, which then
pressed ahead for political and economic reform in
South India. Throughout the 1850s, the period of
its active existence, the MNA remained a vigilant,
if unsparing, critic of the government's policies
and actions. In 1852 it had called for a full-
scale inquiry into Indian affairs before the Charter of the Company be renewed. This demand was
supported by other similar associations in India,
as well as the Indian Reform Society which had been
formed in London in March 1853, but the British
Government rejected the request.

The MNA was not despondent. In October 1853,
when Danby Seymour, Chairman of the Indian Reform
Society visited India to make an on-the-spot investigation, the MNA nominated two of its leading
members to accompany him on a tour of the *mofussil*.
The party visited a number of centers, including
Cuddalore, Trichinopoly, Kumbaconam, Salem,
Tinnevelly, Calicut, and Mangalore.[61] From the
evidence he gathered, Seymour was convinced of the
validity of the general complaints which the MNA
had listed in its petition to the British

Parliament. On his return to England, Seymour
called for an inquiry into the land tenure system
in South India, and alleged that excessive land tax
had led to many abuses in its collection, including
the use of torture by officials.[62] The Madras
authorities agreed to investigate these charges and
appointed a Torture Commission which found evidence
of torture perpetrated by Indian revenue and police
officials.[63]

One of the problems with which the MNA had to
contend stemmed directly from its relationship with
the local officials. Until the formation of this
body, the Madras authorities had been able to discharge their responsibilities largely immune to
public scrutiny or sustained criticism. The advent
of the MNA altered the situation somewhat, and
officials soon found that they had to face a small,
but active, band of Hindu leaders determined to
probe into governmental affairs, criticize policies,
and eagerly expose official misdemeanors. What
irked officials even more was the MNA's method of
securing redress of its grievances: not by directing its complaints to the local authorities but by
appealing directly to the British Parliament. Such
tactics, the officials lamented, were subversive of
their authority and encouraged unwarranted Parliamentary interference in Indian affairs. Moreover,
they bemoaned that the civil service in India was
being "denigrated from all sides," including by
such respectable organs as *The Times*.[64]

However, official antagonism towards the MNA
did not manifest itself openly until Seymour's
visit to South India. Seymour's inquiries into the
methods of revenue collection, and especially his
efforts to gather evidence of the use of torture,
annoyed local officials. Also irritating was the
attempt of the two leaders of the MNA who accompanied Seymour to establish branch associations in
the *mofussil*. Local leaders in Cuddalore, Trichinopoly, Salem, and Tinnevelly were persuaded to
start branches as a means of helping the MNA with
funds and information.[65]

In South Arcot, the Collector intervened to put an end to what was called "this Extortion."[66] In 1854 a more effective way was found to undermine political activity in the *mofussil*. Following the discovery in the Guntur district of a case where certain agents, claiming to represent the MNA, had raised subscriptions on promises of securing tax remission, the Madras Government issued a proclamation throughout the districts warning agents and subscribers that such actions were liable to criminal prosecution. The MNA protested its innocence, and the Torture Commission absolved it of any connection with the Guntur agents, but the Madras authorities steadfastly refused to withdraw the proclamation, the effect of which was to frighten the branch associations into abandoning their ties with the parent body in the metropolis.[67]

Despite this clash with the local authorities, the MNA showed no perceptible signs of abdicating its role as the watchdog of Hindu interests in South India. Petitions were regularly sent to the British Parliament. Public meetings were held from time to time to discuss local grievances. Addresses were presented to important dignitaries enumerating the demands of the Association or acknowledging their services to the country. One such address was presented to Lord Canning in February 1856 on his assumption of the governor-generalship.[68]

Also, a continuing watch was maintained on the activities of local officials, and misdemeanors or highhanded behavior promptly exposed. One such incident involved a *tahsildar* accused of torturing some weavers in Chingleput district to realize arrears in loom tax. The MNA claimed, in a petition to Parliament in January 1856, that the *tahsildar* had acted on the strength of an order issued by the Collector.[69] The incident was discussed in the House of Lords, while the Madras Board of Revenue initiated its own inquiry which ultimately led to the dismissal of the *tahsildar* and the censure of the Collector.[70] This, however, was not

the kind of justice which the MNA was seeking. It
had only wanted to demonstrate that, contrary to
what the Torture Commission reported, Indian officials resorted to practices of this nature only
under instructions or covert encouragement of their
European superiors.

One subject which continued to generate controversy throughout the fifties was the question of
Christian proselytization. Hindu suspicions about
official collusion with the missionaries were never
completely allayed, and from time to time Hindu
leaders alleged a pro-missionary bias in the
actions of the local authorities.

This underlying mistrust of the executive was
best illustrated during the riots in Tinnevelly in
December 1858. Amid rising religious tension in
South India as a result of renewed missionary agitation against the policy of religious neutrality,
the decision of the European Magistrate in Tinnevelly to allow a Christian burial party to use a
street occupied by the higher castes led to a
violent clash in which ten Hindus were killed and
nineteen wounded. The Madras Government approved
the action of the district officials, and ordered
the rigorous prosecution of those suspected of
rioting.

The MNA was unhappy with this order and convened a public meeting in April 1859 to discuss
this and other related issues. Although boycotted
by Venkataroylu Naidu and his friends, the meeting
attracted many Muslims from the metropolis and some
Hindu leaders from the *mofussil*. The meeting approved a memorial to the Secretary of State for
India which attributed the Tinnevelly disturbance
to the machinations of the missionaries. It was
claimed that the magistrate's decision to reverse
the old ruling, disallowing Christians the use of
the street occupied by the higher castes, was the
result of missionary pressure. The MNA was equally
critical of the way in which the Tinnevelly investigations had been handled. It complained that,
instead of appointing an impartial commission, the

Madras Government had entrusted the task to persons "implicated in the unhappy affair."[71]

Sir Charles Trevelyan, who had just assumed the governorship of the Presidency, accepted the memorial as "a genuine expression of the Native mind" and regarded it as creditable that "the faithful people of the South have had recourse to the legal and constitutional mode of petition" in airing their grievances. Though not always agreeing with the sentiments expressed in the memorial, he nevertheless felt that missionary agitation in England had created widespread fear among the inhabitants of South India that the existing policy might be changed and of the "tremendous machine of the Government being brought into the field against them." Trevelyan believed that a firm and authoritative declaration upholding the policy of religious neutrality would put an end to these fears.[72]

The Tinnevelly riots of 1858 provided the last occasion when the MNA held a mass meeting in Madras. Though not apparent at that time, the active days of the Association were gradually drawing to a close. During the next three years, the MNA functioned in a very sporadic fashion. In April 1860 it memorialized the British Parliament calling for the restoration of the Tanjore Raj,[73] and in the same month petitioned the Indian Legislative Council protesting against the proposed license duty and income tax.[74] In March 1862 a deputation from the Association called on the Governor of Madras to plead the case of the *mirasdars* in respect of rights over waste land.[75] Four months later, the MNA was said to be "practically defunct," and moves were afoot for the formation of a new "Native Association."[76] Thus, after a decade of active life, the MNA had retired into oblivion.

Whatever the reasons for its demise, and these are by no means clear from available evidence,[77] the MNA was the first real attempt at organizing a political association along Western lines in South India. Although founded by the Hindu commercial elite in Madras, which felt its established traditions threatened by the actions of the Christian missions, this association cannot be regarded as the mere mouthpiece of the narrow interests of this group, nor was it the platform for the ventilation of specifically religious grievances. In effect, its signal contribution lay in its elaborate criticisms of the high level of public taxation in South India and its graphic portrayal of the corrupt machinery through which revenue was being collected. That the Madras Government took heed of these criticisms, reflected for instance in its decision to reduce land tax in 1855, is a testimony to the adroitness of the leaders of the MNA in harnessing the instruments of modern political protest to secure redress of their grievances.

The dissolution of the MNA symbolized the decline in the importance of the Hindu commercial elite in the civic life of Madras. Propelled into prominence in the 1840s on the crest of the anti-missionary sentiment then prevailing in South India, this elite had given institutional expression to its power by organizing the MNA. However, as anti-missionary feelings slowly subsided during the 1860s, the influence of this elite also waned, and a rival group emerged to provide an alternative focus of leadership in the Madras Presidency. Members of the latter group were products of the Madras High School who had achieved distinction in the service of the British Indian administration. To understand the influence that this group wielded it is important to have some idea of its educational background as well as the strategic position that it occupied in the government.

2. The New Learning and the Advent of the Administrative Elite

BIRTH OF AN ELITE SCHOOL

In April 1841 an event was celebrated in Madras which was to have important consequences, not only for the metropolis, but for South India as a whole. This was the formal inauguration of the so-called High School of the Madras University, better known as the Madras High School. At a ceremony of pomp and grandeur, attended by the Nawab of Arcot and "the principal members of Society at the Presidency, both European and Native," the Governor of Madras, Lord Elphinstone, told his audience that the proceedings they were witnessing should be regarded as "the dawn of a new era rather than the opening of a new school." He went on to say that the success of this institution would be the true vindication of British commitment to work for "the improvement and welfare of the country."[1]

Although Elphinstone might have exaggerated the significance of a venture in which he was largely instrumental, his sentiments reflected the view of many contemporary observers who saw the launching of the Madras High School as the first serious attempt to disseminate Western education in South India. Elphinstone, when he assumed the governorship in 1837, was perturbed to discover that more than three decades of British rule in the

Madras Presidency had only yielded a plethora of
educational schemes which at best had only been
partially implemented. In effect, all that the
government could show was a Normal School started
recently in Madras to train teachers. Elphinstone
was dissatisfied with the role that the government
had played in fostering education, convinced as he
was that Western education provided a splendid instrument for the regeneration of the subject
peoples. Cautious not to repeat the errors of the
past, but nevertheless ambitious to formulate a
comprehensive and lasting educational scheme, he
devoted much time to studying the official papers
on the subject, acquainted himself with contemporary thinking on education, and consulted both
officials and nonofficials in Madras, and elsewhere,
as to ways in which the government could advance
education in South India.

The result of Elphinstone's labors was the
production of his "Minute on Education" of December
1839. This document was notable not so much for
originality as for its concise and clear definition
of what the state should do in the field of education. Elphinstone echoed two important ideas which
had by now become orthodox official thinking at the
highest policy-making levels. First, he accepted
Bentinck's proposition that "the great object of the
British Government ought to be the promotion of
European literature and science among the natives
of India, and that all funds appropriated would be
best employed on English education alone."[2] Second,
Elphinstone subscribed to the "filtration theory"
of education which had been strongly championed by
the Court of Directors in London for some years.
He did not believe in mass education, nor did such
experiments seem feasible to him given the scarce
resources at the disposal of the government. His
scheme was designed to train an elite, a chosen few
from the higher strata of Indian society, which was
to receive the high literary culture of the West
through the medium of the English language. On
completion of its educational training, this elite

group was expected to play the dual role of diffusing its enlightenment to the rest of the community
and of shouldering the responsibilities of high
office in the government.

The scheme which Elphinstone proposed was
modelled on the Scottish educational system, consisting of a college to impart instruction in the
higher branches of Western literature, philosophy,
and science, and a high school to give more elementary courses in the above subjects, besides teaching the vernacular languages. The high school was
to be launched immediately, and a University Board
was constituted in May 1840 to help in its organization.[3]

The first President of the Board was George
Norton, Elphinstone's own choice and a popular one
among the Hindus in Madras. Elphinstone was discerning enough to recognize that the success of his
scheme depended to a large extent on winning Hindu
cooperation. Norton's selection went some distance
in securing this, while the reservation of seven of
the fifteen seats in the Board for Hindus and
Muslims also helped. At the same time, Hindu fears
about the subversion of their religion were allayed
by the ruling that no religious doctrines would be
taught in the institution, nor religious books supplied for that purpose. Admission was open to all
creeds and groups, although care was to be taken
"to avoid whatever may tend to violate or offend
the religious feelings of any class." These conditions were embodied in the "Fundamental Rules"
which the University Board drafted in 1841 to regulate the internal workings of the Madras High
School.[4]

Started with such assumptions, it was inevitable that social distinctions would come to dictate the character of this institution. On the one
hand, school fees were fixed at the inordinately
high rate of four rupees per month, primarily to
prevent "a large influx of Pupils from an inferior
class" who might deter "the more respectable
families" from sending their children to the Madras

High School. Attempts to reduce the fees were resisted by the University Board for almost a decade
on the plea that such a step would defeat the very
purpose for which the institution was founded.[5]
Also, students from the "polluting castes" were denied admission by the University Board which appeared overzealous in respecting the susceptibilities of the high caste Hindus.

It was not until 1851 that the first Harijan
students entered the portals of the Madras High
School, and their arrival was greeted by a loud
Hindu protest which led to the exodus of some high
caste students, while a Hindu member of the University Board tendered his resignation. The Board was
embarrassed by this opposition but stood firm to
weather the crisis, while belatedly declaring that
social distinctions would not be recognized in the
institution.[6]

However, this change did not alter in any
radical sense the composition of the Madras High
School. Its students continued to come mainly from
Brahmin and higher non-Brahmin caste groups, with a
small sprinkling of Indian Christians, Eurasians,
and Muslims.

The man who more than anyone else stamped his
personality on the Madras High School was Eyre
Burton Powell, the Headmaster, and subsequently
Principal of Presidency College. The University
Board had wanted a head who possessed not only
"scholastic acquirements" but also "a willingness
to bend those faculties for a time to the patient
tuition of Native Youths emerging from a total ignorance of civilized learning." Help was sought
from Mountstuart Elphinstone, a former Governor of
Bombay, and he recommended Powell who had recently
taken his B.A. from Cambridge with "the highest
grade of honor."[7]

Powell was anxious to mold the Madras High
School along the lines of an English public school,
an ideal which was shared by George Norton, President of the University Board. The Headmaster was
invested with unshackled discretion to carry out

instruction and discipline in the school. He interviewed youths seeking admission, and his recommendations were invariably accepted by the standing sub-
committee responsible for student admissions.
Within the institution, strict rules governed the
conduct of the students.

Powell did not believe in the efficacy of physical punishment, nor were his colleagues similarly
disposed. Instead, discipline was to be enforced
by winning the confidence of the pupils, by cultivating friendships, and by seeking the help of
senior students who were appointed Praeposters with
general authority over student discipline. Powell
took almost a parental interest in the welfare of
his students, listened to their problems, helped
them in their studies during his spare time, and
coached them in sports. He was very fond of astro-
nomy, and he invited interested students to his
observatory to tell them about the mysteries of the
solar system and the eclipses of the moon. The
importance of literary and debating societies was
also recognized. Powell urged his students to
organize regular debates and lectures, and sometimes participated in these activities to set a
personal example. Students found in him a model in
the development of their ideals, values, and tastes,
and a generous patron when in financial trouble.
Powell evinced particular interest in the bright
boys who were often marked out for special awards
and other favors.

Not surprisingly, many of his students regarded him with affection and attachment which they
treasured for much of their adult life. One of
Powell's distinguished students, T. Madava Rao,
said of his Headmaster in 1883: ". . . I love him,
I respect him, I admire him, I reverence him as my
great 'Guru' . . . How he laboured for us! What
singular devotion--what rare enthusiasm was his!
He made our study literally a pleasure."[8] Indeed,
as Kamesvara Aiyar says, Powell was "a typical
Acharya of the old days of India, whose relation to
the pupil was a life-long tie."[9]

The courses offered in the Madras High School were obviously aimed at imparting a certain quality of substantive knowledge of Western science and literature. However, it was not the intention of the founders of the institution to equip students for any particular calling, except perhaps the public service. The aim was to stimulate and develop the intellectual faculties of the students which was believed to be the hallmark of civilized existence. During the first two years, students were taught grammar, reading exercises, arithmetic, and writing. Mastery of these subjects would provide the students with the necessary foundation to pursue courses in history, natural philosophy, moral philosophy, geography, and mathematics.[10] Normally, a student would take four years to complete the entire course and secure the Proficient's degree. Those who aspired to an honors degree spent an additional year doing intensive work on certain subjects, including the study of prescribed texts. Powell and his colleagues were rigorous in the standards they set, and promotions from one class to another were only granted when all the requirements were met with.[11] This factor, coupled with the large drop-out of students in the lower classes owing to financial and other reasons, severely restricted the numbers obtaining the Proficient's degree. Indeed, between 1841-55, that is the period before the college branch was opened, only 36 students had secured this degree, although student enrollment had grown steadily from 67 to 221 over the same period.[12] The institution, then, remained loyal to Elphinstone's ideals: only the deserving few, an elite group, were to be honored with degrees.

When the Madras High School was launched, it was the ambition of its sponsors that it should ultimately "surpass all that had been done or attempted before in India."[13] Drawing on their knowledge of educational experiments in India and United Kingdom, Elphinstone and his coadjutors had given considerable thought to the eventual

formation of a full-fledged college giving courses
in science, natural philosophy, law and jurispru-
dence, medicine, and engineering. The collegiate
branch, which was an integral part of the original
Elphinstone scheme, was to be organized as soon as
the first batch of Proficients graduated from the
High School, with departments of science, philosophy, and law. Plans for the opening of engineering and medical colleges were finalized in 1842,
the details largely drawn up by the University
Board and approved in principle by Elphinstone before he relinquished his governorship in the same
year.[14]

But as it turned out, these schemes were left
unattended for a decade after the departure of
Elphinstone. The reasons for this inaction are
many and complex, and little purpose will be served
to discuss them here at length. George Norton and
his friends in the University Board believed that
Tweeddale was the main obstruction and alleged that
he had allowed his pro-missionary bias to influence
his educational policies.[15] Tweeddale claimed that
the scheme of his predecessor was too ambitious and
that the anticipated support from Indian benefactors had not materialized. As relations between
the Tweeddale Administration and the University
Board deteriorated, a bitter conflict started in
Madras between the missionaries and their opponents
over such issues as the introduction of religious
education in the Madras High School, the reduction
of school fees, and the extension of preference to
Proficients seeking admission into the public service. This controversy continued into the governorship of Sir Henry Pottinger, and it was not until
the reconstitution of the University Board in April
1852 that any concrete steps were taken to implement some of the plans chalked out a decade earlier.

One result of this controversy was the concentration of state patronage on a single educational
institution, the Madras High School. Expenditure
on this school averaged Rs 30,000 annually during
the 1840s,[16] which meant the accumulation of a fair

surplus over the years from the original educational apportionment of Rs 50,000 per annum. The
University Board would have welcomed it if this
surplus could have been utilized to build suitable
premises for the school. Initially, the institution had rented out the former post office building
in Egmore, but the University Board found this
arrangement unsatisfactory and called for the construction of a suitable structure which would not
only provide adequate classrooms but also staff
quarters, playgrounds, and other facilities. The
Court of Directors was sympathetic, as it felt that
such an edifice would have "a powerful effect in
attracting public confidence, and giving stability
and popularity to the establishment."[17] But
Governor Tweeddale remained skeptical, and the new
buildings were not constructed until the early
1870s.

Of greater importance was the dispute over the
starting of the so-called "superior provincial
schools" in the *mofussil*. Elphinstone had proposed
in 1841 the establishment of four such schools to
cater to the needs of the four linguistic regions
which made up the Madras Presidency. His departure
led to inaction, stemming partly from the opposition of the Court of Directors who wanted the consolidation of the Madras High School before embar-
king on other ventures.[18] More than a decade
elapsed before the provincial schools were established, but this delay gave the Madras High School
a headstart and ensured that its graduates would
receive in the 1840s the benefits from higher education available to the others during the 1850s and
after.

What were the social origins of these graduates? Of the thirty-six students who had obtained
the Proficient's degree up to 1855, no less than
twenty were Brahmins, twelve non-Brahmin Hindus,
three Eurasians and one Indian Christian.[19] It is
significant that the Brahmins, constituting a
little over 3 per cent of the population of the
Madras Presidency, accounted for over half the

total Proficients. This trend was to continue
throughout the nineteenth century and will be explained later. However, it is worth noting here
that the Brahmin subcastes which took advantage of
the opportunities offered by the Madras High School
were the Desasthas, Sri-Vaishnavas, and Smarthas.
These were the groups which had wielded administrative power in the Presidency and, doubtless, they
recognized that Western education was essential for
their continued access to the public service. In
fact, a significant number of the Proficients came
from families of administrative backgrounds, from
sons of Dewans of Indian States to those whose parents were low-paid clerks in the Madras Revenue
Department. In many cases, these families lived in
Madras or nearby districts like Chingleput and
North Arcot, although in some instances students
came from more remote areas such as Tanjore.

RECRUITMENT INTO THE ADMINISTRATION

It was widely assumed by those closely connected with the Madras High School that the alumni
of this institution would furnish the new generation of administrators capable of holding important
positions in the government. Both Elphinstone and
George Norton were confident that this new corps of
administrators would be men of a different breed,
equipped not only with Western knowledge but also
imbibing a new ethos alien to India.
    No doubt, altruistic considerations demanded
that this new corps of Indian officials be raised.
If British commitment to the idea of the regeneration of its conquered subjects was to have any
tangible meaning, it was essential that an honest
and efficient Indian civil service be created,
especially as the old administrative elites have
been found to be singularly deficient in these
attributes. However, British policy was also governed by reasons of expediency and self-interest.
Elphinstone and Norton were convinced that the new

learning would produce an elite group fundamentally
loyal to the British Raj, one which could be expected to play a mediative role between the alien
ruler and the subject people. In the words of
George Norton, Western education was the panacea
"to the very regeneration of the (Indian) people,
and their permanent loyalty and amalgamation with
the British nation."[20] It was to be a loyalty not
founded on narrow self-interest but born out of a
common attachment to values inherited from Western
culture.

No one showed greater consciousness of the
need to imbue the rising generation with these
values than Powell himself. Convinced that his
students were the chosen ones, he nurtured in them
the virtues of moral rectitude, a sense of responsibility, and a capacity for sustained work. These
virtues he continued to stress even after his students had left school and attained high positions
in life. Powell also set rigorous academic standards as he believed that intellectual attainment
was an essential element for success in public service.[21] He also tried to impress on the general
public and the local authorities in particular that
the Proficient's degree was only conferred on those
who had demonstrated high intellectual attainment.
Part of the examination for this degree was held in
public, lasted many days, and attracted several
Europeans and Indians. High government functionaries were also enlisted as examiners, and in this
way officials came to have a first hand knowledge
of the ability of the scholars.

However, when the first Proficients appeared
on the scene, little had been done at an official
level to receive them into the public service.
This was as much the result of Elphinstone's departure as the reluctance of the heads of departments
to surrender their control of patronage. Elphinstone had taken some preliminary steps to give education its due place in administrative recruitment.
He had discussed with his senior official colleagues the desirability of "requiring all Natives

and others to pass an educational examination before they are admitted into the public service."
The University Board was asked to report, and it
prepared a scheme for holding these tests in Madras
before extending them to the *mofussil* as well.[22]
But Elphinstone left before these proposals were
accepted by the government and his successor,
Tweeddale, began to drag his feet. In 1845, when
the University Board reiterated its call for some
kind of educational tests for entry into the administration, the Tweeddale Administration retorted
that as education was backward in the *mofussil* it
would be "premature and detrimental to public interests" to institute such tests.[23] The matter
rested there for another decade.

To the early graduates of the Madras High
School this was a hard decision to take. They had
been led to believe during their student days that
they could seek a place in the public service consistent with their academic attainments. Now they
found that their degrees did not earn them automatic entry, and they were compelled to depend on
their own devices or court the goodwill of influential European officials. The first Proficient,
C. V. Ranganada Sastri, for example, found a patron
in G. J. Casamajor, a judge of the Provincial Court
of Appeal and Circuit, who not only financed his
education but also helped him to secure his first
appointment as head clerk in the Subordinate
Judge's Court at Chittoor.[24] Another Proficient,
V. Rama Iyengar, obtained his appointment, as
translator in the Mahratta *Kacheri* of the Madras
Board of Revenue, largely with the help of its Secretary, Thomas Pycroft, who was impressed with the
academic attainments of the young candidate.[25]
Some Proficients, like Seshia Sastri, had to cultivate the friendship of their European patrons the
hard way. Sastri waited for several days at the
gate of Henry Montgomery, Member of the Board of
Revenue, and "*salaamed* the *Saheb* whenever he drove
out or returned from his morning drive or ride."
He was eventually rewarded with an acting clerkship

in the Board of Revenue.[26] Appointments at such
subordinate levels were the rule rather than the
exception, the Proficients accepting such humble
positions as clerks, writers, translators, and interpreters in the hope of rapid promotions.

From the select band of thirty-six Proficients
who had passed out from the Madras High School, no
less than twenty-five had secured appointments in
the judicial or revenue line of the Madras administration. As Elphinstone had predicted, and as
George Norton and Powell had fondly hoped, the public service had proved to be the largest employer
of the first generation of Western educated class
in South India. This stemmed partly from absence
of opportunities elsewhere,* but to a greater extent it should be attributed to the high esteem in
which public service was held among the upper caste
Hindus.

No doubt the subordinate positions in which
the Proficients found themselves at the start
caused unhappiness and even resentment. They complained that their scholastic attainments had not
been adequately rewarded nor their talent suitably
employed. To such graduates, Powell and Norton
counselled patience and loyal service. *"Sacrifice
the Present and secure the Future,"* wrote Powell to
Seshia Sastri in 1849. Norton advised Sastri that
his career could best be advanced by faithful

---

*C. Karunakara Menon's characterization of
these Proficients is worth quoting here: "The young
men with whom Seshia [Sastri] studied were all of
one mind in this respect. Their thoughts and aspirations were moulded alike, and they were all
trained in the same manner. There was then no public life in which they could distinguish themselves.
There were no parliamentary laurels awaiting them.
They had no intention to shine as scholars or
writers. They could not think of shining as warriors or heroes." See his *A Critical Essay on Sir
Seshia Sastri, K.C.S.I.* (Madras, 1903), pp. 1-2.

service to his European superior: "If you make the
best use of your opportunities—in sedulously attending to all that Mr. Elliot directs or explains,
and to all the duties he requires of you, you will
learn those qualifications which will raise you to
a high post perhaps eventually and at any rate ensure your profitable employment hereafter." Seshia
Sastri took heed of the advice and within three
years of joining service was elevated to the post
of *tahsildar* at Masulipatam.[27] This was not an isolated instance. Many of Seshia Sastri's fellow
graduates were equally quick in climbing the administrative ladder. It was this quick mobility which
led the University Board to claim in 1851 that
there was "no instance of any Proficient having
failed to gain a position likely to lead to a pros-
perous, and possibly to a distinguished, career in
life."[28]

However, not every Proficient believed that
the avenues of rapid advancement lay within the
administrative setup of the Madras Presidency. T.
Madava Rao, for example, decided to throw up his
subordinate position in the Accountant-General's
Office in Madras to become tutor to the princes of
Travancore. This was to prove the turning point in
his life, and the beginning of a distinguished
career in this Indian State. Sadagopah Charlu, a
classmate of Madava Rao, began his career as a
translator in the Sadr Court, but, unhappy with the
prospects, he switched to law, became a qualified
Pleader and built up a lucrative practice in Madras
before his death in 1863. P. Rangiah Naidu began
his life in an almost identical fashion. After
serving for a few years as a translator in the
Small Cause Court, he turned to law which enabled
him to take an active part in public movements. Of
course, there were some Proficients who had never
trespassed the corridors of the Madras administration. One of them was Basil Lovery, a Eurasian,
who became a teacher in Pachaiyappa School and a
few years later its Principal.

However, there was no doubt whatsoever that

prestige and influence belonged to those Proficients who had staked their fortunes on public service. Their emergence as a powerful elite group in
South India after the Mutiny was due to several
factors, but principally to the thoroughgoing administrative changes initiated at the level of the
Indian agency. In an earlier chapter, it was shown
that widespread corruption had permeated the district administration and that, consequently, the
Madras authorities had attempted to cleanse the
system by revising the methods of recruitment into
the Indian agency and by stressing the importance
of Western education as a factor in improving the
moral tone of the administration. These far-
reaching changes were only taken under considerable
pressure from the Board of Control in London. Sir
Charles Wood, who as President of the Board of
Control had borne the brunt of the criticisms directed against the Company rule during the Charter
agitation, was anxious to promote some "internal
improvements" in South India. In 1854 he chose
Lord Harris as Governor of Madras to "infuse new
blood" into the administration of that Presidency.[29]
Among the reforms which Wood advocated was the recasting of the Indian agency, and especially the
reduction of the influence of the Mahratta
Brahmins.

On his arrival in Madras, Harris lost little
time in carrying out an inquiry into the state of
the local administration. The revelations of the
recent years and the report of the Torture Commission convinced him that some reforms were necessary
and urgent. In 1854 he abolished the use of
Marathi as the language of revenue accounts, an
obvious blow at the pervasive influence of the
Mahratta Brahmins. In the following year, he accepted the recommendations of the Torture Commission
to relieve revenue officials of their police duties,
thereby reducing the concentration of power which
in the past was a fruitful source of abuse.[30] A
few months later, Harris won support of his local
advisers to create the posts of Deputy and

Assistant Collectors along the lines of other
Indian provinces. Sixty such posts were requested
from the Indian authorities, to be evenly distributed among the twenty districts in the presidency,
and recruitment to these positions was to be on the
basis of proven administrative experience or educational merit. Although not sanguine about over-
turning immediately the dominance of the Mahratta
Brahmins at the level of the district administration, Harris was convinced that the proposed
changes would eventually achieve the same result
as other social groups acquired Western education.[31]
There was little doubt that his hopes were pinned
on the Madras High School becoming the nursery for
the new cadre of district administrators.

Differences between the Indian and Madras
governments held up the implementation of the
scheme for the appointment of Deputy Collectors.
The bone of contention was the number of such positions to be established, as Calcutta thought that
the number demanded by Madras was excessive. An
impasse resulted, and it was not until January 1859
that Calcutta finally yielded. Meanwhile, the
Madras Government had drafted rules for holding
competitive examinations for the Uncovenanted
Service. Graduates of Arts and Law were exempted
from the tests, while it was stressed that those
aspiring for posts above Rs 50 per month should be
proficient in English.[32] The first examinations
were held in November 1858: 492 candidates presented themselves, of whom 206 passed. The Madras
Government, in a circular to all heads of departments, made it clear that future vacancies should
only be filled by successful candidates, with the
restriction that Tamils should not as a rule be
appointed in Telugu districts and vice versa.[33]

It was now apparent that at long last a clean
break had been made with the old system of recruiting Indians into the administration. Caste, kinship, and matrimonial ties were finally discarded
in favor of an open system of recruitment wherein
the claims of aspirants would be assessed on the

basis of competitive tests or educational qualifications. Without doubt, this system favored those
who had gone through an English-type education. In
effect, the impetus which advocates of Western
education in South India had been demanding for
some time was now supplied, and the consequences of
this change were far-reaching for the coming generations of Indian youth seeking high office and
social prestige.

For the moment, it was the products of the
Madras High School who emerged as the main beneficiaries of these changes. This was especially
evident when the Madras Government began to look
for "the most efficient men" to fill the newly-
created posts of Deputy Collectors. Of course,
some of the posts went to the older Indian officials holding positions of Head and Naib Sheristadars. They did not have superior English
education, but their accumulated experience over
the years and their record of loyal service made it
difficult for the Madras Government to ignore their
claims. But among the ranks of the outgoing Head
and Naib Sheristadars were also a breed of younger
men, essentially products of the Madras High School,
who had joined service after 1845 at very subordinate levels, but through industry, honesty, and the
help of their European patrons, had gained swift
promotions to catch up with their elder, erstwhile
compatriots.

It was from this younger group that some of
the Deputy Collectors were chosen. Prominent in
the first batch of forty Deputy Collectors appointed in March 1859 were A. Seshia Sastri, V. Rama
Iyengar, C. Ranga Charlu, M. Sadasivam Pillay, A.
Ramachandra Rao, T. Durmaroyan Mudali, R. Raghunatha Rao, and C. Sama Rao, all students of the
Madras High School.[34] Subsequent appointments included T. Muthusamy Iyer, P. Varada Chari, A.
Srinivasa Rao, and V. Rajagopala Chari, also from
the same institution, as well as P. Chentsal Rao,
who had studied in the Scotch Mission School at
Nellore. Nor did these younger men suffer by way

of seniority in relation to their elder and more
experienced colleagues. Of the half dozen Deputy
Collectors who held the rank of First Class in
1863, three were Proficients of the Madras High
School, namely, Rama Iyengar, Seshia Sastri, and
Ranga Charlu, each drawing a monthly salary of
Rs 600.[35]

Indicative of the measure of confidence which
was commanded by this new breed of administrators
was the way in which the Inam Commission was constituted in 1859. The Madras authorities had long
wrestled with this controversial question which had
led to interminable disputes with the *inam* holders
and even precipitated an insurrection in Cuddapah
in 1846 when the government attempted to resume
some *inam* lands.[36] Eventually, the authorities decided on a full-scale inquiry and the Madras Inam
Commission was set up to investigate all *inam*
titles and extend proprietory rights to holders
who could adduce evidence of long possession. Sir
Charles Trevelyan, who succeeded Harris as
Governor in 1859, felt that the task would "require
trustworthiness and intellect of a high order.
Fortunately the sifting which the Uncovenanted Service has lately undergone for the selection of
Deputy Collectors places a large body of highly-
qualified officers at our disposal."[37] He urged
G. N. Taylor, the Inam Commissioner, to select his
assistants from this class of officers. Taylor
chose eleven Indians, all Deputy Collectors, of
whom ten were products of the Madras High School
and the other a student of the Scotch Mission
School at Nellore. Among those whom he chose were
Ranga Charlu, who was to be one of the two Special
Assistants to the Commission, Rama Iyengar, Seshia
Sastri, Muthusamy Iyer, and Chentsal Rao.[38] It was
apparent to many in Madras in which direction the
winds of official favor were then blowing in South
India.

The work of the Inam Commission lasted for
seven years. The Commission went from district to
district, listening to claims submitted and

recognizing those which met its requirements. At
the outset there was much suspicion and even hostility to its operations, partly caused by ill-
founded fears as to what the Commission was seeking
to do.[39] The first task of Taylor's assistants was
to dispel these fears, and this was done fairly
quickly by patient talks with *inamdars* and by the
care exercised in dealing with every claim. Progress was naturally slow, but both Trevelyan and
Taylor were happy with the progress of the Commission and were lavish in their praise of the work of
their Indian assistants. Taylor testified later
that the success of the Inam Commission was "undoubtedly due to the admirable native agency it was
my good fortune to employ." He claimed that without his Indian assistants' "intimate knowledge of
landed tenures, the eminent ability, and indefatigable industry," the work of the Commission could
never have been accomplished. He was particularly
impressed by Ranga Charlu's ability, and bestowed
high praise on his "intimate knowledge of native
character, his excellent judgement, [and] his won-
derful capacity for affairs."[40]

By now such praise from the European superiors was almost commonplace. This was, indeed, the
vindication of the confidence which a few European
officials had placed on the products which Powell
had trained in the Madras High School. Others, who
had entertained doubts about the fitness of the
Proficients, were now willing to acknowledge that
this new breed of administrators was infinitely
superior to their predecessors in industry as much
as in integrity.

Trevelyan gave expression in 1860 to the general view that "the rising generation of Native
officers who have been educated in the [Madras]
High School and have since acquired a few years'
administrative experience, are a remarkable set of
men." They possessed, in his opinion, "more
thoughtfulness--more stability of character than
the corresponding Class in Bengal--and have already
acquired the confidence of their European Superiors

and of their own Countrymen." In fact, he saw in
these Indian administrators the kind of men who
could be nominated to the Legislative Councils when
the proposed constitutional changes were completed.
Trevelyan was convinced that the virtues of this
administrative elite could be traced to their
Western education, which had instilled in them "a
higher standard of morality" than what was prevalent in the country.[41]

This view was shared by John Bruce Norton,
Government Pleader and an advocate of Western education in India. Norton contended in 1855 that the
Indians who had acquired English education perforce
"exhibited quite a new phase of a Hindu character.
They are actuated by a European feeling of honour:
they entertain an English sense of the meaning of
the word Duty." He praised the administrative
elite for creating "a new morality; that Office is
no longer looked upon as the legalised opportunity
for plunder, bribery extortion, intimidation, [and]
corruption."[42]

Once it had won such laurels from its European
superiors, the administrative elite gradually
annexed positions in the official hierarchy, which
in the past were inaccessible to Indians. By the
1850s, it was recognized that educated Indians
ought to be slowly introduced into the special
departments of the Uncovenanted Service, notably,
Salt, Sea Customs, Stamps, Registration, and Education; but headships of these departments were the
monopoly of Europeans, often Covenanted Civilians.
The first Indian to break into this European preserve was Rama Iyengar who in 1867 was appointed as
Superintendent of Stamps at a monthly salary of Rs
1000. Eight years later he became Inspector-
General of Registration, still the only Indian to
head a department in the Madras Presidency.[43] It
was a similar story in the judicial line. Here,
the highest position thrown open to qualified
Indians was that of the Principal *Sadr Amin*. But
this was not for long. In 1859 Ranganada Sastri,
the first Proficient of the Madras High School, was

given the acting Judgeship of the Court of Small
Causes in Madras, largely at the prompting of
Governor Trevelyan. Three years later he was confirmed and he continued to hold this office until
his retirement in 1880.[44]

A Proficient who attained greater eminence in
the judicial service was T. Muthusamy Iyer. He had
worked in several departments after entering government service in 1854. In 1859 he was one of the
many graduates of the Madras High School to be
appointed Deputy Collector, but, unlike his colleagues, he showed greater interest in judicial
rather than revenue work. He had passed the
Pleader's Test in 1856, and a decade later he took
the degree of Bachelor of Law, obtaining a First,
which was all the more remarkable because he had
studied part-time. His superiors decided to use
his talents to the best effect and appointed him a
Judge of the Court of Small Causes, first in Madras
and later in Madura. The apotheosis of his career
came in July 1878 when he was appointed Sub-protem
Judge of the Madras High Court, the first Indian to
attain this status in South India, and thereby,
breached what had, thus far, been the preserve of
Covenanted Civilians and European barristers.
Muthusamy Iyer was confirmed at the Bench in 1883,
officiated briefly as Chief Justice in 1891, and
"died in harness" four years later. For one who
had started life as an assistant to a village
accountant in Tanjore district, Muthusamy Iyer's
rise was indeed meteoric.[45]

Despite the many opportunities that came their
way in the Madras Presidency, it was nevertheless
in the Indian States that this "galaxy of notable
administrators" was able to display its varied
talents and achieve the kind of fame which earned
it the accolade of posterity.[46] The man who blazed
this trail was T. Madava Rao, who in 1849 had
accepted the post of tutor to the princes of
Travancore. Obviously, he found his usefulness in
this position somewhat restricted, and decided to
enter administrative service in 1853 as Deputy

Peshkar. Promotions came swiftly: in 1855 he was
made Dewan Peshkar, and two years later duly elevated to Dewanship, thus emulating his father and
uncle who had both been dewans of Travancore
earlier in the century. This position was the
summit of Indian aspirations in the nineteenth century, at least in so far as the Proficients of the
Madras High School were concerned. As William
Robinson, Senior Member of the Madras Revenue Board,
remarked to Seshia Sastri in 1872, the dewanship of
an Indian State was "quite the highest [post] open
to the natives of this Presidency. For *there* you
are truly a native ruling your own countrymen."[47]
Indeed, here was a relatively large state, inhabited by millions of people, entrusted to the care
of a young man of thirty who had barely four years
of real administrative experience. But Madava Rao
was equal to the occasion, and during his sixteen
years as Dewan, he made Travancore "the Model State"
in India.   In 1873 Madava Rao accepted the Dewanship of Indore, and two years later moved to a
similar position in Baroda. By the time he retired
in 1882, Madava Rao had devoted twenty-four years
of his life as ruler of three of the most important
States in Central and South India. Undoubtedly, he
was the outstanding statesman of South India during
the nineteenth century--Fawcett called him "the
Turgot of India."[48]

Madava Rao's contemporaries in the Madras High
School followed his lead. Seshia Sastri was Dewan
of Travancore from 1880-87; Runga Charlu was Dewan
of Mysore from 1881-83; and Raghunatha Rao was
twice Dewan of Indore, in 1875-80 and 1886-88.
Another student of Powell who attained prominence
in the service of an Indian State was Sadasivam
Pillay, who became Chief Justice of the Travancore
High Court.

Having reached the heights of administrative
fame, these men were frequently called upon to
serve in legislative councils, commissions of inquiry, and in public and charity work under the
aegis of the government. Rama Iyengar, for example,

was a nominated member of the Madras Legislative
Council for twelve years; Seshia Sastri served in
the same chamber in 1878-79; while Ranganada
Sastri's tenure in the Madras legislature was cut
short to seven months by his death. Madava Rao,
who had repeatedly turned down offers of a seat in
the Imperial Legislative Council, was chairman of
the Malabar Land Tenure Commission, set up in 1885
to investigate into the causes of agrarian unrest
in that district. Muthusamy Iyer, for example,
presided over the Malabar Marriage Commission in
1891 and the Hindu Religious Endowments Committee
in 1893. For such distinguished service, the
administrative elite was granted honors which in
the past had been reserved for ruling Princes and
eminent European civilians. Madava Rao, Muthusamy
Iyer, and Seshia Sastri received knighthoods; Rama
Iyengar, Runga Charlu, and Raghunatha Rao were
made Companions of the Order of the Star of India.

ATTITUDE TOWARDS SOCIAL CHANGE

It was inevitable that the administrative
elite, because of its superior Western education
and its wide experience of the conditions of its
own society, should thrust itself forward as a new
leadership group committed, however vaguely, to
certain social and political objectives. Basically,
it saw its social goal as one of trying to reconcile the ways of a tradition-ridden society with
the dynamic and egalitarian values of its alien
rulers. In attempting to make some essential adjustments in Hindu social behavior, the administrative elite was seeking not only to rid its
society of some archaic usages but also to remove
the obstacles standing in the way of India's regeneration.
Some of these adjustments would involve a
radical break with tradition, but this elite group
was quick to deny the charge that it was seeking
to reorder Hindu society along Western lines.

Indeed, it always claimed that the changes it advocated had the sanction of ancient Hindu scriptures,
an argument often employed to placate the conservative elements of Hindu society. However, despite
invoking the authority of the Shastras and other
Hindu religious texts, it could not disguise the
fact that the changes urged aimed a blow at some
cherished canons of upper caste Hindu social behavior. By rejecting infant marriage and enforced
widowhood, the administrative elite seemed to undermine the style of life of the Brahmins and higher
non-Brahmin castes, and even endanger the ritual
supremacy of these caste groups. It is not surprising that this social program generated so much
hostility in South India, not only from the ranks
of the religious elite but also from the upper
Hindu castes as a whole.

It is interesting to note that the social
ideas of the administrative elite have their roots
in its student days at the Madras High School.
Swept away to some extent by its initial admiration
for Western institutions, and no doubt influenced
by the views of its European teachers, this elite
group gave a radical twist to its prognostications
on the evils afflicting the country at large. T.
Madava Rao, in an essay written in 1845, attributed
India's backwardness and cultural stagnation partly
to the misrule of the "sceptred tyrants" of the
past and partly to the tenacious hold of certain
ancient institutions and rites. He went on to
argue that the country's regeneration lay in the
renunciation of these social evils and the gradual
assimilation of the values and norms of the West.
The importance of Western education as a means of
achieving this end was stressed: the study of a
Western language was regarded as "the key to the
repositories of the literature and science of the
western world" and the acquisition of this knowledge was believed to raise India to the level of
Western prosperity and power.[49] This was the re-
curring theme in the writings of many of Madava
Rao's contemporaries in the Madras High School.

While they were dazzled by the achievements of the
West, they felt humiliated by the helplessness of
their country, its economic plight, and its social
and sectarian divisions.

Once their scholastic life ended, these Proficients showed little urgency in pursuing their
social objectives. Indeed, their preoccupation
with official duties and furthering their administrative careers seemed to have left them with
little time for anything else. However, by the
1860s the administrative elite began to feel mounting pressure for some action on the social plane.
Partly, this pressure came from its European
patrons and sympathizers who became growingly critical of its continued inaction. Also, the example
set by reformist groups in other parts of the
country could not be ignored. Especially important
was the Brahmo Samaj of Bengal. Seeking to spread
its message to the other provinces, the Brahmo
Samaj sent its secretary, Keshub Chandra Sen, on an
extended tour of southern and western India in 1864.
In a lecture at Madras, Sen exhorted educated
Hindus to remove "the gigantic evil" of caste,
promote female education, and to form associations
to give direction to reformist activity.[50] This
speech, according to a local paper, "created quite
a sensation amongst a large portion of our Hindoo
Community,"[51] and barely three months later, two
young law students, who had recently passed out of
the Madras University, organized the Veda Samaj
along the lines of the Brahmo Samaj of Bengal. A
covenant was drafted, to be signed by all members
of the Veda Samaj, pledging support for theism,
female education, and widow remarriage, while disa-
vowing idolatry, child marriage, and "all sectarian
views and animosities."[52]

Although the organizers of the Veda Samaj had
clearly stolen a march on their elder and more influential counterparts in the administration, it
was, however, soon apparent that their ideology was
too radical to have any significant appeal among
their countrymen. A frontal attack on Hinduism,

from its post-Vedic doctrines to many of its current social practices, did little to recommend the
Veda Samaj either to the mass of conservative Hindus or to the small progressive element which
wanted change along more realistic lines. However,
the launching of the Veda Samaj did seem to have
had the effect of stirring one member of the administrative elite, C. V. Ranganada Sastri, to initiate a concerted agitation against one of the
glaring social evils of South India, that of infant
marriage.

It was almost universal practice among
Brahmins to marry their children in their teens,
often before they had attained the age of ten, and
to a lesser extent this practice was also prevalent
among the Vellalars and Komatis. According to one
contemporary description, infant marriage "consists
in tying the Tally over the neck of a child which
cannot speak, eat or drink, or sit well when the
awful ceremony of marriage is going on, not to say
anything about the solemn and binding obligations
under which it is placed. If the child cries for
milk or is terrified at the scene, the marriage is
effected by placing a plantain in the hand. This
is familiarly known among the Hindoos as a Plantain
Marriage." The burden of reformist objection to
this marriage was that it swelled the numbers of
Hindu widows who were prohibited by strict caste
injunctions from remarrying. The injustice of this
practice, especially when it applied to child
widows, as well as the many disabilities and pri-
vations to which they were subjected for the rest
of their adult lives, struck a sympathetic chord
among reformist-minded Hindus. Others argued that
enforced widowhood had introduced "a flood of im-
morality" into Hindu society by compelling widows
to seek illicit liaisons and, in the event of an
illegitimate offspring, resort to infanticide.[53]

Ranganada Sastri had utilized his knowledge of
Sanskrit to delve into the sacred writings of the
Hindus in an attempt to establish the validity of
some of the social rites which had become an

essential part of Hindu life. In so far as infant
marriage was concerned, he found that it was not
only opposed to common sense but also "contrary to
the sentiments and doctrines expressly promulgated
in the sacred formula pronounced on the celebration
of the marriage itself." In a letter to a local
newspaper, Ranganada Sastri announced his intention
of seeking the abolition of child marriage. He
claimed to have enlisted the support of many "able
Pundits," and gave formal notice of mooting the
subject in the presence of the Sankaracharya, the
Head Priest of Madras, with the help of Sanskrit
scholar, C. Ananda Rama Sastri.[54] A pamphlet was
produced for circulation among the Pundits and
other interested parties.

The cause of infant marriage was championed by
a Telugu scholar, G. Venkanna Sastri. He argued
that the reformers had referred to "the wrong
source of evidence in support of their cause" and,
consequently, had arrived at "a most extraordinary
[sic] illogical conclusion with respect to the
meaning of the passages" they had cited.[55] He persuaded the Sankaracharaya to defer decision on the
issue until he produced a pamphlet. Two months
elapsed before the pamphlet was published, but when
the long-awaited confrontation took place in
October 1865, it proved to be something of an anti-
climax. Each party blamed the other for failing to
settle the issue decisively: the reformers felt
that their opponents had resorted to dilatory tactics, while the latter contended that the reformers
had not abided by their undertaking to refer the
dispute to a committee of learned men drawn from
the various parts of South India.[56] This abortive
encounter ended, at least temporarily, the agitation against infant marriage.

Ranganada Sastri must have sensed the strong
feelings which this issue had engendered, especially within the Brahmin community, but he did not
allow this to interfere with his other reformist
schemes. One issue which had been attracting some
interest was female education. Since the 1850s

female education had made some headway in South
India, but reformers were concerned about the premature withdrawal of high caste girls from schools.
This stemmed partly from early marriage and partly
from parental objection to their daughters being
taught by male teachers once they had attained
maturity. Reformers had long recognized the weight
of the latter objection, but it was only with the
arrival of Mary Carpenter in Madras in November
1866 that a way was found to surmount this difficulty.

Miss Carpenter, whose acquaintance with Ram
Mohan Roy had roused her "ardent interest in the
regeneration of India," visited the country to mobilize support for a number of schemes, including
female education. In Madras, she convened a meeting of local leaders in the house of E. B. Powell,
then Director of Public Instruction, and persuaded
them that a female normal school was "absolutely
necessary" to prevent high caste girls leaving
school without completing their education.
Ranganada Sastri and Rama Iyengar were among those
who supported Miss Carpenter, and it was agreed
that a public meeting would be called to memorialize the authorities to establish such an institution.[57]

When the meeting took place in January 1867,
there was a sharp division of views as to what
ought to be the medium of instruction and who ought
to be admitted into the school. The meeting ended
without taking a decision.[58] Mary Carpenter, who
was then in Calcutta, convened a fresh meeting on
her return and secured support for a memorial to
the Madras Government calling for the establishment
of a female normal school. The authorities agreed
provided that part of the maintenance costs were
met from private sources. An appeal for public
contributions generated little response, and the
fate of the project hung in the balance until the
Maharajah of Vizianagram offered to subscribe Rs
12,000 annually.[59] The Female Normal School was
started in 1869, with admission restricted to girls

from the higher castes and classes.

Besides infant marriage and female education, the other issue which attracted attention was widow remarriage. Reformers in Madras, having failed in their campaign against infant marriage, recognized that something ought to be done in the way of relieving the plight of the child widows. Sanctioning remarriage of virgin widows seemed to suggest an effectual remedy, but little advance was made in this direction despite a desultory discussion of the issue in the press. Indeed, it was the reformers in the neighboring Indian States who demonstrated greater courage and earnestness in promoting widow remarriages. In 1867, a Mahratta Brahmin in Bangalore remarried his widowed daughter despite threats of excommunication.[60] Similarly, in 1873, Sesha Iyengar, a Sri-Vaishnava Brahmin Pleader in Nagercoil, Travancore, married off his widowed daughter according to Hindu rites. After the marriage, the entire family was outcasted, denied the services of priests, barbers, and washermen, barred from entering temples, and prevented from drawing water from wells.[61] To withstand these social pressures, Sesha Iyengar announced the formation of a widow remarriage society in Nagercoil which would offer financial help and advice to those arranging widow remarriages.[62]

Sesha Iyengar's efforts in remote Nagercoil must have been something of an embarrassment to fellow reformers in Madras. As the metropolis of South India, and boasting of many educated Hindus in positions of influence and wealth, Madras was expected to provide the lead in political as in social matters rather than following on the heels of the *mofussil* and Indian States. The reformers in Madras realized that a new initiative was overdue, and in April 1874 a meeting was convened to inaugurate the Madras Hindu Widow Marriage Association. Its aim was to encourage "the marriage of Hindoo widows to the extent of its means and opportunities and so far as may be compatible with the preservation of the hold on and their influence in

orthodox Hindoo society." Believing that success
would depend on obtaining religious sanction, it
was decided to publish relevant extracts from the
Shastras which expressly approved of widow remarriage. Any idea of seeking inter-caste marriage or
of overthrowing the caste system was vigorously
disclaimed. Among the active sponsors of this
association were Rama Iyengar and Muthusamy Iyer,
both of whom were elected to the Managing Committee,
while P. Chentsal Rao was made Secretary.[63] Despite its modest aims, the Madras Hindu Widow
Marriage Association failed to rally any significant support, and little was heard of its activities in the ensuing years.

The collapse of this association reflected,
according to some contemporary critics, the very
timidity of the reformers. As reformist bodies
languished for want of support, and as reformers
almost everywhere seemed reluctant to run into any
headlong conflict with their opponents, criticisms
of the reformist movement became harsher and more
vociferous. The founders of the Madras Hindu
Widow Marriage Association, for example, were
accused of being insincere, and their efforts were
described as "a sham to please the European
public."[64] Others charged the reformers with lacking the courage to practice what they boldly
preached on the platform and in the press. A
"Native Critic" claimed in 1878 that although the
great majority of the Brahmins deplored infant marriage, that same majority would persecute anyone
who departed from the practice. He contended that
even Hindus who had risen to high administrative
positions in Madras were as timid as their uneducated brethren, and would shrink away from challenging "popular opinion and prejudices." This was
an obvious reference to Ranganada Sastri, Rama
Iyengar, and Muthusamy Iyer, men of high ritual
status and enjoying much influence in the administration, but who were found wanting in courage and
dedication in pursuing their goals. The "Native
Critic" concluded that unless Hindu reformers

displayed "moral courage and above all *action*"
their endeavors would "evaporate into empty speculation."[65]

Indeed, the crux of the matter was to find
someone who had the courage of his convictions and
who would be willing to sacrifice his comfort for
conscience and humanity. Such a person was K.
Viresalingam Pantalu, whose pioneering efforts in
the Northern Circars represented the most significant breakthrough yet in the field of social reform
in South India. Born into a Niyogi Brahmin family
in Rajahmundry in 1848, he studied in the local
high school and eventually became a Telugu Pundit
in the Rajahmundry Arts College. From the outset,
he set his mind firmly on the cause of social reform. His mastery of Telugu enabled him to wield
his pen persuasively against wrongs and injustices
of any kind, and this was especially evident in
his writings in the *Vivekavandana,* a Telugu weekly
he had started in 1874. Four years later, he and
his close associates organized the Rajahmundry
Social Reform Association to collect funds and disseminate information on social questions.

Although a number of different issues were
discussed, it was the condition of the child widows
which stirred their innermost sympathy. Viresalingam prepared a memorandum to demonstrate that
there was no religious objection to the remarriage
of virgin widows, and he widely circulated it in
the Northern Circars. This soon touched off a
fierce controversy in Rajahmundry, with the reformers clearly in a minority. Viresalingam was not
dissuaded, and in December 1881 two widow marriages
were performed in Rajahmundry according to Hindu
rites. Although excommunication followed, the reformers rode the storm, and by June 1884 they had
celebrated their tenth widow marriage in Rajahmundry.[66]

With the excitement generated by events in
Rajahmundry, reformers in Madras gradually began to
shake themselves out of their apathy. Although a
younger and more vocal element had appeared on the

scene, it was still the administrative elite which
continued to lead the reformist agitation. Two of
the prominent figures of the earlier years were,
however, absent: Ranganada Sastri, who died in 1881,
and Rama Iyengar, who assumed the Dewanship of
Travancore a year earlier.

In their place came Rubgundai Raghunatha Rao,
a member of a distinguished Mahratta Brahmin family
whose ancestors had served the British for three
generations. He had studied under Powell, was appointed Deputy Collector in 1859, and later secon-
ded to Indore as Dewan in 1875. When he returned
to Madras as Deputy Collector five years later, he
plunged into the reformist movement with a zeal and
devotion rarely found among his counterparts. His
interest in the movement was stimulated by his
study of the religious writings of the Hindus. The
more deeply he delved into "Aryan religion and
sociology," the more convinced he became of the
Hindu departure from the simple and pristine quality of Vedic life. It was in the treatment of
Hindu women that he noted the greatest departure
from early Aryan practice. Although the Shastras,
the divinely inspired writings of the Hindus, had
placed women in a position of equality with men,
Raghunatha Rao was appalled to see that most of
their civil rights had been eroded away and they
were forced into infant marriage and enforced
widowhood, customs which did not have the sanction
of the Shastras.[67] He attributed these changes to
the centuries of decay and chaos following "the
golden age" of the Vedic period, and the resulting
degeneration of the intellectual quality of the
pundits and priests. Some of the latter he held
responsible for importing "sinister" textual
changes in their commentaries of the Vedas which
he believed were "prejudicial to the happiness of
the people."[68] Raghunatha Rao believed that this
orthodox elite, which held custom as more authoritative than the Shastras, to be the major obstacle
to social reform in South India.

Raghunatha Rao was equally disenchanted with

the attitude of the Western-educated class. For
many years, he had assumed that reforms would logi-
cally follow with the spread of Western education,
but by the early 1880s he came to the contrary view
that the new learning was an impediment rather than
a help. He regarded the younger Western-educated
class as atheists and iconoclasts, so enamored by
the ways of the West that it despised its own religious and social heritage. It held in contempt the
Shastras which it took for "a code of repealed
rules . . . utterly unsuited to these days of re-
fined civilization." With such zealots Raghunatha
Rao had little sympathy as he felt that their radicalism was essentially destructive and threatened
the basic cohesion of Hindu society. His hopes for
constructive change were placed on that section of
Hindu opinion which wanted the Shastras to be the
sole determinant of Hindu social behavior.
Raghunatha Rao believed that this group was larger
than the "orthodox section" or the radicals,[69] and
it was its support he courted when he organized
the Hindu Women's Remarriage Association in 1882,
although he was not prepared to shut out the radicals entirely from this body.

The admission of the radicals meant an uneasy
partnership of two groups which, though agreed on
certain social reforms, derived their inspiration
from widely divergent sources. The dominant faction was the group led by Raghunatha Rao, known as
the "traditional school" of reformers whose source
of inspiration was the Shastras. Other leaders of
this group were Chentsal Rao and S. Subramania
Iyer, a *vakil* in the Madras High Court who later
became a judge. Unlike its younger opponents, who
were called the "rationalist school," as they
wanted reason and common sense to be the guidelines of reform, the traditional school called for
"an inflexible conformity with the Shastras" in
the pursuit of reformist goals.[70] At times,
Raghunatha Rao went as far as to reject the term
"reform" in preference to what he called "the revival of our old rules of conduct." This attitude

stemmed to some extent from reasons of expediency.
He did not believe that change could be achieved by
merely "proclaiming ourselves to be clever men and
calling upon others to obey us." The success of
any cause, Raghunatha Rao argued, depended on
"preaching to the people that the practice is not
only pernicious but is opposed to the Shastras."[71]
It was only by invoking the authority of the sacred
Hindu texts that he felt that any progress could be
achieved in social reform.

The most important positions within the Hindu
Women's Remarriage Association were filled by reformers of the traditional school, with Raghunatha Rao
elected President, and the aims and activities of
the Association largely mirrored the thinking of
the traditional school of reformers. The Association disapproved of infant marriage where the bride
was below ten years of age. Its main aim, however,
was to promote widow marriages. Marriage, according to the rules of the Association, was only
"completed by sacrifices and by consummation," and
widow marriage "with Vedic marital rites" was per-
missible "*provided* she is a *virgin*."[72] The Association pledged "to advocate and encourage, celebrate
and pay for, the marriage of girls who are or who
may be widowed before the consummation of marriage
with their husbands, and to receive them, their
supporters and sympathisers into society."[73]

During its early years of existence, the Hindu
Women's Remarriage Association displayed commen-
dable activity which was in marked contrast to its
predecessors. In May 1883 the idea of seeking a
modification of the Hindu Widow Remarriage Act of
1856 was mooted. The Association submitted to the
Indian Government a Draft Bill, the aim of which
was to annul the clause which imposed forfeiture of
inheritance rights on widows who remarried. The
reformers argued that this clause had encouraged
many parents to keep their widowed daughters in a
state of enforced widowhood.[74] At the same time, a
propaganda campaign was launched to mobilize public
support for widow marriages very much along the

lines of what Viresalingam had done in the Northern
Circars. But there was one difference: the reformers in Madras offered monetary incentives to anyone who negotiated widow marriages or gave information of virgin widows seeking marriage.[75] In June
1883 the Association celebrated its first widow
marriage with some eclat, culminating in a procession through Mylapore.[76] This stirred the ire of
the religious heads who promptly excommunicated six
reformers who had participated in a dinner given to
the married couple. An attempt to settle the differences amicably at a conference in September 1884
failed, owing to the insistence of the Head Priest
of Triplicane to be the sole judge of the discussion.[77]

Among the declared objectives of the Hindu
Women's Remarriage Association was the forging of
closer links between reformers in different parts
of South India. In the past little premium was
placed on this, but the example set by political
leaders must have gone a long way to convince
social reformers that cooperation was an essential
factor in furthering their aims. The opportunity
to make a modest start came in December 1884, when
a political conference was held in Madras. The
Hindu Women's Remarriage Association sent out invitations to *mofussil* leaders welcoming them to a
conference to discuss ways of promoting widow marriage. When the Conference met on 31 December,
participation, for reasons not apparent, was restricted to graduates, while other reformers like
Raghunatha Rao, Chentsal Rao, and Viresalingam were
invited as guests. Another unexpected move was to
broaden the scope of the Conference to include such
subjects as female education and infant marriage.
Three main resolutions were passed: every graduate
should actively promote female education; infant
marriage should be discouraged; and graduates
should support widow remarriage and signify this
in writing. The last resolution was heatedly debated and was only carried after an attempt to
defer it for future consideration.[78] A similar

Conference was held in Madras in December 1885, and on this occasion there was no restriction on those wishing to attend.[79]

Conferences of this kind had come to stay, and there were many reformers in South India who even began to feel that the scope of such meetings should be broadened to embrace other regions of India as well. Among the advocates of this idea was Raghunatha Rao, who was doubtless influenced by the success of the politicians in organizing the Indian National Congress. For some time he and his supporters tried to get social issues discussed at the Congress, but, having failed to do so, they decided to go ahead on their own. The result was the convening of the National Social Conference in Madras in December 1887. Like the Congress, this Conference soon established provincial committees in the various parts of India. In Madras, the Hindu Committee of the National Social Conference was formed in December 1888, with Madava Rao as President and Raghunatha Rao as Secretary.[80] Although this Committee became the focus of reformist activity in Madras, the Hindu Women's Remarriage Association continued to fulfill its limited role of promoting widow marriages.

THE APPROACH TO POLITICS

What emerges clearly in studying the involvment of the administrative elite in the public movements is the obvious contrast between its activist role in the field of social reform and its deep reluctance to promote change in the country's political institutions. In social reform, as already noticed, the administrative elite had displayed zeal in forming associations, convening conferences, and attacking certain established usages and customs. Here, this group was to a considerable extent keeping pace with the thinking of the more numerous, younger, Western-educated class that was graduating from high schools and colleges

in South India after the Mutiny. A measure of its
success in winning the loyalty of the younger element was the readiness of the latter to entrust
leadership of the reformist movement to such elders
as Raghunatha Rao, Madava Rao, and Chentsal Rao.
However, in the field of politics, the reverse
seemed to have been the case. Here, the administrative elite displayed a marked degree of inaction,
sometimes even hostility. By its failure to compre-
hend the importance of the political developments
of the 1880s, it forfeited whatever chances it had
of influencing the course of events, if not providing constructive leadership. Indeed, this decade was to witness a running political conflict
between the elder, status conscious administrative
elite and the younger, politically conscious professional elite.*

In trying to explain the attitude of the administrative elite towards politics in general and
the professional elite in particular, it is important to bear in mind that its members had spent the
better part of their lives in public service in the
course of which they had been entrusted with the
responsibilities of high office and rewarded with
honors and titles by their British masters. If
anything, this was an experience which had convinced them that the most effective way of promoting the country's welfare was by good government
management and pragmatic policies rather than inno-
vative legislation and structural changes in an
administration based on alien doctrines. Essentially, the administrative elite saw the ends of
government as basically custodial rather than creative, with emphasis on political stability rather
than trying to keep pace with the newfangled
Western concepts of individual liberty, parliamentary democracy, and social justice. In stressing
political stability, these elder administrators

-----

*The origins of this elite group are discussed
in the next Chapter.

wanted the Western-educated class to play a kind of
mediative role between the rulers and the ruled,
removing possible misunderstandings and helping the
former to formulate the right policies on which depended the continued progress of the country. It
was this mediative role which the administrative
elite chose to play, both during the period of its
active public service and during its years in retirement.*

To play this role effectively, the administrators made conscious efforts to establish their
credentials with the rulers. Their long and devoted service to the Raj was helpful for a start
but by itself was quite inadequate. It was equally
important to affirm periodically their unflinching
loyalty to the British Empire; this helped counter
the rising antigovernment clamor of the professional elite, which had led to official doubts
about the loyalty of the educated class.[81]
Muthusamy Iyer, for example, exhorted the graduates
of the Madras University in these words: "Let your
thought and action be always guided by a profound
feeling of loyalty to our gracious Sovereign and to
the British nation to whom you owe a debt of gratitude which you can never adequately repay." He
asserted that in India the two branches of "the
Aryan race" had come together "under God's Provi-
dence," and he expressed confidence in Britain's
ability to discharge its great mission in India,
"the grandest of all spectacles and the noblest of
all triumphs."[82] At the same time, the virtues of
British rule were constantly reiterated. Said
Madava Rao in 1887:

---

*Seshia Sastri said in 1882: ". . . the edu-
cated natives, whether engaged in Government service or in other walks of life must, for a long
time to come, continue to be interpreters between
their own countrymen and the rulers." Cited in
Kamesvara Aiyar, *Sastri,* pp. 255-56.

The truth must be frankly and gratefully admitted that the British Government of India is incomparably the best Government we have ever had.

It is the strongest and the most righteous and the best suited to India's diverse populations and diverse interests.

It is the most capable of self-maintenance, of self-renovation and self-adjustment, in reference to the progressive advancement of the subject-race.[83]

Seshia Sastri was no less generous in his praise of what the British Raj had done in recognizing Indian talent since the Mutiny. He wrote in 1882:

Nor is it possible for me to forget the fact that twenty-five years ago there was not a single native exercising Revenue and Magisterial functions higher than those of Tahsildar of Head of Police. What is the case now? All these functions excepting the highest have been transferred to Native Deputy Collectors and Magistrates. Twenty-five years ago no native was trusted with the charge of a Treasury and now there is none but a native in charge of all Treasuries all over India. Again twenty-five years ago in the Judicial Department even the Principal Sudder Amins had but a limited jurisdiction. Now there is hardly a District Judge exercising original jurisdiction, the whole work of original jurisdiction has passed to a native agency.[84]

At the same time, attempts were made to win the goodwill of the rulers by cultivating closer social ties with senior European officials. Rama Iyengar, for example, endeavored "to keep his house in European style, to teach English to the female members of his family and to invite European gentlemen to parties at his residence."[85]

Perhaps the most significant attempt which the

administrative elite made at developing cordial
ties between Europeans and Indians was the foundation of the Cosmopolitan Club in October 1873. Its
aim was to give "greater facilities for personal
intercourse between Indian and European Gentlemen
in Madras," and to provide for "introducing European visitors to Madras to the principal residents
and thereby affording some insight into Indian
Society." Lectures and discussions were to be held
from time to time, and a library and recreational
facilities provided. All leading officials in
South India, from members of the Governor's Executive Council to Deputy Collectors and *Tahsildars*,
were invited to join, and membership during the
first year jumped from 41 to 177. Among those who
took a prominent part in the formation of this club
were Rama Iyengar, Raghunatha Rao, and Muthusamy
Iyer, the last named having the distinction of becoming the first Indian President.[86] M. G. Ranade,
who had visited the Cosmopolitan Club no less than
five times, said in 1887 that "gentlemen of all
shades of opinion do assemble regularly every even-
ing for discussing the general topics of the day."[87]
In the absence of other similar institutions, the
Cosmopolitan Club long continued to fulfill the
role of providing the means for informal exchange
of views between groups of diverse ethnic and
social origins.

       Such social associations, coupled with its
pro-British sympathies, naturally precluded the
administrative elite from fully participating in
the political movements unleashed by the professional elite during the 1880s. The idea of agitating for reforms, which in its eyes amounted to
nothing more than confronting the government with
unrealistic demands, was repugnant to a group which
had so long employed different tactics to achieve
its ends. Equally distasteful were the efforts of
the professional elite to organize itself into
political camps, as a kind of permanent opposition
to the government. Such associations, including
the Indian National Congress, appeared to divide

the rulers from the ruled whereas the administrative elite would have preferred to bring the two
parties together. Moreover, the idea of holding
public meetings, of rubbing shoulders with the common folk and seeking their support, did not appeal
to the genteel and aristocratic ways of the administrators. But underlying all these was the latent
hostility towards the professional elite, which,
though lacking in wealth or prestige, was nevertheless asserting its dominance over political movements and claiming to speak for the people as a
whole. Not surprisingly, the administrative elite
regarded its younger rivals as "upstarts," or in
the words of Seshia Sastri "penniless patriots,"[88]
whose extravagant rhetoric and radical posturing
betrayed their youthfulness, inexperience in public
affairs, and an impatient idealism. To cast their
fortunes with this group appeared to many elder
administrators to be an act of folly, subversive of
the long-term interests of the country and even
prejudicial to the stability of the Empire.

However, one prominent member of the administrative elite was broadly in sympathy with the
activities of the youthful politicians. He was
Raghunatha Rao, who, in his efforts to mobilize
support for social reform, came to establish useful
friendships with some prominent members of the professional elite. He had a reputation, both within
the public service and outside, for candor and
plain speaking, which had often "brought him into
collision with the [European] officials." As W. S.
Blunt recorded in his diary in 1883, Raghunatha Rao
was not easily overawed by his European superiors
as he knew their weaknesses and was affluent enough
to look after himself if something went amiss.[89]
As a student of the Madras High School, he had
closely followed the activities of the Madras
Native Association. In later years he often publicly acknowledged his admiration for the political work of Lakshmanarasu Chetty.

As an official, he never hesitated to express
his views on questions he deemed important. In

1860, for instance, he addressed a letter to
Trevelyan in which he upheld the rights of the *mirasdars* to the soil, a stand contrary to that held
by senior Madras officials.[90] When he was Dewan of
Indore, at the height of the famine then sweeping
Central and South India, he penned a memorandum in
which he argued that the high government assessment
had impoverished the peasants and discouraged agricultural production.[91] In 1880 he was elected
President of the Triplicane Literary Society, which,
during the next few years, became the leading
critic of the policies of the Madras authorities.
There is little doubt that Raghunatha Rao, despite
his official status, was increasingly identifying
himself with the aspirations, if not the activities,
of the professional elite, perhaps from his dissatisfaction with the growing European disregard
for "the feelings and opinions of the [Indian]
people." He told Blunt in 1883 that this alienation was a recent occurrence, which was very unlike
the old times when Indians and Europeans were "on a
footing of something like equality."[92] Not surprisingly, when the Congress first met in Bombay in
1885, Raghunatha Rao was among the few officials
who attended it as *amici curiae*.* In later years,
his ardor for the Congress diminished somewhat when
it adamantly refused to consider social questions.
    Raghunatha Rao's involvement in political
movements did not remove the underlying antagonism
between these two elite groups which came to the
surface when the elder leaders, including Madava
Rao, Muthusamy Iyer, and Raghunatha Rao, gave a
farewell reception in honor of the departing Member
of the Governor's Executive Council, D. F.
Carmichael, in December 1883. This reception
touched off a heated controversy with the professional elite which opposed the idea of "a public

----

*In February 1888, at a speech in Indore,
Raghunatha Rao even claimed to be the originator of
the Congress. See *Hindu*, 9 March 1888.

reception" on the grounds that Carmichael had not
championed Indian interests. The sponsors of the
reception were urged to abandon the "odious movement" or run the risk of "a direct and open collision" with their opponents.[93] When the warning was
ignored, the professional elite proposed to test
popular reactions to the reception. A committee
was formed which reported that reaction to honoring
Carmichael was adverse. Convinced that popular
opinion was behind it, this elite group convened a
public meeting which resolved that Carmichael's
services "have not been such as to entitle him to
any special recognition."[94]

Whatever ill feeling this incident had caused,
and however deeply the administrative elite dis-
trusted its more aggressive rivals, it was not
always easy for the former to maintain an attitude
of noninvolvement in political issues. On the one
hand, there was little doubt that popular opinion,
as far as it was capable of articulation, was
sympathetic to the causes which animated the activities of the professional elite. Issues like
local self-government, Ilbert Bill, higher education, and greater Indian participation in the administration, were supported by public opinion. Nor
were the elder leaders always opposed to these demands: indeed, they had a sneaking sympathy for
many of these demands and some gave public expression to their views. Then again, there were
occasions when the administrative elite had to dis-
card its posture of aloofness from political
demonstrations. One occasion was the visit of Lord
Ripon to Madras in January and February 1884. The
professional elite wanted a popular reception,
ostensibly to honor the Viceroy, but, in reality,
to demonstrate its support for the policies of
Ripon which had been strongly criticized in the
Anglo-Indian press. The elder leaders were aware
of the political nature of the celebrations, but
they could hardly remain aloof without seeming to
snub a popular Viceroy. Madava Rao led the way,
first by presiding over a public meeting to decide

what ought to be done, and then by heading the welcoming party to receive Ripon on behalf of the
Indian community in Madras.[95]

There is no doubt that from this point onwards,
Madava Rao, for one, was being gradually drawn into
the vortex of regional and national politics. His
family, like that of Raghunatha Rao, had in the
past produced many distinguished administrators,
and he had carried on this tradition by becoming
Dewan of three different Indian States, where he
had governed in the paternalistic tradition of the
British Raj. When he retired in 1882, he settled
in Madras to a life of comfort and quietude. But
his solemn resolution to live "in placid retirement"[96] was shattered by calls from the government
to serve in various committees and by urgings from
the professional elite to take a more prominent
part in political questions of the day. For some
time Madava Rao resisted the wooing of the younger
politicians whom he regarded as harsh critics of
the government and considered "too theoretical" in
their remedies, deficiencies which he attributed to
their lack of the "sobering experience in the
actual management of [public] affairs." He constantly exhorted the professional elite that to be
useful guides it must "not too much outrun the mul-
titude," but lead it "from step to step."[97] At the
same time, he wanted this class to divert its
energies to nonpolitical issues as well, like
social reform, agriculture, and industry. When
this evoked little response from "the fiery patriots," Madava Rao wrote in despair in 1885: "But I
am afraid their goal is a Parliament of B.A.'s,
Native Viceroys, Native Governors, Native Lieut.-
Governors, Native Chief Commissioners."[98]

Despite these inner reservations about the
professional elite, the events of the next few
years drove Madava Rao into the camp of the youthful politicians. The real moment of decision for
him came in 1887, when the third Congress met in
Madras. There was considerable enthusiasm in the
southern metropolis, and this must have infected

Madava Rao. Hence, when the Chairmanship of the
Congress Reception Committee was offered to him,
Madava Rao, according to a biographer who knew him
intimately then, had "a regular struggle in his
mind" whether to accept it or "cut himself off from
the youthful politicians of New India."[99] Eventually he accepted the offer, played his part in
the arrangements for holding the Congress, and in
his speech of welcome to the Congress delegates
said that "such a gathering must appear the soun-
dest triumph of British administration, and the
crown of glory to the great British nation."[100]

With his reputation as "the Nestor of Indian
Statesmen," Madava Rao's accession to the Congress
was "universally acknowledged to be an event of
the greatest possible importance, and one which
spoke much for the reality and weight of the movement."[101] If the Congress leadership was delighted,
Madava Rao's erstwhile friends were surprised, and
in some circles it was even said that he was
guilty of political opportunism. There might be
some grain of truth in this charge, although a
close examination of Madava Rao's public utterances
since 1882 leads one to the conclusion that he had
always sought some kind of an accommodation.

Nevertheless, it was an accommodation on his
own terms, as his subsequent activities clearly
show. He became a member of the Madras Standing
Congress Committee but he was not prepared to be
tied down by the fetters of party control or direction. In his effusive writings in a local newspaper under the *non de plume* "A Native Observer,"
Madava Rao freely ventilated his opinions on a wide
range of subjects, some of which were critical of
the Congress. In November 1889, for example, he
warned his Congress friends against imitating the
political experiments in Europe, which he felt
might disturb the tranquility of India. Rather, he
wanted the country's welfare to be entrusted to the
British bureaucracy, "a large, practical and highly-
trained body profoundly interested in the continu-
ance of British rule in India as a great blessing

to its vast population."[102] Such gratuitous advice,
given in an organ generally hostile to the Congress,
caused resentment among the professional elite and,
in a sense, foreshadowed the open rupture which
came in 1890 over the question of the introduction
of the elective principle in India.

In February 1890 the British Government introduced a Bill in Parliament to reform the Indian
legislatures. Called the Cross Bill, its controversial clause was the nonrecognition of the
principle of election in the choice of members to
these bodies. Congress leaders in Madras reacted
with anger and dismay and adopted a posture of
defiance so long as the principle of election was
not conceded. Madava Rao, however, took a different view. He argued that the concessions embodied
in the Bill were reasonable and the Congress should
accept the measure "with gratitude." He wrote: "I
do not much care about the non-concession of popular election, because careful observation and
experience convince me that popular election at
present would have ensured the failure of extended
Councils, whereas nomination would probably be
their success."[103] These utterances provoked a
political storm in Madras, with Madava Rao accused
of political inconsistency and naivete, while some
charged him with having "betrayed his party."[104]

Madava Rao reacted angrily to these charges
and in retaliation denounced both the Congress program and its supporters. He deprecated the demand
for the separation of revenue and judicial functions, contending that it was a "mischievous" proposal aimed to benefit the lawyers while imposing
"an intolerable burden on the simple country population."[105] As for elected legislatures, Madava
Rao charged that this was an attempt on the part of
the professional elite to exclude from these bodies
"all men of *property and position* as ignorant and
useless." He warned the British rulers not to
yield to the "impetuous and iconoclastic ambition
of an imperfectly educated and impoverished class."
He felt that "men of property and position and of

common sense in relation to human affairs are
really more eligible for the work of legislation,"
and could be relied upon to apply "the *brake* to
hasty, excessive, or mischievous legislation."[106]
In April 1890 Madava Mao resigned from the Madras
Standing Congress Committee.

Madava Rao's break with the Congress symbolized the fact that the cleavage between the two
elite groups remained as wide as ever. Differences
in age and temperament, attainment and wealth, had
invested these groups with divergent attitudes and
ideologies which no amount of goodwill by either
party could bridge. Madava Rao's attempt to reach
a kind of accommodation with the professional elite
demonstrated that both sides were not totally
averse to reaching compromise. But, in the long
run, the compromise proved to be tenuous, partly
because the mood of the times called for political
militancy and partly because the credentials of
one group were suspect because of its long and intimate association with the British Raj. Moreover,
the professional elite was not prepared to be led
by the apron strings of its elders, however distinguished and able they might be, as it offended
its sense of dignity and pride. Indeed, a true
insight into the relations of these two groups can
only be gained by examining more closely the
origins of the professional elite.

3. The Origins of the Professional Elite

It was the controversy over the reception for Carmichael in 1883 which highlighted, rather dramatically, the emergence of the professional elite on the political scene in South India. The spectacle of a minor issue assuming the character of a major political controversy bemused many contemporary observers, but, in retrospect, the incident marked the first real confrontation between two groups aspiring for leadership within the Indian community in Madras. In the normal course of things the action of the administrative elite in holding a farewell reception for an English official would have evoked little comment. But, coming as it did at the height of the unpopularity of the Madras Government, aggravated no doubt by the passions aroused by the European agitation against the Ilbert Bill, the celebration to honor publicly an official whose reputation had been tarnished by these controversies* appeared in the professional elite's eyes to be obtrusively sycophantic, if not wounding to the self-respect of an embattled subject community.

In taking issue over the reception, the

---

*The political controversies which convulsed South India during the early 1880s are discussed in Chapter 4.

professional elite went to some lengths to emphasize the fact that issues of public importance
ought to be decided in accordance with public opinion as expressed through the press, platform, and
voluntary associations. Doubtless, it was trying
to lay the ground rules for a new style of political agitation where the stress would be on organizational unity and ideological purity. With such
sentiments, however, the administrative elite had
little sympathy, but this did not deter the younger
elite group from rigorously pursuing its ideals to
their logical conclusion. The formation of the
Madras Mahajana Sabha in May 1884 was the first
significant attempt on the part of the professional
elite at attaining organizational unity by affiliating the numerous political bodies which had
sprung up in different parts of South India, while
the decision to hold a conference of these associations a few months later represented the first
tangible effort at reaching a political consensus
on the important issues of the day.

EXPANSION OF COLLEGIATE EDUCATION

The origins of the professional elite can be
largely traced to the rapid expansion of collegiate
education in South India during the second half of
the nineteenth century. Unlike the 1840s, when
bitter religious controversies restricted the educational endeavors of the government to the maintenance of the Madras High School, the succeeding
decade saw the gradual resolution of points of conflict and the formulation of guidelines of policy
which were largely responsible for the significant
educational advance made over the next generation.
The Wood despatch of 1854 provided for the
formation of the Department of Public Instruction
in Madras, gave sanction to the liberal use of the
grants-in-aid system to stimulate private enterprise in education, envisaged the establishment of
universities in the three presidency capitals of

India, and approved the institution of examinations
to test the fitness of candidates for public service. In 1858 the Madras authorities finalized
arrangements for holding competitive tests for
those seeking entry into all levels of government
service. In the same year the issuing of the
Queen's Proclamation reaffirmed the official policy
of religious neutrality. Henceforth, missionary
agitation for Bible lessons in government schools
subsided, while Hindu fears about the pro-
missionary bias of British officials also gradually
disappeared.[1] Western education, reorganized on a
more efficient basis, removed from the realm of
controversy, and given its due rewards, was in a
position to assert its hold over South India.

The diagram in Chart 1 indicates the broad educational structure that prevailed in South India
during the second half of the nineteenth century.
The base of the educational pyramid was formed by
the vast network of primary schools scattered
through the length and breadth of the presidency,
embracing not only the towns but also most of the
villages. Instruction at this level was in the
language of the region, with English taught to a
limited extent whenever there was a demand for it.
Pupils learned reading, writing, and arithmetic,
and, in most cases, this was all the formal education they would get. Eventually, only about one in
ten managed to reach the secondary level. Several
factors accounted for this high dropout rate.
Besides having to cope with the difficulties of
passing examinations, paying fees, and even learning their family craft, pupils in the rural areas
had to contend with the fact that the secondary
schools were almost always located in the towns and
cities. It was beyond the means of most rural
families to educate their children in these urban
based institutions.

Secondary education began at the middle schools
and ended in the high schools, which prepared students for matriculation. Instruction here was increasingly in English, while pupils were given

STRUCTURE OF EDUCATIONAL SYSTEM

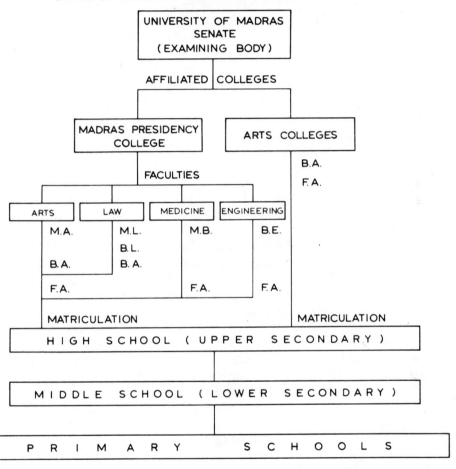

F. A. FIRST ARTS
B.A. BACHELOR OF ARTS
B. L. BACHELOR OF LAW
B. E. BACHELOR OF ENGINEERING

M.A. MASTER OF ARTS
M.L. MASTER OF LAW
M.B. BACHELOR OF MEDICINE

limited opportunities to pursue technical and
scientific studies. As McCully rightly points out,
it was these secondary schools which "constituted
the basis of the English educational pyramid which
was crowned by the universities."[2] Increasingly,
these institutions saw themselves as feeders to the
colleges, concerned with preparing students to
clear the matriculation hurdle and secure a place
in a college.

The colleges of South India, located in the
larger urban centers, were essentially teaching institutions affiliated to the University of Madras.
Except for the Madras Presidency College, all
others were Arts colleges offering instruction in
the liberal arts or science subjects up to First
Arts (F.A.) or Bachelor of Arts degree (B.A.). In
the Madras Presidency College, however, degree
courses were also available in law, medicine and
engineering, as well as facilities for postgraduate
training in these fields. Therefore, this college
earned the reputation of being the premier institution in South India, attracting the best teachers
and students alike in the presidency.

The functions of examining and awarding degrees were entrusted to the University of Madras,
set up in 1857. Modelled upon the University of
London, this institution, through its Senate, ensured that there was uniformity in the curriculum,
teaching methods, and academic standards of its
various affiliated colleges.[3] Indeed, situated as
it was at the apex of the educational pyramid, the
University of Madras wielded a decisive influence
in shaping educational development in South India.

The following table shows the progress of
higher education in South India during the decades
immediately after the setting up of the University
of Madras:

Table 3.1
Progress of Higher Education in South India 1857–1896

Period	Matric. Passes	First Arts	B.A.	Law	Engi- neering	Medi- cine	Total
1857–66	937	149	62	16	5	1	1,170
1867–76	4,968	1,371	401	88	9	9	6,846
1877–86	12,880	2,983	1,214	161	31	58	17,327
1887–96	15,526	7,257	2,917	434	34	157	26,325
Total	34,311	11,760	4,594	699	79	225	51,668

Source: *Madras University Calendar,* for relevant years (1857–1896).

The first decade of university education in South India was one of slow growth, at least in comparison to Bengal where five times as many students matriculated and four times as many secured the B.A. degree.[4] The small number in South India can be attributed partly to the narrow base on which Western education rested in 1857 and partly to the attraction of the public service to students leaving schools. Particularly significant was the institution of the General Test in 1858 which siphoned off into the Uncovenanted Service many potential college students.[5]

However, these factors did not seem to have exercised the same influence during the years 1867–78 when collegiate education achieved a rapid growth rate. Passes in matriculation quintupled, while the increase in the numbers getting degrees was even higher.

The growth rate over the next decade, though not of the same magnitude, saw the momentum nevertheless maintained. South India caught up with Bengal (the latter produced 12,363 matriculates in this period as compared to 12,880 by South India), and official optimism that higher education was "developing at a rate far beyond the expectations of the most hopeful well-wishers of educational progress in India" was fully justified.[6]

During the decade 1887–96 the pace of expansion, at least in the Arts, eased off somewhat.

With the new emphasis on commercial and scientific
education, and the narrowing of employment opportunities in the public service, demand for literary degrees began to recede gradually.

This sharp growth in the output of graduates
was matched by the corresponding proliferation of
colleges in South India. In 1858, when the first
graduates passed out of the Madras University, the
Presidency was served by a single college, the
Presidency College. By 1871, however, eleven new
colleges had sprung up in different centers of
South India giving courses up to the First Arts
(F.A.) or B.A. degree. In many instances it was
merely a question of raising existing high schools
to the status of colleges as in the case of Kumbaconam, Calicut, Bellary, and Mangalore.[7]

During the decade 1872-81, the number of colleges doubled to twenty-five, largely as a consequence of the official policy of decentralizing
higher education by establishing institutions in
the less accessible parts of the region. In 1885-
86 only eight of the twenty-two districts of the
Madras Presidency were without a college of their
own, but, of these, seven were situated close to
Madras or had too easy rail connections with the
metropolis to warrant a college of their own.[8] As
McCully observes, South India during the eighties
"offered greater provision for collegiate instruction than did Bengal despite the earlier lead of
the latter Presidency in the field of higher education."[9]

A feature of higher education in South India
was its uneven spread among the various linguistic
groups inhabiting the Presidency. Superior educational facilities and a more efficient system of
communications permitted the Tamils to establish an
early lead in the race for collegiate education.
In 1866, for example, about 75 per cent of the
students in the Presidency College, the premier institution in South India, came from the Tamil-
speaking areas.[10] The situation was unchanged during the early seventies when the Tamil districts of

Madras and Tanjore dominated higher education. Possessing half the total colleges in South India, and all but one of the first-grade colleges instructing up to B.A. standard, Madras and Tanjore, by their easy accessibility to the Tamil districts, provided an enormous advantage to the Tamils seeking higher education.

By contrast, the Malayalam-speaking district of Malabar failed to make any progress in collegiate education until a decade after the foundation of the Madras University. Cut off from the metropolis by the high peaks of the Western Ghats, and without the benefit of rail or road links, Malayali youths were long deterred from migrating eastwards for their collegiate instruction.

Equally isolated were the northern Telugu districts. Especially affected was the Northern Circars. "This province," observed the Director of Public Instruction in 1876, "with a population twice as great as that of Scotland and an area one-fourth greater, has yet derived no benefit from the introduction of the railway into the Presidency, and although the establishment of coasting steamers has rendered these districts less inaccessible than they used to be to Europeans, the strong prejudices which many Hindus and most Brahmans have against sea-voyages have not been overcome, and very few students come down and prosecute their studies at Madras." Indeed, after two decades of higher education, the Northern Circars could hardly boast of half a dozen graduates.[11]

It was the recognition of these inter-regional disparities which precipitated the decision by the government to decentralize higher education in South India. Conscious of the impetus which colleges had to higher learning in their immediate environs, the Director of Public Instruction advocated in 1876 the establishment of colleges in every district of the Presidency. The first fruit of this new policy was the decision a year later to elevate the Rajahmundry College to the status of a first-grade institution. Within a decade it became

"a nucleus for the high education over a large
tract of country," drawing its students principally
from the surrounding Telugu districts.[12] At the
same time second-grade colleges, training students
for the F.A. examination, sprang up in rapid succession in other Telugu centers, namely Vizianagram
(1877), Vizagapatam (1878), Cocanada (1884), and
Guntur (1884). The needs of the Malayali-speaking
areas were also met with. In Malabar, Calicut became the center of higher learning with the establishment of two second-grade colleges in 1868 and
1879, while a third was started in Palghat in 1888.
Facilities for collegiate instruction were also
provided in Travancore, where a first-grade college
existed in Trevandram since 1869 and a second-grade
college in Ernakulam since 1877.

No accurate statistical compilation has been
made of the advance registered in higher education
by the different linguistic groups of the Presidency during the nineteenth century. Rough estimates, however, seem to confirm the popular view
that Tamils never surrendered the early lead they
had established. Between 1858 and 1894 a total of
1900 Tamils graduated with the B.A. degree from
Madras University, a figure which exceeded the combined total of all the other linguistic groups of
South India. The Malayalis came next with 500
graduates, though numerically they constituted a
third of the Tamil population. The Telugus, numerically equal to the Tamils, could only boast of 450
graduates, while the Kanarese, equal in population
to the Malayalis, accounted for 300 graduates.[13]

In an age when political consciousness stirred
mainly the Western-educated class, Tamil preponderance in higher education led to their domination
of the political movements in the Presidency. To
an equal extent, the Tamils also dominated the
public service, and this was nowhere more apparent
than in the Indian States of Cochin, Travancore,
and Mysore. It was a situation which gave rise to
anti-Tamil sentiments in these areas from the 1880s
onwards, finding expression in the cry "Mysore for

Mysoreans" and "Travancore for Travancoreans."
Equally significant in political terms were
the varying responses of the different communal
groups to collegiate education. The table below
gives the communal composition of the graduates on
the rolls of Madras University in 1894:

Table 3.2
Composition of Graduates

Communal Group	No. of Graduates	Percentage of Total Graduates	Percentage of Total Population in 1891
Brahmins	2,393	68.8	3.1
Non-Brahmin Hindus	660	19.0	86.6
Indian Christians	287	8.2	2.3
Europeans & Eurasians	115	3.3	0.1
Muslims	26	0.7	6.3
Others	2	0	1.6
Total	3,483	100	100

Source: *University of Madras. Calendar for
1893-94*, 1, pp. 405-19; *Madras Census*, XIII
(1891): 65, 259.

The Brahmin preponderance was quite overwhelming. The domination of this caste was apparent at
every level of higher education in South India,
whether literary, scientific, or professional, and
it was consistently sustained throughout the nineteenth century. But it should be stressed that not
all Brahmin subcastes accepted Western learning.
In Malabar, the Namburdiri group held aloof, scorn-
ing the attractions of secular pursuits and maintaining pride in its claim to be "the truest Aryan
in Southern India."[14] In the Northern Circars, the
Vydiki Brahmins adopted a similar stance and
stoutly resisted any encroachments into their traditional sacerdotal status. However, by and large,
the Brahmins flocked to the colleges to take advantage of the new range of employment opportunities
afforded to those with superior Western education.
The pace was initially set by the Mahratta
Brahmins, at the time when the Madras High School
was started, and their example stimulated two other

important Brahmin groups in Tamilnadu, the Smarthas and Sri-Vaishnavas, to apply themselves to the new learning with even greater zeal. These two groups had been traditionally associated with the higher Sanskrit culture, and the fact that they together formed a relatively affluent landholding class, especially in Tanjore, enabled them to surmount the financial burdens of collegiate instruction more easily than any other caste group. Equally important was the founding of a college in Kumbaconam, the stronghold of the Brahmins of the region and the center of Sanskrit culture in Tamilnadu for many centuries. This college "long had the monopoly of all the best Native teaching talent in the presidency," which was entirely Brahmin, while 90 per cent of its students were also Brahmins.[15] According to one calculation, no less than 144 out of 599 Arts graduates of the Madras University between 1858 and 1877 were natives of Tanjore[16] and they were principally Sri-Vaishnava or Smartha Brahmins.

After the 1870s Niyogi Brahmins began to enter the mainstream of higher education in the Northern Circars, aided no doubt by the starting of a first-grade college in Rajahmundry, while in Malabar the Pattar Brahmins showed a similar devotion to Western education and came to occupy influential positions in the administration and the professions.

In comparison to the Brahmins, the achievements of the other groups pale into relative insignificance. To an extent, the Indian Christians matched the Brahmins in the race for higher education. Though forming only 2 per cent of the total population, they accounted for over 8 per cent of the total graduates of Madras University. Their performance was all the more remarkable as they started from humble economic backgrounds and had to contend with social prejudices of the communities from which they had broken away. However, under the fostering care of the Christian missions, and their own readiness to adapt themselves to the changes brought about by British rule, the Indian

Christians successfully overcame their difficulties
and won general acceptance as a progressive community. Christian women were the most literate in
South India, and Christian men ranked second only
to the Brahmins in their performance in collegiate
education relative to their proportion of the population.[17]

Trailing far behind the Brahmins and Indian
Christians were the non-Brahmin Hindus. Although
the latter constituted over four-fifths of the population of the Presidency, their proportion of the
total graduates was only one-fifth. Whatever the
popular myths about Hindu response to Western education, there is nothing to obscure the fact that during the nineteenth century substantial sections of
the non-Brahmins and Harijans remained untouched by
the new learning. While the Harijans were given
hardly any opportunity to excel, effectively shut
out of Western education by poverty and high caste
opposition, the wealthy non-Brahmin trading castes,
whether the Chettis of Tamilnadu or the Komatis of
Telugu country, showed little interest in the new
learning. A similar spirit of unconcern was also
displayed by the great agricultural castes of South
India who were more content with their traditional
pursuits than interested in coming to terms with an
alien culture, although it must be said that some
of the wealthier agricultural families, especially
the Vellalars, did send their sons to colleges.
But throughout the nineteenth century, the in-
grained habits of social and occupational behavior
militated against zealous acceptance of Western education, especially at a collegiate level, by the
non-Brahmins and Harijans.*

---

*The performance of the Muslims in Western ed-
ucation will be examined in Chapter 6.

SEARCH FOR OFFICIAL EMPLOYMENT

By 1886, after three decades of university education, a total of 18,785 had passed the matriculation examination in South India.* Although this number was small in relation to the population of the Presidency (1:1,700), it was nevertheless high in terms of opportunities available in the public service, commerce, and industry. Hence, the question of employment for the educated became one of the central issues by the 1880s, affecting not only the very structure of the educational system but also having important political implications in the Madras Presidency.

During the 1860s and 1870s Indians passing through the portals of higher learning had their eyes fixed on the public service. A graduate was reported as saying in 1864:

Education has been made to subserve this end, viz. the creation of an intelligent class of Government servants. Hence for a long time the notion has prevailed and even now I think it is prevailing in some parts that the object of education is Government service. If we ask a Hindu Gentleman why he sends his son to school, his answer will be that his son may obtain his livelihood in future, that he may secure some employment under Government and pass his days in quiet and ease without being put to the necessity of begging for his bread.[18]

Without doubt the notion that Western education was the passport to official employment was widely prevalent at this time. In part, this belief was stimulated by the early advocates of Western education in South India: Elphinstone, George Norton and Powell had all sought to

---

*See Table 3.1, p. 109.

popularize the new learning by assuring the Indians
that preference would be given to those who were
trained in Western culture. The institution of the
General Test in 1858 reinforced this belief. Also,
the notion gained currency from the performance of
the Proficients of the Madras High School. The success of the administrative elite in achieving fame
and prestige in government service, under the active auspices of the Madras authorities, impressed
on the minds of the succeeding generation that
public service held the key to success and influence. The feats of Madava Rao, Muthusamy Iyer, and
Rama Iyengar doubtless inspired many graduates who
followed them to believe that they would become the
next generation of dewans, High Court judges, and
heads of departments.

But this is not the entire explanation. The
norms and values derived from caste also determined
the choice of occupation. The bulk of the graduates of South India came from the upper Hindu
castes, notably, Brahmins. For centuries these
castes had been dominating the learned and administrative professions. They despised manual work and
held in contempt commercial and industrial pursuits.
In turning to Western education, these castes were
largely endeavoring to perpetuate their traditional
life styles and occupations.

About the time that the first graduates were
emerging from the portals of the University of
Madras, policies of recruitment into the administration of the British Raj were being radically recast.
Two basic changes (made after 1850) were to have
important consequences for Indian graduates in
search of official employment. First, there was
the removal of all barriers against Indians entering the administrative service, especially at the
higher levels. Second, there was the British acceptance of the principle that all but the most menial
positions in the public service must be filled on
the basis of open competition. Although the actual
implementation of these policy changes did not always satisfy Indian opinion, their effect

nonetheless was to pave the way for educated elements in South India to infiltrate into many of the
middle ranking positions in the administration of
the Madras Presidency.

Indian representation was weakest at the apex
of the Indian administrative structure, known as
the Covenanted Civil Service.* This prestigious
service was manned by a select corps of largely
European officials, numbering less than a thousand.
Called Covenanted Civilians, these officials controlled the key positions both in the central and
provincial secretariats as well as in the district
administration. In 1853 the Covenanted Civil Service was thrown open to competition and in the
following year racial disabilities were removed by
law. Though these were important concessions to
Indian aspirants, the fact that the competitive examinations were held in England and the prescrip-
tion later on of a low age limit almost nullified
these concessions. For Brahmins and some high
caste non-Brahmin Hindus, ritual taboos against sea
travel ruled out the possibility of going to England to compete. For many other groups, the substantial outlay that was required to undertake such
a visit made it hardly a worthwhile proposition.
To add to the difficulties, the progressive reduction of the age of entry into the Covenanted Civil
Service placed Indian competitors at a disadvantage
vis-a-vis their British counterparts. In 1864 the
upper age limit was reduced from twenty-two to
twenty-one and in 1876 it was further reduced to
nineteen. At this youthful age, Indians had yet to
gain a sufficiently, strong foundation in English,
or the other branches of substantive knowledge to
stand a chance against their English rivals trained

---

*The term is derived from the word "covenant"
which every official in this service was expected
to sign with the Secretary of State for India,
swearing loyalty to the British Crown and pledging
to uphold the rules of the service.

largely in the public schools. Viceroy Ripon testified in 1883 that the effect of the 1876 age reduction had "undoubtedly been altogether to shut
the door of the competitive examinations in England
to natives of India."[19] Indeed, after three decades of competitive examinations, South India could
only boast of a single successful entrant into this
service.

Hence, when nationalist opinion became organized in the 1880s, the Covenanted Civil Service became one of its prime targets. The Indian National
Congress passed resolutions annually calling for
the raising of the age limit and the institution of
simultaneous examinations in England and India.
The former demand was conceded by the Public Service Commission in its report of 1888 and was implemented four years later, but the latter continued
to be a nationalist grievance for several more
decades.

Placed below the Covenanted Civil Service was
the Statutory Civil Service, a new branch created
in 1870 by a Statute of the British Parliament
which empowered the Indian Government to appoint
Indians to any position in the public service without having to resort to competitive examinations.
The intention here was to provide an alternative
outlet for Indians who were being practically shut
out of the Covenanted Civil Service. When the
rules of this service were drafted by the Indian
authorities in 1879, they obviously wanted to recruit Indians of high social status without showing
too much concern for educational attainments. In
Madras, the government largely adhered to this
principle and between 1879 and 1886 made eight appointments of "Statutory Civilians" from "young men
of good family or social position."[20] This mode of
selection aroused strong criticism in several
quarters. However, the Statutory Civil Service offered far too few openings for the educated and its
abolition in 1892 was hardly mourned, even in official circles.

The base of the Indian administrative pyramid

was formed by the Uncovenanted Service, so styled
because its officers were not required to sign a
covenant. It was this service which came to provide the main outlet for educated employment in
South India during the second half of the nineteenth century. A large and complex establishment,
the Uncovenanted Service came to include multifarious subordinate grades that existed within the
district administration, on the one hand, and in
the special departments, on the other. It is not
possible here to give a detailed listing of these
various grades. However, in the district administration, except for the handful of top positions,
like those of the Collector, Sub-Collector, Head
Assistant, or Zillah Judge, which were filled by
Covenanted Civilians, the rest of the posts were
designated Uncovenanted and were largely held by
Indians. In the special departments, like Registration, Education, Settlement, Revenue Survey,
Police, Public Works, Salt, Forest, and Jail, the
heads were invariably Covenanted Civilians while
the subordinate staff were designated Uncovenanted
officers.

Selection into the Uncovenanted Service was on
the basis of merit and proven ability. From 1858
onwards, Indian aspirants to this service, except
for very menial posts, had to pass the General Test
examinations conducted by the Madras Government or
possess a university qualification.[21] Recruitment
into the district administration was entrusted to
the Collector, while in the special departments it
was the responsibility of the respective departmental heads. Only in the case of the elite officers in the service, notably, deputy collectors,
subordinate judges, district *munsifs,* and *tahsildars,* was selection either done by or required the
sanction of the Governor-in-Council.[22]

Ever since the new system of recruitment into
the Uncovenanted Service came into operation in
1858, it became evident that there would be more
qualified candidates than jobs available. This invested considerable discretion in the heads of

departments as to who among these qualified aspirants they should recruit and at what point in the
service hierarchy. Some heads exercized their discretion by selecting almost exclusively from among
those who had passed the General Test, often at a
very low grade, and then promoting them according
to performance and experience. Such a policy
placed those with university qualification at some
disadvantage. Other departmental heads tried to
relate different educational attainments to the
different grades in the Uncovenanted Service.
While filling the lower rungs with those having a
pass in the General Test or matriculation, they reserved the higher posts almost entirely to graduates. Consequently, while some departments had
only a sprinkling of graduates, others were heavily
populated by such elements.

The different recruitment policies of the departments in the Madras Presidency were revealed at
the inquiry undertaken by the Public Service Commission in 1886–87. At the level of the district
administration, which was divided into the executive and judicial branches, it was found that there
was a higher proportion of graduates in the judicial than in the executive line. Of a total of 120
judicial officers, called subordinate judges and
district *munsifs,* 34 were graduates, 14 had passed
First Arts, 32 were matriculates, and the remaining
40 had no university qualification. In the executive service, on the other hand, out of 255 officers who were either deputy collectors or *tahsildars,* only 10 were graduates, 18 had passed First
Arts, 52 were matriculates, and the remaining 175
had no university qualification.[23] Hence, while 1
in every 4 of the judicial officers was a graduate,
only 1 in every 25 of the executive officers had a
similar qualification.

Such variations were even more marked in the
special departments of the Madras Government, reflecting largely the different recruitment policies
of their heads. Some departments became virtual
preserves of graduates. One such department was

Registration. Organized in 1865, its first
Inspector-General made it a deliberate policy to
attract educated applicants, whether in the cleri-
cal side or at the level of special registrars and
subregistrars. In 1884, of the 260 special and
subregistrars in the department, 117 were graduates,
102 had passed First Arts, 36 were matriculates,
and the remaining 5 had no university qualification.[24]

Some departments, however, showed less willingness to employ Indian graduates. The Police Department, though dominated by the Indian element in the
lower ranks, rarely attracted applicants with university qualifications. The generally low esteem
in which the profession was held, the subordinate
level at which recruitment was made, and the alleged partiality shown towards Europeans in promotion served to discourage educated Indians from
joining this department. Of the forty-nine gazet-
ted posts in the department in 1886 only one was
held by an Indian.[25]

A similar situation prevailed in the Salt Department. It was the Department's policy to recruit Europeans exclusively into certain higher
grades on the grounds that they were best fitted
"to govern a large number of [Indian] subordinates
and enforce discipline." Hence, Indian graduates
were a rarity in the Department: in 1884 there were
only 18 graduates in an establishment which had 487
posts carrying salaries of Rs 100 and above.[26]

Besides the Covenanted, Statutory, and Uncovenanted services, the only other area where there was
an outlet for official employment was the administration of the Indian or "Native" States. Little
information is forthcoming about the mode of recruitment into the service of such States as Mysore,
Travancore, Cochin, or Hyderabad. It is known,
however, that since about the middle of the nineteenth century, some of the important executive and
judicial positions in these States began to be
filled by university graduates. Attempts to ra-
tionalize the administration, often under the

promptings of the British Resident in the State, demanded that an efficient and honest corps of officials be recruited. Increasingly such men came
from the ranks of the Western-educated class, who
filled positions of trust and influence, including
that of the *dewan*. In 1891 it was estimated that
174 Arts graduates were in the official employment
of Indian States.[27]

Without a shadow of doubt the public service
provided the largest single outlet for the Western-
educated class in South India during the nineteenth
century. A survey of the occupational distribution
among Arts graduates of all colleges affiliated to
Madras University in 1882 revealed that 416 out of
971 (or 43 per cent) were public servants. Figures
compiled for the Madras Presidency College in this
period confirm this overall trend of graduate
employment in South India: of its 387 graduates in
1882, a total of 175 (or 45 per cent) were in official employment. Estimates for the eighties are
not available in isolation. However, of the 2,386
Arts graduates on the rolls of the Madras University in 1891, no fewer than 1,019 (or 43 per cent)
were public servants.[28] These figures reveal the
continuing attraction of government employment
among Indian graduates, and there were few signs of
any weakening in the government's position as the
leading employer of educated talent in South India.

A feature of administrative recruitment was
the preponderance of the Brahmins (see Table 3.3).
In 1886 the Brahmins held 42 per cent of all posts
in the Madras Government carrying a monthly salary
of over Rs 10. Brahmin domination was even more
marked at the higher level of the Uncovenanted Service: of the 349 elite posts in the executive and
judicial line in 1886, no less than 202 (or 58 per
cent) were in Brahmin hands.[29] In certain special
departments, Brahmin representation was just as
preponderant. In the Registration Department, for
example, 217 out of 365 officers were Brahmins, although since 1880 it was the policy of the Department "to reduce the number of Brahmans and to allow

all classes [to] have a fair share of the appointments."30 However, so long as competition remained
the main criterion for recruitment, especially for
posts carrying salaries of Rs 10 and above, Brahmin
supremacy in higher education ensured their domination of the public service.

Table 3.3
Composition of the Public Service

Caste or Communal Group	Percentage of Total Population	Percentage of Appointments Held of Over Rs 10 per Month	Percentage of Appointments Held of Rs 10 and Below per Month	Total
Brahmins	3.1	42.2	4.4	19.2
Non-Brahmin Hindus	86.6	36.5	67.7	55.4
Muslims	6.3	5.5	24.1	16.8
Indian Christians	2.3	4.9	3.5	4.1
Europeans & Eurasians	0.1	10.9	0.3	4.5
Others	1.6	0	0	0
Total	100	100	100	100

Source: *MEP*, Vol. 3045, No. 386 (Table covers
the year 1886).

To those British officials who had assumed
that open competition would ensure a fair distribution of government jobs among the various communities in South India, the results were manifestly
disappointing. W. R. Cornish, the Census Commissioner in 1871, noted that the introduction of competition had only "tended to strengthen their
[Brahmin] position in the executive," which he
attributed to the fact that the Brahmins were the
first to recognize "the necessity of educating
their youths to qualify for admission into the
civil service."31 Official concern over the working of the competition system found expression in
1887 following a detailed inquiry into the strength
of the various caste and communal groups in the
Uncovenanted Service of the Madras Government. The
inquiry revealed that while non-Brahmin Hindus,

Harijans, and Muslims were underrepresented, Brahmins, Eurasians, and Europeans enjoyed more than
their fair share of official patronage. It was
found that in certain departments, especially
Settlement, Registration, Education, and Revenue,
Brahmin preponderance was excessive.

While unwilling to create the impression that
it was hostile to Brahmin admission into the public
service, the Madras Government nevertheless felt
compelled to draw the attention of heads of departments to the inexpediency of allowing "any single
class to monopolise the whole patronage of Government."[32] In 1890, when the Provincial Civil Service scheme was being worked out in South India,
the Madras authorities decided that free competition to fill the vacant posts of deputy collectors
should be modified to enable the government to
appoint one-third of the vacancies on the basis of
selection from among persons of proved merit and
ability. Even this restriction did not halt the
influx of the Brahmins, compelling the Madras
Government to impose further restrictions on open
competition in 1896. Henceforth, appointments of
deputy collectors by competition were limited to
one per year, an arrangement which the local authorities felt would "afford opportunities for correc-
ting the distribution of these appointments among
the various classes of the community, from time to
time."[33]

Although British officials regarded Brahmin
domination of the public service in the late nineteenth century as essentially a continuation of
what had prevailed in earlier decades, they failed
to grasp the fact that open competition had at
least brought about significant changes in the distribution of administrative power within the Brahmin community in South India. Particularly
significant was the relative decline in the position of the Desasthas, who no longer held the keys
to administrative influence in the districts. Instead, other Brahmin groups had increasingly come
to the forefront, notably, the Sri-Vaishnavas and

Smarthas of Tamilnadu and the Niyogis of the Northern Circars. The pervasive influence of the former was nowhere more apparent than in Tanjore
district:

> Of all the several Brahmanical communities in
> Tanjore, the Dravidas or Tamilians, notably
> the Aiyangar section, are by far the most in-
> dustrious and thrifty, as well as intelligent;
> they are at present the most rising and pros-
> perous. There is hardly a pursuit, literary,
> industrial or professional, to which they do
> not apply themselves with remarkable success.
> They are found in all departments of the
> Government service; as pleaders they are pre-
> eminently successful. No class of people have
> availed themselves, to the extent the Tamil
> Brahmins have, of the education imparted by
> the Combaconum College and other schools scat-
> tered over the district.[34]

DIVERSIFICATION OF THE EDUCATIONAL SYSTEM

The public service, despite its capacity to absorb large numbers of educated Indians, could not
conceivably hope to find suitable positions for the
ever-growing numbers of Indians graduating from
high schools and colleges in South India. This
created a social problem of considerable magnitude
as the literary character of the educational training, coupled with higher caste aversion to commercial and manual pursuits, inevitably drove many to
seek refuge in teaching, journalism, or other lowly
paid positions. The problem of finding employment
for the educated commensurate with their attainments
had attracted notice during the 1860s, but it was
not until a decade later that it compelled more
serious consideration at the higher levels of the
Madras Government. In 1875, while speaking to the
students at the Presidency College, Governor Lord
Hobart warned that those who studied for the sake

of official employment would face "a bitter disappointment." He went on to say that the primary object of education was not to clothe graduates "with official authority, but to adorn and invigorate the current of their lives."[35] But such exhortations did little to relieve the pressure for state employment which was felt in its most acute form at the level of those passing the General Test. In 1879 the Director of Public Instruction admitted that the number passing this test was "enormously in excess of the number of appointments available."[36]

University graduates, though not in the same predicament, nevertheless found themselves accepting positions which they would have scorned a few years before. T. Muthusamy Iyer, in a speech to the Presidency College students in 1886, indicated the kind of prospects which they would have to encounter after their college career:

> When I left the College 32 years ago, there
> were about 75 highly educated men whose at-
> tainments may be said to be co-extensive with
> those of our graduates. At present there are
> upwards of 1,500 B.A.'s besides 7,000 under-
> graduates and matriculates. Public offices
> are largely filled with educated men and the
> Bar is crowded. The church, the army and the
> navy are not available to you as a profession
> as they are to Englishmen in England.[37]

By the 1880s it had become commonplace to talk of the diminishing opportunities of the university graduates, and to infer that such qualifications no longer commanded the market value of the earlier years. Indeed, at the hearing of the Public Service Commission in Madras in 1887, both officials and nonofficials, Indians and Europeans, testified that graduates were greatly in excess of jobs and that they could be recruited at salaries as low as Rs 15 per month. At the same time, fears were expressed in various circles that the presence of an

educated unemployed or underemployed class would
"breed only an element of dangerous discontent in
the community."[38]

In their efforts to come to grips with the
problem, the educational authorities in South India
decided to raise the academic standards of the university and Uncovenanted Service examinations, impose higher fees on those seeking collegiate
instruction, and insist on candidates producing certificates of having studied in recognized educational institutions.

Though these measures were introduced with the
ostensible aim of improving the quality of instruction, their real purpose was to restrict the numbers passing university and public service examinations. As examination standards began to be raised,
failure rates began to soar, in some years reaching
inordinately high levels. In 1889, for instance,
89 per cent of those presenting themselves for the
F.A. examination failed and the *Journal of Education* commented, with some understatement, that the
examiners of late were showing "an increasing tendency towards severity."[39] A high failure rate was
also evident in the Pleader's examination, brought
about by the raising of the pass mark and the repeated revision of the curriculum. Between 1888
and 1892, only 99 succeeded in passing the First
Grade Pleader's examination out of a total of 888
candidates, an average pass rate of 11 per cent.[40]
Not unnaturally, examinations came to be regarded
as "something like a lottery. In some years the
percentage of passes is fair; in others it is hor-
ribly low."[41] Failure in one attempt was not taken
as the signal to bow out of the examination altogether. Like the intrepid gambler, those who
failed continued to press their luck over a number
of occasions, on borrowed time and sometimes on
borrowed money. Some took casual jobs to tide them
over their financial problems.

The tightening up of academic standards was at
best only a negative remedy to the problem of educated unemployment and at worst could produce

equally serious social consequences. More important in tackling the problem from the long range
point of view was the decision to diversify the educational system in South India by strengthening
such courses as medicine, science, and engineering
and by introducing more practical courses to meet
the demands for trained personnel in agriculture,
industry, and commerce.

Indeed, it was the constitution of the Education Commission in 1882 which provided a much
needed opportunity to reappraise some of the premises on which Indian educational policy had been
evolving for over a generation. Although its terms
of reference disavowed the need for any inquiry
into "the general working of the Indian Universities" or the state of technical education, the
Education Commission could hardly ignore these
weighty subjects, especially as they were attracting an element of political controversy.

In its recommendations, the Education Commission emphasized the need for "diversity of culture,
both on the literary and on the physical side." At
the level of secondary education, it urged that:
"in the upper classes of high schools there be two
divisions, one leading to the Entrance examination
of the Universities, the other of a more practical
character, intended to fit youths for commercial or
non-literary pursuits." As for higher education,
the Education Commission felt that greater provision should be made for the study of science in
government and aided colleges.[42] These proposals
found general acceptance among the educational
authorities in Madras, and the next decade witnessed a concerted attempt on their part to reorien-
tate the educational system along the lines
suggested by the Educational Commission.

The main task was to recast the entire curriculum of the secondary schools, and ensure the popularity of the new courses by awarding jobs in the
public and related services. In March 1886 the
higher examinations in Science, Art, Industries and
Commerce were instituted in the hope of encouraging

instruction "in those kinds of knowledge which bear
upon the different branches of the industry now
existing in this Presidency or suitable for it."
Among the subjects prescribed were mechanical drawing, metallurgy, minerology, animal physiology,
forestry, painting, design, and surveying. In the
following year, the Middle School examination was
revised. The changes divided the examination into
"a general side" and "a technical and industrial
side." Incorporated in the latter section was a
whole range of new subjects to equip youths for
technical, commercial, and industrial pursuits.[43]
Changes in curriculum were also announced for the
Upper Secondary forms in 1889, aimed at stimulating
"secondary and technical education, of improving
its character and of widening its scope." Included
among the optional courses were such subjects as
hydraulics, mechanical drawing, agriculture, forestry, printing, bookkeeping, and banking. Those successful in these examinations were to receive
certificates from the Commissioner of the Uncovenanted Service Examination, a necessary passport for
public employment.[44]

Among those who welcomed these changes were
some of the more influential private and aided institutions of learning. There had been a growing
recognition in Madras of the need to divert educated talent into commercial and industrial vocations.
Symptomatic of this change of attitude was the decision of the Trustees of Pachaiyappa Charities to
encourage commercial education. Thus far, the commercial world had been wholly neglected by the
Western-educated class, and the few who had tried
to enter the profession as *dubashes*, bankers, or
clerks were a disappointment to their employers.
It was a common complaint that educated applicants
knew "nothing of book-keeping, and their hand-
writing is bad, and that they are in many cases unable to compose a simple letter."

The remedy lay in providing a commercial training, and the arrival of John Adam as Principal of
Pachaiyappa College in 1884 proved timely. He

drafted a scheme for commercial education* and persuaded the Director of Public Instruction to incor-
porate it in the revised curriculum for the Middle
School examination. A shorthand class was started
in Pachaiyappa College in 1884, and the favorable
response emboldened its Trustees to launch a separate commercial school two years later. This lead
was followed by other educational agencies, including the Christian missions, and between 1890 and
1894 a total of 154 students had obtained certificates in bookkeeping, correspondence or banking.[45]
The idea of raising "a commercially educated middle
class, which will not, on the one hand, think business details beneath its dignity, nor, on the
other, find them above its capacity,"[46] thus found
a modest realization before the nineteenth century
drew to a close.

Simultaneously, conscious attempts were made
to encourage industrial education. In 1883-84
there were barely 400 students receiving training
in six schools throughout the Madras Presidency, of
which some partook "more the nature of charity
schools designed to feed, house and clothe a certain number of poor children, than of schools where
young people are taught on scientific principles
the theory and practice of some of the industrial
arts." Under the new policy, these schools were reorganized, provided with equipment and trained
teachers, while students were awarded scholarships

─────────────────

*John Adam, a graduate of Cambridge, was
hailed as "the father of commercial education" in
South India for his attempts to stimulate commercial training both within the Pachaiyappa College
and elsewhere. In 1891 he relinquished the princi-
palship of the College to read law and subsequently
became a barrister at the Madras High Court. He
was an active participant in Congress affairs for
many years, and was its spokesman on commercial and
technical education. *Journal of the National
Indian Association*, No. 164 (August 1884): 384.

to complete their training. In some institutions,
the government decided to introduce a course on
some recognized craft, as was the case in Rajahmundry College where a carpentry class was started
in 1885. This experiment, though of a modest kind,
was significant in so far as it helped "to break
down the prejudice among the caste Hindus against
manual labour."[47]

The educational authorities also welcomed any
private support to stimulate industrial education.
In 1887 at the celebrations to mark Queen Victoria's
Jubilee, over Rs 100,000 was raised from private
sources in Madras in the cause of technical education. The Madras Government agreed to subscribe an
equal amount, and the result was the erection of the
Victoria Technical Institute.[48]

The need for a shift of emphasis away from
purely literary education was also recognized at
the level of collegiate instruction. It had long
been a source of complaint that "university education is a literary education as contrasted with
technical education." Although there was provision
for B.A. students to read a course in Physical
Science, it was not popular and the Madras Provincial Committee of the Education Commission felt compelled to draw attention to the absence of "an
opportunity for students to graduate in a scientific course."[49]

But over the next decade little was done to
provide a degree course in science, partly due to
the conservative Senate of the Madras University,
although in the revision of the B.A. curriculum in
1891-92 more options were added to the science
division. In 1895, there were 472 students in the
science division of the B.A. class who, on gradua-
tion, were expected to apply their knowledge to
"arts, industries and manufactures." Although the
changes hardly went to the extent that many had
hoped, there was nevertheless confidence in official
circles in the ability of the existing colleges in
South India to turn out "young men imbued to some
extent with the scientific spirit and more or less

with scientific facts, laws and methods."[50]

Also indicative of the trend towards educational diversification was the growing popularity of medicine and engineering. The Madras Medical School, established in 1835 to train subordinate medical staff, was unpopular among some Hindu castes during the early years because of the opposition to Western medical science and ritual taboos associated with the profession as such. Despite the abstention of the Brahmins, a total of 603 students had passed out of the institution between 1835 and 1851 and entered service as hospital assistants and apprentices.[51] With the establishment of the Medical College in 1857, facilities were now available for advanced training. However, the long duration of the course and the preference shown to those graduating in English universities checked the progress of the college and only eleven candidates succeeded in taking the degree between 1858 and 1878.

However, the situation changed during the eighties with the growing popularity of science and diminution in employment prospects for those in literary pursuits. Hence, between 1878 and 1894 a total of 186 doctors graduated from the Medical College. The engineering profession, though it did not show the same growth rate, also began to attract more students during the eighties. While only 24 students had graduated from the Engineering College between 1858 and 1880, a total of 55 passed out during the next fifteen years.* The growth rate would have been faster but for the fact that graduates had great difficulty in finding "an opening at all commensurate with the time, labour and expense involved in securing their professional education."[52]

---

*See Table 3.1.

RISE OF INDEPENDENT PROFESSIONS

The diversification of the educational system
was only one consequence flowing from the inability
of the public service to absorb the growing Western-
educated class in South India. Another consequence,
albeit of an indirect kind, was the remarkable
acceleration in the growth of three independent professions, namely, law, teaching and journalism.

The important role that the members of these
three professions played in the political and
social movements of South India, especially after
1880, can hardly be exaggerated. In the words of
the *Hindu:* "School-masters, lawyers, and journalists form the most important and active members of
political bodies or associations."[53] This was a
claim which was admitted on all sides, not the
least by the ruling authorities who were constantly
endeavoring to find ways and means to combat the
political radicalism of these groups and circumscribe the limits of their agitational activity.

While the administrative elite, and indeed all
Indians in the service of the government, were reluctant to be drawn into any kind of overt political agitation for fear of government reprisal,
these three professional groups presented themselves as obvious foci of political leadership.
Their commitment to secular, nonsectarian politics,
their all-India orientation, and their genius for
organization and propaganda combined to transform
the style of politics in South India during the
1880s and brought the presidency into the mainstream of nationalist politics as represented by
the Indian National Congress.

Of these three professional groups, the lawyers exercised the strongest influence. Their
training acquainted them with the intricacies of
the British legal system, including constitutional
law and history, as well as with the highly-compli-
cated Hindu law. If one gave them an insight into
the British political system, the other enabled
them to shake the proverbial "pagoda tree," largely

at the expense of the litigious-minded landed
gentry of South India. The relative affluence of
the lawyers, while increasingly attracting the
best brains into the profession, also ensured their
robust independence in political issues. In the
words of one European barrister in Madras, "the
best political intellect in the country is, in the
main, to be found in the keeping of the Vakils
. . . . On the whole, the best educated men in the
country are the lawyers. They are also the most,
if not the only independent men in the [Madras]
Presidency."[54] The legal profession, more than
any other independent pursuit, also provided an
opportunity to travel, especially to the lawyer in
the metropolis. Visits for professional reasons
were used to establish links with political groups
in the *mofussil* towns. Indeed, by their training,
affluence, and enterprise, the lawyers had equipped themselves as leaders in the quest for political power.

The growth of the legal profession in South
India was to a considerable degree influenced by
British policies. During the early years of the
British Raj, Indian pleaders or *vakils* were allowed
to practice on receiving "a sunnud of appointment
duly authenticated by the court to which they may
be respectively attached." At this stage, entry
into the profession rested on no proven tests of
ability or knowledge, although this was partially
rectified in 1817 by the decision to establish
"native classes to study the hindoo and mahomedan
law and the regulations passed by Government, and
for the periodical examination of students in those
classes."[55] Despite this provision, judges in the
mofussil courts still could grant *sunnuds* of appointment to anyone whom they deemed to be "a fit
and proper person," and these "private" or "uncer-
tified" pleaders continued to practice throughout
the nineteenth century.

However, the overall tendency, especially during the second half of the century, was to institute more regular and rigorous examinations in

order to raise a better quality of Indian pleaders.
The first major step in this direction was taken in
1856 with the introduction of the pleadership examinations. Candidates were required to read Hindu
and Muslim law, the law of evidence, and the regulations and acts of government. Those successful
in these examinations were allowed to practice in
the Sadr courts and after 1861 in the district
courts. In subsequent years the pleadership examinations underwent frequent changes, invariably to
raise the qualifications of those wishing to compete. When the Legal Practitioners Act came into
operation in 1879, the right of sitting for this
examination was confined upon those who had passed
the matriculation. Successful candidates were divided into first and second grade pleaders, based
on their performance, with the former allowed to
practice in district courts and the latter in district *munsif's* courts.[56] During the latter decades
of the nineteenth century, it was this class of
legal practitioners who dominated the *mofussil*
courts, although some "private" *vakils* were still
allowed to appear in certain cases.

A second mode of entry into the legal profession was the Bachelor of Law (B.L.) examinations
instituted in the Madras University in 1858. Here
the training was far more rigorous than in the case
of the pleaders, and the degree course was obviously designed to produce a superior class of
legal practitioners. The recipients of the B.L.
degree were allowed to appear both in the High
Court and in the district courts and consequently
enjoyed a much higher status and prestige than the
pleaders. Not surprisingly, it was from the ranks
of the law graduates that the Madras Government
recruited its Indian judges of the High Court and
Government Pleaders. A third route of entry into
the profession was the bar examination in England.
The Europeans practicing in South India invariably
entered through this route. However, few South
Indians attempted this path; the costs involved and
the strong ritual objections on the part of the

higher castes against sea travel severely restricted the numbers proceeding to England to take the
bar examinations.

During the 1850s and 1860s the Madras bar was
dominated by the European barristers. Early in the
field and possessing superior training and grasp of
the law, many European barristers were able to collect "handsome incomes." There were instances of
single fees amounting to Rs 30,000, and many of the
European lawyers in Madras were earning about
Rs 10,000 a month. Their Indian rivals were slow
in challenging this supremacy; indeed, many of the
vakils were acting as juniors to their European
counterparts, often on very moderate incomes.[57]

The turning point came during the 1870s when
many *vakils* decided to go on their own and to exploit their knowledge of Hindu law. By mastering
the intricacies of Hindu law, often buried in
ancient Sanskrit texts, the *vakils* became "better
equipped than the Barristers and Attorneys in respect of laws of special applicability to Indian
cases."[58] Suits involving inheritance and property
rights were increasingly referred to them, and by
the 1880s the Original Side of the Madras bar was
under virtual *vakil* control. Some even began to
encroach on the Appellate Side, long the preserve
of the European barristers.[59] The "Vakil Raj," so
often used to describe *vakil* domination of political movements in India, was first established in
the legal profession, largely at the expense of
European practitioners.

The practice of appointing private pleaders
rules out the possibility of accurately assessing
the growth of the legal profession in South India.
According to the census returns in 1881, there were
4,705 legal practitioners in the Madras Presidency,
which included not only private pleaders but also
petition writers. Of these 64 were barristers,
solicitors, and attorneys with British qualifications, while 2,516 were classified as *vakils*.[60] As
only 164 had graduated with a law degree from the
Madras University up to 1882, it is obvious that

the vast majority of the *vakils* were pleaders,
practicing in the *mofussil* courts. Despite claims
that the bar was getting crowded, the profession remained lucrative throughout the eighties and the
envy of those in other vocations. An indication of
its popularity was the output of law graduates in
the Madras University: while only 85 obtained the
degree during the 1870s, a total of 269 passed during the ensuing decade. The pleadership examinations also reflected a similar trend: 21 passed in
1883, 135 in 1889 and 233 in 1892. With this accel-
erated expansion the profession became more competitive and less remunerative. This provoked the
Madras Law Journal to voice its unease about the
state of the profession in 1900:[61]

> The ranks of the profession are rapidly length-
> ening out. Competition is getting day by day
> keener, and the law courts being the only
> sphere where a man of education can earn his
> livelihood apart from the public service, per-
> sons of varying degrees of moral elevation
> crowd into the ranks of the profession without
> any adequate check or control or undergoing a
> proper process of sifting.

There was an element of exaggeration in this
claim that the ethical standards of the profession
had declined. If anything, the contrary was true,
for, as the profession became more lucrative and
prestigious, there were more insistent demands for
enforcing a rigid code of professional conduct. As
early as 1882 Muthusamy Iyer had called for a
vakils' association in Madras which would "bring
the whole body of legal practitioners in the country under wholesome professional control" along the
lines of the Inns of Court in England.[62] However,
the response to this appeal was slow in coming, and
it was not until March 1889 that the Madras High
Court Vakils' Association was formed. Representing
that group which had gained most in terms of prestige and wealth, this body was largely successful

at enforcing agreed rules of professional conduct.[63]
It also became a pressure group agitating for the
interests of the *vakils*, especially for the latter's
entry into such positions as Official Trustee,
Government Pleader, Officer of the Clerk of the
Crown and Official Assignee, Crown Prosecutor, Law
Reporter, and Attorney-General, which even in the
1890s were still the preserve of the European barristers.[64]

Established on a less lucrative footing, but
nevertheless possessing political influence, was
the teaching profession. The role of the teacher
in the work of India's regeneration was performed
on two distinct planes. Within the classroom, the
teacher molded the thinking of his pupils, and instilled in them the values and motivations which he
idealized. Outside the classroom, the teacher
shouldered some of the burden of public work, em-
ploying his spare hours either in managing religious institutions, settling caste disputes, running the affairs of municipal and district boards,
or organizing debating societies or political meetings. The teacher was often recruited to speak on
important issues, especially in the more remote
areas of the *mofussil*, and at times he also contributed to the local newspaper. Hence, in many parts
of South India, "the most competent and trusted
adviser in matters [of] politics was the schoolmaster."[65]

The teaching profession, despite the growing
popularity of education during the second half of
the nineteenth century, always retained a certain
fluidity. Low salaries, poor promotional prospects,
and absence of any retirement benefits divested the
profession of many of its attractions. Indeed,
teaching was only the last resort of the Western-
educated class, and even then many used it as a
springboard to other professions. Disgruntled
teachers spent their spare hours, and sometimes
even their teaching time, studying for university
or public examinations. Often the schoolmaster was
not professionally qualified to teach, nor did he

show any disposition to undergo such training. The
problem was most acute at the level of primary instruction where trained teachers, as the Madras
Provincial Committee of Education Commission remarked in 1884, were "a pressing want."[66] Even among
graduate teachers, many did not have a teaching
qualification, admittedly performing a makeshift
duty and awaiting the earliest escape to a more re-
warding profession.

However, the teaching profession began to
attain some measure of stability and respectability
during the 1880s, partly with the diminution of
employment prospects in public service and partly
with new opportunities being created for private
initiative in secondary and higher education. The
latter stemmed directly from the official policy of
withdrawing from higher and secondary education,
and this provided a challenge and opportunity to
Indians anxious that the momentum of Western education should not be lost. Aided by public subscriptions, some Indian graduates established high
schools in centers where there was a demand for
education. One successful venture was the Native
High School in Kumbaconam. Founded in 1876 by
three Brahmin graduates, this school overcame some
of its teething troubles and by 1889 had produced a
total of 350 matriculate passes.[67] The success of
this venture inspired other graduates to establish
similar schools elsewhere.*

Accurate estimates of the growth of the teaching profession are difficult to obtain, largely
owing to the absence of reliable data about
teachers in indigenous schools. According to the

---

*K. Subba Rao, who started his career by estab-
lishing a high school in Coimbatore in 1882, says
that the example of the Native High School in Kumbaconam "awakened a keen desire in several of the students to take to the profession of teaching and to
open new schools wherever needed." K. Subba Rao,
Revived Memories, pp. 47-48.

census returns of 1891, a total 103,970 people were
employed in teaching, inspecting, and managing educational institutions in the Madras Presidency.[68]
Obviously, the vast majority were teachers of primary and village schools. Barely one in ten were
involved with secondary or higher education. Those
holding degrees from a university were a small
minority. In 1891 only 371 of the B.A. graduates
of Madras University had entered the profession,
either as principals of high schools, or lecturers
in colleges, or as inspectors of schools.[69]

As the teaching profession grew in strength
and came to attain some measure of stability, there
were growing demands for the improvement in the
status and pay of teachers. John Adam, drawing on
his experience in Pachaiyappa College, stated in
1895 that the elevation of the teaching profession
would depend ultimately on pay and promotional
prospects. So long as public service and other related professions were accorded a better treatment,
he felt that teaching would remain "the refuge of
the destitute, the last resort of those who find
themselves unable to pass the portals of law or
medicine or special test."[70]

V. S. Srinivasa Sastri, a member of the profession which he believed had "fallen from its high
dignity," argued that the ability of teachers
should not be assessed on the basis of examination
results. He felt that inspectors of schools, and
indeed parents, laid too great a stress on students
passing examinations rather than how they were
being instructed. Character building, the inculca-
tion of civic and social responsibilities, and the
development of the capacity for clear thinking were
all ignored. Srinivasa Sastri felt that so long
as these aspects of education were neglected the
teaching profession would not command much esteem
nor the coming generation play any more constructive role in promoting social and political reforms.[71]

Others believed that the status of the profession could only be improved by forming teachers'

associations. The *Educational Review*, a monthly
journal published in Madras, argued that such associations would serve "to create a pride in the
teaching profession, to awaken an interest in educational questions, [and] to disseminate views on
the methods of teaching and the theories of Education." Active canvassing led to the formation of
the Madras Teachers' Guild in November 1895, and
this body was expected to fulfill the dual function
of improving the material prospects of its members
and of providing a platform to discuss such educational issues as curricula, textbooks, and teaching
methods.[72]

Unlike law and teaching, journalism was a
wholly "foreign plant" engrafted on Indian soil,[73]
and its remarkable growth during the closing years
of the nineteenth century epitomized the kind of
transformation which Western rule had effected in
the subcontinent. During the early years of the
British Raj, the press had subserved a religious
function as well as meeting the social and commercial needs of the European community. Christian
missionaries had long grasped the importance of the
printed word in disseminating their doctrines and
they had set up their own presses to translate the
Bible into Indian languages and publish periodicals
and newspapers. In fact, the first vernacular
printing press in South India had begun functioning
during the early years of the eighteenth century,
and soon the missionaries were publishing transla-
tions of well-known English works for use in
schools, compiling grammars and dictionaries, and
enlarging the vocabulary of the Indian languages by
coining new words.[74] This lead was taken up by the
Europeans in commerce and administration who saw
the need for regular information about the state of
business and what the government was doing. In
1785 the *Madras Courier* made its appearance as a
weekly, and it was followed by the *Madras Gazette*,
Madras Male Asylum Herald, and the *Madras Conservative*. None of these publications managed to survive for any great length of time, troubled as they

were by official restrictions and the absence of a
consistent public demand.[75]

Early Indian ventures into journalism in South
India were doubtless influenced by the desire to uphold Hindu religious and social order in the face
of bitter missionary onslaught. Nevertheless, the
importance of disseminating information of local
importance and elevating community life were ideals
that were kept in mind. For instance, the *Carnatic
Chronicle*, first published in 1833 and carrying
articles in English, Tamil, and Telugu, attempted
to discuss local issues without descending into religious controversies.[76] Similarly, the *Native Interpreter* was launched in 1840 with the avowed
object of diffusing "useful knowledge amongst the
Hindoo community through the medium of English
language, and the opening of a channel through
which Hindoo claims might be urged on the notice of
the Government." However, during the religious
convulsions of the forties, this organ increasingly
assumed the role of the guardian of Hindu religion
and heritage and vehemently attacked the Christian
missionaries and their publications.[77] Even more
militant were the Hindu religious societies, especially the Sadur Veda Siddhanta Sabha, which had
its own press issuing a stream of publications in
defence of Hinduism. Journalism, at this stage of
its evolution in South India, could not escape from
being drawn into religious disputes and to that
extent it appeared to subserve religious rather
than the secular needs of its readers.

However, as these theological controversies
died out during the 1850s, journalism in South
India came to assume an increasingly secular character. Especially significant in this transition
was the appearance of a fresh crop of English Language newspapers. The *Athenaeum and Daily News*
(1845), *Madras Times* (1858), and *Madras Mail* (1867),
all European owned and edited, came to have a major
share of the circulation in the Madras Presidency
throughout the nineteenth century.

By contrast, Indian attempts in English

journalism at this juncture had less permanence.
The *Crescent* (1844) and the *Rising Sun* (1853)
folded up after a period of precarious existence.
Their successors in the sixties, namely, the *Hindu
Chronicle* and *Native Advocate*, fared even worse.
During the 1870s the *Native Public Opinion* and
Madrassee functioned as organs of Indian opinion until they merged into the *Madras Native Opinion* in
1877. However, this move did not save the new
paper from extinction a few years later.[78] Nor
were early Indian attempts in vernacular journalism
any more successful, although in this field there
was no European competition. Indeed, in February
1877 there were only thirteen vernacular newspapers
in South India, with an estimated circulation of
4,000, catering to a population of about thirty
million.[79]

The new era in the history of Indian journalism
dawned in Madras with the launching of the English
language *Hindu* in September 1878 by "six ardent
youths just out of college." Undaunted by failures
in the past, the sponsors of this attempt believed
that with luck and dedication they would be able to
surmount whatever difficulties might stand in their
way. Starting publication as a weekly, the *Hindu*
soon acquired popularity by its fearless advocacy
of Indian interests. In 1883 this paper was converted into a tri-weekly, and six years later it
became a daily--the first Indian-owned daily in
South India. As its editor explained subsequently,
the success of the *Hindu* stemmed from the fact that
it "fell harmoniously with the spirit of the
times."[80]

The success of the *Hindu* persuaded its editors
to try their hand in the field of vernacular journalism. In 1881 a Tamil weekly called *Swadesamitran* was started with the aim of educating the
Tamils on the political questions affecting the
country at large. By slow stages this newspaper
built up its circulation and popularity, and in
1899 it was made a daily--the first vernacular
daily in South India.

Stimulated by the example of the *Hindu* and *Swadesamitran*, and taking advantage of a growing reading public, a host of Indian-owned newspapers emerged during the 1880s, published either in English, vernacular, or Anglo-vernacular. Two English newspapers which were started in the metropolis were the *People's Friend* (1881) and the *Hindu Observer* (1883), but neither survived long as they were unable to make much headway against the already entrenched newspapers. Besides, certain communal associations also started their own organs. The Madras Anjuman-i-Islamiah was served by the *Ittifaq*, the Eurasian and Anglo-Indian Association of Southern India by the *Eastern Guardian*, and the Indian Christians by the *Eastern Star*.

In the *mofussil* it was the vernacular and Anglo-vernacular press which achieved some degree of success. Edited largely by men who lacked higher education, and with very small capital outlay, the vernacular newspapers managed to survive by minimizing their costs and by catering to local needs. Some of the larger towns had more than one vernacular paper: Calicut in 1894 was served by three Malayalam weeklies. But the great majority of the *mofussil* towns had room for only one newspaper, and these towns largely accounted for the eighty-two vernacular and Anglo-vernacular papers circulating in South India in 1890.[81]

With the rapid expansion of the press in South India, journalism began to shed its amateur status and to emerge as full-fledged profession. The early Indian newspapers had failed partly because those who were responsible for their running were unable to "give their whole time" to the work.[82] Even the *Hindu* was run for some years as a part-time concern, with both its editor and proprietor continuing their teaching duties. Similar instances were common in other such ventures. To a large extent this was a reflection of the hazards of the profession. Competition from Europeans, defaulting subscribers, and the refusal of the Indian capitalists to invest in the press kept the Indian-owned newspapers in a state of precarious existence for much of the nineteenth century. The *Hindu* commented thus in 1903:[83]

> Newspaper enterprise in this country has not so far attracted the attention of capitalists and speculators. It has thriven by the efforts of patriotic men who disregarding the rewards of the legal profession or of the public service have affianced themselves to it. This is peculiar to journalism in India. It has been specially so to the *Hindu*.

In these circumstances, the profession held few attractions for the Western-educated class. Some graduates joined it as "a stepping stone for something better."[84] But the great majority who took to journalism were prompted more by political fervor than by material prospects. As the *Hindu* observed in 1897, "Journalism to [an] Indian is a means to public good."[85] If the profession lacked stability and financial attraction, it was not devoid of political influence and glamor.

THE PROFESSIONAL ELITE

In seeking to define the term professional elite, there are two fundamental problems which ought to be recognized at the outset. First, it is not possible to define this elite group in terms of formal positions, roles, or institutions of which it would form a part. Instead, it would be more pertinent to view this elite as a flexible category, as a social group in the process of attaining a corporate status. As such, the professional elite can be regarded as an aggregate of people sharing certain similarities in education, occupation, and norms of social behavior. For purposes of this study, the professional elite in late nineteenth century South India can be taken to mean those who had received a high level of Western

education and had equipped themselves with the
special skills so essential for the functioning of
a modernizing society. By this definition, the
professional elite would include lawyers, teachers,
editors, journalists, writers, doctors, and
engineers.

A second difficulty in studying this elite
group is the absence of data to assess its exact
size during the nineteenth century. Census returns,
the only detailed statistical enumeration of the
professions undertaken during this period, provide
at best only a rough and ready system of classifi-
cation, and even then the value of this source is
greatly diminished by its failure to furnish information on the educational or other qualifications
of those listed under the various professions.

However, evidence from other sources, notably
figures about the growth of Western education as
provided by the Department of Public Instruction,
makes it apparent that the size of the professional
elite was small, even in relation to the so-called
"Learned and Artistic Professions" listed in the
decennial censuses of the period. That barely
19,000 candidates passed the matriculation examinations in South India up to 1886[*]--a prerequisite
for entry into university and professional training
--is generally indicative of the numbers passing
out as lawyers, teachers of high schools and
colleges, doctors, and engineers. The relative
weakness of this group of 19,000 is also emphasized
when it is realized that the larger group they
were part of, the "Learned and Artistic Professions,"
as enumerated in the 1881 census, totalled
188,783.[86]

Although small, the professional elite was
considerably more numerous than the administrative
elite. No doubt this could be attributed to the
significant expansion of higher education in South
India following the elevation of the Presidency

---

[*]See Table 3.1.

College to university status in 1857 and the growing demand for trained personnel to fill such callings as law, medicine, and teaching. However, in
social origins, there was little actual difference
between the two elite groups. Both groups came almost exclusively from the upper Hindu castes, with
Brahmins--be they Sri-Vaishnavas, Smarthas, Niyogis,
or Desasthas--predominating, while the rest belonged to the higher non-Brahmin castes, notably,
Vellalars, Chettis, Kammas, and Nairs. The caste
origin of the professional elite determined the
social values of the group. This was especially so
in its attitude towards job selection. True to
upper caste ancestry, the professional elite regarded official employment in universal esteem;
then came such "polite" professions as law, medicine, teaching, and journalism; trade was still
regarded as vulgar, while manual labor was shunned
at all costs.

Reinforcing this social coherence of the professional elite was the experience of a common
educational training. As Western education held
the key to the esteemed professions, and its
acquisition was regarded as something of a status
symbol, high caste families went to great lengths
and made many sacrifices to get their sons educated.
Parents living in remote *mofussil* areas sent their
sons over hundreds of miles to towns which had a
high school or college, often at great family
expense and sometimes even drawing on the generosity of relatives and friends. Colleges in Madras
commanded great prestige throughout South India,
and, not surprisingly, such institutions as the
Presidency College, Christian College, and Pachaiyappa College had a high proportion of *mofussil*
students, some coming from such remote districts
as Malabar and Tinnevelly. Students of these institutions, and particularly of Presidency College,
developed close ties of friendship and an *esprit
de corps* which often found institutional expression
in the formation of literary societies, reading
rooms, and debating clubs. *Mofussil* students were

invariably the more active participants of such
activities, denied as they were of home and family
life. When their educational training was completed, they either searched for an opening in the
metropolis or migrated to some *mofussil* town which
offered a lucrative position in any of the esteemed
professions. Here they continued the habits they
had cultivated during their college days, founding
literary societies, participating in debates, or
writing to the local newspapers.

What gave the professional elite a sense of
identity, and set it off from the rest of the
Western-educated community in South India, was its
attitude towards the ruling power. In part, the
educational training had instilled among the members of this elite group an appreciation of democratic values and a knowledge of the skills of
effective political action. Inevitably, higher
learning tended to emphasize the value of civil
liberties while creating misgivings about the efficacy of authoritarian rule. Equally, the callings
to which the professional elite belonged provided
opportunities for resisting arbitrary government
action and upholding the sanctity of the rule of
law. The legal profession in particular came to
occupy an honored place because of its role as the
guardian of the values and rights of society. The
astuteness of the Indian lawyers in mastering the
complex judicial procedures which the British had
introduced in the country, coupled with their knowledge of Hindu law, enabled them to serve as a
buffer between the government and society and to
soften somewhat the excesses of centralized rule
which increasingly impinged upon the everyday life
of the people through proliferation of economic and
social controls. Similarly, editors and journalists of newspapers and periodicals rose in popular
estimation because of their willingness to articulate the aspirations of society and criticize
freely the actions of the government. By the 1880s,
when a series of developments in the Madras Presidency and outside called for new dynamic leadership,

the professional elite had rapidly become so politicized that it was able to lead the battle for enlarged political rights for the subject peoples.

4. The Politicization of the Professional Elite

A new school of critics had then [1883] sprung
up in Madras. A new journal to voice the opinions and aspirations of the Indian community
had come into existence. To attack the foibles
of the older men, some of whom assiduously paid
pujah to officials, sometimes at the sacrifice
of great interests, was the aim of the new
party.

C. Karunakara Menon[1]

THE VOICE OF THE PROFESSIONAL ELITE

It is somewhat ironical, in view of the sharp
antagonism which developed between the administrative and professional elites during the 1880s, that
the immediate reason for the starting of the "new
journal"--the *Hindu*--in 1878 was the controversy
surrounding Muthusamy Iyer's elevation to a judgeship at the Madras High Court. Even before the appointment was formally announced in July 1878,
opposition to it was voiced in the columns of the
local press. Except for the *Madras Times*, which
under William Digby's editorship* had expressed

---

*W. Digby (1849-1904), editor of the *Madras
Times* between 1877-79, was an active participant in

"great satisfaction" with Muthusamy Iyer's appointment,[2] the other Anglo-Indian organs in Madras were
unanimously critical. The *Madras Mail*, the mouthpiece of the European-dominated Madras Chamber of
Commerce, claimed that the choice of Muthusamy Iyer
was a concession to Indian agitation for greater
participation in the government. At the same time,
it objected to Indians in such high positions being
paid the same emoluments as Europeans. It felt
that as a rule "native officials should not draw
the same rate of pay as Europeans in similar circumstances" and urged the government to introduce differential pay scales in such instances.[3] These
views found support in the *Athenaeum and Daily News*,
the other Anglo-Indian daily in South India. While
expressing regret over the appointment, this paper
cast doubt on the ability of an Indian judge to try
certain types of suits that might come up before
the High Court. "In some of these cases especially
those relating to matrimony," argued the editor of
the *Athenaeum and Daily News*, "it would be most difficult for a native judge to enter into the feelings and motives of the European parties before
him."[4]

Even more extreme were the sentiments ventilated in the correspondence columns of these Anglo-
Indian newspapers. "Subordination to a Brahmin,"
wrote an irate European correspondent, "is an outrage which makes the blood boil in the veins of a
European."[5]

If Anglo-Indian hostility to Muthusamy Iyer's
appointment was not entirely unexpected, what was
surprising to some contemporary observers was the
opposition emanating from certain sections of Hindu

---

local public movements and is best remembered for
his services in the famine relief operations in
1878-79 for which he was awarded a C.I.E. In later
years he was to be closely associated with the
British Committee of the Indian National Congress.
Hindu, Weekly Edition, 29 September 1904.

opinion in Madras. In a letter published by the
Madras Mail, a "Sudra correspondent" contested
official claims about Muthusamy Iyer's knowledge of
Hindu law and customs. The correspondent claimed
that the judge only moved within the restricted
circle of his Brahmin relatives and friends and had
little actual knowledge or experience of the habits
and ways of the rest of the Hindu community.
Doubts were also raised as to the wisdom of conferring such high posts on Indians at this juncture.
The correspondent argued that despite progress in
Western education and other fields, Hindus were
still too actuated by "caste feelings" to be expected to discharge their official responsibilities
impartially.[6]

Another opponent of Muthusamy Iyer's elevation,
styling himself "A Dravidian correspondent," contended that the Brahmin was "least fitted of all
castes to deal fairly with the masses . . . since
he considers himself as a god, and all others as
Milechas." Moreover, the writer argued that since
the Brahmins were holding over 70 per cent of
public appointments it would be unwise to invest
them with such high positions and thereby strengthen their position in the government vis-a-vis the
other castes.[7] These views found an echo in the
Madras Native Opinion, the only Indian-owned newspaper in English in Madras. Its editor, an Indian
Christian, was of the firm opinion that Indians
had not sufficiently advanced, socially or otherwise, to assume the responsibilities of high office
in the government.[8]

While the Madras authorities refused to be
drawn into this controversy, it was evident that
the Brahmins, especially the Western-educated section, resented the criticisms which had been
levelled against Muthusamy Iyer's elevation to the
High Court and the imputations cast on the community as a whole. The Brahmin reply came from the
pen of G. Subramania Iyer, an Arts graduate then
teaching in Pachaiyappa School. In a letter to the
Madras Times, Subramania Iyer asserted that

Muthusamy Iyer's appointment had given rise to
"much unjust and invidious criticism." He regarded
the question of differential pay scales for European and Indian officials as "a grave question" but
dissented from the stand taken by the editor of the
Madras Mail. "When two officials whose duties are
attended with the same responsibility and difficulty are unequally paid," he argued, "one who is
underpaid is sure to murmur and grow discontented;
and this will grieviously tell upon the efficiency
with which he is expected to discharge his duties."

However, for reasons of economy, he favored a
reduction in the pay of Indian officials so long
as this was accompanied simultaneously by steps
transferring to Indians certain positions so far
held exclusively by Europeans. Subramania Iyer
believed that such posts as assistant collectors
and district judges could be safely transferred to
Indian hands, and, if the pay structure was revised, then it would mean a considerable saving to
the treasury.[9]

Turning to criticisms of the Brahmins in the
public service, he felt that it had "become the
fashion to cry down Brahmans." He agreed that as a
class the Brahmins were the "objects of envy" because of their progress in education and their pre-
dominance in the public service where they were
challenging even the primacy of the Europeans. As
for corruption and abuse in the public service,
Subramania Iyer contended that this was not confined to the Brahmins alone. He attributed such
practices to officials who lacked a superior Western
education, many of whom were found in the subordinate executive and police service. He felt that
progress in education would not only produce a
superior quality of civil servants but also bring
about a more equitable distribution of public appointments to all classes, non-Brahmins included.
He also denied that there was an absence of mutual
sympathy between Brahmins and non-Brahmins:

What an enormous change has come over the

social fabric of the Hindus, and how their
caste antipathies are being levelled down into
harmony, ever since the dawn of English influence in this country, are quite beyond the
comprehension of these [European] gentlemen.
To say that the educated Brahmans hate Sudras,
and that they consider it a sin to touch them,
is no more true of the modern state of society
in India, than to say that the Druids in
England still continue to burn human beings
before their mistletoe God under the oak tree,
is true of the modern state of society in
England.[10]

Subramania Iyer's disquisition, while seeking
to defuse any possible eruption of caste antagonisms in South India, was also an adroit attempt at
appealing to the essential unity of interest which
the Western-educated class as a whole shared. By
singling out this class from the rest of the Indian
community and by stressing the changes that its
educational training had wrought on its attitudes
and social values, Subramania Iyer was clearly ad-
vertising the credentials of this class for a
favored treatment in government recruitment. Like
other members of the professional elite, he believed that the Western-educated Indian was a
superior being, had imbibed new virtues and values,
and possessed the qualifications and ability for
high office. He felt that this class should assert
its just claims to the ruling authorities and defeat any insidious attempt to stir up old caste
animosities which might endanger the growing
fellow feeling which this class as a whole had come
to share.
    In the context of the times, Subramania Iyer's
appeal was also a protest against the lack or organized political activity in South India. Much of
the subcontinent at this juncture was in the grip
of a severe famine. In the Madras Presidency, two
out of every three districts were drought stricken
since 1876, and the final death toll after two

years reached four million.[11] While the country
was in the depth of this crisis, the Government of
India seemed to be pursuing policies out of tune
with the exigencies of the moment, particularly the
grand celebration marking the Queen's assumption of
the Throne of India in 1876 and the sparking off of
conflict with Afghanistan a year later. Equally unpopular with the Western-educated class was the
reduction of the age of entry into the Covenanted
Civil Service in 1876 and the enactment of the
Vernacular Press Act and Arms Act two years later.
For these actions Lord Lytton was held largely responsible and he became the target of hostile criticism throughout India. However, in Madras, unlike Calcutta or Bombay, there was no concerted
action to mobilize opposition to Lytton's policies,
owing to the absence of any "medium through which
the energies of the educated Indian could be focus-
sed and by which the masses of the population could
be educated." There was no voluntary association
or newspaper which could consistently voice the interests of the Indian people as a whole.[12] It was
an inadequacy which the professional elite began
to experience during the time of Lytton's controversial viceroyalty, and the controversy over
Muthusamy Iyer's appointment merely heightened this
feeling.

     As the need for some kind of concerted action
began to be felt, leaders in Madras began to float
a number of schemes both in the press and on the
platform. One school of opinion advocated the formation of a political organization to represent the
interests of South India. Among the exponents of
this idea was William Digby, the popular editor of
the *Madras Times*. In March 1877, when he first
broached this subject, Digby called for a broad-
based, noncommunal organization embracing both Europeans and Indians.[13] When this appeal brought no
response, he modified his scheme and suggested a
purely Indian body along the lines of the Poona
Sarvajanik Sabha.[14] This proposal accorded with
the sentiments expressed by the *Madrassee* in April

1877 when it called upon "the educated natives
scattered throughout the Presidency" to organize "a
strong association to watch over and protect the
interests of the people."[15] Another school of
thought in Madras believed that what was needed was
a well-conducted newspaper to educate public opinion and thereby make its voice heard in the ruling
circles. To this school belonged the "six ardent
youths" who started the *Hindu* in September 1878.
As one of them recounted many years later:[16]

> We knew that public feeling, not only politi-
> cally and morally, but socially, is influenced
> in all countries by the tone of their public
> journals, as the community is bound however
> unconsciously to imbibe the spirit of the news-
> paper which its members daily read; and rea-
> lised the responsibility of the undertaking,
> and the immense evil that would be inflicted
> on the community if we failed to develop those
> qualities of political moral and social well-
> being which are so essential for the advance-
> ment of the nation.

The six who jointly launched the *Hindu* were G.
Subramania Iyer, M. Viraraghava Chari, N. Subba
Rao, T. T. Ranga Chari, P. V. Ranga Chari, and D.
Kesava Rao Pant. They were all Brahmins, having
just completed or being about to complete their
collegiate education, and were eventually to branch
off into one of the three independent professions,
namely, law, teaching, or journalism. They were
also members of the Triplicane Literary Society,
founded some years ago as a forum for lectures and
discussions among the younger sections of the
Western-educated class in the metropolis.

The actual task of conducting the *Hindu* fell
on the shoulders of Subramania Iyer and Viraraghava
Chari. These two Brahmins came from families of
relative poverty, and it was with some difficulty
that they were able to complete their higher education. G. Subramania Iyer was born in 1855 in

Tanjore district, two years before Viraraghava
Chari saw the light of day in Chingleput district.
Their paths merged in 1874 when they came to Madras
to join the Government Normal School in Saidapet.
In the following year they passed out as teachers,
and while Viraraghava Chari enrolled in the Presidency College to read for an Arts degree, Subramania Iyer became a teacher while at the same time
reading for his degree part-time. When they graduated, they taught in Pachaiyappa School while
continuing as prominent members of the Triplicane
Literary Society.[17] In starting the *Hindu* they
were not only cementing a developing friendship but
were also finding a calling in which they could
harness their individual talents in the cause of
realizing their political ambitions.

In the first issue the editorial policy of the
Hindu was clearly defined by G. Subramania Iyer.
He stressed at the outset that he and his friends
had embarked on this enterprize with "great diffi-
dence," conscious as they were of past journalistic
failures. However, he contended that the great
changes that had taken place in India had encouraged them to believe that there was scope as well
as necessity for a fresh attempt in this direction.
While lamenting the absence of organized public
opinion in South India, Subramania Iyer asserted
that the *Hindu* was aspiring to fill this lacuna by
not only giving expression to public opinion but
also modifying and molding it according to events
and circumstances. The paper was to be devoted to
Indian subjects which were to be discussed on the
principle of "fairness and justice." At the same
time, the *Hindu* would endeavor "to promote harmony
and union" among the Indian people and "interpret
correctly the feelings of the natives and to create
mutual confidence between the governed and the
governors."[18]

The general reaction to this journalistic venture was at best a mixed one. The appearance of
the *Hindu* went unnoticed in the Anglo-Indian press
in Madras. Among the Western-educated Indians

there was skepticism about the ability of these
young graduates, without journalistic training,
capital resources, and with a limited grasp of public questions, to manage as exacting and responsible a job as a weekly newspaper. While on the
one hand many well-wishers agreed with the need for
such a newspaper, they did not try to disguise
their inner misgivings. In the words of Viraraghava Chari:[19]

> Oh! I well remember the various letters of
> encouragement and congratulation that came
> from all parts of India. I should, however,
> not omit to mention the discouraging remarks
> of some of our well-wishers who foresaw many
> evil consequences from the enterprise; they
> considered that the profession of a journalist
> was hazardous in the extreme, and that in the
> then condition of the Presidency could not
> financially pay its way. The fate of the
> "Native Public Opinion" and the "Madrassee"
> was predicted for "The Hindu." But nothing
> daunted, we continued to work on.

The fact that the *Hindu* survived and prospered
despite these early forebodings was in no small
measure due to Subramania Iyer and Viraraghava
Chari. In a partnership extending over two decades,
they blended their talents to subserve the long-
term interests of the paper.* Subramania Iyer took
sole charge of the editorial responsibilities.
Gifted with a fluent if pungent style, he gave expression to the ideals, aspirations, and fears of
the professional elite then emerging on the

---

*W. S. Blunt, a British M.P. who interviewed
Subramania Iyer and Viraraghava Chari in November
1883, found them "intelligent, clear-headed men,
contrasting by no means unfavourably with men of
their profession in London." Blunt, *India Under
Ripon*, p. 36.

political scene of South India. His honesty and
courage, which were reflected in his editorial
writings, earned the *Hindu* the reputation of being
"a sober, vigilant and honest critic of men and
measures."[20] Viraraghava Chari, for his part, managed the business side of the newspaper. Since he
was known for his "tact, energy, and business
ability,"[21] it fell on him to arrange for the publication of the paper, secure advertisements, and
seek ways and means of boosting circulation. He
established wide contacts with the members of the
Western-educated class and often appealed to their
sense of patriotism to mobilize support for the
newspaper.

   The *Hindu* was also fortunate in attracting
assistance from various and unexpected quarters.
The editor of the defunct *Madrassee*, A. Ramachandra
Iyer, was of "immense help" in freely offering his
advice and the benefit of his experience in conducting a newspaper. He also introduced a certain
Surgeon-Major Nicholson to Subramania Iyer and
Viraraghava Chari. It was this retired official
who instructed the editor and his colleague in the
complexities of bringing out a newspaper while at
the same time he sent regularly "valuable contributions on various topics."[22] Also important was
the help rendered by the "journalistic fraternity"
which Subramania Iyer had slowly built up in order
to secure a more comprehensive coverage of news in
South India. This fraternity, consisting of his
old college friends or well-known public figures in
the *mofussil*, submitted at regular intervals reports and newsletters of happenings in their towns
and districts.[23] Stress was laid on the activities
of the professional elite, and such events as the
formation of literary societies, proceedings of
public meetings, and municipal and district board
elections received prominent mention. At the same
time, a close watch was kept on the activities of
officials, both Indians and Europeans, and acts of
misdemeanor and highhandedness were promptly reported. As these contributors remained anonymous,

they were able to comment on any local occurrence
without fear of possible reprisals.

The question of solvency, which bedevilled
all Indian journalistic ventures during the nineteenth century, did not spare the *Hindu*. None of
the six who had founded the paper had any capital,
and, as those with wealth were not prepared to invest in the paper, Subramania Iyer and Viraraghava
Chari had to turn to the aid of generous and
patriotic fellow Hindus from time to time. Among
those who generously assisted the *Hindu* to find a
secure footing were officials like Raghunatha Rao,
lawyers like P. Ananda Charlu, S. Subramania Iyer,
and P. Rangiah Naidu, industrialists like A.
Sabapathy Mudaliar, merchants like S. Savalay
Ramasamy Mudaliar, and members of the landed aristocracy, notably, the Maharajah of Vizianagram and
the Raja of Ramnad. It was largely due to the
generosity of S. Subramania Iyer that the *Hindu*
acquired its own press in 1883, called the
"National Press."

About this time the *Hindu* also shifted to its
newly-rented premises at 100 Mount Road, which was
soon to become the nerve center of political activity in South India. In the words of Viraraghava
Chari, the *Hindu* Office "used to be visited by members of Parliament who happened to visit Madras;
there it was that the Mahajana Sabha met and trans-
acted business for a long time. It was to 100,
Mount Road, that people with grievances reported.
. . . Memorials and pamphlets in the thousands on
the questions of the day were printed and circulated at the time from 'The Hindu' Office."[24]

During its early years, at least until it became a tri-weekly in 1883, the *Hindu* was in reality
an opinion sheet rather than a newspaper. Its
content was heavily political, with hard news
clearly occupying a secondary place. In its proclaimed role as the tribune of the people, it discussed political, economic, and social issues of
immediate and long-term significance to the Madras
Presidency. Founded as it was at the height of the

famine, the *Hindu* showed an obvious concern for
the problems of the peasant class. It called for
urgent and radical measures to prevent such disasters, advocating particularly the reduction in
assessment and more liberal tax remissions during
times of natural disasters.[25] Here, the editor of
the *Hindu* saw himself as the guardian of the interests of the masses, who, ignorant and docile as
they were, needed some kind of a protective shield
to safeguard their well-being from being threatened
by an omnipotent bureaucracy.

If its role as the tribune of the masses was
somewhat unreal, the *Hindu* was undisguisedly the
voice of the professional elite in South India.
Here, the format of the paper bore the heavy im-
print of its editor, Subramania Iyer. During his
unbroken tenure of twenty years, he came to be
widely acknowledged as "the father of South Indian
Journalism."[26] This distinction was conferred on
him not merely for his success in transforming what
began as a precarious weekly periodical into a
successful daily but also for making the *Hindu* a
recognized social institution of the Presidency,
both helping to shape as well as being a vehicle of
elite thinking. To Subramania Iyer, the former was
the more important function of his paper, as he
once said:[27]

> The Indian Press is not representative of mature
> public opinion. To represent mature public
> opinion is only a subordinate function of it,
> because public opinion has no constitutional or
> regular channel of making itself felt in the
> Councils of the Empire. Its more serious and
> important function, is to form public opinion,
> and to direct it along the channels of public
> utility and public improvement; and this pecu-
> liarity of the Indian Press was most particular-
> ly felt at the time when the *Hindu* was started.

It was this educative function which Subramania
Iyer held as most important, even sacrosanct, in his

role as the editor of the *Hindu*. In his editorial
writings, he argued rationally and with moderation
that political regeneration of the Indians depended
on their readiness to make the necessary sacrifices,
in terms of time, energy, and wealth, and in their
ability to reform their social institutions in the
light of the values which Western rule had introduced in the country.

His message was primarily directed at the
professional elite which he believed should be in
the vanguard of all political and social movements.
He often reminded this elite group that, as beneficiaries of a superior education, it had special
responsibilities in stimulating orderly change and
providing enlightened leadership to the tradition-
bound Indian masses. Where there was apathy or
selfishness in the ranks of the professional elite,
Subramania Iyer was merciless in his criticisms.
Not surprisingly, he acquired a reputation, even
among his friends, of "harshness and undue severity
of judgement and action." To those who took exception to his editorial severity, he was said to have
retorted: "I place the highest value on national
progress . . . I want to impress on my countrymen,
high and low, that, whenever any man's career or
conduct runs counter to national interest, he can
expect no mercy from us, however high he may be."[28]
He deliberately kept his social distance from officials, lest friendship circumscribe his editorial
freedom or warp his judgment. He urged the professional elite to do the same, in order that it might
develop the habits of self-reliance and independence of thought and action.[29]

In the history of Indian newspapers this was
very much the era of personal journalism. Like
editors elsewhere in the country, Subramania Iyer
sought to mold society through strongly expressed
editorial opinion, to sustain the interest of his
readers by starting appropriate political and
social crusades, and to ensure the stability of the
paper by building up circulation on the basis of a
personal following. Although sobriety was regarded

as a virtue, the *Hindu* was not expected to be
always neutral on nonpartisan. Subramania Iyer
wished the paper to be controversial, even drama-
tize issues and situations, in order to involve its
readers, and to display a spirit of independence,
even if it meant courting official disapproval.

A measure of the editor's success was reflected in the growing popularity of the *Hindu*. By
1885 it had the second, largest readership in South
India, and was challenging the entrenched position
of the Anglo-Indian dailies. It was "the favourite
paper of the Vakils and native officials throughout
the Presidency" and was being read in almost every
reading room and literary society in the Madras
Presidency.[30] Equally important was its acceptance
as the authoritative organ of the professional
elite. The latter's continued patronage of the
Hindu, the readiness of its members to subsidize
its operations, and their willingness to subscribe
to the political beliefs expounded in the paper,
especially during the troubled times of the early
1880s, were ample evidence that the credentials of
the *Hindu* were wholly accepted by the professional
elite. For this, the editor had to be thankful for
the events that occurred at this time, notably, the
administrative blunders of the Grant Duff Administration in South India and the organized European
onslaught on Lord Ripon's liberal policies. Helped
by the ferment caused by these events, the *Hindu*
successfully galvanized the professional elite into
concerted political action.

"THE GRANT DUFFIAN ERA"

In the summer of 1881 the Gladstone Ministry
announced the appointment of Mountstuart Elphinstone Grant Duff as Governor of the Madras Presidency. This announcement, coming in the wake of
the Liberal Party's electoral triumph of the previous year and so soon after Lord Ripon's assumption
of the viceroyalty of India, was greeted by Indian

politicians in Madras as "the dawn of a new epoch
in the administration of the country." There was a
general belief, especially among the ranks of the
professional elite, that these high-level appointments represented a repudiation of the military and
domestic policies associated with the Lytton regime.
The discerning members of the Triplicane Literary
Society, in a message of welcome to Grant Duff,
were already testifying that Ripon's measures had
"won back public confidence"; they expected the new
governor to reinforce the viceroy's policies by
formulating "various measures of reform in the internal administration of the country calculated to
promote the prosperity, freedom, and contentment of
the people."[31]
    No doubt, "the antecedents" of Grant Duff
served to heighten these expectations. Being the
son of the illustrious historian of the Mahrattas,
a prominent member of the Liberal Party, and for
five years an Under-Secretary of State at the India
Office during the previous Gladstone Ministry,
Grant Duff's reputation had travelled ahead of him
to his Indian principality. The *Hindu*'s welcoming
remark of the new governor reflected the mood of
the Indian politicians in South India: "His ante-
cedents have roused the sanguine expectations of
the Native community, and his arrival is very conspicuous."[32]
    While welcoming the new governor, no time was
lost in spelling out the pressing problems that
awaited his attention. The effects of the famine
of 1876-78 had been gradually erased by the relatively good harvests that followed immediately the
years of drought. However, complete recovery was
not expected yet, and there were hopes that the
new administration would accelerate the process by
initiating fundamental changes in the existing
revenue policy. The Triplicane Literary Society,
in its address to the governor, charged that the
shortsighted policies of the Madras authorities had
resulted in the "growing impoverishment of the agricultural class" in the Presidency. It alleged that

the authorities were only interested in augmenting
revenue and had consequently enhanced the assessment at every fresh settlement, imposed new cesses,
and had collected taxes with "unusual rigidity."
In urging a new policy, the society advocated
"fixity of tenure, consolidation of the several
assessments, reduction of assessments wherever
necessary," and proper maintenance of irrigation
works. Also, concern was expressed at the lack of
supervision of the "ill-paid subordinates" in the
revenue line. It was claimed that the activities
of the latter had led to "complete demoralization"
of the cultivators of South India.[33]

Indicative of the kind of official harassment
was an incident which for some months prior to
Grant Duff's arrival was achieving a certain
notoriety in the press as "the Chingleput Scandal."
The district of Chingleput, situated at the "back-
door" of Madras, was famous in earlier times as the
resort of Hindu pilgrims and the center of a
flourishing weaving industry. However, by the
latter half of the nineteenth century, much of its
past splendor had vanished and, although it still
continued to function as a popular temple city, its
weaving industry was almost completely extinguished
by machine-produced goods from Manchester. Agriculture became the mainstay of the district, but
inferior soils and the rack-renting practices of
absentee *mirasdars* denied the "pauper sub-tenant"
of any initiative to maximize production.[34] To
aggravate matters, the district was a frequent
victim of seasonal vagaries, and during the nineteenth century it was afflicted by severe famines
on no less than five occasions. In these circumstances, the cultivators in the district constantly
defaulted in paying their assessments and revenue
officials were often compelled to resort to "co-
ercive process by distraint and sale" to realize
the dues.[35]

Indeed, the Chingleput Scandal had its origins
in the decision of the *tahsildar* of Conjeeveram
taluk, Seethapathy Naidu, to attach the holdings of

certain Brahmin *ryots* living in Vadagaput village
for their failure to pay their dues on time. The
ryots alleged that the attachment was illegal, as
they had still a week to clear their arrears, and
asserted that the *tahsildar* had acted in retaliation of their refusal to pay a bribe.[36] Failing
to get any redress from the local officials, the
ryots petitioned the Madras Government which ordered a local inquiry. The inquiry turned out to
be a protracted affair, over 250 *ryots* were sum-
moned to give evidence, and ultimately the *tahsildar* was cleared. The aggrieved *ryots* protested
that the inquiry was not impartially conducted,
while those who did not answer the summonses to
give evidence were arrested and sentenced to varying terms of imprisonment.[37]

It was at this juncture that Grant Duff
assumed the reins of office. The Madras press,
which had become critical of the manner in which
the Chingleput case was being handled, appealed to
the new governor to institute an impartial inquiry
to get at the truth of the complaint. The *Madras
Mail*, for example, urged Grant Duff to "shake himself clear of his surroundings," especially the
civil service.[38] Early in December 1881, a small
deputation of *ryots* from Chingleput called on the
governor to lay their grievances in person.[39] However, Grant Duff was not prepared to intervene
personally in this case and instead allowed the
Board of Revenue to handle this complaint in the
normal way. The latter accepted the results of the
local inquiry and called for the rigorous punishment of those who had brought false charges against
the *tahsildar*. Among those who were charged was a
village *munsif* who had submitted an adverse report
on Seethapathy Naidu. Dismissed from office, the
munsif was subsequently arrested on charges of giving false evidence and sentenced to eighteen months
rigorous imprisonment.

Some sections of opinion in Madras were out-
raged by these actions of the officials and rapidly
lost patience with Grant Duff's "passive policy."

The *Madras Mail* renewed its appeal to the governor
to intervene and "nip evil in the bud" rather than
facing "serious embarrassments" later.[40] The
editor of the *Hindu* was critical of the governor's
handling of the issue, and asserted that his inaction had allowed the affair "to branch off into
episodes, each sufficient to cast dirt on the fair
face of British justice."[41] In January 1882, despairing of securing any justice from the Grant Duff
Administration, a group of six prominent Indian
leaders in Madras, including G. Subramania Iyer and
R. Balaji Rao,* launched the "Chingleput Ryots Relief Fund," aimed at raising funds to meet the
trial expenses of those *ryots* who were already sus-
taining heavy losses owing to their enforced
absence from their farms.[42] The contributions, de-
posited with the *Hindu* office, reached the total of
Rs 900 by March 1882.[43]

In May 1882 the Chingleput case took a new
turn when the *tahsildar* filed a charge of giving
false evidence against another *ryot*, B. Rangasamy
Iyengar. Unfortunately for Seethapathy Naidu, his
former superiors had left the district on transfer,
and his case was heard by the new sub-collector
Arthur F. Cox. In his inquiry, Cox found enough
evidence in the village accounts to entertain serious doubts as to the legality of the *tahsildar*'s
original attachment in May 1881. He discovered "a
singular array of irregularities" in the village
records and improper attachments in the case of
certain *ryots*. Satisfied that there were reasonable grounds to accept the *ryots'* testimony, he

---

*R. Balaji Rao (1842-1896) was born in Tanjore
district and had his early education in Kumbaconam
before migrating to Madras where he read law. He
was enrolled as *vakil* in the High Court in 1870 and
soon acquired a considerable practice. An active
public figure, he served for several years as an
elected member of the Madras Municipality. *Hindu*,
3 February 1896.

acquitted Rangasamy Iyengar and drafted a report to the Board of Revenue in which he questioned the legality of Seethapathy Naidu's attachment of May 1881.[44] A few days later, the report disappeared without a trace, and suspicion fell on the *tahsildar*. Pending investigations, Cox decided to suspend Seethapathy Naidu from duty. Hearing the news the latter took flight, and a warrant was issued for his arrest. The trial for theft of the documents was heard in July 1882, and Seethapathy Naidu was found guilty and sentenced to two years' rigorous imprisonment. This curious episode, by now "a *cause celebre*," came to an end in May 1883 when the Madras Government remitted the rest of his sentence and ordered his release.[45]

To students of South Indian history, the Chingleput affair will always remain something of an enigma. Was the *tahsildar* a victim of a conspiracy to unseat him or was he guilty of indiscretion? The district officials took the former view, at least until Cox made his disclosures. The professional elite, judging by the sentiments of the *Hindu*, took the side of the *ryots*, although it was prepared to welcome an independent inquiry along the lines suggested by some of the European newspapers. In the long term, the significance of this episode lay in the way it affected relations between the professional elite and the Grant Duff Administration. The latter's handling of the affair drove the first wedge between the two and dissipated the grandiose hopes which the Indians had entertained about the new governor.

An event which stirred even stronger passions in South India was the communal violence which flared up in Salem town in July-August 1882. The seeds of Hindu-Muslim tension in this town were sown in 1878 when the Muslims erected a mosque in "a conspicuous part" that had long been "a pathway of all the Hindu processions." The Hindus, resenting the enforcement of the official ban on music, appealed to the High Court to exercise a right that they had enjoyed "from time immemorial." The High

Court ruled in their favor and ordered the local
magistrate to fix hours when Hindu processions
could pass the mosque with music. Undecided between official regulations and the High Court
ruling, and showing neither firmness nor tact in
mediating between the opposing factions, the
Salem officials lost control over a rapidly deteriorating communal situation. When serious rioting
broke out in August 1882 for a second time within
a month, the local authorities watched helplessly
while an angry Hindu mob proceeded to destroy the
mosque.[46]

The Madras Government, convinced that the
Salem outrage was a symptom of "the rising spirit
of religious intolerance and lawlessness" in South
India, ordered a full-scale inquiry to bring the
rioters to book. Lewis McIver, Head Assistant to
the collector of Nellore, was selected to lead the
inquiry, supported by "the best detectives" that
the Inspector-General of Police could furnish.[47]
Investigations began promptly, followed shortly by
a steady stream of arrests.

The trials began in September under Herbert
Wigram, Additional Sessions Judge of Coimbatore.
In all, twenty-four "ring-leaders" were charged
"with abetting the destruction of the Shevapett
Mosque, and, in so doing, with abetting the commission of culpable homicide." McIver, the counsel
for the prosecution, contended that the accused had
organized "a Hindu League" with the avowed purpose
of waging a crusade against the Muslims. He
claimed that they had hatched a conspiracy to destroy the mosque, raised funds from all Hindus, and
recruited gangs from neighboring villages to carry
out their design. On the day of the event, said
McIver, "the whole adult male Hindu population,
augmented by contingents from out villages, turned
out as a man, armed, and animated by a common purpose: that purpose being an attack on the persons
and property of Mussulmans." He also claimed that
there was an "absence of all warning before the
event."[48]

The judge, while acquitting the accused of abetment to murder, found fifteen Hindus guilty of abetting the destruction of the mosque. One was sentenced to transportation for life, and the rest to varying periods of transportation and fines. Besides, many others were convicted on lesser charges and total convictions, after some were quashed by the High Court, stood at 154, of whom one was a Muslim and the rest Hindus.[49]

Retributive punishment did not end there. The Madras Government moved swiftly in dealing with those officials suspected of complicity or withholding information about the riots. Eight officials in the revenue line, including a *tahsildar* and a *huzur sheristadar*, were dismissed and fifteen of their colleagues were either demoted or transferred out of the district. Dismissals from the police force, for "neglect and treachery," numbered fifteen while twenty-two others were demoted.[50] Nor were inhabitants of Salem who had helped the rioters spared. A special levy was imposed on twelve villages for the purpose of maintaining a "Punitive Police Force" in the district.[51] In May 1883 the Madras Government dismissed three elected Hindu municipal commissioners for their part in the Salem riots. In its report to the Secretary of State, the Grant Duff Administration asserted that it had punished the Salem rioters with "the utmost rigour of the law."[52]

The professional elite viewed these official proceedings with some degree of dismay, if not alarm. The official thesis that the riots were the result of a deep-laid conspiracy was received with skepticism, even by the Anglo-Indian press. The *Hindu* believed that there had been a miscarriage of justice. It claimed that the innocent had been punished and the guilty had escaped. At the same time, it criticized the official assumption that the Hindus were the culpable party, and as such they should be punished with severity. The *Hindu* also contended that the local officials must take some of the blame for the breakdown of law and order but was dismayed that the Grant Duff Administration instead of censuring them had commended their work:

> The worst enemies of England in India are such
> weak and incompetent administrators--those,
> who by tyrannical and arbitrary acts give room
> for the belief that those European officials
> who delight in the oppression of the people do
> so under the previous assurance of impunity
> and protection from Government. The Hindus
> will never forget the Salem Riots and they
> will continue to bitterly hate those Englishmen
> who were the cause of the most severe and un-
> just punishment of so many of their respectable
> and honoured countrymen.[53]

Much of this bitterness was directed against the Collector of Salem, C. D. Macleane. He had emerged as the most controversial figure of this entire episode, and sections of the local press held him largely responsible for the unfortunate events which occurred in Salem in July-August 1882. In May 1883 the *Hindu* even published a letter from a correspondent who alleged that Macleane was at the Bangalore races when the first riots broke out in July and not on "kacheri business" as he claimed. While challenging Macleane to controvert this charge, the editor of the paper urged the Madras Government "to wash off the stain of their past deeds" rather than standing on "the false idea of dignity and prestige."[54] Such pleas evoked no response from the Grant Duff Administration. Equally devoid of immediate result were the appeals which many literary societies and local associations made to Lord Ripon when he visited South India in January 1884.

Although Ripon's refusal to intervene was a blow to Hindu hopes, the agitation for the release of the Salem prisoners continued to gain momentum in the ensuing months. In February 1884 the *Athenaeum and Daily News* published a semiofficial letter from McIver to a member of the Madras

Executive Council in which he urged the government "to use every legitimate weapon" in its power to uphold the Salem judgment. Writing at a time when appeals of certain convicted Hindus were before the High Court, McIver alleged that a section of the Bar, the High Court, and the local press were all seeking to overturn the Salem sentences. Proclaiming the dictum that "it is attack that generally wins," he wanted the Government Pleader to be roused to fight against any acquittals.[55] This letter caused a sensation in Madras and in some circles it gave credence to the suspicion that "the gentlemen employed by the Government to enquire into the case of the riots, one and all seem to have been animated by the desire, not to administer justice, but to get convictions."[56]

In May 1884 C. Vijiaraghava Chari sued the Madras Government for wrongful dismissal from the Salem Municipality a year previously. Born in 1852 to an orthodox Sri-Vaishnava Brahmin family in Chingleput district, Vijiaraghava Chari had taken his B.A. at the Presidency College and had become a teacher in Bangalore and then in Salem. But finding little scope for his talents in this profession, he switched to law and built up a successful practice in Salem. Like many other members of the professional elite, he decided to devote some of his energies and time to politics. He was mainly instrumental in the formation of the Salem Mahajana Sabha in 1881, and in the following year, he together with seven other members of this body, contested and captured all the elective seats in the Salem Municipality.

After the August riots, Vijiaraghava Chari was among those convicted of conspiring to destroy the mosque and was sentenced to ten years' transportation. On appeal, the High Court quashed the conviction and ordered his release. His dismissal from the Municipality compelled him to renew his encounter with the authorities. The latter contended that they had powers for such action without explanation or justification, but the High Court rejected

this contention and awarded Vijiaraghava Chari
damages of Rs 100 and costs.[57]

Heartened by this success, Vijiaraghava Chari
then decided to vindicate the innocence of his im-
prisoned compatriots by impugning the evidence
given by certain witnesses during the Salem trials.
The Madras Government opposed his application, only
to be overruled by the High Court. The perjury
trial was heard in Coimbatore in July 1884, and
seven of the nine accused were found guilty and
sentenced to imprisonment. The District Judge, in
his summing up, attributed their perjury in part to
"the undue influence of the Police and Subordinate
officials."[58] By this time, with the confidence in
the Salem trials severely undermined, public clamor
for the release of those still in prison in the
Andamans gained greater force and conviction. Almost every shade of public opinion in Madras, including some sections of the Muslim press, came to
believe that there was some miscarriage of justice
and urged a review of the sentences in the light of
recent revelations. With mounting political agitation, some of which emanated from outside the
Presidency, and sustained pressure from Lord Ripon,
the Madras Government eventually agreed to the release of all prisoners in October 1884, thus bringing to an end an issue which had convulsed South
Indian politics for more than two years.

The unpopularity of the Grant Duff Administration did not however stem solely from its mis-
handling of the Chingleput Scandal and the Salem
Riots. A further cause of its unpopularity was its
legislative program, notably, the salt, forest, and
kudimaramat bills. Some of these enactments,
though accepted as desirable in principle by the
professional elite, aroused opposition because
their implementation was harsh.

The Forest Act of 1882 was a case in point.
It was inspired by the need to arrest the almost
alarming denudation of forests that was taking
place in South India as a result of growth in human
and cattle population. The Act invested forest

officials with powers to set the limits of forest
reservation, arrest offenders, and seize cattle
straying into reservations.[59] It was inevitable
that the implementation of this measure would
create friction in the rural areas where the villagers, from the powerful landlord to the menial
ryot, had long enjoyed customary rights to fuel and
pasture. The situation was aggravated by the overzealous way in which the forest officials discharged their duties, especially enclosing common
lands and impounding cattle grazing in the reservations. Not surprisingly, there were protests everywhere that the enforcement of the Forest Act was
"needlessly violent."[60] Equally widespread was the
opposition to the Salt Act of 1882. There had been
a long history of Indian agitation against the
official salt policy, directed partly against the
arbitrary price fixing of the government and partly
against the state's claim to monopoly of production.
The latter had led to the formation of a separate
Salt Department in Madras in 1878 aimed at stamping
out illicit manufacture of salt and the guarding of
the salt pans and other saliferous areas.[61] Under
pressure from this department, the Grant Duff Administration had agreed to tighten the salt laws which
allowed officials to search houses without warrants,
arrest and detain suspects, and demand from magistrates more stringent penalties for offenders.

    Neither the reorganization of the Salt Depart-
ment nor the tightening of the laws was popular.
The former meant that certain districts, especially
in the Telugu areas, would for the first time feel
the impact of the government salt monopoly. The
provisions of the Act of 1882 also raised the fear
of official abuse of power, especially by the lowly-
paid Indian subordinates seeking self-enrichment.
Nor was the professional elite happy with the new
law. In an age when it anticipated enlightened
policies, this legislation seemed to be illiberal
both in conception and execution. Not surprisingly,
when Ripon visited Madras in January 1884, almost
every address that was presented to him alluded to

the severity of the salt laws and the hardships
which the common folk underwent as a consequence.[62]

A measure that was neither liberal in conception nor carrying a conviction of necessity was the
Kudimaramat Bill. Prompted by the suggestion of
the Indian Famine Commission to revive "the custom
of statute labour" to repair neglected irrigation
works, the Grant Duff Administration drafted a Bill
which provided for the recruitment of unpaid labor
to repair bunds that were breached and clear vegeta-
tion and silt blocking sluices and channels of
tanks. The right to commute labor in money payment
was recognized, but the Bill disallowed any intervention by the civil courts in disputes arising out
of its working.[63]

When the Bill was made public in May 1883, protests were heard from the press and political
associations in South India. The recently-
resuscitated Madras Native Association, in a memorial to the government, argued that the measure was
"altogether unsuited to the altered condition of
the time," if not "absolutely repugnant" to enlightened opinion. It claimed that, as the *ryots* were
already paying their share of taxation, it would be
unfair to impose an additional burden in the shape
of *kudimaramat*, which would "demoralise as well as
impoverish them."[64] The agitation against the Bill
was intensified when Ripon visited South India, and
the latter persuaded Grant Duff "to let the Kudimaramat Bill sleep."[65] In discussing the abandonment of this measure, the editor of the *Madras Mail*
observed:[66]

A seven months child, it produced many pains
of gestation; it was born without a back-bone;
. . . it died unregretted. . . . In a word it
was smothered in child-bed by the heaps of addresses presented to the Viceroy.

By the early months of 1884, there was a general consensus of opinion in South India that Grant
Duff, far from fulfilling the great expectations

that were entertained of him at his arrival, was a
decided failure. The *Madras Times* commented editor-
ially that since Grant Duff's arrival there had
prevailed in the Presidency "a discontent which had
become more and more profound."[67] Another European
daily, in a postmortem into the governor's unpopularity, argued that Grant Duff had made the error
of identifying himself too closely with European
officials instead of observing "an attentive and
sympathetic neutrality in questions that have forced Europeans and natives into hostile camps."
Though convinced of his ability, the paper felt
that the governor had "yet to come out of his shell,
and make himself directly and easily accessible to
representatives not of the governing as much as the
governed classes."[68] The Indian-owned press attributed Grant Duff's unpopularity to his desertion of
his liberal creed. The *Hindu* noted that, after two
years of Grant Duff's rule, it found it difficult
to reconcile his policies to the doctrines of his
political party:[69]

> All that philosophical radicalism, the maxims
> of democracy, of representative government, in
> fact of good government itself, are all good
> to European people; but to the semi-civilised
> races of India paternal despotism is the only
> good government possible. On this conviction
> he [Grant Duff] has ever endeavoured to uphold
> the measures of individual European officers,
> especially the executive, and has shown utter
> contempt for public feeling.

The breach between the governor and the vocal
sections of opinion in South India was almost complete. Dissatisfaction with the Grant Duff Administration had led to unceasing agitation and even
personal attacks on the governor in which the organs of the professional elite played a prominent
part. The political consequences of such agitation
were far-reaching. On the one hand, the credibility of the government was damaged almost

irreparably. As crisis after crisis confronted the
Grant Duff Administration, it was found to be lacking imagination and resoluteness in tackling them.
Moreover, the handling of the Salem riots had cast
doubts about the evenhandedness of British justice.
The *Hindu* complained that while the rioters were
punished with "uncommon severity," no action was
taken against European officials who were guilty of
"serious offences against public morality." In the
eyes of this paper, the Grant Duff Administration
was "a singularly weak Government, distinguished
neither for administrative ability nor regard for
the requirements of honest public service."[70]

RIPON'S REFORMS AND INDIAN DEMONSTRATIONS

Although Ripon and Grant Duff shared much in
common in public life, notably, a long attachment
to the Liberal Party and a deep interest in Indian
affairs, it is difficult to conceive, based on
their actions in India, of two men of such contrasting attitudes and temperament. If Grant Duff
believed that Western liberalism had no place in
India and that the country should be ruled by a des-
potic government,* Ripon held the view that changes
brought about by British rule called for modifica-
tions in the authoritarian structure of the Indian
government. If Grant Duff was "all for a soothing
cautious nay even dull policy of peace & public

---

*Grant Duff wrote privately to A. C. Lyall:
"We imagine that we can govern here on the principles which are recognized as best for Western so-
cieties--Call them Liberal principles or what you
will--forgetting that our being here at all is if
this country were a fit theatre for these excellent
principles an usurpation & atrocity." *Lyall Collection*, MSS. Eur. F.132, Grant Duff to Lyall, 19
June 1884. I am indebted to Mr. E. Chew for this
quotation.

works," Ripon boldly advocated changes to bring the
administration "into harmony with the extended education, the free public discussion, and the growing
public opinion" which British rule had steadily
fostered in India.[71]

In particular, Ripon stressed the importance
of recognizing the emergence of the Western-educated
class on the Indian scene. He argued that unless
this class was provided with outlets for its talents and political aspirations, unless it was given
a share in the administration of the country, it
would become alienated from the British Raj.

It is not that I want to *please* these men: it
is that I want to make them useful citizens instead of discontented and hostile agitators;
it is because I believe that to rely upon
force alone to keep down the aspirations and
curb the ambitions of men like these is to
trust to a reed which will break under our
hand; and that if we do not, by timely foresight, take steps to supply legitimate outlets
for those aspirations in a manner consistent
with the maintenance of our authority, we
shall find in a few short years that we have
raised up a power we cannot control.[72]

Grant Duff, on the other hand, remained largely unimpressed by such arguments. He believed
that the Western-educated class--"the small clique
of wire-pullers in the Presidency & some of the big
Towns"--exerted "little influence" over the masses
in India who only wanted "quite sensible things,
bridges, roads, railways & so on."[73]

While Grant Duff was incurring the wrath of
many in South India by his excessive reliance on
the bureaucracy, Ripon was clearly intent on being
his own master and began to undo some of the measures associated with his predecessor. In the
first two years of his viceroyalty, Ripon ended the
war with Afghanistan, repealed the Vernacular Press
Act, reduced the duty on salt, and resisted the

efforts of the British Government to burden India
with the charges of the Egyptian campaign. These
actions of the Viceroy won applause of the enlightened section of the Indian population, and a
feeling of euphoria began to grip the Western-
educated class. The days of Lyttonian repression
were regarded as things of the past, and nothing
fortified this new mood more forcefully than
Ripon's celebrated resolution on local self-
government of May 1882.

Ever since his arrival, Ripon had given considerable thought to the question of utilizing the
talents and energies of the growing Western-
educated class. Local government provided one
obvious field where he believed a start could be
made without endangering the stability of the
British Raj. But more importantly, the viceroy's
liberal instincts demanded that his subjects ought
to be instructed in the art of self-rule. Ripon
believed that it was the duty of the British
rulers "to raise the people of the country politically and socially, and not to merely content ourselves with providing them with the good administration of a benevolent despotism."[74] Not
surprisingly, the Indian Government's resolution of
May 1882 stressed that what was sought in the reform of local institutions was not administrative
efficiency but "political and popular education"
and the development among the people of "a capacity
for self-help in respect of all matters." Executive interference was to be kept minimal, and
wherever possible elected representatives were to
tax themselves and undertake local works and improvements. It was not expected that in a country
of such diversity that a uniform system of local
institutions could be evolved; rather the institutions were to be adapted to the peculiar wants of
every locality. To achieve this, provincial governments were urged to initiate the widest possible
consultation with nonofficial opinion before final-
izing the details of local government.[75]

Ripon was aware from previous experience that

such experiments were popularly regarded more as an exercise in shifting financial burdens to local authority than in transferring political power. However, the language in which the resolution was couched, and the viceroy's popularity in Indian circles, helped to erase this impression and even generate some enthusiasm from the members of the professional elite. The Triplicane Literary Society claimed that the resolution of May 1882 was received with "a general demonstration of joy and gratitude," and it was confident that there was "a willingness to take the utmost advantage" of this concession.[76] Even more rapturous was the comment of the *Hindu Reformer and Politician:* "A new era of political independence has dawned on India and the harbinger of good news is the Government of India Resolution on Local Self-Government."[77] Doubtless, the favorable reaction of the Madras Government also helped to create an atmosphere of euphoria. Before making up its own mind over details, the Madras Government set up a mixed committee of officials and nonofficials to submit a report, while at the same time inviting the Madras Native Association to sound out public opinion in the Presidency.

The MNA prepared a detailed questionnaire, eliciting information on various aspects of local government, and circulated it widely to political associations, literary societies, and influential leaders throughout South India. At the same time, it sent G. Subramania Iyer on a tour to the Tamil districts to explain the significance of the resolution of May 1882 and rally support. Subramania Iyer's mission of July-August 1882 took him to Cuddalore, Chidambaram, Trichinopoly, Tanjore, Kumbaconam, Mayaveram, Negapatam, Madura, Tinnevelly, and Tuticorin. Local associations in these centers gave willing cooperation by convening public meetings to discuss the local self-government scheme, while others sent written replies to the MNA. On the basis of these submissions, the association drafted its proposals which were forwarded to the Madras Government in December 1882.[78]

Subramania Iyer's visit to the *mofussil* had a deeper significance than one of merely mobilizing public support for the resolution of May 1882. As the editor of the most influential Indian newspaper in the Presidency, and the rising star in the ranks of the professional elite, Subramania Iyer commanded a unique authority among political circles in South India. His visit to the *mofussil* towns excited interest among local leaders who were anxious to know his views on important public questions.

Subramania Iyer in his discussions and speeches explained the aims of Ripon's policies, and stressed the long-term implications of the local self-government scheme, particularly in laying "the foundation of the great future Representative Government" in India. He also emphasized that unless Indians demonstrated their ability to shoulder the responsibilities which these changes would thrust on them, unless leaders of high calibre and integrity would be willing to labor and sacrifice in the public cause, progress towards political enfranchisement would be a slow process.[79] At the same time, this visit enabled Subramania Iyer to meet local leaders and ascertain their reactions to public issues. In some centers, he was impressed by the enthusiasm that marked his visit. In Tanjore the meeting to discuss local self-government was widely publicized, with notices stuck in all parts of the town, and the large crowd which attended the meeting included lawyers, officials, merchants, and municipal commissioners.[80]

The issue of local self-government also provided the more astute leaders of the professional elite with an opportunity to stimulate political activity in the Presidency. By convening public meetings and by skillful propaganda in the press, a concerted effort was made to get local leaders in the *mofussil* to take a more active interest in the political issues of the day. The attempt was not entirely unsuccessful. According to the *Hindu*, within a year of the publication of the resolution of May 1882 "nearly a thousand public meetings have been held all over the country, for one or other public object," while "a network of such [political] associations" had sprung into existence in South India. To the editor, this development was "a certain sign of the people's advancement in political knowledge."[81]

There was little doubt that the tempo of political activity had quickened considerably since the publication of the scheme for local self-government. Not long before, the province had been labelled "the benighted Presidency" on account of its political apathy. The *Hindu* admitted as late as January 1881 that there was in South India a "miserable apathy in studying and discussing public questions."[82] But within two years a perceptible change had resulted: associations and societies sprouted in almost every town; public meetings were held in increasing frequency; and public opinion began to gain greater force and coherence.

The nerve center of much of this activity was Madras, where a small but able band of leaders drawn from the ranks of the professional elite were giving direction to the growing, political ferment in the Presidency. G. Subramania Iyer's tour of the *mofussil* to mobilize support for local self-government was evidence of such direction, but more significant were the series of political demonstrations that were organized in Madras during the eventful months from April 1883 to January 1884.

Three important demonstrations were organized in this period and they all concerned Lord Ripon or some aspect of his policy. The first demonstration took place in April 1883 and its aim was to petition the Queen to extend Ripon's term of office by another five years. The idea probably originated in Poona, and Bombay led the way by holding a successful meeting in February 1883. It was about this time that Madras awoke to the idea and a small representative committee was formed to make the necessary preparations with Salem Ramaswamy

Mudaliar* as secretary. A man of tact and modesty,
he had come into prominence when he became secretary of the resuscitated Madras Native Association
in 1881. It fell on him largely to make all due
arrangements. He sent out invitations to various
associations in South India urging them to send
delegates to the demonstration in the metropolis or
else to hold simultaneous meetings in their respective centers. In Madras itself, steps were taken
to give due publicity to the event. Almost a week
before the meeting, "placards and small fly-leaves"
in English, Telugu, and Tamil were freely distributed, while notices were "pasted on walls in the
busiest centres of the city."[83]
     On the day of the meeting, Pachaiyappa Hall
could barely accommodate all those who flocked to
demonstrate their support for Lord Ripon. Among
the prominent leaders from the metropolis were P.
Somasundram Chetty, "the conservative veteran,"
whose connection with local politics went back to
the 1850s when he was associated with the Madras
Native Association; P. Rungiah Naidu, a Proficient
of the Madras High School, who had preferred the
legal profession to service with the government;
P. Ananda Charlu,** G. Subramania Iyer, M. Viraraghava Chari, R. Balaji Rao, and Salem Ramaswamy

---

     *Salem Ramaswamy Mudaliar (1852–1892) was born
into a Vellalar *mittadar* family in Salem. His
father, a respected *tahsildar*, had sent him early
to Madras to pursue his education. After a distinguished academic career, taking his law degree in
1875, Salem Ramaswamy Mudaliar worked in the judicial service of the government for some years before establishing his own law practice in Madras.
For further biographical details, see Paramaswaran
Pillai, *Representative Men of South India*, pp.
167–79.

     **Ananda Charlu was born in 1843 to a Brahmin
family in Chittoor, North Arcot. He joined

Mudaliar. Also present at the meeting were delegates from Coimbatore and Negapatam, while other *mofussil* associations had sent telegrams and letters expressing sympathy with the movement.

The meeting endorsed three resolutions: that Ripon's rule had been "conspicuously marked by an earnest desire to promote the material, intellectual and political condition of the people of India"; that the many judicious reforms inaugurated since 1880 were "entirely in accordance with the policy laid down by the Imperial Majesty in her proclamation of 1858 of gradually raising the political status of the people of India and of abolishing distinctions and disabilities founded simply on considerations of race, creed or colour"; and lastly, that in order to enable Ripon "to carry out to completion the various measures of reform which he has with such statesmanlike foresight inaugurated," a memorial be sent to Queen Victoria asking for an extension of his viceroyalty.[84]

The day after this event, the Triplicane Literary Society at a special meeting decided to celebrate the first anniversary of the publication of the resolution on local self-government by holding a similar demonstration in Madras. A sub-committee was formed, and "the public of Madras and of the Mofussil" was invited to participate.[85] The response, however, was not as encouraging as was hoped: no *mofussil* center was represented at this meeting, while leaders of the Muslim and Eurasian

---

Pachaiyappa School in Madras, and came under the influence of C. V. Ranganada Sastri, a close friend of his father. After taking his B.A. he taught for a few years before switching to law and soon built up a flourishing practice in Madras. Endowed with a strong physical constitution and an incisive mind, he was to feature in regional and national politics for almost three decades. M. Venkatarangaiya (ed.), *The Freedom Struggle in Andhra Pradesh*, I, (1800-1905) (Hyderabad, 1965), pp. 235-44.

communities also kept aloof. However, the occasion
was observed by some leading towns in the *mofussil*,
and resolutions were adopted supporting local self-
government.[86] The demonstration in Madras was attended by the prominent leaders of the professional
elite, notably, G. Subramania Iyer, Ananda Charlu,
Salem Ramaswamy Mudaliar, and Viraraghava Chari.

Fittingly enough, G. Subramania Iyer was the
main speaker on this occasion, as no one had done
more to popularize local self-government in South
India. While discussing the manifold benefits that
had flowed from Ripon's farsighted scheme, he contended that it had "breathed a new life into the
people" and fostered "a sense of union and responsibility." He went on to claim that even the village
folk had begun to take an interest in the question,
while nearly fifty associations had been formed in
South India since the resolution was published--
associations which were "diffusing useful knowledge,
inculcating correct views on public questions, [and]
creating a wholesome habit of activity and public
spirit." At the same time, he was confident that
the scheme would revive the village system and provide a strong impetus "to the development of Municipal Government throughout the country, and the
consequent advantages in the shape of education,
public spirit and the elevation of moral tone, will
be immense." Subramania Iyer felt that the seeds
which Ripon had sowed would soon "acquire wider and
wider development, gathering strength and permanence as it grows, and bringing to bear on the conduct of administration, the wholesome force of
public opinion."[87]

The success of these political demonstrations,
organized in vindication of Ripon and his policies,
doubtless reflected the popularity and esteem which
the Viceroy commanded in Indian circles at this
time. To an equal extent, however, these political
displays also symbolized a concerted Indian reaction to the growing Anglo-Indian opposition to the
Viceroy's reforms. Ripon's appointment had always
been suspect in Anglo-Indian eyes, especially with

his conversion to Catholicism and his strong commitment to Gladstonian liberalism. Suspicion began
to turn to hostility when the Viceroy began to dismantle his predecessor's policies, while his advocacy of local self-government raised the fearful
prospect of political power being transferred to
the despised "educated Babu."

What brought matters to a head was the promulgation of the so-called Ilbert Bill in February
1883, aimed at removing "the absolute race disqualification" of Indian judges in the *mofussil* trying
Europeans on criminal charges.[88] This measure
precipitated a political storm of an unprecedented
scale. Starting from Bengal, where a demonstration
was held in February under the aegis of lawyers,
planters, and journalists, the latent forces of
European discontent found a focus to rally together
all sections of Anglo-Indian opinion to mount a
fierce assault on the Viceroy and his reforms. An
Anglo-Indian Defence Association was organized to
spearhead the agitation as well as to collect funds
to defray expenses of the campaign in India and
England. In Madras, where European opposition to
the Ilbert Bill was described as "deep, bitter, and
enduring," a protest memorial was widely circulated
for signatures in April 1883.[89]

Although the Viceroy bore the brunt of Anglo-
Indian wrath, part of this European anger was directed against the Indian people. Moderate Anglo-
Indian opinion took the view that, as conquerors,
the British could preserve their supremacy only by
keeping certain crucial positions in European hands,
even though it was conceded that this would render
nugatory past pledges of equality of treatment to
Indians in the administration. A more extreme
school of European opinion argued with considerable
vehemence that Indians, for reasons of heredity and
environment, would never attain the degree of intellectual or moral capacity to deserve equal treatment with Europeans. Anglo-Indian superiority was
justified on openly racialistic grounds, and in
elaborating this thesis some Anglo-Indians indulged

in the free abuse of the Indian, his character, his
morals, and his social habits.

Even more vehement was the attack on Ripon.
In their strong hostility towards the Viceroy, the
Anglo-Indians indulged in such tactics as boycot-
ting his functions, openly insulting him in the
streets, and even issuing threats of violence to
his person.[90] What came to be called the "White
Mutiny," the agitation against the Ilbert Bill, continued uninterrupted throughout 1883, actively encouraged by a body of European officials in high
positions, and ultimately compelled the Indian
authorities to agree to a compromise.

The professional elite, while not resorting to
platform oratory for tactical reasons, waged a running propaganda battle with the Anglo-Indian
critics of the Ilbert Bill through the columns of
the press. The *Hindu*, as expected, provided the
lead, with the vernacular press giving consistent
support. From the outset, the *Hindu* assailed any
suggestion of abandonment or compromise on this
issue. It asserted that the principle embodied in
the Ilbert Bill was so "simple and fundamental" as
to permit no viable compromise.[91] It dismissed
European opposition as founded on racial arrogance
and a jealousy of Indian advancement to a position
of equality with the Anglo-Indian. It believed
that to conciliate this lobby would not only be
"unfortunate" but also would "lower the prestige of
Government in the eyes of the people. . . . It will
create a belief that the admitted interests of
justice and good administration have been sacri-
ficed to the selfish clamour of a few planters."[92]

During this affair the proprietors of the
Hindu announced in June 1883 their intention of
converting the paper into a tri-weekly. They contended that the "organized attempts" to discredit
Ripon's reforms had made it "more than ever necessary that the real feelings and wishes of the
people should be correctly interpreted to the
people of England."[93]

However, when the vicissitudes of the Ilbert

Bill affair produced the Concordat in December 1883,
an event hailed by an Anglo-Indian organ as "the
surrender of the Viceroy and Mr. Ilbert to the
Defence Association," there was the inevitable dismay among the Indian supporters of the measure.
The *Hindu*, seeing that its campaign was largely in
vain, described the amended Bill as a "mangled
skeleton" and "a veritable apology for the proposed
measure."[94] What was more painful was the decision
of Ripon to initiate negotiations with the Anglo-
Indian Defence Association to reach an agreed
settlement. "That an irresponsible body of men,"
moaned the *Hindu*, "should dictate the policy of a
civilised and responsible Government is without a
parallel even in the history of this country."
Ripon was charged with having introduced "Government by Compact." "There is no denying," observed
the *Hindu*, "that a compact had been made, that a
novelty had been introduced into the administration of this country."[95]

Although immediate Indian reactions to the
Concordat were almost everywhere hostile and even
sharply critical of the way in which Ripon had handled the issue, there was an equal recognition of
the dangers of any course of action on the Indian
side which might be interpreted as disowning Ripon
or his policies. The dilemma, as one Bombay leader
saw it, was that while Indians must criticize the
Concordat "openly and strongly," they must do so
without embarrassing a government which had done
"too much good to the country." Leaders in Bombay
decided against protest demonstrations and instead
suggested that the Indians should make known their
views "in respectfully but emphatically worded
memorials."[96] Leaders in other Indian centers
generally accepted this line of action, and by the
first week of January 1884, there were hopes in
Bombay that their decision would assume "the shape
of a national expression of confidence in Ld.
Ripon's Government."[97]

To the leaders of the professional elite, the
announcement of the Viceroy's visit to South India

in late January 1884 provided a welcome opportunity
to demonstrate their confidence in Lord Ripon and
his policies and show to their Anglo-Indian counterparts that the Viceroy's popularity had in no way
diminished as a result of the Concordat. The enthusiastic reception that had greeted Ripon during
his recent visit to Calcutta and Allahabad set a
precedent that the leaders in Madras wished to
emulate.

A small committee drawn from the leaders of
the professional elite was formed to initiate plans
for Ripon's welcome,[98] and it was anxious that all
shades of Indian opinion should cooperate to make
the occasion fully representative of the Presidency.
There was some speculation as to whether the administrative elite would join the celebrations, especially after the bitter controversy which had
occurred over the reception to Carmichael a month
before. However, to the relief of the leaders of
the professional elite, their elders, as well as
leaders of the Eurasian, Muslim, and Indian Christian communities, agreed to participate in the
demonstration.

The meeting to make the final arrangements
took place on 19 January. Attended by all the
recognized leaders of Madras, and presided over by
T. Madava Rao, this meeting decided to give the
viceroy's party "a suitable reception at their
landing" in the city and "a public entertainment"
during their stay. It was also agreed that a deputation should present an address "setting forth
the views and wishes of the native community, in
regard to the general administration of the
country." A large Ripon Reception Committee, with
Ananda Charlu as secretary, was elected to make
arrangements for the reception.[99]

The idea of a grand demonstration to welcome
the Viceroy found enthusiastic response both in the
metropolis and in the *mofussil* towns. In Madras
support for the cause came from the numerous literary and reading room societies, including the
Triplicane Literary Society, Chintadripetta

Literary Association, and the City Union. More
significant was the readiness of the *mofussil* towns
to participate in the demonstration. Some, like
Tanjore, decided to send a deputation to Madras.
Others indicated their intention to celebrate the
occasion in their respective towns or villages.
The man who was chiefly instrumental in coordi-
nating the entire celebration was Ananda Charlu.
It fell on him, as secretary of the Ripon Reception
Committee, to invite the various associations,
raise funds to meet expenses, ensure that the
pandal (or special tent) where the Viceroy would be
received was completed in time, and arrange for the
seating of the dignitaries. Much of this work had
to be done in less than two weeks' notice, but
Ananda Charlu succeeded with the help of a small
band of volunteers. On the eve of the Viceroy's
arrival, preparations were complete, and as one
paper observed, Madras was "in a state of enthusiasm."[100]

The Ripon demonstrations exceeded even the expectations of those who had organized them. Madras
shed its habitual inertia and turned out in large
numbers to welcome the viceroy, either by crowding
the pier to see Ripon come ashore or by lining the
decorated streets to cheer the viceroy's cavalcade
as it passed on its way to Government House. Celebrations were also organized in almost every district, taking the form of street illuminations,
erection of triumphal arches, acts of charity, or
special temple services. A number of *mofussil*
towns responded to the invitation of the Ripon
Reception Committee by sending deputations to the
metropolis. Only the Anglo-Indians kept aloof, although there were some notable exceptions. Indeed,
as Grant Duff observed, Ripon was "as well received
by the population as Vishnu himself could have been
--probably better."[101]

The success of the Ripon demonstrations filled
the leaders of the professional elite with a sense
of achievement. The *Hindu*, which in the past five
years had done more than any other organ to shake

South India from its political torpor, observed
that the Ripon celebrations were "a marvellously
enthusiastic and unanimous demonstration." In its
view, these festivities "really signalised a new
turn in the development of loyalty and political
education among the people of India."[102] A
European daily, which had witnessed the occasion
from the sidelines, remarked that the demonstrations were quite unprecedented and even spontaneous. As for the new ferment sweeping the Madras
Presidency, the paper commented thus:[103]

> It is not connected with rupees, annas and
> pies; it does not arise from their having been
> fed and clothed. It is gratitude for an at-
> tempt to recognise the political right of
> natives to exercise such political functions
> as they shall be deemed fit or nearly fit to
> exercise. It shews that the natives do value
> political liberty and rights, and are, there-
> fore, in some measure fit for them; that they
> are intensely grateful for even the attempt to
> treat them with respect and fairness, and that
> there is something of a national feeling, not
> springing, but sprung up, among them.

5. Provincial Organization and Conferences

Amidst the fierce political controversies of
the early 1880s, stimulated on the one hand by the
unpopular actions of the Grant Duff Administration
and on the other by the formidable Anglo-Indian opposition to Ripon's reforms, the cry was heard
among various political groups in South India for a
voluntary association to represent the interests of
the presidency as a whole. The source of this demand can be largely traced to the professional
elite, or more specifically to that small group of
activists in Madras who had organized successive
political demonstrations in 1883-84. As this embattled group found itself drawn increasingly into
the vortex of the sharpening political conflicts of
the time, the idea began to dawn in its mind that a
cohesive organization, established on a representative basis and endowed with adequate financial resources, would be an invaluable auxiliary in any
continuing struggle against the government or the
European community.
  The reasons why this idea began to take such a
firm hold on the mind of the Indian politicians in
Madras are not far to seek. Especially important
in influencing their thinking was the European triumph in the Ilbert Bill campaign. This episode
revealed, among other things, the effectiveness of
organization and unity in securing group demands.
The Indians realized that they too must organize if

they wanted to obtain their rights. In this respect, the Bengal and Bombay presidencies had shown
the way by establishing their respective associations. The Indian Association in Calcutta and the
Poona Sarvajanik Sabha had shown themselves to be
capable of rallying under their banner elements
sharing common interests in their regions. Madras
Presidency, on the other hand, lacked such a political organization. It seemed only logical that
steps should be taken to redress this deficiency.
What gave a sense of urgency to such a move was the
fact that politicians in the three presidencies
were slowly awakening to the importance of all-
India unity. If Indian national unity was to be
seriously entertained, the formation of provincial
organization in the three presidencies appeared to
be an essential prerequisite.

THE DEMAND FOR A PROVINCIAL ORGANIZATION

The need for a voluntary association had been
felt in South India ever since the MNA became defunct during the early 1860s. In 1862, for example,
certain Hindu leaders in Madras were reported to
have had consultations on starting a new political
association, but these talks did not prove fruitful.[1] In the ensuing years, the idea continued to
be canvassed in the press as well as on the platform, but it was not until 1872 that anything tangible happened. Then, amid the excitement caused
by the enactment of the Brahmo Marriage Bill, the
MNA was resuscitated.[2] However, this revival was
short-lived, as little was heard afterwards of its
existence.

The absence of a recognized vehicle of political expression in South India, and the disadvantages that stemmed from it, were sharply emphasized
during the 1870s when the Indian Association in
Calcutta was beginning to make an impact on the
Indian political scene by its determined opposition
to unpopular policies associated with Lord Lytton's

regime. The reduction of the age of entry into the
Covenanted Civil Service in 1876, the enactment of
the Vernacular Press Act in 1878, and the remission
of the cotton duties a year later provided sufficiently provocative issues around which the Indian
Association was able to mount an all-India agitation. Inevitably, South India was called upon to
support the campaign. In January 1878, Surendran-
ath Banerjea, a prominent member of the Indian
Association who had been making extensive tours to
various parts of the country, arrived in Madras to
canvass support for the civil service agitation.
His plea for a public meeting failed, and he had to
be content with "a conference of leading men"[3]
which endorsed the resolutions of the Indian Association.* This was not the only expression of political apathy in Madras. Later in the year, when
the Indian Association was directing a concerted
agitation against the Vernacular Press Act, leaders
in Madras refrained from registering any public protest against the measure.

If these larger, albeit all-India, issues
caused little flutter in South India, the same cannot be said of the more specific local questions
which were troubling the Presidency during this
period. Overshadowing all other problems was the
famine of 1876-78, which not only called for massive state relief but also a measure of voluntary
public service and charity. A large, representative Madras Famine Relief Committee, consisting of
Indians and Europeans, had been set up in the metropolis and it functioned with reasonable efficiency
with the help of branch committees established in
different districts in the Presidency. Although
suffering had been reduced and deaths minimized, it

---

*A belated public meeting was held in Madras
on 30 January 1878 when a petition on the civil service issue was endorsed for submission to the British Parliament through the aegis of the Indian
Association. *Madras Times*, 31 January 1878.

was glaringly apparent to discerning observers that
a task of such magnitude and urgency had evoked so
little independent initiative on the part of the
Indians themselves. Some attributed this to the
absence of a well-organized voluntary association
in South India. William Digby, the energetic secretary of the Madras Famine Relief Committee, took
this view in a speech he gave in March 1878. Impressed by the energy and imagination which the
members of the Poona Sarvajanik Sabha had showed in
combating famine in the Deccan, he urged his South
Indian friends, with whom he had closely worked in
famine relief, to organize a similar association to
work for the welfare of the Presidency.[4]

What gave Digby's call a sense or urgency was
the decision of the Madras Government to increase
local taxation to carry out improvements in conser-
vation and sanitation in the metropolis. Local
taxation had always been unpopular among the
Indians, not merely because of its financial burden
but also because of the petty official exactions
that accompanied its collection and the fact that
it breached the traditional secrecy surrounding
business operations of the mercantile and artisan
classes. But despite opposition, by the 1870s,
local taxation had been extended to almost every
major town in South India and in Madras it had come
to affect almost every section of the nonofficial
class, from the indigent weavers to the wealthier
merchant and professional classes. In April 1877,
in spite of vigorous opposition from the chamber of
commerce, press, municipal commissioners, and nonofficial members of the local Legislative Council,
the Madras authorities decided to raise the tax on
houses and landed property in Madras. The irate
citizens of the metropolis called a public meeting
to protest against the increase and called upon the
Viceroy to veto the legislation.[5] One Indian newspaper, the *Madrassee*, angered by the way the government had defied "the unanimous voice of the Madras
citizens and the unanimous voice of the native members" of the Legislative Council, advocated the

formation of "an active and respectable association" which could agitate incessantly against official iniquities and seek redress from the highest
British authorities, including Parliament.[6]

As the demand for a political organization became more insistent, some Hindus decided to revive
the Madras Hindu Debating Society. Founded originally during the 1850s as a forum for lectures and
debates, especially for the Hindu youth, this body
had been defunct since the death of Venkataroylu
Naidu in 1863. The decision to resuscitate it
came from some Hindu merchants and officials, of
whom V. Rajaratnam Mudaliar was the most prominent,
while Digby was made its Patron.[7] A month later,
the name of the society was changed to the Southern
Indian Association, and its newly-defined objectives revealed its overtly political character.
The association pledged itself to consider political and social issues of the Indian community,
while at the same time serving "as a medium between
the Government and the non-official native community on all matters affecting its interest."[8] However, the Southern Indian Association was short-lived,
disappearing from public view in the same myster-
ious way as other similar ventures over the past
decade.

A more successful attempt at revival was that
of the MNA. Informal discussions to reactivate
this body for a second time had begun in 1877, but
it took almost four years before the process of
resuscitation was completed. Among those actively
associated with its revival were C. V. Ranganada
Sastri, who was elected as President, and Salem
Ramaswamy Mudaliar, its Secretary. Ranganada
Sastri died in July 1881, and the presidentship was
assumed by V. Bhashyam Iyengar, a Sri-Vaishnava
Brahmin, born into the well-known Vembakkam family
to which also belonged V. Sadagopah Charlu and V.
Rama Iyengar. After taking his B.A. degree from
Presidency College in 1864, Bhashyam Iyengar had
entered government service but abandoned it a few
years later to become a lawyer. He acquired a

mastery of Hindu Law, especially the law relating
to land tenures and inheritance, and built up a
clientele around wealthy merchants and *zamindars*.[9]
By the eighties he had become the unchallenged
leader of "the Native Bar" in South India, reputed
to be earning annually Rs 100,000.[10]

The MNA threw open its membership to all
Indians in the metropolis, both officials and nonofficials, irrespective of caste or communal affiliations. A special effort, however, was made to
recruit prominent public figures, notably, members
of the Madras Legislative Council, officials in
high positions, and the leading lawyers in the city.
Social prestige, education, and wealth were the distinguishing characteristics of its members, and not
surprisingly the MNA earned a reputation for political moderation and a conciliatory attitude
towards the government. Its headquarters for some
time was at Mylapore, the residential suburb of the
leading Indian lawyers and officials in the city.[11]
When its premises were shifted to Mount Road in
December 1881, the association was reported to have
within its ranks "many learned and influential
native gentlemen" in the city.[12]

As a body aspiring to represent the political
interests of the Indian community, the MNA held
periodical meetings to discuss issues of local importance. Subjects, like the admission of qualified Indians into the higher ranks of the judicial
and revenue service and the disestablishment of the
English Church in India,[13] were discussed with a
view to persuading the authorities to adopt a more
equitable policy.

Undeniably, it was in furthering the cause of
local self-government that the MNA did signal service. By circulating questionnaires to various
bodies and leaders, and by sending a delegate to
tour the Tamil districts, the association not only
equipped itself with a mass of useful data and
opinion but also helped to dispel Indian reservations about Ripon's scheme. Its own memorandum on
the subject was an exercise in moderation and sound

judgment. It suggested that the elective system
should be adopted, except in the hilly and agency
tracts, with the majority of members of municipalities and *taluk* boards elected on a territorial
basis. Where seats were to be filled by nomination,
the association was anxious that minorities and
special interests should be fairly represented. As
regards the choice of presidents and vice-
presidents, the association recommended their election in the case of municipalities, while in the
taluk boards the president was to be nominated and
the vice-president elected.[14]

Another issue which attracted its attention
was higher education. For some years before the
appointment of the Education Commission in 1882,
fears had been created in Indian circles that the
government, under pressure from Christian missionaries and the European press, might feel compelled
to withdraw entirely from higher education. Taking
advantage of the hearings instituted by the Education Commission, the MNA presented a lengthy memorial in which it expressed the hope that "no re-
actionary policy will be adopted with regard to
higher education which has produced such signal
results." While accepting the transfer of high
schools to private control, the association declared its opposition to any similar transfer of
government colleges, notably, those in Madras,
Kumbaconam, and Rajahmundry, on the ground that continued private financial support was uncertain. It
was claimed that not only did wealthy *zamindars*
show little interest in education, but Hindu charity had "generally taken a religious form." Moreover, the association felt that the government
allocation for education was "an insignificant proportion" when compared to European countries, and
the Indian authorities were urged to make greater
provision for education by reducing expenditure in
other fields.[15]

That the MNA continued to function in 1883 is
certain, although less and less was heard of its
activities as the year progressed. In part this

can be attributed to the failure of the association
to keep pace with the changing political situation
in South India. At a time of sharpening conflicts
between the government and certain sections of Indian public opinion, the Association's efforts to
maintain a moderate posture seemed to convey the
impression of mendicancy, if not a fear of the
government. Nor were its relations with the government always cordial. Since the early months of
1882, when the government came under mounting public criticism, relations between the Grant Duff
Administration and the metropolitan politicians had
become strained. This jeopardized continued official participation in political work, fearful as
officials were of government reprisal, and the MNA
with its sizable official element was particularly
affected. The *Hindu* commented in November 1883:
". . . the Government has of late become so jealous
of any public spirit among Native gentlemen that
those who are anxious to stand well in the estimation of Government shrink from taking part in public movements."[16] W. S. Blunt, who visited Madras
at this time, drew a similar conclusion. "The
natives in the public service," Blunt recorded in
his diary, "are completely under the thumb of the
Government, and unless they have means of their own
dare not offend their English superiors."[17]

A body of different origin and political com-
plexion was the Triplicane Literary Society. It is
not clear when exactly this body was founded; probably it was the outgrowth of the Triplicane Native
Literary Society started in 1868. It was at this
time that literary societies, as one newspaper remarked, were "becoming the order of the day amongst
educated natives" of South India.[18] With the
steady expansion of colleges and high schools, students in search of some form of intellectual and
corporate activity had begun to organize literary
societies, debating clubs, and reading rooms in the
various centers of the Presidency. Often encouraged by their principals and teachers, students
assumed management of these societies, invited

distinguished lecturers to address them, organized
debates, and provided facilities for reading and
even games. Though overtly political themes were
avoided, there was nevertheless enough opportunity
for a wide ranging discussion of topical issues.
Many of these students, when their scholastic
careers were over, continued their association with
these societies; others founded new societies to
cater to their special needs. In almost every town
in South India, where there was a nucleus of educated Indians, there was a literary society, debating club, or a reading room. In 1886 at least a
hundred such societies were strung over Madras
Presidency with memberships ranging from ten to one
hundred.[19] Many of these societies existed pre-
cariously, often on fluctuating membership and uncertain incomes, but their importance should not be
underestimated. They were not only a source of informed Indian opinion but also the nursery of the
latter-day political leadership of South India.

Undeniably, the best known of these societies
in the nineteenth century was the Triplicane
Literary Society. It had been reorganized on a
more efficient basis in 1874 by some graduates residing in what was claimed to be the intellectual
heart of Madras. Triplicane, a conjested suburb,
was in effect the Muslim quarter of the city. However, a significant Hindu population had always
lived here, close to Sri Parthasarathy temple,
which, as one of the oldest and most sacred Hindu
shrines in the metropolis, attracted a regular
stream of pilgrims from various parts of the
Presidency. In more recent years, with the location of the Presidency College and Senate building
of the University of Madras along the Triplicane
beach, college students and graduates had come to
reside in this suburb, among them G. Subramania
Iyer and Viraraghava Chari. It seems unlikely that
either had a hand in the reorganization of the Triplicane Literary Society in 1874, but there is no
doubt that they were soon to be among its most
active members.

The society rented modest premises, subscribed
to select newspapers and periodicals, and depended
on benefactors and the government to supply books
for its small library. Membership remained around
seventy,[20] almost all graduates trained in such
vocations as teaching, law and journalism. Officials were not excluded, and, indeed, some of the
important positions in the society were filled by
officials in the service of the Madras Government.
But there was no mistaking its real character:
it was a society of young intellectuals of the sort
then filling the ranks of the professional elite--
persons who were known for their radical political
orientation and organizational skill, attributes
which were to make them the focus of political
movements during the 1880s. In the *Hindu*, they had
already found a vehicle to express their thoughts.
The next stage in their political evolution was to
establish a voluntary association.

For a time, however, they decided to operate
within the framework of the Triplicane Literary
Society. Its literary character was gradually discarded after 1880, and it increasingly assumed the
outward forms of a voluntary association. Among
those who had a hand in this change were Raghunatha
Rao, Ananda Charlu, G. Subramania Iyer, and Viraraghava Chari, all holding important positions in
society and becoming conspicuous in Madras for
their work in journalism, politics, or social reform. They were delighted with the triumph of the
liberals in the elections of 1880, had visions of
a new epoch in India, and were anxious to play a
creative role in enabling the rulers to frame the
right policies. One way to achieve this was to submit regular memorials and addresses. In November
1881, for example, the Triplicane Literary Society
presented an address of welcome to Grant Duff in
which it urged the reduction of land assessments,
encouragement of agricultural education, separation
of revenue from judicial functions, improvement of
the management of religious endowments by fresh
legislation, and lessening of the rigors of salt

and forest laws.[21] None of these demands were new,
but in skillfully presenting them in a single document, the Triplicane Literary Society was obviously
highlighting the kind of issues around which a concerted political agitation could be mounted.

The travails which South India experienced
during the years of Grant Duff's governorship did
not embarrass the Triplicane Literary Society in
the same way that they affected the MNA. If anything, the former seemed to have gained in vigor
during these turbulent times. Provided with a
raison d'etre for its recently acquired political
status, the Triplicane Literary Society emerged as
a fearless critic of the government, advocating in
the process greater restraints on the power of the
bureaucracy. No doubt this feeling stemmed from
the widely held view that the Chingleput Scandal
and Salem Riots were the outcome of inadequate
checks on the power of officials. In an address
that it presented to Evelyn Baring, the retiring
Finance Member, in December 1882, the Triplicane
Literary Society concerned itself largely with the
way in which the administration was functioning in
South India. Not only were the administration's
glaring anomalies exposed, but the Society also
called for some system of appeals against the rul-
ings of district officials, especially on revenue
matters. Equally, the favorable reaction to
Ripon's local self-government scheme, though partly
inspired by the fact that it would provide "the
means of imparting political education to the
people," also stemmed from the belief that it would
remove official interference in one area of government.[22] These sentiments were undoubtedly an expression of the suspicions and distrust which the
professional elite was beginning to show towards
the Indian bureaucracy. As one author remarked in
1886, the bureaucracy was likened by "Young Madras"
to "an immense vampire" which sat brooding over
India and "draining her almost to her heart's blood
during the last century and more."[23]

It is difficult to be certain for how long and

to what extent the Triplicane Literary Society was
able to fulfill the hope of its leaders that it
function as a provincial organization along the
lines of the Poona Sarvajanik Sabha. In certain
circles, at least, it was being discounted, before
long, as a serious alternative to a voluntary association capable of rallying together the various
centers of political activity in the Presidency.
The *Hindu*, which had access to the thoughts of the
leaders of the Triplicane Literary Society, had
since 1881 repeatedly called for a new organization
which would be more representative of the Madras
Presidency as a whole and prevent the dissipation
of energy and time "in random and unorganised
efforts often misdirected and abortive."[24] The
editor was obviously alluding to the plethora of
associations, societies, and clubs mushrooming in
South India and working without any coherence or
central direction. The political demonstrations
which were staged in 1883 in defence of Lord Ripon
and his policies were also an attempt on the part
of the metropolitan politicians to supply an element of coherence which they felt was lacking in
these literary societies and clubs. As G. Subramania Iyer explained at the first anniversary meeting of the publication of the Resolution on Local
Self-Government, such demonstrations would stimulate provincial unity "by gathering in the metropolis leading Native gentlemen from all parts of the
Presidency to discuss questions affecting the
public weal, and by diffusing that patriotism and
liberality of thought which are sure to result from
the periodical contact, on public business, of men
from the mofussil with their compatriots of the
capital city."[25]

Once this political insight was gained, it was
only a short step to recognition that to lend unity
and vigor to any continuing political agitation
would demand the formation of a provincial organization that embraced the metropolis as well as the
mofussil. In November 1883 the *Hindu* made a strong
appeal for such an association "to watch the

administration of the districts and bring to light
any failure of justice or grievance of the people
to be forwarded to England." The editor asked
whether the entire Presidency could not furnish a
hundred men who would be willing to "lend their
time, thought and money for such a purpose."[26]
What gave this appeal an element of poignancy, and
indeed urgency, were two events which occurred at
this juncture and acted as a kind of a catalyst in
bringing to a consummation the long-felt need for a
Presidency-wide organization.

The first of these two events concerned the
reception given to D. F. Carmichael in December
1883. The fierce controversy that broke out, while
highlighting the cleavage between the administrative
elite and its younger rivals, also brought to the
surface the simmering discontent and ill-feeling
which the latter had come to entertain towards
Grant Duff and his close official advisors. In its
opposition to the reception, the professional elite
represented Carmichael as the key figure in the
recent policies of the Grant Duff Administration.
Carmichael's commissions and omissions were duly
catalogued, including his declared opposition to
the Ilbert Bill, his prominent part in enacting
"the most illiberal and unpopular Madras Municipal
Bill" of 1883,[27] and his failure to protect those
who had suffered in the Chingleput Scandal and the
Salem Riots. The *Hindu* remarked that Carmichael
was "an object of the people's intense dislike."
It protested in "unqualified language" against "the
poojah" which the supporters of Carmichael were
constantly offering to their official deities,
pleaded with them against making "native demonstrations such cheap articles," and appealed to the
people not to associate with what it termed "this
odious movement."[28]

The agitation was to no purpose. The reception took place with the usual pomp associated with
such events, graced by the governor and attended by
Europeans and Indians of wealth and social eminence.
The anti-Carmichael faction watched the proceedings

with a mixture of scorn and anger. Although the
presence of "the titled rajas and knights" was dismissed with derision, it was not possible to adopt
the same attitude towards the participation of
Raghunatha Rao, Bhashyam Iyengar, and other leaders
connected with metropolitan politics. The Triplicane Literary Society had declared its opposition
to the reception, but this did not restrain its
President, Raghunatha Rao, from attending the function. It is not clear what attitude the MNA
adopted, but its president and secretary found
themselves in opposing camps. If any lesson was
derived from this episode, it was that neither of
these bodies had shown any capacity for united
action. In their failure to command the loyalty of
their prominent members to an agreed line of action,
they had destroyed their credibility to be truly
Presidency-wide organizations.

The other event which heightened the need for
a provincial body was the European triumph in
securing the compromise on the Ilbert Bill in
December 1883. While many Indians regarded the
Concordat with dismay as a case of the government's
sacrificing the principle of racial equality on the
altar of European supremacy, what was more alarming
to many discerning Indians was the long-term implications of this event. The *Hindu*, which claimed
that the Concordat had filled "every thinking mind
with gloomy forebodings," was apprehensive as to
what would happen if a weak Viceroy succeeded Ripon.
It was obvious to the professional elite that henceforth the Anglo-Indians were a factor to be reck-
oned with in Indian politics. If their influence
in the past was not always apparent, the Ilbert
Bill had provided a foretaste of the kind of opposition which liberal Viceroys like Ripon must encounter in the future. With their wealth, their
organizational skills, and their determination to
defend the privileges which they had long enjoyed,
the Anglo-Indian planters, lawyers, and merchants
were regarded as a formidable element capable even
of dictating official policies. No doubt some of

their power was derived from the fact that they enjoyed the support of British officials in India,
the India Office in London, and influential sections of the press and ruling classes in England.
For the professional elite to combat the Europeans whom it regarded as "enemies of reform and
progress,"[29] it was essential that the elite equip
itself with the kind of weapons which the Anglo-
Indians had so successfully brandished at the
government. Agitation through the press alone, as
the *Hindu* admitted, was inadequate. What was
needed was organization. Lamenting the absence of
voluntary associations, the *Hindu* asked: "Had such
Associations existed, would not the united voice of
two hundred millions of India's people drowned
even the London Thunderer [*The Times*], and rendered
it unavailing against Ilbert's Bill or any other
useful reform in India?"[30]

FORMATION OF THE MADRAS MAHAJANA SABHA

There is no record of when and where the decision was taken to organize a new provisional association. Like those who started the Indian
National Congress, the leaders who were behind the
formation of the Madras Mahajana Sabha had revealed
nothing to the public until they published a prospectus of the proposed body in March 1884. Circum-
stantial evidence suggests that the actual decision
to form a provincial association was taken sometime
before Ripon visited Madras late in January 1884,
although there was to be prior consultation with
mofussil leaders before its formal launching to ensure that adequate support was forthcoming for the
venture.
The inspiration and driving force behind this
decision was that small band of metropolitan leaders who had organized the political demonstrations
and had actively campaigned against the Carmichael
reception, notably, G. Subramania Iyer, Ananda
Charlu, Rangiah Naidu, Salem Ramaswamy Mudaliar,

Balaji Rao, and Viraraghava Chari. Balaji Rao was
named Provisional Secretary of the new association
and was entrusted with the task of ascertaining the
reactions of local associations and leaders in the
Presidency. He sent out letters to every association in which he explained the objects of the new
venture and enquired whether support would be forthcoming.

However, the real task of mobilizing support
for the new association was done during the Ripon
demonstrations when over 100 politicians from the
mofussil had arrived at the metropolis.[31] Informal
consultations took place, and Balaji Rao and his
colleagues were able to explain in some detail what
their proposed association intended to achieve. To
some extent, their task was made easier by the very
success of the Ripon demonstrations; in coming to
the metropolis at considerable effort and expense,
the *mofussil* leaders had shown that provincial
unity was possible where common interest was at
stake.

In the addresses these local delegations presented to the Viceroy, there was further proof of
provincial unity. These addresses gave expression
to "certain grievances felt by the whole country at
large." Commenting on "a family resemblance"
among the addresses, an Anglo-Indian daily observed
that the Indians were "taking a leaf out of the
Anglo-Indian book by organising in view to defence
and self-support."[32]

In March 1884, almost six weeks after Ripon's
visit to Madras, the sponsors of the Madras
Mahajana Sabha issued a prospectus formally announcing their decision to establish this body. Emphasis was laid on its nonofficial character, with
membership to be thrown open to graduates, pleaders,
dubashes, and landholders. The declared aim of
this body was to "watch public interests and to
take such steps to promote them from time to time."
It was to hold regular public meetings, arrange for
lectures, and issue tracts in the vernaculars of
the Presidency. While seeking the cooperation of

all local associations in South India, the founders
of the Madras Mahajana Sabha disavowed any interest
in supplanting them with branch associations. All
local bodies were to retain their individual identity and were to function in the fashion they had
before. It was not clear from the prospectus what
would be the rights or obligations of those associations affiliating, excepting their right to be
represented in the deliberations of the parent body
and their obligation to pay a certain sum as subscription.[33]

The meeting to inaugurate the Madras Mahajana
Sabha was held on 16 May 1884. Dominating the proceedings were G. Subramania Iyer, Viraraghava
Chari, Ananda Charlu, Rangiah Naidu, Balaji Rao,
and Salem Ramaswamy Mudaliar. Balaji Rao, while
moving the main resolution, explained that his inquiries in recent months had satisfied him that
there was wide support for the organization. In
seconding the motion, Rangiah Naidu contended that
the Madras Mahajana Sabha, unlike the Madras Native
Association, would only have nonofficial members
who would "represent fearlessly the wishes of the
people." The objectives of the new body were defined at the meeting. Balaji Rao envisaged a dual
function for the Madras Mahajana Sabha. First, it
was "to bring before our rulers the views of the
public, and to correctly represent to Government
what our needs are and to suggest remedies."
Second, it was to devise means "to improve the condition of the people." Rangiah Naidu, on the other
hand, suggested that the association should establish ties "with institutions of a similar nature in
sister-Presidencies."[34]

One of the earliest tasks that faced the founders of the Madras Mahajana Sabha was to draft its
rules. The constitution that was adopted in 1884
contained seventeen clauses, setting out in detail
the objectives of the body and ways of attaining
them, the composition and fees of membership, the
strength and functions of the office bearers, and
the mode of enlisting the cooperation of local

associations in South India. Membership was to be
restricted to those above twenty-one years of age;
those accepted into the association were to pay an
annual subscription of not less than one rupee.
The executive control of the body was to be vested
in the hands of a Committee, elected annually,
while each affiliated association had the right of
nominating one member to sit in an ex officio capacity. This committee was empowered to "bring about
the objects of the Sabha by means of memorials,
deputations, public meetings and such other means
as it deems fit." Provision was made for the quarterly meetings of the Madras Mahajana Sabha which
would review the work done over the past three
months.[35]

The nucleus of the early leadership of this
association came from that small band of metropolitan politicians who had so strongly resisted the
unpopular policies of the Grant Duff Administration and opposed with equal vehemence the reception
to Carmichael. Elected as the first President of
the Madras Mahajana Sabha was Rangiah Naidu, and
he continued to fill this office until his death in
1902. Balaji Rao, who had worked tirelessly in enlisting support from the *mofussil* associations, was
chosen as one of the Vice-Presidents. The Joint
Secretary positions were filled by Ananda Charlu
and Viraraghava Chari, both of whom had been active
participants in the recent political demonstrations
and who for many years to come were to remain in
the inner circle of Madras politics. Among those
elected to serve in the Committee of the Madras
Mahajana Sabha were G. Subramania Iyer and Salem
Ramaswamy Mudaliar, two of the most dedicated young
politicians of South India and two who had contributed their share in developing public opinion in
the Presidency.

Unfortunately, no complete list of office
holders of the Madras Mahajana Sabha for the first
year of its existence has survived. However, Appendix 1 provides a list of those elected to the Committee of the Sabha for the year 1886-87. Despite

obvious gaps in the data provided in this table, it
is still possible to draw certain conclusions about
the leadership of the association.

First, it is clear that the majority of the
leaders belonged to a relatively young generation,
being born after 1840. The notable exceptions were
Rangiah Naidu, Somasundram Chetty, and Sabapathy
Mudaliar. These three leaders, men of wealth and
social standing, had also shown strong sympathies
for the causes associated with the younger politicians. Though these considerations must have
weighed in their selection, there is no doubt that
their age was also an important factor. The charge
of youthful impetuosity, which the critics so often
levelled against the professional elite, had to be
countered by recruiting older, more mature politicians into the leadership of the Madras Mahajana
Sabha. But this did not conceal the preponderance
of the younger politicians, mostly in their twen-
ties and thirties, who had grown up in the more
tranquil times of the post-1858 era. These young
leaders had no firsthand experience of the violence
released during the conflagration of 1857-58, and
not surprisingly, some European critics argued
that this group could never fully appreciate the extent of British contributions to the prevailing stability and security in the subcontinent. Monier
Williams made this point in 1878: "The longer we
continue to hold the country, the more its condition before we took it in hand is forgotten. In
those parts of the Madras Presidency which have
been longest under our rule, the people, having had
no personal experience of the evils which their
fathers were delivered through our intervention,
are unable to cherish due sense of gratitude towards us."[36]

As might be expected, education played an important part in the selection of the leaders of the
Madras Mahajana Sabha. No less than nineteen of
the thirty-six Committee members of the Sabha had a
university degree or its equivalent, and of these
all but one of them belonged to one of the

independent professions--law, journalism, or medicine. This was a measure of the strength of the
professional elite in South Indian politics at this
time, and there is no doubt that it was this group
which wielded decisive influence in the actual management of the Madras Mahajana Sabha. However, the
professional elements saw the need to enlist the
support of other influential groups in Madras. A
strong contingent of merchants and *dubashes*, thirteen in all, was represented in the Committee of
the Sabha. It was not expected that these merchants would exercise the same degree of power in
the civic life of Madras that they had done during
the middle of the century, but it was nonetheless
widely recognized that their wealth and social
status would add weight to any political movement
in South India.

Prominent among the merchants who were elected
into the Committee of the Madras Mahajana Sabha
were P. Somasundram Chetty, A. Sabapathy Mudaliar,
and P. S. Ramaswamy Mudaliar. Somasundram Chetty
came from a wealthy merchant family in Madras. He
had studied English privately under an European
tutor, then entered the service of Arbuthnot & Co.
as a *dubash*, and eventually returned to his family
business. A successful businessman, he had always
shown an interest in public affairs. In the early
1850s, he had joined the Hindu Reading Room and
later became a member of the Madras Native Association.[37] Known to be "a strictly orthodox Hindu,"
Somasundram Chetty was noted as a man of "striking
geniality and humour," which to some extent accounted for his popularity in Madras.[38]

A. Sabapathy Mudaliar of Bellary was a self-
made man. He had entered official service at a
very subordinate position, but dissatisfied with
this, he joined a European firm which opened his
eyes to the prospects of a commercial and industrial career. Speculating intelligently and investing his profits shrewdly in cotton presses, spin-
ning wheels, and sugar factories, Sabapathy
Mudaliar emerged during the 1880s as one of the

most enterprising and wealthy men in South India.[39]

Savalay Ramaswamy Mudaliar, a *dubash* in the firm Arbuthnot & Co., had acquired his fortunes through long and loyal service in this firm. A regular contributor to various charitable causes in Madras, he was reported to have spent over Rs 44,000 to feed starving people flocking into Madras during the famine of 1876-78.[40]

Another characteristic of the leaders of the Madras Mahajana Sabha was the fact that most of them whose birthplace is known were *mofussil* born. A sizable number came originally from Tanjore district, while others were born in districts as widely dispersed as Malabar in the west, Madura in the south, and Bellary in the north. It was education that had brought them together. The leading educational institutions in Madras, notably, the Presidency College, not only commanded great prestige throughout South India but also offered professional courses, like law, which attracted many bright and ambitious students from the *mofussil*.

When their educational career ended, these students decided to settle in Madras, attracted among other things by professional prospects, by the comforts of urban living, and by the varied social and cultural life of the city. Lawyers in particular seemed to favor Madras, especially during the 1870s and early 1880s when the profession was lucrative and when Indian *vakils* were effectively challenging the dominant position of the European barristers. Some lawyers, however, had resisted the pull of Madras for many years only to succumb to it in the end. S. Subramania Iyer, for instance, had established his law practice in Madura, his native town, and he built up a rich clientele which was the envy of even the metropolitan lawyers. However, in 1884 he decided to shift his practice to Madras, ostensibly to facilitate his attendance at the meetings of the Madras Legislative Council.[41] He never returned to Madura, except for professional or social reasons.

A breakdown of the communal groups represented

in the Committee of the Madras Mahajana Sabha
shows that twenty were non-Brahmin Hindus, thirteen
Brahmins, two Indian Christians and one Muslim.
Judged in terms of population strength, the Brahmins were palpably over-represented. However, the
idea of proportional communal representation seemed
to have counted least among those who organized the
Sabha. Greater importance was accorded to such considerations as the individual merit of those seeking office, their past contributions to public life,
and the economic and social influence they wielded
in the Presidency. Education was an important criterion, especially if those who had acquired it had
entered an independent calling which would enable
them to participate fully in political activity
without fear of official reprisal.

A further point which deserves notice is the
fact that a fair number of the leaders of the
Madras Mahajana Sabha had served in statutory
bodies, charitable organizations or literary societies and clubs. At least fifteen of the leaders
were known to have served in a municipality or district board. Somasundram Chetty, for instance, had
been a member of the Madras Municipality since the
1860s. Rangiah Naidu became a member of the
Chingleput District Board in 1871 and later was
elected to the Madras Municipality. Another long-
serving member was S. Subramania Iyer. First elected to the Madura Municipality in 1870, he was its
Vice-President in 1884. Sabapathy Mudaliar, who
dominated the civic life of Bellany from the seventies onward, was Chairman of the Bellany Municipality in 1885.

Charitable organizations, like the Monegar
Choultry and Pachaiyappa Charities, also drew on
the services of these leaders. Somasundram Chetty
was Chairman of Pachaiyappa Charities for many
years and he was associated with the Monegar
Choultry for a similar length of time. Balaji Rao
became a Fellow of Madras University in 1877, while
Savalay Ramaswamy Mudaliar had the distinction of
being the first Indian to be appointed Sheriff of

Madras in 1886. Hence, many of the prominent members of the Madras Mahajana Sabha had a tradition
of public service and they were known beyond their
immediate circles of friends and relatives.

It is not possible, owing to lack of relevant
data, to extend this analysis to those who became
ordinary members of the Madras Mahajana Sabha. The
framers of the constitution of this body had explicitly laid down that admission would be restricted
to nonofficials only. The right of entry to nonofficials was not automatic, no doubt reflecting
the uncertainty of the organizers as to who should
be welcomed into the association. When the prospectus of the body was published in March 1884, the
sponsors went so far as to specify their preference
for the proficient of the High School, the graduate
of the university, the pleader of the district
court, the *dubash* of the agency house, and members
of the landed gentry. It was obvious that the association was to be essentially elitist in character,
drawing its membership from the ranks of the professional elite and the wealthier classes in the
region. However, when the constitution was finally
adopted in May 1884, the restrictive clauses were
generally discarded. Annual subscriptions were reduced from three to one rupee, while membership was
thrown open to "any Native of more than 21," provided he was recommended by any two members.[42]

In retaining the principle of recommendation
in admitting members, the Madras Mahajana Sabha
still had a built-in safeguard against any indis-
criminate stampeding of its portals by unwanted elements. Although there is no actual evidence of any
interest or social group being deliberately refused
admission, there is no mistaking the fact that the
Madras Mahajana Sabha remained an elitist body with
a fairly small membership. In June 1885, a year
after its formation, it had 205 members on its
rolls.[43] By May 1886 the total had climbed to 796,
aided largely by accessions from *mofussil* areas.[44]
However, for the rest of the century, the membership figure remained almost static.

It would be wrong to measure the influence of the Madras Mahajana Sabha purely in terms of the number of members on its rolls. A truer index of its influence would be to assess the strength of its affiliated associations spread out over the various parts of the Presidency. The constitution of the Madras Mahajana Sabha had empowered its leaders to "affiliate with itself any other Association in Madras or in the mofussil aiming at the same object."[45] The obvious advantage of this scheme of affiliation was that it provided a formula for the central association to link itself with the numerous societies and clubs already functioning in South India. The alternative to this would be to set up branch associations, but this posed many difficulties, including the danger of stirring up an element of friction with the already existing associations. This was the kind of danger which the leaders of the Madras Mahajana Sabha were anxious to avoid, lest it threatened their aims of fostering the slowly developing sentiments of provincial unity. Hence, wherever possible, they opted for the affiliation scheme and stressed to the local leaders that affiliation with the central association would not necessarily impede the local leaders' freedom of pursuing their own objectives. However, where there were no local associations, the Committee of the Madras Mahajana Sabha had to take the initiative in organizing branch bodies, either by writing letters to local leaders or by sending one of its own members to visit the *mofussil* centre. Such efforts appear to have had a fair degree of success in the early years. By August 1888 a total of eighty-two local associations or branch bodies had come to be linked with the central body in Madras.[46] Almost every town in the Presidency could now boast of its own local association, and the Madras Mahajana Sabha provided the common thread linking them together.

The kind of ties which developed between the central association and its widely dispersed affiliates depended to some extent on the personality of

the "Corresponding Member." The latter was the
link through whom the central leadership maintained
liaison with the affiliated associations. It is
not clear as to who chose the Corresponding Member
or on what basis the selection was made. Presumably, the same considerations which influenced the
selection of the Committee of the Madras Mahajana
Sabha also determined the choice of the Corresponding Members. Education was an important factor:
of the forty-two Corresponding Members selected for
the year 1886-87, twenty- nine had a university degree or passed the pleadership examinations. Not
surprisingly, the lawyers were the dominant occupational group: no less than twenty-four of the forty-
two were lawyers practising in the *mofussil* courts.
Of the remaining eighteen, four were teachers, two
journalists, two merchants, one *zamindar*, while the
vocations of the rest were not known.[47] Clearly,
the professional elite was exercising the same
decisive influence in *mofussil* politics as in the
metropolis. Wherever a small nucleus of this group
existed, it hastened to organize a political association, and link its fortunes with those of the
Madras Mahajana Sabha.

More often than not, it was the most energetic
and talented politician in the *mofussil* who was
chosen as the Corresponding Member. Among those
who served in this position in 1886-87 was C. Vijiaraghava Chari, "the Salem Patriot," whose legal
battles to vindicate the innocence of the Salem
prisoners had earned him an all-India reputation.
In December 1881 he and a few other local leaders
had organized the Salem Mahajana Sabha. However,
with the outbreak of communal violence, the Salem
Mahajana Sabha became dormant, but it was reacti-
vated in the early months of 1884, when Vijiaraghava Chari led the fight for the release of the
prisoners.

Another prominent name in the list of Corresponding Members was N. Subha Rao, representing
Rajahmundry. He was one of the six young men who
conceived the idea of starting the *Hindu*, but on

passing his law examinations he had decided to return to his native district where he established a
lucrative practice. He was an active figure in
local affairs, but it was his association with
Viresalingam Pantalu in the widow remarriage movement which earned him more than a local renown.[48]
    Another well-known figure in *mofussil* politics
was S. V. Subbarayudu, Corresponding Member of
Masulipatam. A lawyer by profession, he was a member of the Local Fund Board and Municipality, and
contributed generously to charities and public
movements.[49]
    A man of similar stature in Tanjore district
at this time was S. A. Saminatha Iyer. For many
years he had been a Pleader in Negapatam, where he
was a member of the Municipality, and helped in
organizing the Native Association in 1882. Later,
he moved to Kumbaconam, and in September 1885 was
elected President of the Tanjore People's Association.[50]
    Dominating the political scene in Gooty,
Anantapur district, was P. Kesava Pillay. A Pleader, he was involved in almost every public movement in the district, and at the time was an
occasional correspondent of the *Hindu*.
    Others who featured in this list of Correspon-
ding Members included C. Jambulingam Mudaliar, a
Pleader in Cuddalore, S. P. Narasimulu Naidu, editor of the Anglo-Vernacular paper called *Coimbatore
Crescent*, K. Venkata Rao, Pleader in Bellary, Paul
Peter Pillay, a teacher representing Srivilliputtur,
Tinnevelly district, and C. Kunhi Raman Menon, editor of the *Kerala Patrika* of Calicut.

EARLY PROVINCIAL CONFERENCES

    A significant innovation in the evolution of
agitational techniques in South India was the decision of the Madras Mahajana Sabha to convene "a
Conference of Gentlemen representing various parts
of the Presidency" in order to bring about "a

periodical exchange of thoughts between Madras and
the Mofussil."[51] Unlike earlier associations in
South India, whose activities were restricted to
public meetings, deputations, lectures, and memorials, the Madras Mahajana Sabha took a new leaf out
of the book of constitutional agitation by convening periodic conferences, attended by delegates
from the affiliated associations in the Presidency,
to formulate an agreed upon program for political
action.

To some extent the very character of the
Madras Mahajana Sabha demanded this new departure.
Being an organization embracing a large number of
disparate local associations, it could not easily
frame a readily acceptable political program. The
constitution of the Madras Mahajana Sabha had vested immediate responsibility for policy formation
in the Committee which had some built-in provisions
to guide it in its efforts to ascertain the feelings of the affiliated bodies before committing
them to any line of policy or action. The appointment of Corresponding Members offered one channel
of contact between the Committee and the scattered
affiliates, while the right of the latter to nominate members to sit on the Committee furnished
another means of contact and consultation. If the
former was a rather tenuous link, the latter right
was rarely invoked. Indeed, neither of these provisions afforded scope for a regular and systematic
exchange of views between the central caucus and
the affiliated associations.

It was partly an appreciation of these shortcomings that persuaded the Committee to convene a
provincial conference in Madras in December 1884.
All affiliated associations were notified in September. There was guarded optimism about the response to this invitation, especially since the
Madras Fair was scheduled to take place at the same
time.[52] Moreover, the Christmas season witnessed
the annual Convention of the Theosophical Society
in Madras, and this event was bound to attract a
number of influential *mofussil* leaders who were

also members of the Madras Mahajana Sabha.

The Conference, delayed slightly by the inter-
ruption of rail services, started on 29 December,
attended by over seventy delegates. The great
majority came from the *mofussil*, especially from
the Tamil districts, notably Salem, Tanjore, Madura,
Tinnevelly, and Chingleput. Also significant was
the response from such remote Telugu centers as
Bellary, Gooty, Anantapur, and Rajahmundry. The
presence of three delegates from Bangalore also provoked interest, especially as affairs concerning
the Indian States remained outside the scope of the
gathering. Conspicuous by their absence were the
west coast districts of Malabar and South Kanara,
while the extreme northern districts of Vizagapatam
and Ganjam also went unrepresented at the Conference.[53]

The Conference was opened by the President of
the Madras Mahajana Sabha, Rangiah Naidu, who gave
a brief speech of welcome to the delegates present.
Ananda Charlu, one of the two Joint Secretaries,
then explained that the realization of the objectives of the central body necessitated "a free and
frequent interchange of thought" between its affiliated members. He felt that such meetings permitted
the leaders to participate in "the process of stock-
taking and self-improvement," and at the same time
to "enlighten the public with their knowledge and
the result of their labours." Moreover, he believed
that such gatherings were "a crying emergency" to
prevent "a widespread misunderstanding" between the
rulers and the ruled and between "the races making
up the latter." If this "mere alienation of feeling" was allowed to take deep roots, Ananda Charlu
feared that it might develop into "positive antipathy" and might have serious repercussions for the
entire country.[54]

Much of the Conference sessions was devoted to
the reading of lengthy papers on the reform of the
Indian legislative bodies, the separation of revenue from judicial functions, the condition of the
agricultural masses in South India, and the

structure of the Indian Government and the changes
desired.

Of particular interest to the professional
elite was Viraraghava Chari's paper on "Indian legislation and Indian Legislative Councils." In recent years, this subject had attracted growing
attention from the articulate section of the Indian
community anxious to have a voice in the policy-
making organs of their country. Viraraghava Chari
gave expression to the disenchantment of his colleagues with the functioning of the legislatures.
He argued that the Indian Councils Act of 1861 had
only invested limited powers on the legislatures,
while excessive executive interference had almost
reduced them to "a simple Registration office where
the projects of the Executive, however unpopular
and ill-suited as regards time and place, are correctly copied and recorded and preserved." Another
complaint was the imposition of undue restrictions
on nonofficial members. Viraraghava Chari claimed
that nonofficials had not been encouraged to voice
their "independent and conscientious convictions,"
nor had they been nominated to the extent allowed
under the provisions of the Act. Hence, he concluded that nonofficial opinion had not exercised
the degree of influence in legislation anticipated
in 1861. Also he attributed the "several undesir-
able laws" that had been enacted to the "sole and
single circumstance that the Indian legislatures
are not constituted so as to shed on them the light
--the heavenly light--of popular opinion and local
knowledge."

In calling for a fresh installment of constitutional reform, Viraraghava Chari alluded to the
many changes that India had undergone since 1861.
The Indians, he claimed, were "no longer a station-
ary people" and had "to a very great extent out-
grown the conditions of the past." He believed
that the Act of 1861 offered "little scope for improvement" and could not be adapted to the demands
of a changed situation. The important change which
he wanted to be incorporated in the future was the

recognition of the principle of popular representation. "No evil is likely to follow from such a
course," he assured his audience, "but much
strength to Government, as more confidence will be
reposed in them by the people."[55]

The Conference agreed in a resolution that the
existing legislatures provided "little room for the
successful expression of popular opinion and fail
to command that degree of confidence which is so
needful for their efficient working." It was also
agreed that a draft scheme on the reform of the
legislatures was to be prepared for submission to
the government after adoption at the next provincial conference. The other resolution that was
accepted related to the question of executive officers having magisterial functions. The delegates
agreed that "the union of the revenue and magisterial functions in one and the same officer is pro-
ductive of much evil and hardship, and that early
measures should be adopted for their separation."
The Conference spelled out the substance of a memorial which the Committee of the Madras Mahajana
Sabha was to prepare for endorsement at the next
gathering.[56]

The main criticism that could be levelled
against this Conference was the undue amount of
time that was expended in discussing lengthy papers
on fairly general themes rather than formulating
clear-cut resolutions on more specific issues. It
was argued in some circles that the Conference, instead of devoting its energies to all-India issues,
should have discussed subjects of more immediate
concern to the Presidency, notably, the question of
local self-government and the operation of salt and
forest laws.[57] Indeed, when the circular announcing the Conference was issued in September, both
these latter issues had been listed in the agenda.
While the question of salt and forest laws was
touched upon in a general way by delegates discussing the condition of the agricultural classes, the
subject of local self-government was entirely
omitted without any explanation being offered.

Another surprising feature of the Conference
was the omission of the civil service question.
This issue had hung fire ever since the age of entry into the Covenanted Civil Service was reduced
in 1876, and as late as March 1884 a deputation had
waited on the Secretary of State seeking redress.
But Lord Kimberley's blank refusal to restore the
previous age limit gave rise to a renewed outburst
of agitation in India, and in Madras the *Hindu* led
an onslaught on the India Office which continued
almost uninterrupted for four months. At one point,
it attributed Kimberley's refusal to the "unjust
and unfounded jealously of the political advancement of the Natives," and warned that disregard of
past pledges was causing "silent discontent throughout the country."[58] The Madras Mahajana Sabha decided to memorialize the Secretary of State on this
question in October 1884. Expressing "deep regret
and disappointment" over his refusal to raise the
age limit, it contended that the reduction of 1876
had "practically shut out the natives of India from
the Covenanted Civil Service."[59]

If the India Office had hoped to neutralize
the odium that it had incurred over the reduction
of the age limit by creating the Statutory Civil
Service, it must have been disappointed by the
Indian reaction to the experiment. In South India,
the government's insistence on adopting a system of
nomination of candidates, giving priority to considerations of "birth, character, services of
family," rendered the experiment unpopular, especially in the eyes of the professional elite.
Fearing abuse of official patronage, it urged Ripon
in January 1884 to replace the system of nomination
by open competition. Ripon promised to revise the
rules, but when he left the country he had only succeeded in suspending the old rules, which had in
effect given provincial governments wide discretion
in the selection of candidates.[60]

Ripon's promise, not unnaturally, created the
fallacious impression in the mind of the professional elite that the era of patronage had come to

an end. Hence, when the Madras Government selected
three Statutory Civilians on the basis of "limited
competition" in January 1885, there was a fresh
outburst of protest. The Committee of the Madras
Mahajana Sabha called upon the Indian Government to
veto the nominations, contending that the examinations were neither wholly competitive nor the results adequately publicized. The process of
selection, the Committee said, was "highly unpopular with the Native community" and would only discourage "able and intelligent candidates" from
competing.[61] Protests also came from other public
bodies in the Presidency, including the Madras
Graduates Association. The Government of India,
while regretting that the Madras authorities had
not fully explained their procedure of selecting
candidates to the public, upheld the right of the
local administration to devise whatever system it
thought proper.[62]

This reply did not satisfy the leaders of the
Madras Mahajana Sabha who decided to carry their
protest a stage higher by appealing directly to the
Secretary of State. In a memorial to the India
Council in August 1885, the Committee of the association spelled out in detail its views as to how
the rules governing entry into the Statutory Civil
Service might be rendered more equitable. The
basic change that was advocated was to limit selections "compulsorily in the first instance" to those
who had attained "eminence in Government service or
in a learned profession." Only if these two sources of talent had been "earnestly searched and exhausted" was the government to turn elsewhere.
Where the latter was necessary, the Committee of
Madras Mahajana Sabha felt that the "competitive
examination should be accepted as the sole and
final test" in the selection, thereby minimizing
"the chances of abuse of patronage and injustice to
the public at large."[63]

However, when the Committee met in September
1885 to draft the agenda for the second provincial
conference to be held at the end of the year, the

civil service issue was again omitted. This gathering was committed to discuss two subjects which had
been deferred at the last meeting, namely, the reform of the Indian legislatures and the separation
of revenue from judicial functions. Besides, three
other themes were listed in the agenda for discussion: the operation of forest and salt laws in
South India, the establishment of an Arbitration
Court, and the promotion of indigenous industries
in the Presidency.[64] The inclusion of the latter
themes was partly the outcome of recent developments. The constitution of the Bombay Forest Commission earlier in the year led to demands in the
press for a similar inquiry in South India. The
Madras Times had first put forward this suggestion
and had urged the Madras Mahajana Sabha to undertake the task of collecting information and bringing to light "authentic cases of hardship" resulting from the operation of the forest laws. The
proposal was welcomed by the *Hindu* which urged the
Committee of the association to include the issue
in the agenda of the forthcoming conference.[65] The
Committee agreed, framed interrogatories on forest
and salt laws, and circulated them to all its
affiliated bodies.[66]
    The inclusion of this subject was welcomed by
the affiliated associations. In many towns, the
leaders of associations convened public meetings to
explain the objectives of the provincial conference
and to discuss the proposed agenda. At the same
time, steps were also taken to gather data on the
working of the forest and salt rules. In many instances, small teams were sent out into the rural
areas to interview the *ryots* and ascertain on-the-
spot the grievances of the villagers. In Coimbatore, for example, a deputation of six leaders,
including Narasimulu Naidu, made an extensive tour
of the villages in the district to collect data on
the operation of forest laws. Most of the information that was gathered was forwarded to the office
of the Madras Mahajana Sabha, while petitions and
other written complaints also flowed in from

independent sources.[67]

The second provincial conference assembled in
Madras on 23, 24 and 25 December 1885. The *mofussil* was adequately represented, with twenty-one
centers sending a total of forty-four delegates.
Especially heartening to the organizers was the presence of large delegations from Gooty and Anantapur,
while Tanjore district retained its reputation as
the politically most advanced in the *mofussil* by
sending the largest number of delegates. Although
Ganjam was represented in this Conference, Viza-
gapatnam, Malabar, and South Kanara had sent no
delegates.[68] A novel feature of the gathering was
the presence of *ryots*. Both Coimbatore and Vellore
had included a number of *ryots* in their deputations
to give weight to the evidence which they had amassed about the forest and salt laws.[69]

The opening day of the Conference, after in-
troductory speeches from the President and Joint
Secretary of the Madras Mahajana Sabha, was devoted
entirely to the discussion of the two draft memorials that had been prepared on the reform of the
Indian legislatures and the separation of revenue
from judicial functions. The former memorial departed little from the proposals which Viraraghava
Chari had made a year earlier. This document, endorsed by the Conference without any modification
and forwarded to the Secretary of State, urged the
introduction of the elective principle in the selection of nonofficials to the legislative councils.

One of the difficulties was the question of
the electorate. It was at once conceded that universal franchise was not feasible, but it was believed that a start could be made with "a limited
electorate, provided that such an electorate might
be shown in its turn to have been formed on an
elective basis." The obvious choices were the municipal and local boards, and it was claimed that
these bodies could be converted into electorates on
a territorial or population basis. Other institutions, like universities or chambers of commerce,
if they had acquired "a fairly pronounced

representative status," were to be given seats in
the provincial legislatures. The importance of
minority representation was stressed and the scheme
adopted called for representation of communal minorities in proportion to their numerical strength.

Increased powers were also to be invested in
the legislative bodies, with elected members enjoying the right of interpellation "on matters of
administration, finance and other vital topics."[70]
One obvious gap in this scheme was the failure to
specify the proportion of elective seats in the re-
formed legislatures. Another shortcoming was the
ambiguity surrounding the reconstitution of the
Supreme Legislative Council: the scheme approved by
the Conference appeared to be concerned almost
wholly with provincial legislatures.

The other memorial that was adopted at the
Conference related to the separation of revenue
from magisterial functions. There was some unhappiness among delegates over the government's
refusal to consider this reform because of financial reasons. In deciding to petition the Indian
Government, the Conference wanted to evolve a
scheme which would show that the financial problem
was "not such an insurmountable difficulty as is
generally supposed." It was estimated that the
reform would involve an additional outlay of Rs
50,000 per annum for the Madras authorities. To
offset this new burden, the Conference suggested
certain administrative adjustments to set free the
necessary funds, namely, the amalgamation of Registration and Revenue departments, abolition of the
post of Inspector-General of Registration, and
dissolution of the District Court at Kurnool, as
recommended by the Judicial Reorganization Committee.[71] G. Subramania Iyer, in proposing the
adoption of the scheme at the Conference, asserted
that the proposed reform would end "a relic of
barbarous times" and relieve the district collector
from his multifarious duties and enable him to
"acquaint himself with the feelings and wishes of
the people."[72]

The second and third days of the Conference
were almost exclusively dominated by the controversial forest and salt questions. Emotion-charged
speeches were heard at the Conference for the first
time, emanating not only from *ryots* but also from
delegates who had conducted an independent inquiry
into the working of these laws. Paul Peter Pillay,
speaking from "personal experience," accused forest
officials of conniving with speculators "at the
wanton and unfair denudation of trees for their
illegal income." He contended that forests in
zamindari areas, where these irksome laws did not
exist, were "better controlled and managed."[73]
Narasimulu Naidu, who had carried out a special inquiry into the working of the forest laws in
Coimbatore district, asserted that the Forest
Department was "a costly establishment, and the
gain to Government nil." He described in vivid
terms the hardships which some of the villagers
suffered, especially those who lived in the hills.
Being very poor and knowing no English, they were
victims of persecution by forest officials. He
ended his speech with an impassioned appeal on behalf of his constituents who had sent him and some
others "for representing their grievances to this
assembly hoping sincerely thereby that you at least
would appeal to the proper authorities and have
their grievances redressed: you may thus see that
we don't crave for a higher civilisation in our
country, for the introduction of a greater number
of coaches, chairs, railways, watches and other
luxuries."[74] Speeches in a similar vein, though
not with the same degree of intensity, were made
against the salt laws. The Conference ended by
passing resolutions calling for separate government
inquiries into the working of the forest and salt
rules in South India.[75]
    Though the discussion of the salt and forest
issues was a concession to a deeply felt rural
grievance, it should not conceal the fact that
these provincial conferences constituted essentially the forum of the professional elite. These

young urban-based politicians, who owed their existence to the professions which British rule had
largely created in South India, were pragmatic reformers seeking to influence British policy rather
than revolutionaries intending to overthrow the Raj.
In the main, the reforms that they advocated were
designed to give Indians a larger voice in the administration of the country, notably, through recasting the legislatures by admitting a nonofficial
element elected on the basis of a limited franchise.
The professional elite felt confident that such a
change would not only acquaint Indians with the
processes of government but would also enable them
to ventilate more effectively their grievances and
even seek their removal from within.

That there was a deeply seated distrust of the
executive among the ranks of this elite is evident
in the sentiments that were voiced in these provincial conferences. With memories of the excesses
of the Grant Duff Administration still fresh in
their minds, the delegates at these sessions devoted considerable attention towards finding ways
and means of checking the power of the bureaucracy.
The proposed reform of the legislatures promised to
be one source of check. The popularly elected
element was expected to probe deeply into official
iniquities of any kind. Another check was the separation of revenue from judicial functions. The
fusion of these functions had long been regarded as
a source of official abuse, with the agricultural
classes left to the mercy of grasping revenue officials. Moreover, in the eyes of the professional
elite, this fusion was an anachronism, inconsistent
with modern governmental practice.

As the curtain came down on the second provincial conference, an important era in the political
evolution of South India also drew to a close.
This era had begun with the search by politicians
in Madras for a new and cohesive presidency-wide
organization. Following the successful inauguration of the Madras Mahajana Sabha in 1884, the
metropolitan leaders moved quickly to forge ties

with the plethora of local associations and literary societies which had already come into existence
in the *mofussil*. That the latter agreed to join
the Sabha was in some measure due to the fact that
their leaders shared a certain identity of interest
with their counterparts in Madras, attributable in
large measure to their shared educational and professional backgrounds. Just as compelling were the
tangible benefits that could be derived through
united action. Politicians in Madras and the *mofussil* recognized that their coming together under the
umbrella of a single provincial organization would
allow them to widen their political horizons: they
would no longer be local leaders concerned with
local problems. For the same reason, these politicians also welcomed the idea of provincial conferences. Such gatherings would elevate them from the
status of local politicians to leaders of provincial fame.

Equally revealing, in this period of rapid
political change, was the fact that barely within
hours of the termination of the second provincial
conference, no less than seventeen of the delegates,
ten from the *mofussil* and seven from Madras, took
the train bound for Bombay to attend the first
meeting of the Indian National Congress scheduled
to begin a few days later. This transition from
provincial to all-India politics might seem sudden,
but it was a transition for which the prominent
leaders of the professional elite had prepared
themselves during the past few years.

6. The Congress and Communal Politics in South India

The growth of national political consciousness was an event of recent origin and was largely the creation of that small class of Western-educated Indians congregating in the larger urban centers of India. In the South, it was the professional elite which consistently espoused the cause of all-India unity. In the speeches of its leaders, in its writings in the press, and in the activities of its associations, this elite not only stressed the importance of national unity for the political regeneration of the country but also discussed the practical ways in which such unity ought to be realized. What imparted a sense of urgency to such designs was the Ilbert Bill episode. If some of the manifestations of the European agitation against this measure had divided the rulers and the ruled along racial lines, the decision of the government to go back on its proposals emphasized to the Indians their own disunity and organizational weakness. This feeling of inadequacy prompted some Indian groups to seek more effective forms of political expression. The convening of the Indian National Congress in 1885 demonstrated the determination of these groups to surmount the traditional barriers of caste, language, and region in their bid to offset the tide of European reaction in India.

THE CONVENING OF THE INDIAN NATIONAL CONGRESS

Prior to 1880, politicians in South India could hardly claim to have been zealous advocates of inter-regional cooperation. This stemmed less from the absence of opportunities than from the infancy of political life which made it almost impossible to build up any kind of durable links between the different regional centers of political activity. For example, at the height of the Lex Loci agitation in 1850, talks between the leaders of Calcutta and Madras on the feasibility of making a united protest failed despite the fact that the issue had stirred strong Hindu emotions.[1] Ultimately, Bengal and Madras submitted separate protest memorials against the measure. Similarly, when the British Indian Association sought to enlist the cooperation of the different Indian centers in making joint representations on the Charter question, the attempt floundered on the rocks of regional suspicions and misunderstandings. While Poona and Bombay formed their separate associations, Madras endured a short and uneasy partnership with Bengal before going its own way in 1852. When these associations drafted their petitions to the British Parliament, it was clear that, though they were seeking broadly similar objectives, they either lacked the will or had not found the means to translate their common purpose into some kind of united political action.

If the politicians recoiled from further ventures for some years after these early failures, the social reformers did not appear to display a similar reticence. The lead was taken by the Brahmo Samaj which during the 1860s made a bold attempt to carry the torch of its reformist message beyond its Bengali frontiers. In February 1864 Keshub Chandra Sen was deputed by the Brahmo Samaj to go on a lecture tour of South and Western India. His powerful and eloquent oratory, as well as his persuasive skill, had the desired effect. In Madras his appeal led to the formation of the Veda

Samaj a month after his departure. Bombay also
responded, and the Prarthana Samaj--described as "a
sister church" of the Brahmo Samaj--was organized
in 1867.[2] By this time, similar inroads were being
made into the North-Western Provinces and the Punjab owing to the exertions of Sen and his "itiner-
ant missionaries" from Bengal, and an expanding
network of Brahmo Samaj branches was beginning to
link the important centers of British India. Sig-
nificantly, Sen had also established in Calcutta a
new "Brahmo Samaj of India" in 1866 which was indicative of his confidence in enlisting countrywide
support for his movement.

Keshub Chandra Sen, however, was more than a
mere social reformer engaged in overthrowing idolatry, changing marriage customs, or combatting caste
exclusiveness. He was also an ardent believer in
the cause of all-India unity and he looked to the
Western-educated class, or the "Young India" as he
called it, to bring about the "national reformation." In his speeches, he stressed the degenerate
state into which the country had sunk, suggested
ways of finding a remedy, and urged the educated
class to take the lead.[3]

Make a small beginning. Let there be a dozen
men in Bombay, a dozen in Madras, and a dozen
in the Punjab, and we shall form the nucleus
of a general confederation--one caste for all
the educated natives of India,--and then we
shall take in all other classes of the native
communities, and unite in a vast and mighty
confederation.

Similar sentiments were also voiced by the regular
stream of Bengali reformers spanning the subcontinent during the 1870s and after. South India received its due quota of such missionaries who
organized congregations, became teachers in areas
where there was a shortage of qualified English
teachers, and participated in charitable and social
work, especially during the famine years of 1876-78.

Such activities, though of a modest nature, nevertheless demonstrated that there were areas of common interest in which men from different regional backgrounds could cooperate meaningfully. Also, the barriers of regional exclusiveness, for long nurtured by lack of personal contacts, began to collapse gradually as Bengali Samajists began to roam the subcontinent and recruits from different parts of the country went to Bengal for their training.

Some of the Bengali Samajists who came South were also members of the Indian Association which, since its foundation in 1876, had been zealously pursuing its declared objective of unifying "the Indian races and peoples upon the basis of common political interests and aspirations." One member of the Indian Association who made a strong political impact on Madras was Bipin Chandra Pal of the Sadharan Brahmo Samaj. On his way to Bangalore in September 1881, Pal delivered a stirring speech in Madras on the subject of "National Improvement." Much of his speech was a plea for all-India unity to redeem a people "groaning under foreign misrule." Though he agreed that India in the past was a mere "geographical entity," he was confident that one day it would become "one homogeneous nation."[4]

> It is an Utopian idea. It is a chimera, but from history I have learnt that India, notwithstanding our 100 religions and 200 languages, will prosper and flourish. The histories of Germany, Italy and Switzerland tell us that we should not despair, and there shall be a day when the Madrassee shall embrace the Bengalee and walk hand in hand with each other. That day is not far off.

There is no doubt that politicians in search of all-India unity found much that was instructive in the achievements of the Brahmo Samaj. In establishing branch bodies, in undertaking lecture tours, and in cultivating personal ties with leaders in other parts of the country, Keshub Chandra Sen and

his fellow Samajists had provided a model of action
which the Indian Association imitated with considerable success during the late 1870s. Utilizing
every opportunity to stir up political activity inside and outside Bengal, the Indian Association
seized upon the unpopular measures of Lytton's viceroyalty to mount an all-India agitation. The reduction of the age of entry into the civil service in
1876 provided the first important cause to organize
"a national movement." The views of its branches
were ascertained, a memorial was drafted, and S. N.
Banerjea was deputed as special delegate to enlist
support of other centers throughout the country.
Banerjea's extensive tours took him to Madras in
January 1878 where he urged the leaders to submit a
protest memorial on the civil service issue.[5] This
procedure was repeated, with some variations in detail, when the Vernacular Press Act was passed in
1878 and duties on cotton imports were partially
abolished a year later.[6] In these issues, the
Indian Association had sought to demonstrate that
there were areas of common interest in which inter-
regional cooperation was feasible.

Politicians in South India, particularly the
members of the professional elite, were sufficiently impressed by the dedication and organizational
skill of their Bengali counterparts to explore some
practical ways of achieving all-India unity.
Ananda Charlu, while speaking on the cotton duties
issue in June 1879, advocated the formation of an
"Indian Association having branches in every town
where intelligent men can muster together, for the
purpose of forming and disseminating their opinions." He expressed regret that because of "the
want of intercommunication between the different
Presidencies, or rather between the different towns
where men of intelligence ought to be found, movements are made in one part without any consultation
whatever with parties in the other."[7]

Ananda Charlu's idea of an all-India organization was echoed by N. Sivasamy Iyer, a graduate of
Madras University. In a scheme he outlined in May

1880 for the formation of a "National Congress" or "Hindu Mahajana Sabha," Sivasamy Iyer called for the setting up of an all-India body with branches in every village, district, and region, supported by a National Fund to be collected with the help of editors of newspapers throughout the country. He claimed that only through organization could India achieve "true regeneration," as well as advance towards the goal of representative government.[8]

The editor of the *Hindu* agreed. Citing the example of Ireland, the editor argued in May 1881 that India's political regeneration depended upon the people's capacity "to combine for national purpose." The work of the British Indian Association and the Poona Sarvajanik Sabha was praised, but the editor wondered whether

. . . India's interests, so varied and so vast as they are, [can] be successfully fought by one or two political bodies acting at random and at great distance from one another, however able and patriotic these Associations may be? We fear not. To carry home, therefore, to the mind of the English public the strength of public opinion in India on any public question, there ought to be a large number of Associations scattered through the various parts of the country, whose duty is to create public opinion and represent it to the Government.[9]

The editor of the *Hindu* was obviously more concerned with the need to stimulate political activity through better organization than with devising a scheme whereby Indian people could "combine for national purpose." However, in January 1883, when a number of associations had emerged on the Indian political scene, the editor was prepared to indicate the kind of all-India cooperation he thought was feasible. He had learned of the proposal of the Indian Association to hold "an annual national congress" in some central city to which "native gentlemen from different parts of the country were to be invited." If this idea was impractical, the editor of the *Hindu* asked whether "the associations that have been started in several important towns throughout the country cannot arrange to depute delegates to meet in a central place. They can devise a scheme of perpetual constitutional agitation and thereby provide a means of bringing the united Indian public opinion to the notice of Government or Parliament in a manner the force of which it will be impossible for the Anglo-Indian or the English public to mistake." The editor contended that the moment had arrived for concerted action:[10]

At present much of our energies are scattered and wasted by want of organised action. What an individual association or a local population represent to government as a grievance of the country is generally treated as the outcome of some intriguing and ambitious mind and consequently the representation though possibly based on existing facts is little heeded by Government. Therefore those various local energies should command an organised and central outlet which will command the attentive hearing of the authorities as being the genuine public feeling.

What gave this appeal a note of conviction was the European agitation against the Ilbert Bill. The rapidity with which the Europeans had formed the Anglo-Indian Defence Association, the skill and intensity with which they mounted the assault on the measure and its authors, and the disdain they showed towards Indian claims for equal rights were enough to create widespread Indian alarm throughout the country. Even if the Indians for tactical reasons decided against counterdemonstrations, for fear of aggravating racial tensions, it was nevertheless apparent that some kind of all-India cooperation was necessary to neutralize the propaganda of the Anglo-Indian Defence Association and put forward the authoritative opinion of the Indian people as a whole. The editor of the *Hindu*, moved by these considerations, wrote in July 1883:[11]

> The time for half-measures, and half-hearted action is gone; that for united and sustaining efforts has arrived. The two hundred and fifty millions living in this vast continent should no longer regard themselves as inhabitants of different provinces bound together by no common interest or common grievances. They have become the nation of a great and flourishing empire; their interests have been unified; and they must henceforth stand or fall together.

This was preaching to the converted. By now, such exhortations had almost given way to the formulation of practical schemes for all-India cooperation. One scheme that was widely discussed at this time was the starting of an Indian journal in England. The editor of the *Hindu* believed that this scheme was feasible and urged that provincial committees be formed to find subscribers and contributors.[12]

Another scheme that was floated at this juncture was the National Fund. The Indian Association had launched such a fund in July 1883 to find resources to continue its political work. The editor of the *Hindu*, while welcoming any proposal to promote "native interests as distinct from those of the Anglo-Indians," urged the leaders of the various provincial organizations to initiate consultations so as to determine "the objects on which the fund is to be spent, the amount of the fund, and the rules to direct its distribution and apportionment among the different provinces of the country." The projects to which the editor wanted this fund to be applied included running of a weekly journal in London, providing Indians with scholarships for competing in the civil service examinations and undergoing technical education, and maintaining of permanent delegates in England for "creating public

opinion on Indian questions and obtaining redress
for Indian grievances."[13]

However, it was the Indian Association's idea
of holding "an annual conference of representatives
from various parts of the country" which appealed
most strongly to the editor of the *Hindu*. Such
gatherings, the paper believed, would "have the invaluable effect of harmonising local feelings, diffusing public spirit, and creating and consolidating native public opinion. Backward provinces will
be stimulated into activity and those that are advanced will lend the benefit of their experience
and knowledge."[14] When it was announced in November 1883 that the International Exhibition was to
be held at Calcutta in the following month, the
Hindu was quick to remark that this occasion provided "a splendid opportunity for having a grand
National Conference in Calcutta." Urging the
Indian Association to take full advantage of this
chance, the paper advised that leaders from all
parts of the country be invited for this gathering
to discuss such important issues as the National
Fund, local self-government, civil service examinations, mass education, and the Arms Act.[15] It is
clear that the *Hindu* was not entirely happy with
the way in which the first National Conference was
organized and it remarked that the Indian Association should hold the next session at "a more central place and in a more favourable season of the
year."[16]

There is little doubt, looking at this plethora of schemes and projects for achieving all-
India cooperation, that Indian politicians were by
and large still groping in their attempts to give
concrete expression to their all-India identity.
In part, this plethora of schemes stemmed from the
existence of different political groups all simultaneously engaged in pushing their particular projects without adequate consultation with each
other.

One such group was the leadership of the Indian Association. Since its foundation, this body

had thought of an all-India memorial on the civil
service question, floated a National Fund, and convened the National Conference. These schemes had
a mixed reception from the other centers of political activity in the country, largely because the
leaders of the Indian Association had not allowed
for prior consultation with their counterparts in
other provinces.

A second group, functioning independently of
the Indian Association, gathered around A. O. Hume,
generally recognized as the "father of the Indian
National Congress." Since his retirement from the
Indian Civil Service in 1882, Hume had established
his home in Simla and had begun to turn his energies to politics and philantrophy. He became a con-
fidant of Lord Ripon and some of the viceroy's advisers who wanted a trustworthy agent to establish
ties with the Indian politicians. The latter, as
Anil Seal says, "esteemed Hume as the man who could
tell them what Viceregal Lodge was thinking."[17] It
is difficult to be precise as to who were Hume's
friends, but there is no doubt that he sought his
friends from the Western-educated class--whom he
called "the soul of the [Indian] nation"[18]--which
included prominent officials, lawyers, and newspaper editors. In a letter to the *Pioneer* in April
1883, Hume listed as his "friends" the editors of
the *Hindu Patriot, Indian Mirror, Hindu, Indian
Spectator, Amrita Bazar Patrika,* and *Tribune*. Sig-
nificantly, there was no mention of the editor of
the *Bengalee,* S. N. Banerjea, the prominent leader
of the Indian Association.[19] Hume was also connected with the Theosophical Society, which had established branches in leading Indian centers after
1879 and held annual conventions attended by European and Indian members. Hume was President of an
Anglo-Indian branch in Simla, and although his connections with the Theosophical Society ended soon
afterwards, there is no doubt that his friendship
with many Indian Theosophists survived this rupture.[20]

Hume's intervention in Indian politics, as

judged from his letters of the time, sprang from
his fear that continuing alienation between British
authority and the subject people might eventually
lead to a dangerous catastrophe. In a private
letter to Ripon in 1882, Hume claimed that "for
years past India has been becoming more or less
saturated with discontent--with dissatisfaction if
not positive disloyalty . . . Day after day the
saturation was & is increasing partly owing to the
gradual change in the character of our Govt., partly to the gradual change in the relations between
district officers & their people, partly to the
growth of education & partly to other causes too
numerous to mention. Sooner or later as things
were going a catastrophe was inevitable."[21] However, to Hume's relief, Ripon's viceroyalty had
"changed everything for the better." According to
Hume, Ripon had succeeded in converting "as though
with the wand of a magician, universal sullen discontent into widespread and enthusiastic loyalty,"
and "restored the people's waning belief in British
honesty of purpose and good faith." Equally, Hume
believed that Ripon's reforms had had the effect of
rendering "the whole country once more wholly amenable to the intellectual guides." He regarded the
latter as "the brains of India" who were also
"unwaveringly on the side of the British Government." To ensure that this class continued to play
its role in maintaining the political equilibrium
in India, Hume wanted it to be justly treated, lest
its task of keeping "the pulses of the body at an
equal flow" be made more difficult.[22]

Hume was anxious that the Western-educated
Indians should organize themselves, partly to overcome their own numerical weakness and partly to
demonstrate on important occasions that they were
capable of speaking with one voice for the country
as a whole. It is not known with what kind of pre-
conceptions Hume set about to achieve this, though
it is evident that he favored the idea of setting
up caucuses consisting of trusted friends in the
important centers of the country. Nothing is known

as to how many such caucuses were set up or who exactly was recruited into them. However, by the early months of 1883, Hume's handiwork was beginning to attract the public eye through the movement set afoot to secure an extension of Lord Ripon's viceroyalty by sending numerous memorials to Queen Victoria. Meetings were held in all prominent Indian cities, and addresses were adopted expressing India's confidence in the ability and the policies of the Viceroy. In May 1883 Hume informed Ripon that he had seen several of these addresses and said that they would be submitted "through the usual channels." Hume also expressed his suspicions that the Queen might be "against us" but felt that these addresses *"might* have some effect upon her ideas."[23]

In 1884 Hume's caucuses went through the same motions in supporting Ripon's efforts to raise the age of entry into the civil service. In April 1884, at Ripon's suggestion, Hume had called upon his Indian allies throughout the country "to strengthen the Viceroy's hands by numerous and influential memorials couched in moderate language and addressed to the Secretary of State."[*] The suggestion was accepted, and in the months that followed meetings were held and memorials were adopted by every important Indian association in the country.

However, it was the occasion of Ripon's departure from India that provided Hume's caucuses, or "head centres" as he called them, with an unrivalled opportunity to demonstrate their latent capacity for organization and united political action. In September 1884 the Simla correspondent of the

---

[*]Hume's letter was published in the Anglo-Indian papers, though they failed to identify the writer. Hume remarked to Ripon's Private Secretary: "There having been *some* treachery *somewhere.*" *Ripon Papers,* Add. MSS. 43616, Hume to Primrose, n.d.

Indian Mirror, most probably Hume, called for "a grand farewell demonstration to Lord Ripon for his large-hearted, liberal, and statesmanlike policy, which he has tried to inaugurate in this country."[24] The proposal was warmly welcomed by the Indian press throughout the country. The *Hindu*, while calling for strong support for the demonstrations, enumerated the many debts which India owed to the departing Viceroy:[25]

> He has created in this short period in the minds of the people of this country an interest in its affairs; he has put into their minds the notion quite new to them that they have an interest in the manner in which their country is governed . . . He has also brought home to us the idea of self-government, an idea quite foreign in its present form to our national traditions and instincts. He has given a shape and a mould to national aspirations and has pointed to us not only a legitimate goal of ambition, but the road that lies to it.

For almost two months, the Indian press waged a publicity campaign to stir up popular enthusiasm for the farewell demonstrations. In November 1884 a large public meeting, attended by all shades of Indian opinion, was held in Madras in which it was resolved that an address would be presented by a deputation to Lord Ripon at Bombay.[26] Similar meetings were held in other *mofussil* towns in South India, as indeed throughout India as a whole. Ripon's final journey from Simla to Bombay, stretching over five weeks and linking the main towns of North India, proved to be, in the words of one observer, "a triumphal march, such as India had never witnessed--a long procession, in which seventy million people sang hosanna to their friend."[27] Bombay climaxed the entire demonstration. To this western metropolis came countless deputations from various parts of the country, including twelve from

South India.

Neither discerning European observers nor Indian politicians had any fundamental misconceptions about the significance of the farewell demonstrations for Lord Ripon. W. A. Porter, for many years Principal of Kumbaconam College, told an Indian audience in Tanjore: "In the last days of Lord Ripon's Viceroyalty you found out that native opinion had surprising unanimity and volume. All over India men were moved by the same feeling and spoke the same language. Opinion had organised itself."[29] To those who conceived the demonstrations, the success of their venture was hailed as the "first achievement of national India." According to the *Hindu*, whose editor was a prominent participant in the affair, the demonstrations were not merely the expression of Indian gratitude to the departing Viceroy but also aimed "to prove to the world the existence of a powerful native opinion which is capable of organisation and which has acquired a consciousness of its importance and strength." The demonstrations, the paper claimed, were "a distinctly political movement" intended to show "the change that has come over the political feeling and knowledge of the people, and its growing intensity and width."[30]

If the testimony of some of the Madras leaders who attended the Bombay demonstrations is to be believed, it was on this occasion that the idea of the Indian National Congress was actually mooted. In March 1888 the editor of the *Hindu*, countering Raghunatha Rao's claim that the Congress was conceived at Madras following the Convention of the Theosophical Society in December 1884, asserted that it was during the Bombay demonstrations that members of the Madras deputation "had a talk with their Bombay friends about a meeting of reformers from different Provinces." Hume was present in these discussions and it was he who was largely instrumental in implementing this idea.[31] Supporting testimony came from another Madras member who had gone to Bombay to bid farewell to Lord Ripon.

Ananda Charlu, in an article he published on the
Indian National Congress in 1903, claimed that it
was at the Bombay demonstrations that the convening
of the Congress "actually took shape and met the
eye." He recounted what actually took place:

> I was a member of the deputation from Madras;
> and among many interesting events, which took
> place on that occasion, was an evening party
> given us all . . . Many and stalwart were the
> men whom I there witnessed and mixed with. It
> was there and among these that for the first
> time, the idea found expression, in terms,
> that an annual gathering should be convened of
> all India, beginning with the next ensuing
> year, so far as delegates might be willing to
> be induced to come to a central city, to dis-
> cuss questions in which the country, *as a
> whole*, may be said to be interested and on
> which a practically unanimous opinion would be
> arrived at and declared.

Ananda Charlu went on to claim that this meeting dispersed without deciding either on the location or the date when the annual convention would
be held. Later, the initiative was taken by the
leaders of Poona, supported by Hume, and it was
they who matured plans to hold the first Congress
there in December 1885.[32]
From the rather fragmentary evidence, it is apparent that Hume played the dominant role in the
organization of the Congress. According to G. Subramania Iyer, who was intimately associated with
the Congress since its birth, Hume not only conceived "the idea of an annual assembly of leading
Indian politicians" but also "worked out a scheme
which included the idea that the Governor of the
Province where the assembly was held should preside
over its deliberations."[33] The latter part of the
scheme was vetoed by Lord Dufferin in May 1885,
but by this time Hume had already helped the Bombay
leaders in forming the Bombay Presidency

Association, visited the various regional centers in the country to consult the leaders and enlist their support, and finally, secured the Viceroy's sympathy for his scheme "to assemble a Political Convention of delegates."[34]

Satisfied with arrangements in India, Hume set sail for England in August where with characteristic energy he met important leaders to inform them of his plans and secure whatever assistance was necessary.[35] The intervention of the British General Elections in November gave Hume and his Indian allies a chance to publicize India's cause before the British electorate. Six political associations, including the Madras Mahajana Sabha, published and distributed "a general address to electors of the United Kingdom on behalf of India."[36] At the same time, three Indian delegates representing Bengal, Bombay, and Madras presidencies were dispatched to England "to interest and inform the British public on Indian matters" and support the candidature of the "friends of India."[37]

When Hume returned to India early in December, it was formally announced that "a Congress of native gentlemen from different parts of India" would be held in Poona at the end of the month.[38] However, the outbreak of cholera in the city led to the change of location to Bombay.

THE SEARCH FOR COMMUNAL SUPPORT

From the preceding discussion, it is clear that the strongest advocates of the cause of all-India unity in the South were the group of politicians who had played an active part in organizing the Madras Mahajana Sabha and the provincial conferences of 1884 and 1885. The *Hindu*, the authoritative spokesman of this group, had been increasingly vocal in its pleas for some concrete scheme for inter-regional cooperation ever since the Anglo-Indians unleashed their campaign against the Ilbert Bill in the early months of 1883. To some extent, this demand was met by the holding of joint public meetings in the various Indian centers to express Indian solidarity on issues of common interest. Without doubt the most successful of such meetings was the staging of the farewell demonstrations to Lord Ripon when numerous delegations from different parts of the country converged on Bombay in December 1884. Hence, when the first Congress met there a year later, the delegates who came belonged mainly to that small group of activists who in the past three years had worked closely with Hume and had been most prominent in holding demonstrations in vindication of Ripon's policies.

Invitations to attend the first Congress were issued by the Poona Sarvajanik Sabha and the Bombay Presidency Association. In response to an invitation, the Madras Mahajana Sabha met on 12 December 1885 and nominated six delegates to represent the metropolis, namely, S. Subramania Iyer, G. Subramania Iyer, Rangiah Naidu, Ananda Charlu, Viraraghava Chari, and T. Nemberumal Chetty.[39] The last named dropped out, but three others were added to the Madras deputation, namely, C. Singaravelu Mudaliar, M. E. Sriranga Chari, and S. V. Athalye, all active members of the Madras Mahajana Sabha. It is apparent that only members of this association were elected as delegates. The *mofussil* nominated thirteen delegates representing twelve towns, and every one of them was either a member of an affiliated body of the Madras Mahajana Sabha or had attended the provincial conferences. Among the conspicuous *mofussil* figures who participated in the Bombay Congress were Sabapathy Mudaliar, Kesava Pillay, Paul Peter Pillay, Saminatha Iyer, Narasimulu Naidu, and Venkata Subbrayudu.[40]

The presence of a relatively large delegation from South India at this Congress gathering, and the active role that its leaders played in the proceedings, did not go unnoticed in the press. The *Indian Mirror*, whose editor was also a delegate, remarked that "Benighted Madras" was "the strongest in point of numbers" and claimed that "in course of

time, Madras will outrun not only Bengal, but every
other Province in the race for progress, though preserving its national characteristics more prominently than any other Province."[41] These sentiments were echoed by the *Tribune:*

> Madras sent the greatest number of delegates,
> all of good education and high social standing.
> They completely enchanted the audience with
> their liberal views and impressive eloquence.
> Clad in conservative Hindu garments, with
> their shining foreheads rubbed with sandal
> after the orthodox Hindu fashion, and speaking
> in eloquent English about the various ways in
> which India should improve her political
> status, they exhibited a spectacle at once
> charming and instructive; charming in as much
> as it was a glorious sight to behold genuine
> Hindus (preserving intact ancient custom of
> their great race) holding the most radical
> views about politics; instructive in as much
> as it was capable of infusing a belief that
> India could improve, to the highest extent de-
> sirable, its political status without becoming
> *Anglicised.*[42]

Although the pro-Congress organs like the *Hindu* hailed the convening of the Congress "as a memorable day in the annals of our national career,"[43]
they could not conceal the fact that the secrecy
that surrounded this gathering had given some credence to the critics' charge that it was "a hole-
and-corner Conference."[44] A controversy soon
started in which the critics of the Congress challenged its claim to speak for all-India, denied
that its delegates represented the country at large,
and cast doubts as to whether the resolutions
passed at Bombay faithfully reflected the will of
the people of India. This controversy convinced
the leaders of the Congress that secrecy was hardly
consistent with a movement seeking to represent all-
India interests. Hence, soon after the delegates

left Bombay, the formal resolutions passed at the
gathering were circulated to the various political
bodies for endorsement by the country at large. In
South India, public meetings were held under the
aegis of the Madras Mahajana Sabha and its affiliates to explain the aims and program of the Congress, and some of them were addressed by delegates
who had participated in the Bombay Congress. These
meetings, to some extent, helped towards enlighten-
ing public opinion in South India as to what the
Congress was attempting to do.

Equally significant was the decision of the
Congress leadership to institute a system of elec-
ting delegates for the second gathering in Calcutta
in December 1886. It was agreed that the practice
that had obtained at the first Congress, when delegates came as "volunteers in the good cause, uncom-
missioned, as a rule, by any constituencies, local
or general," should be replaced by a system where
delegates "ought to receive some public authorisa-
tion from the bodies and communities (or leading
members of the latter) whom they were to represent."[45] When these instructions were received in
October 1886, the Committee of the Madras Mahajana
Sabha transmitted them to its affiliated and other
associations throughout the Presidency urging them
to convene public meetings to elect delegates.
Elections got under way almost immediately, and by
the end of November the names of thirty-six *mofussil* delegates, representing fourteen districts,
were forwarded for submission to Calcutta.[46]
Though perhaps satisfactory in securing some sem-
blance of territorial representation, these elections did not broaden the base of Congress support
in South India by securing the representation of
the various factional and minority groups in the region. In effect, the delegates elected belonged in
large measure to that group which had been actively
associated with the Madras Mahajana Sabha and the
provincial conferences.

However, it was the decision to hold the third
Congress in Madras which stimulated the political

leadership in South India to make an earnest attempt to broaden the base of Congress support in
the Presidency. The success with which the first
two sessions had been staged imposed a responsibility as well as a challenge upon the leaders in
South India. On the one hand, as the *Hindu*
stressed, the Presidency had to demonstrate to the
country at large that it was "not behind any other
part of India in discharging her part of public
obligations."[47] Like Bombay and Calcutta before
her, Madras had to prove that she possessed "a real
capacity for organization and union," qualities regarded as vital to the ultimate success of the
Congress movement. On the other hand, South Indian
politicians were anxious to nurture the continued
growth of "the national principle" and convert the
Congress into "a really representative movement."
It was now freely admitted by the pro-Congress
organs that the attainment of all-India unity was
a gradual process, with every year witnessing "a
triumphant advance in the work of the year preceding." The Calcutta gathering, in the eyes of the
Congress leaders, had had one obvious shortcoming:
the failure to secure Muslim support, an occurrence
which the *Hindu* attributed to "an insidious attempt
. . . made to sow discord and foment sectional
jealousies among the Mohammadan community."[48] The
politicians of South India were anxious to avoid
repetition of this event in Madras.

Muslim politics in South India during the
1880s showed a certain fragmented character. A number of associations had been established, advocating almost identical objectives and sometimes even
involving the same personalities. The first to be
formed was the Anjuman-i-Islamiah, founded in 1876
at a time when there was Muslim anxiety about the
future of Turkey in the face of external aggression.
When Russia declared war on Turkey in 1877, the
leaders of this body launched the Turkish Relief
Fund to remit money to their embattled brethren in
Turkey. However, with the termination of the war
in 1878, the Anjuman-i-Islamiah became dormant

until it was revived in May 1881.

On this occasion, the leaders showed greater concern for their local problems. They wished to ventilate the grievances of the Muslims, work towards reforming "such customs and usages as are injurious to Mussulmans and obstructing their progress," and "establish good fellowship between several sects of Islam, and between the Mussulmans and members of other classes of the community."[49] Humayun Jah Bahadur,* a descendent of Tipu Sultan and a wealthy Shia with large landed and business interests in Madras, was elected as President. Ahmad Mohidin, a member of the Prince of Arcot's staff, was named Secretary, while Mahomed Abdullah Badsha, a wealthy merchant, filled the post of Treasurer. By July 1884 this association had about 500 members on its rolls, had started two schools to educate Muslim youth up to middle school level, and conducted an Urdu paper, called *Ittifaq*, to voice the claims of the community.

A second Muslim association was founded in September 1883 with the inauguration of the Madras Branch of the Central National Mahomedan Association. The parent body had been founded in Bengal in 1878, but its activities had attracted little attention in the South until the arrival of Syed Abdur Rahman in Madras in March 1883. A Bengali Muslim, he had qualified as a barrister in England, and had migrated southwards to practice in the Madras High Court. He was said to belong to "the advanced party" who wished "to create a similar movement in the community as was created by that Irish Barrister who organised the Catholic

---

*Humayun Jah Bahadur (1837-1893) was born and educated in Calcutta before he settled in Madras. He enjoyed the confidence of the local government and was constantly consulted on questions affecting the Muslim community. He served as the Muslim member of the Madras Legislative Council for almost twenty-five years. *Hindu*, 16 December 1893.

Association in Ireland."[50]   In launching this association, one of its founders contended that there
was "no proper channel" for Muslims to communicate
with the government, and he went on to claim that
the body was necessary for the "social, intellectual and political improvements" of the community.
Oddly enough, Humayun Jah Bahadur was elected
"Permanent President" and Mahomed Abdullah Badsha,
Treasurer, although both continued their connection
with the Anjuman-i-Islamiah. Syed Abdur Rahman was
named Secretary, while Mir Ansaruddin, Presidency
Magistrate, and Mahomed Ishak, Assistant Government
Agent at Chepauk, were elected Vice-Presidents.[51]

In October 1885, a third Muslim association
was founded in Madras, called the Anjuman-i-Mufidi-
Ahla-i-Islam. Although the main aim of this body
was to promote industrial education among the Muslims by starting workshops where such crafts as
carpentry, tailoring, and embroidery would be
taught, its leaders also aspired to further the
general interests of the Muslim community. The
President of this body was Lieutenant-Colonel T. O.
Underwood, Paymaster, Carnatic Stipends, who was
largely instrumental in getting industrial workshops established. The post of Secretary was
filled by Syed Mahomed Nizamuddin, a lawyer practicing in the Madras High Court.[52]

With three Muslim associations in the metropolis, all working for broadly similar objectives,
there were the inevitable demands for a single
association to give greater solidity to the demands
of the Muslim community. One advocate of this idea
was C. D. Macleane, Collector of Sea Customs and
Chairman of the Mahomedan Educational Endowment
Fund. In April 1886 Macleane invited the leaders
of the three associations to form a central association. Two of them agreed, but the Anjuman-i-
Mufidi-Ahla-i-Islam refused to join on the grounds
that the committee of the new body had not been
democratically elected.[53] The Central Mahomedan
Association was formally launched in August 1886
with Humayun Jah Bahadur as President and Mohidin

Sheriff, a doctor at a Triplicane hospital, as Secretary.[54] But Muslim solidarity was far from being
achieved as yet in Madras, despite a growing Muslim
concern with the escalating political agitation of
the Hindus through such organizations as the Madras
Mahajana Sabha and the Congress.

In spite of their divisions, which often mirrored personality differences, these Muslim associations were doubtless inchoate expressions of the
community's concern with maintaining its own identity. Although Islam with its institutional controls provided a high degree of inner cohesion, the
Muslims in South India felt themselves to be vulner-
able in the new situation which British rule had
created in the country. While in the past political power and economic influence had compensated
for their lack of numbers, during the nineteenth
century both these sources of strength had been
eroded away. Those who felt this loss most acutely
were the Muslim conquerors and administrators who
had settled in the larger urban centers of South
India. For a time, the loss of political power was
concealed somewhat by the retention of the Nawab-
ships of Kurnool and Arcot which provided employment for a large number of retainers. However, the
Nawabship of Kurnool was abolished in 1839 when the
Nawab was found to be conspiring to overthrow the
British Raj. In 1855 the Nawabship of Arcot was
also abolished, much to the dismay of many Muslims
in the Presidency. Although the Nawab was henceforth recognized as "the first nobleman at Madras,"[55]
that did not disguise the fact that he was a mere
pensioner of the British, shorn of his patronage
and influence. Many Muslim families which in the
past had depended on the Nawab's bounty now swelled
the numbers of Muslim stipendiaries of the state;
some migrated to Hyderabad and other places in
search of a livelihood, while others bore down heavily on those families with landed property or fixed
income.[56]

Economic impoverishment was accompanied by a
marked diminution in the share of high administrative

positions in Muslim hands. In the heyday of their
political power, high appointments in the government had been one source of their affluence, but
such opportunities vanished with the appearance of
the British Raj, while in the middle and lower
rungs of the administrative ladder the Muslims had
to encounter competition from the Hindus. As time
went on, the Muslims fared worse, a condition aggravated no doubt by the introduction of the competitive tests in 1858. Having shunned Western education, the Muslims seemed to have virtually abdi-
cated the field to the more adaptable Hindus. In
1872, when Governor Hobart ordered an inquiry into
the condition of the Muslims in South India, it was
found that Muslims held only 19 out of the 485
elite positions in the judicial and revenue line.
Hobart, concerned that the extinction of the Muslim
element from the higher public service might throw
strong temptation "to disaffection and (should
occasion occur) to conspiracy against the state,"
argued that the revival of Muslim fortunes lay in
their acceptance of Western education.[57]

For almost three decades prior to Hobart's
arrival, that is, since the founding of the Madras
High School, Muslims in South India had set their
face against Western education either through indifference, poverty, or hostility. The coastal Muslims, especially the Mappillas and Labbays, preoccu-
pied with their commercial pursuits and with no
literary tradition, were fundamentally apathetic to
the new learning. They continued to send their
children to the traditional religious schools where
the latter were instructed in the tenets of the
Koran, acquired the rudiments of knowledge, and
learned the local Dravidian language. The Urdu-
speaking Muslims, descendents of the former rulers,
regarded Western education with hostility. Pride
in their own past, resentment of their present
rulers, and opposition to secular instruction as
such, all combined to keep these Muslims away from
the schools and colleges which the British had
established in South India. Hence, by 1872-73 only

sixty-one Muslims had passed their matriculation
while only a single Muslim had taken a B.A. degree.[58]

　　To　tackle this Muslim malaise, Hobart suggested a two-fold remedy. First, he wanted Muslim objections to the existing educational system to be
taken into account. Hobart felt that the system of
instruction was "framed with exclusive reference to
the Hindoos," which left the Muslims at a "serious
disadvantage." To redress this bias, he persuaded
the Department of Public Instruction to establish
special schools for Muslims in areas where they
were numerously concentrated. In such schools, instruction was to be provided in Urdu and English.
Arrangements were to be made to train Muslim teachers, while suitable textbooks were to be secured
from other provinces if necessary. Thus, the so-
called system of "special agency" came into vogue
in 1872, and during the next decade this system was
developed to provide further facilities for Muslim
students, including fee exemptions, reservation of
scholarships, and appointment of Muslims as inspectors of schools.[59]

　　The other remedy which Hobart prescribed for
the Muslim malaise was to remove the general Muslim
impression that the government was disinclined to
admit them into the public service. He secured the
consent of his Council to circulate orders to all
district officers, as well as heads of departments,
calling on them to dispel this impression "in the
most speedy and convincing manner by the employment,
as opportunity offers, of a fair proportion of
those Mahomedans who may have passed the prescribed
tests of qualification, and by the promotion, according to their merits, of those who are already
employed."[60] This gesture, Hobart argued, would
convince Muslims that the government was interested
in their welfare, while at the same time inducing
them to educate their children with a view to public employment.[61] Hobart's remedies seemed to have
achieved some of the desired results, at least in
so far as Western education began to gain in

popularity among the Muslims.

Hobart's endeavors, and the changes in official policy towards Muslim education, created over the next decade or so an incipient class of Western-educated Muslims in South India who were either absorbed into the administration or became lawyers, journalists, teachers, or doctors. It was this class which showed an acute sensitivity to the problems that faced the Muslim community as a whole. Its education had opened its eyes to the fact that in the not too distant past Muslims had enjoyed political power and economic strength and the Hindus were in a position of subservience. But all this had changed radically since the advent of the British Raj, with the Hindus asserting their economic power while their acceptance of Western learning had given them a virtual stranglehold of the modern professions and the middle and lower rungs of the administration of South India. Also alarming to these Muslims was the emergence of Hindu nationalism, finding expression through provincial and all-India associations during the early 1880s, which heightened Muslim consciousness of their own political effeteness and minority status.

In this feeling of helplessness, the Muslims turned outwardly to the British and inwardly to themselves. In the British, they saw an ally who would not only act as impartial arbiters in the distribution of official patronage but would also keep Hindu nationalism within proper bounds. In turning inwardly, the Muslims recognized the importance of unity and organization in preserving their identity and resisting certain Hindu demands, notably, for increased representation in the legislatures and the higher echelons of the civil service. Muslims, already alarmed at the growing Hindu influence in the administration, had no wish to see the highest organs of executive and legislative power in the country transferred from "the hands of the neutral classes" to the Hindus.[62]

Two other minority groups in South India whose support the Congress politicians wanted to enlist

were the Indian Christians and the Eurasians. The
former, constituting just over 2 per cent of the
population of the Presidency, did not allow their
numerical weakness to stand in the way of their
improvement. Education provided them the main
avenue to upward mobility. In 1885-86, 52 per cent
of the Indian Christian boys were attending schools,
an average which placed them second only to the
Brahmins.[63] By this time, educated members of the
community were found in every important profession,
holding their own in a highly competitive world
without seeking government patronage or depending
on the goodwill of other communities. Surprisingly,
their leaders had been slow in organizing communal
associations and, indeed, some of them had identified themselves with the Hindus by joining the
Madras Mahajana Sabha and participating in its
activities.

However, the seeds of communal solidarity did
eventually take root. An expression of this was
the National Church Movement, the brainchild of
Pulney Andy. A medical practitioner who retired in
1882, Pulney Andy had settled in Madras "to work in
the land of my birth to strengthen the cause of
Christianity among my brethren." He deplored the
sectarian divisions in the community, divisions
which he attributed in India to "the mere accident
of Baptism." After he had consulted prominent leaders of the community in Madras as to the feasibility of organizing "an Indian Church on Non-
Sectarian principles," a preliminary meeting was
held at his home in November 1885, and a scheme to
organize the national church was accepted. In September 1886 the National Church was formally
launched, with Pulney Andy as President. Its constitution allowed its members to continue their
affiliations with their respective churches, while
ministers were to be recruited from any church so
long as they agreed to be nonsectarian. Regular
services of the National Church were held, a weekly
paper called the *Eastern Star* was started, and expenses were met by voluntary contributions.[64]

There is little doubt that the National Church movement in South India was a conscious attempt on the part of the Indian Christians to assert their own identity and not be too closely tied to the apron strings of their European pastors. Pulney Andy, who wanted Christianity in India to be "moulded into an eastern form," believed that a united church was "suited to the national peculiarities and instincts of the people" and would encourage habits of "independence, and self-reliance" and introduce "a system of self-help, self-work and self-government in the ministrations of the Church, without depending on foreign aid and the charity of the people of Europe and America." Excessive dependence on the latter countries, Pulney Andy pointed out, had cast "reproach and contempt" on the community, offended its sense of self-respect and pride, and even discouraged Hindus from joining Christianity on the belief that it was "a mere asylum for forlorn creatures."[65] For this state of things, the European missionaries were held largely responsible. It was claimed by the advocates of the National Church that these missionaries had imported into India "the sectarian bigotry of English Churches" and had molded Indian Christianity "too much after European patterns."[66] Others complained that Indian Christians were not given a voice in managing the affairs of their own community. W. L. Venkataramiah, a founding member of the National Church, admitted that one of the reasons which prompted him and his friends to act was their exclusion by the European missionaries "from anything like a fair share in the management of church affairs." He alleged that some of the missionaries had lost touch with their congregations and had consequently endangered the development of "a healthy church life."[67]

By their attempts to blur the sectarian divisions, by renouncing foreign financial support, and by criticizing the management of the European missionaries, the founders of the National Church stirred up hostility in certain powerful quarters

in South India. The European missions, still the
source of much of the funds and patronage, were
clearly alarmed by the rhetoric of those associated
with the National Church. The Indian pastors, very
much under the control of the European missions, became the outspoken critics of the National Church
and urged the laity to keep aloof from the services
of the National Church.[68]

The community thus appeared to be divided and
those opposed to the National Church formed the
Madras Native Christian Association in November
1887. This body hoped to promote the secular interests of the community without meddling with spiritual questions or interfering with the way that the
various churches were run. In its prospectus, it
claimed that as the community as a whole had "increased both in numbers and importance" it was
essential that it have a recognized channel to
voice its claims. At the same time, this body was
to work towards uniting a community widely dispersed
in the Presidency.[69] N. Subramaniam, a lawyer in
the Madras High Court and the guiding spirit behind
the formation of the association, was elected as
its first President, while Rev. John Lazarus filled
the post of Secretary. By December 1888 a total
of 114 members had enrolled with the Association,
the majority being *mofussil* residents.[70] Pulney
Andy admitted that the formation of the Madras
Native Christian Association had "caused a split in
the camp of the Native Christians community," and
was a blow to his hopes of achieving communal solidarity through the National Church.[71]

The Eurasian community, despite its numerical
smallness, had long displayed a capacity for organization. As early as 1862 an East Indian Association had been organized in Madras "to watch over
the interests of the East Indian community,"[72] although little was heard of its activities in the
ensuing years. With the formation of the Anglo-
Indian and Eurasian Association in Bengal in 1876,
there were discussions in Madras for the formation
of a similar body. However, it was not until

October 1879 that the Eurasian and Anglo-Indian
Association of Southern India was formally inaugu-
rated, largely due to the indefatigable D. S.
White, an official in the Department of Public In-
struction in Madras. Elected as President, a post
he was to hold until his death ten years later,
White sought to rally the Eurasian community, assis-
ted by such leaders as W. S. Gantz, a lawyer in the
Madras High Court, B. H. Chester, a professor at
Doveton Protestant College, and B. Lovery, retired
Principal of Pachaiyappa College and a Municipal
Commissioner of Madras.

White was convinced that an Eurasian association was "a political necessity," at least to ensure that the legitimate rights of the community
were not eroded away through the acts of the local
authorities. In theory, the British Parliament had
recognized the "nationality, rights and privileges"
of the Eurasians domiciled in India, but the recent
policies of the government left White with the impression that the community was being discriminated
against. For one, "political representation" had
been denied. White contended that, while the
Muslims enjoyed a permanent seat in the Madras
Legislative Council, the Eurasians had not been similarly favored.[73] A more serious complaint was the
charge that Eurasians had been unfairly treated in
the distribution of official appointments, largely
owing to the mistaken notion that "a native is none
other than a *Pure Asiatic*." In a memorial to the
Secretary of State, White urged that the claims of
the Eurasians be considered "officially and politically apart from that of undomiciled Europeans."
He did not want "special privileges" for his community, but only that they be accorded the status
of "Natives of India" and treated like any other
"permanently settled" community.[74]

However, White did not believe that public service alone would meet the long-term needs of the
community. To him, the future lay in agriculture
and industry and, consequently, much of the energies
of the Eurasian and Anglo-Indian Association of

Southern India were devoted towards providing opportunities for its members in these sectors. Priority
was given to the scheme for establishing agricultural colonies in an effort "to root" the floating
Eurasian population. Lands were acquired in Chingleput district and Mysore State with capital raised
from the community. To promote industrial education, workshops were started in Madras. White
travelled extensively throughout South India exhorting local leaders to start branches and raise
capital to realize the objects of the association.
By 1882 four agricultural colonies had been founded,
twenty-eight branches opened, and a capital fund of
Rs 60,000 had been raised to be expended on the
various schemes connected with the Association.[75]

The true significance of White's leadership
lay in his attempt to identify his community with
India. He had little sympathy with those in his
community who believed that Eurasians must eventually seek their home elsewhere. This attitude,
he reasoned, had given the community the character
of a "floating" population and had reduced it to a
state "bordering on pauperism." In calling upon
the Eurasians to identify themselves with the
peoples of India, White believed that there were
many issues on which cooperation was feasible. He
strongly supported the Indianization of the civil
service wherever Indians of talent and competence
were found and he accused the Madras authorities of
recruiting nondomiciled Europeans into the higher
ranks of the Uncovenanted Civil Service in defiance
of the restriction imposed by the Secretary of
State's order of 1879. Equally, he supported the
Ilbert Bill on the grounds that its principle was
"unassailable" and that it was merely removing a
race disqualification which had long been disowned
by the British authorities.[76]

His outspoken support for this measure, as indeed his participation in the demonstrations that
had been organized in honor of Ripon, alienated
many members of his community who alleged that he
was demeaning the status of the community by

closely identifying it with the "natives." White
dismissed these charges as evidence of "sickly sen-
timentalism" and urged the community to "go man-
fully for the term native of India." "Why," he
remarked, "it is the most splendid country in the
world, and I am as proud as I can be that I belong
to it." A visionary in some respects, White predicted "a vast change" soon overtaking India when
there would be the "utter disintegration of native
society" and its replacement by another "on the
European model." He was confident that the Brahmins would be in the vanguard of this movement, and
he wanted the Eurasians and Europeans to play their
part in this transformation.77

The wooing of these three communal groups, at
a time when they were each trying to express their
identity in their own distinctive way, was without
doubt the most challenging task that faced the Congress leaders in South India. As early as March
1887, the *Hindu* put out its first feelers for Muslim cooperation in the forthcoming Congress. It
claimed that except in North-Western Provinces and
Calcutta, Hindus and Muslims were living on terms
of amity, and it called upon Muslim leaders sympathetic to the Congress to persuade their friends
who indulged in the "present most uncharitable and
unwise crusade against their Hindu brothers" to dis-
continue their campaign. Imputations about the disloyalty of the Congress were vigorously denied, and
Muslims were assured that with their cooperation
the Congress would be able to formulate a "loyal
and moderate programme."78

Behind-the-scene consultations to mobilize
support of all the communal and factional groups in
the Madras Presidency began in April 1887. Early
in the month, the third provincial conference was
held at Kumbaconam, and the leaders of the Madras
Mahajana Sabha took advantage of this opportunity
to meet their counterparts from the *mofussil* to discuss "the general plan" of organizing the forthcoming Congress meeting. It was agreed that "the only
means of obtaining the requisite funds was by a

wide and complete organisation which would commit
every district and every *taluk* to a vigorous cooperation with the Central Committee at Madras."[79]

In Madras itself, the leaders of minority
groups, prominent members of the landed aristocracy,
and the elder administrators were contacted for support. Response was almost everywhere favorable,
and in May a public meeting was held to elect a
Reception Committee on whose shoulders fell the responsibility for arranging the Congress meeting at
the end of the year. Among those who agreed to
serve in this Committee were Humayun Jah Bahadur
and Mahomed Abdullah Badsha, President and Vice-
President of the Central Mahomedan Association,
Syed Mahomed Nizamuddin, Secretary of the Anjuman-
i-Mufidi-Ahal-i-Islam, B. Lovery and B. H. Chester,
members of the Eurasian and Anglo-Indian Association of Southern India, Pulney Andy and Subramaniam,
prominent members of the Indian Christian community,
Madava Rao, who was elected Chairman of the Reception Committee, and G. N. Gajapati Rao, a wealthy
zamindar from Vizagapatam and a member of the
Madras Legislative Council.[80]

The first round in the battle to win general
support was decidedly in favor of the Congress
leadership. Not only had the most important
leaders of the minority groups in Madras thrown in
their support for the Congress, but, also, such
"conservative" stalwarts of Madras politics as
Madava Rao and Gajapati Rao--who had so far kept
aloof from political involvement--had agreed to
take a prominent part in the coming Congress.

However, it ought to be stressed that these
leaders were not acting upon any mandate from their
constituents or associations; theirs was an expression of their personal inclinations. Consequently,
in the months ahead, they had the task of persuading their immediate supporters to back the Congress and to participate in the gathering of
December 1887. Of the three communal groups, only
the Indian Christians appeared to be in any clear
unanimity in their support for the Congress. The

Eastern Star, organ of the National Church, claimed
that communal relations in the Presidency had always been cordial and there had been a certain
readiness among the leaders to work together to
realize common objectives. It looked upon the Congress as a forum to cement the spirit of communal
goodwill by representing faithfully the grievances
of the people of India as a whole.[81] When meetings were held to elect delegates, most of the
prominent leaders of the Indian Christian community
were chosen, including Subramaniam, Pulney Andy,
Jagga Rao Pillay, and Paul Peter Pillay. Eventually, eleven Indian Christians from South India
attended the *tamasha* in December 1887.[82]

The center of interest, however, were the Muslims. Ever since the Congress emerged as the
champion of all-India interests, the Muslim press
in Madras had made occasional sallies against this
claim and at times had called upon its community to
keep aloof from the movement. But, on the whole,
Muslim opposition to the Congress had been rather
muted, reflecting to some extent the indecision of
the Muslim associations in the Presidency. The
latter, not under any pressure to take sides, had
taken the path of least resistance by remaining
silent.

However, the situation was different in 1887,
with the Congress leaders displaying zealousness to
win Muslim backing and prevent the kind of secession that occurred at the last Congress when Muslim
leaders from Aligarh and Calcutta refused to participate. Their first move was to enroll the Muslim
notables in Madras and this was carried out with
considerable success when the latter agreed to
serve in the Reception Committee. The next step
was to get the Muslim associations to nominate delegates, and directives to this effect were issued
by the Reception Committee in October 1887. Simultaneously, pro-Congress organs launched a campaign
calling upon the different minority groups to participate and show that there was all-India solidarity
despite differences in creed, caste, and language.

This, in effect, was the real moment of decision
for the many Muslims in South India who had thus
far been quiescent. It was also the moment for
those Muslims who had misgivings about the Congress
and its motives to make public their feelings.

It was Ahmad Mohidin, editor of the *Muslim
Herald*, who first raised his voice against Muslim
participation in the Congress. He had once served
the Prince of Arcot, but in October 1884 he entered
journalism by starting the *Muslim Herald* to represent "the views and wants of the Muhammadans" of
South India.[83] An active participant in Muslim
politics, he had been Secretary of the Anjuman-i-
Islamiah and on its dissolution became a leading
member of the Central Mahomedan Association. In
August 1887 he visited Nellore to enlist local support for starting a branch body of the Central
Mahomedan Association, and in his speech stressed
the importance of Muslim unity to secure the interests of the community.[84]

Like many Muslim leaders, Ahmad Mohidin believed that the community had not received a fair
share of official appointments in South India. At
one point he published details in his paper about
Muslim aspirants for office who possessed the necessary qualifications, but was disappointed when the
authorities failed to respond. However, when the
Public Service Commission assembled in Madras in
February 1887, he discussed with his Muslim friends
the kind of demands which the community as a whole
should make for more equitable representation in
the administration. They rejected simultaneous
examinations and instead urged that Statutory
Civilians should be promoted to the Covenanted Service wherever they had shown their worth. At the
same time, Ahmad Mohidin and his friends wanted the
claims of certain "backward classes," namely,
Muslims, Sikhs, Mahrattas, and Rajputs, to be given
special consideration, as they had been slow to
adapt to the changes introduced by British rule.[85]

On this issue of civil service recruitment,
Ahmad Mohidin and his supporters differed

fundamentally with the Congress leaders. If the
one veered towards proportionate representation of
communities and sects, with the British acting as
arbiters in distributing patronage, the other demanded recruitment on the basis of free and impartial competition, unrestrained by any patronage,
however well meant.

As the outspoken critic of the Congress, Ahmad
Mohidin gave vigorous expression to the doubts and
apprehensions which some Muslims entertained about
the movement. He questioned the very assumptions
on which the Congress was founded, ridiculed its
tactics and derided its supporters. He argued that
many of the demands of the Congress were under official consideration and he felt that little would
be gained by harassing the government into taking
precipitate action. Also, he doubted the wisdom of
such tactics in achieving political goals. "We
have often urged," he wrote in the *Muslim Herald*,
"that agitation and noise would never suit us; we
are glad our co-religionists are of our mind."[86]
Ahmad Mohidin also questioned the Congress claim
that India was a nation. "The term is applicable
only to a body made up of a people descended from
one stock, speaking a common tongue, amenable to a
uniform law, and united under one Government."[87]
In India, he argued, the Muslims and Hindus were
deeply and irreconcilably divided:

> No one would venture to deny [he wrote in the
> *Muslim Herald*] that the interests of the
> Indian Muslims and Hindus are more hopelessly
> divergent than those of the Orangemen and the
> Ribbonmen of Ireland. From a religious or
> social point of view, the Musalman differs
> much more from the Hindu than the Irish Catho-
> lic from the Irish Protestant.[88]

Implicit in Ahmad Mohidin's reasoning was the
belief that British India was a hotchpotch of
nationalities and cultures, nourishing a variety of
traditions, languages, and creeds, all held

together by the tenuous circumstance of British
rule. Among the clashing loyalties in India was
the division between the so-called martial and nonmartial races.* The martial races, among whom were
included Muslims, Sikhs, and Rajputs, were regarded
as the victims of British conquest, robbed of their
political power, deprived of their economic
strength, and denied their share of high official
appointments. On the other hand, the nonmartial
races were seen as the real beneficiaries of British rule. The *bhadralok* of Bengal and the Brahmins
of South and Western India had, by embracing Western education, secured a strong foothold in the
lower and middle reaches of the administration, a
position from which they were supposedly manipulating policies and patronage to further their own
sectional interests. Other members of these castes
had entered the new professions, accumulated wealth,
and were exerting influence on the government
through the press and political associations. The
Congress, as Ahmad Mohidin and his school of
thought saw it, was nothing more than yet another
ambitious attempt on the part of these nonmartial
groups educated in the Western learning to find new
levers to exert pressure on the government to gain
their own ends. If they were successful, it was
feared that the martial races, and particularly the

---

*A similar distinction was made by Sir Lepel
Griffin in a speech he gave at the Gwalior durbar
in December 1887. He was reported as saying: "One
of the reasons which I urge you, Mahrattas, to
utilise the educational advantages which we offer
you, is, that you may take your rightful place in
India and keep the Bengalis, who are now everywhere
very active, in their proper place. You are their
superiors in ability, in strength, and in courage.
They are only your superiors in noise and volu-
bility. If they should be your leaders, it would
be an army of lions commanded by grasshoppers."
Madras Mail, 22 December 1887.

Muslims, would face utter ruination.

Ahmad Mohidin's assault on the Congress, and the support that his campaign received from some sections of the Muslim press, did not prove decisive in consolidating Muslim opinion against the Congress; at best, it divided the Muslims between pro-Congress and anti-Congress groups. To some extent, this polarization was the inevitable sequel to the factional rivalries which had bedevilled Muslim politics in Madras since the early eighties. The leadership of the Central Mahomedan Association was clearly divided on this issue and it refrained from giving any clear direction to its members as to whether they ought to participate in the coming Congress sessions. While Humayun Jah Bahadur and Mahomed Abdullah Badsha became delegates, Ahmad Mohidin and Mohidin Sheriff held aloof. The Anjuman-i-Mufid-i-Ahla-i-Islam, on the other hand, accepted the Congress invitation and nominated three delegates, including its Secretary Syed Mahomed Nizamuddin. Eventually fifty-eight Muslims, nominated by associations and public meetings, attended the Madras Congress as delegates.[89] Of these Muslims, the *Muslim Herald* said: "The Congress is welcome to such adherents, but we must ask its promoters not to parade these perverts as a proof that the Muslims, as a body, have joined their camp."[90]

The Congress also aroused a controversy within the Eurasian community. Ever since White came out in support of the Ilbert Bill, two shades of opinion had existed within the Eurasian and Anglo-Indian Association of Southern India, one accepting White's policy of making common cause with the other Indian communities on issues of mutual interest, and the other wishing to tie its fortunes to those of the Anglo-Indians. Although the latter repeatedly criticized White's "pro-Native policy" and even challenged his leadership of the Association at times, it was unable to change the policy so long as White and his close associates kept a tight rein on the leadership of the Association.

White had always evinced a strong sympathy for the
Congress, although his status as a public servant
stood in his way of active participation in its
proceedings. He was a friend of Hume, had been impressed with Ripon's policy, and had cultivated
connections with Congress leaders in Madras and
Bombay. He attended the first Congress at Bombay
in the capacity of *amici curiae*. Hence, there was
optimism in Congress circles in Madras that he
would persuade the Eurasians to join the movement.
The *Eastern Guardian,* which echoed White's political views, had been a steady advocate of Eurasian
participation in the Congress. It claimed in
April 1887 that the Congress was "a forcible ex-
ponent of the patriotism and desire for political
reform" in India. "It would be unwise," it remarked, "to stand aloof from the great movement
that is going forward or to allow personal jealousies or race prejudices to retard the progress
of events."[91]
    However, for over a month after receiving a
formal invitation to participate in the Congress
sessions, no decision was taken by the Eurasian
and Anglo-Indian Association, reflecting to some
extent the indecision arising from White's absence
in Calcutta in connection with the report of the
Public Service Commission. It was left to Hume,
who arrived in Madras on 30 November to look after
his "special pet child the Congress,"[92] to stir
the Eurasian leaders into some kind of action.
With the help of Gantz, the Vice-President of the
Association, a meeting of members was held on 7
December at which the Association agreed to participate in the Madras Congress. Five members, including Gantz, Chester, and Lovery, were nominated
as delegates.[93]
    Attempts were also made to enlist the support
of the Europeans of South India. Hume, in his circular to all Congress committees, had stressed
that every community should be persuaded to participate in the Madras Congress, including nonofficial Europeans.[94] This was in line with the policy

of making the Congress fully representative of
every ethnic and social group, although, in the
case of the Anglo-Indians, it would also mean that
the Congress would have to modify its thesis that
the interests of the Europeans and Indians were
completely antithetical and irreconcilable.   In
South India, the Anglo-Indians lacked an association, and Congress leaders decided to recruit individual Europeans known to be sympathetic to their
cause.   In some instances, Europeans were asked to
preside over meetings where delegates to the Congress were elected.   According to the *Hindu*, many
European missionaries in the districts did in fact
do so.[95]   Also, some European lawyers and teachers
in Madras evinced sympathy.

Of these, the two conspicuous figures were
John Adam and Eardley Norton, both of whom were
elected as delegates.   John Adam, Principal of
Pachaiyappa College, had built up a local renown
for his exertions on behalf of commercial and technical education.   He held the view that every
Englishman in India had "a sacred duty to perform,
viz., to maintain the English character, and to
stand to his belief in justice and equality."[96]

Eardley Norton was a barrister whose father,
J. B. Norton, was warmly remembered by many Hindus
in Madras for his espousal of their cause, notably,
in advancing Western education at a time when it
was still in its infancy in South India.   Eardley
Norton was born in Madras in 1852, acquired his
legal training in England, and joined the Madras
bar in 1879.   He soon built up a lucrative practice,
aided no doubt, by his forensic skill, which lost
little of its lustre in a career extending for almost half a century.[97]   A vivid personality, with a
love for drama and controversy, Norton's first involvement in local politics was in 1883 when as the
"Madras Correspondent of the *Pioneer*" he freely criticized his fellow countrymen for their opposition
to the Ilbert Bill.   Nor did he hesitate to expose
the vagaries of European officials in South India.
The editor of the *Hindu*, without being aware of his

actual identity, praised him for his "invaluable
service to the native community."[98] In April 1885,
when the issue of volunteering was being discussed
throughout India, Norton supported Indian admission
in defiance of general European opinion in the country, as he felt that the government ought "to encourage that loyalty among the natives which has
given such spontaneous evidence of its activity in
Madras."[99]

No doubt, Norton in recent years had witnessed
the rising tempo of Indian politics, which he attributed, in his maiden political speech given in
September 1885, to "a steadily increasing feeling
of discontent" arising from "many legitimate grievances" of the Indian people. He asserted that, if
this discontent was not heeded, the Indian authorities would be "precipitating a crisis, of the
magnitude of which, I do not believe any member of
this or any other Government has an iota of conception." At the same time, he welcomed attempts by
the Indians to secure their legitimate rights
through the accepted norms of political protest.
To Norton, this was a measure of Indians attaining
political maturity and responsibility and their
"ceasing to be children in leading strings."[100] It
was indeed unique for an European in India to hold
such political convictions at this stage in the
country's political evolution, and this was an
important factor in Norton's popularity with the
Western-educated class in South India. Consequently, when he declared his open support for the Congress in 1887, it was not entirely unexpected. However, there was no disguising the fact that his
accession was one of the more dramatic events of
the Madras Congress, and during the next few years
Norton was to emerge as the principal Congress
spokesman in South India, eclipsing many of the earlier Congress stalwarts.

ALIENATION OF COMMUNAL SUPPORT

The prevalent mood after the Congress gathering of December 1887 was one of euphoria. Congress leaders in Madras were quick to enumerate the significant gains that they had made on this third meeting. First, the landed aristocracy and the ruling Princes of South India had shown their sympathy for the Congress by subscribing liberally to its cause. Then, the expected support of the middle income groups had materialized, with contributions coming from even such far off places as Burma and Singapore. Third, European officials in Madras had shown an attitude of sympathetic neutrality towards the Congress, with the governor, Lord Connemara, throwing a garden party in honor of the delegates.* Last, and most important, the support of the minority groups in the Presidency was secured.[101] Congress leaders had been particularly nervous about the Muslims, fearing that the example of Aligarh and Calcutta might be repeated in Madras.

The mood of euphoria in the Congress camp did not last long. Barely had the Congress delegates dispersed from Madras when a fierce controversy started over the issue of Muslim participation in the Congress, sparked off by Syed Ahmad Khan's vigorous denunciation of the movement. In a series of speeches he delivered in North India, Syed Ahmad Khan rekindled many of the fears which the Muslims entertained about the Congress, particularly of the latter's demands for representative institutions and simultaneous civil service examinations.

In South India this was the signal for a renewed campaign against Muslim involvement in Congress activity, spearheaded largely by the Muslim press in Madras. The *Sultan-ul-Akhbar*, an Urdu

---

*Of the Congress delegates, Connemara confided to the Viceroy: "They seem to be a very loyal and harmless set of people." *Dufferin Collection*, Reel 532, Connemara to Dufferin, 28 December 1887.

paper, described the Congress as a Hindu gathering
working in the interests of the Hindus. It claimed
that Islam did "not induce its believers to work
against Government but since Government took India
from the Muhammadans she should help them and give
them special advantages in obtaining posts under
it."[102] The *Muslim Herald*, in welcoming Syed Ahmad
Khan's speeches, hailed them as "the key-note of
our policy."[103]

The Congress leadership in Madras was clearly
alarmed at the possible effects that Syed Ahmad
Khan's rhetoric might have on its Muslim supporters.
Eardley Norton, in a speech delivered in Madras in
January 1888, provided the counter blast to Syed
Ahmad Khan and the editor of the *Muslim Herald*. Of
the former, Norton said that he "talked such nonsense in public and he was doing his best to create
a breach between the people maliciously and perni-
ciously, like Sir Lepel Griffin." As for Syed's
opposition to the reform of the legislatures on the
grounds that the Hindus were in the majority and
ahead in education, Norton replied: "Are the people
to be in a state of collapse until the Mahomedans
become M.A.'s and B.A.'s? Should the whole body
politic, take a dose of political chloroform until
the Mahomedans come to the front?" He also urged
his Muslim friends not to be misled by such organs
as the *Muslim Herald*, which, according to Norton,
indulged in "a series of misrepresentations, which
were intentional and wilful even though the Editor
himself was present at the Congress." He called
upon the Muslims, if they had common sense and self-
respect, to "put off their fantasies and rubbish
notions and throw their lot in life not only with
the Hindus but with Europeans for the purpose of
achieving one common end."[104]

This was Norton displaying his forensic skill,
trading polemics with his Muslim opponents. But,
as an attempt at assuaging Muslim fears about the
Congress or winning new friends among the uncommitted Muslims, this speech was a decided failure.
Norton seemed to have realized this, for, when he

broached the subject again in March 1888, he made
a more reasoned, dispassionate plea for Muslim support. He rejected as "absolutely untrue" the
thesis of Syed Ahmad Khan that Hindus and Muslims
did not see eye to eye on many things. Discussing
the demand for representative institutions, Norton
explained that such a system of government would
not necessarily submerge the voice of the minorities. Nor was Norton convinced that the Hindus
would monopolize all the privileges which the Congress was demanding from the government. If there
were any disadvantages weighing against the Muslims,
he believed that they lay not so much in their
numerical inferiority as in their educational backwardness. Norton contended that the remedy to the
latter problem lay within the Muslim grasp, and
urged Muslims to apply themselves rigorously to
attain educational parity with the other communities.[105]

Meanwhile, Muslim leaders in Madras, who were
opposed to the Congress, were drawing up plans for
a public meeting where the issue of Muslim participation would be discussed. After some preliminary meetings to secure the cooperation of "the
various sects of Islam residing in Madras," a program was formulated for adoption by the general community. The meeting, held on 28 April 1888, was
attended by about one hundred Muslims, including
Mahomed Mahmud Khan, Mohidin Sheriff, and Ahmad
Mohidin. Conspicuous by their absence were Humayun
Jah Bahadur, Mahomed Abdullah Badsha, Syed Mahomed
Nizamuddin, and Walji Lalji Sait.

The meeting adopted a number of resolutions,
including a vote of regret at the approaching departure of Lord Dufferin. The main resolution related to Muslim participation in the Congress. The
meeting agreed that, for "divers reasons," it was
not desirable for the Muslims to be identified with
the Congress. "It is a mistake," read the resolution, "to think that that movement, as at present
constituted and worked, would yield advantage to
the Natives of India in general and the Muhammadans

in particular." The meeting also endorsed the
stand that Syed Ahmad Khan has assumed on the various political questions affecting the community,
and expressed its "entire confidence in the general
tenor of his policy." The meeting further recorded
that "the disinclination of Musalmans to take part
in any political movement set on foot by the Hindus
does not imply race antagonism, but is due to a
diversity of interests." It was made clear that
the Muslims "sincerely hope to live on the best
possible terms with their Hindu, Christian and
Parsi brethren, whatever the differences as to policy that may prevail."[106]

In effect, this was a meeting of Muslims who
felt their basic interests threatened by the activities of the Congress. The meeting was also a
demonstration of support for Syed Ahmad Khan's
efforts to achieve communal solidarity in the country as a whole, while, at the same time, dispelling
Congress claims to have captured Muslim support in
Madras Presidency. There was no doubt that Muslim
opinion on the Congress issue was sharply divided,
a situation which led to increasing pressures being
exerted on uncommitted Muslims to join one or the
other camp.

In some circles, the very intensity of this
campaign aroused fears of possible communal violence. One who feared this was Mir Shujaat Ali,
a Statutory Civilian in Madras, who argued that the
campaign among Muslims was "increasingly fanning
the flames of communal animosities." In a two-
part article he wrote for the *Hindu* in June 1888,
Mir Shujaat Ali appealed for a truce in the agitation that was being conducted among the Muslims,
lest it lead to "worse results." On the one hand,
he advised those Muslims opposed to the Congress
not "to agitate *against* the Congress." Instead,
they should channel their efforts in more creative
directions--formulating their political program and
indicating where they differed with the Congress
leaders. As for the Congress adherents, he recommended caution and moderation in their campaign to

enlist support for their cause, as well as recognition of the existence of an opposition to the Congress.

Analyzing Muslim attitudes towards the Congress, Mir Shujaat Ali asserted that "an overwhelming majority of thinking Musalmans in India have not joined it," though an exception were "the coastal communities of the Bombay side." He attributed this partly to racial differences and partly to Muslim backwardness in Western education. Moreover, Muslim leaders feared that "the ultimate aim of Congress movement is to introduce into India of diverse races and creeds, the political institutions of England of one nationality and religion, because they cannot shut their eyes to the 'colored' carriages and numerous other race inflictions imposed *by law* on the Negro minority of certain States of the great republic of the United States." Nor did he hold much hopes for the future integration of Hindus and Muslims, so deep and fundamental were their differences. Though he believed that Western education might effect a slow change in Muslim attitudes towards the Congress, Mir Shujaat Ali did not expect this to happen for many years, and until such time he wanted the Congress to leave the Muslims alone.[107]

Mir Shujaat Ali was not alone in calling for a truce in the campaign to enlist Muslim support for the Congress. M. D. Habibullah, President of the Vellore Literary Society and a supporter of the Congress, also adopted a similar line of reasoning in a speech given at Vellore in June 1889. He asserted that the "majority of Musalmans" did not support the Congress. "A Tyabji and a Bhimji, names however prominent in themselves, do not make up the whole community of Islam nor even the more influential portion of it." Ascribing Muslim aloofness to their educational backwardness, Habibullah urged his Congress friends to leave the Muslims alone.

They will be a burden to you. They will impede your way, they will mar your progress, leave

them alone, and when the Promethean spark of
knowledge has entered into and revived the
dead bones of Muslim society they will join
you unasked and unsolicited.[108]

Such advice, though distasteful to many Congress leaders, did compel some rethinking on the existence of Muslim opposition to the Congress. John
Adam, while discussing "the Muhammadan question" in
May 1888, conceded that the Muslims were deeply
divided on the Congress issue. While urging the
Congress workers to resolve this Muslim dilemma as
far as possible, Adam also expressed the desirability of recognizing the existence of an opposition to the Congress. He felt that Syed Ahmad Khan
had been "rather badly treated" for expressing his
views, and emphasized the "great advantage" of
having an opponent who was "no hidden enemy."[109]
With the formation of the United Indian Patriotic
Association in August 1888, aimed at rallying anti-
Congress forces in the country, the existence of
an opposition to the Congress could no longer be
denied.
    However, further setbacks lay in store for the
Congress leadership in South India. In January
1888 the draft constitution of the Congress, framed
by a committee set up at the Madras gathering, was
published, providing a body of rules to regulate
the working of the Congress. The draft constitution recommended the division of the provincial
"Congress circles" into a number of "electoral circles," based partly on the territorial principle
and partly on the representation of special and
minority interests. Each of these electoral circles was to be placed under the immediate control
of a subcommittee, with those constituted on the
territorial principle expected "to secure a fair
representation of the intelligent portion of the
community, without distinction of creed, caste,
race, or color."[110]
    While the other provinces were debating the
merits of the draft constitution, the Madras

Standing Congress Committee decided to implement
that part of the constitution which called for the
formation of electoral circles. The entire Madras
Presidency was divided into forty-three electoral
circles, thirty-six based on the territorial principle, and seven representing special and minority
interests. Those electoral circles formed on the
territorial basis consisted "either of portions of
a large city, a large town, a town with a portion
of the surrounding district, or a town with the
whole of the district of which it is the capital."[111]
The process of forming subcommittees in each of
these electoral circles proved to be a slow one,
with the urban centers responding more easily than
the rural areas. Much of the initiative to form
the subcommittees was taken by the Madras Mahajana
Sabha and its affiliated associations, with prominent Congress leaders from the metropolis visiting
the *mofussil* to stir up local action. Of particular importance was the "political mission" of G.
Subramania Iyer. In an extended tour he undertook
in July-September 1888, he visited Wallajanagar,
Erode, Coimbatore, Lalgudi, Palghat, and Calicut,
where he enlisted support for the formation of
local subcommittees. By December 1889 the Madras
Standing Congress Committee claimed that the formation of subcommittees in the urban areas of South
India was complete.[112]

However, a mixed response awaited the Congress
leaders when they solicited the cooperation of
minority and special interests. Invitations were
issued to the Eurasian and Anglo-Indian Association,
the two Muslim associations in the metropolis, the
Madras Chamber of Commerce, the Madras Trades'
Association, and the Madras University to constitute themselves into separate electoral circles.[113]
There was some optimism that the Chamber of Commerce and the Trades' Association would agree, especially as in recent years they had expressed sympathy for some of the reforms urged by the Congress.
But the reaction of these bodies was distinctly
hostile. While both rejected the invitation of the

Congress, some members of the Trades' Association
expressed their "entire disapproval" of the activities of the Congress.[114] This dashed any hopes
of securing European participation in the Congress.

If the European abstention was not entirely
unexpected, the withdrawal of the Eurasians from
the Congress in 1890 came as a surprise to the Congress leaders in the Presidency. Since 1887, when
the Eurasian and Anglo-Indian Association had
joined the Congress, it had continued to send delegates to the annual Congress sessions and nominated
its representatives to sit on the Madras Standing
Congress Committee. This policy of partnership
with the Congress was, however, unpopular with "a
dissentient party" within the Eurasian body, but
White's firm control of the leadership made any
change of policy impossible so long as he remained
at the helm.

However, White died in February 1889, and this
dealt a blow to his policy of partnership with the
Congress. Gantz, elected as his successor, pledged
to continue his predecessor's policy. In defending
the policy, which he termed as "cutting adrift from
the European and making common cause with the
Native," Gantz asserted that the Eurasian leaders
were not "rushing headlong from Scylla to Chary-
bidis." On the contrary, he was convinced that the
Eurasian minority should "form an essential link in
the well woven chain of this great National movement, whose influence has already spread from East
to West, from the long suffering and oppressed
India to the Land of the brave, and the free, and
the just." He declared that the Congress leaders
were "neither Nihilists, Communists, Socialists, or
Moonfighters," but rather "honest, sober-minded men
who have thought out some of the most important
political questions of the day, and who, year by
year, have met and formulated in moderate and constitutional language our demands for reforms, the
reasonableness of which are admitted on all
sides."[115]

Although Gantz's pledge promised a new era of

Eurasian cooperation with the Congress, his policy
came to be challenged, both from within and without
the Eurasian body. In October 1889 the President
of the Anglo-Indian and Eurasian Association of
Bengal criticized the Eurasian leadership in Madras
for its continued participation in Congress activities. He attributed this policy to the "radical
element" that dominated that body, although he felt
that "the great majority of the Madras Association
have not been persuaded by the eloquence of Mr.
White and Mr. Gantz."116 Also, at this juncture,
Gantz's policy was challenged by C. S. Crole, a
senior official in the Madras Government. While
presiding over the anniversary meeting of the Eurasian and Anglo-Indian Association, Crole urged the
Eurasians to look towards the European community
to realize their aspirations. "It was not to the
interest of the Eurasians," remarked Crole, "to
throw themselves into the natives. It was their
interest to join the Europeans, because the Europeans could get their wrongs redressed." As for
the Congress, he believed that it was "a movement
for the native races of the country," still very
much in its "infancy," and afflicted with "childish
ailments."

How far these criticisms weakened Gantz's
authority within the Eurasian body is unknown, but
what undermined the policy of partnership with the
Congress was Gantz's rather abrupt resignation
from the Madras Standing Congress Committee in
December 1890 following a quarrel over his selection to preside over the sixth session of the Congress at Calcutta. The details of the quarrel are
obscure, but Gantz gave the impression that his
selection was balked by the attitude of the Congress leadership in Madras. According to the
Madras Times, Gantz's nomination had been "demurred"
at by the Madras leaders who had "taken offence at
not having been given the voice they wanted in the
election of a President."117

Gantz's withdrawal meant, in effect, the virtual dissolution of the Eurasian connection with

the Congress. White's policy of alliance with the
Congress was finally repudiated in September 1891
when the Association formally decided against sending delegates to the coming Congress session at
Nagpur.[118] The *Eastern Guardian*, while discussing
the reversal of White's policy, asserted that the
"dissentient party" had grown in strength over the
years and converted the majority of the members
within the Eurasian association to the new policy
of noncooperation with the Congress.[119]

Almost simultaneously, Muslim support for the
Congress also began to wane. Since April 1888 the
Congress leadership in South India had come to
rely on some prominent Muslim leaders, notably,
Humayun Jah Bahadur, Mahomed Abdullah Badsha, Syed
Mahomed Nizamuddin, and Walji Lalji Sait, to exert
its influence on the Muslims of South India. However, this policy suffered as a consequence of the
death of some of these Muslim leaders. In June
1891 Mahomed Abdullah Badsha died, and the *Hindu*
mourned the "irreparable loss" to South India of
"an ardent supporter of the national cause" who
during the Madras Congress in 1887 had "laboured
hard to convince his co-religionists of the reasonableness of Congress proposals and converted many
to his opinions."[120] Another blow to the Congress
was the death of Humayun Jah Bahadur in December
1893. He had been the patriarchal leader of the
Muslims in South India for almost a generation and
had remained loyal to the Congress since his accession in 1887. In September 1893 his Congress
friends in the Madras Legislative Council had secured his election to the Supreme Legislative
Council, but death intervened before he was able to
take his seat. The *Hindu* regarded him as "a highly
cultured man, with a shrewd common sense" whose
death would be a loss to his community in South
India.[121]

Muslim attitudes towards the Congress were
also affected by the latter's ability to win certain concessions from the British rulers. The Congress demand for popular representation in the

legislatures was partially granted by the Indian
Councils Act of 1892. The expanded provincial
legislatures were to include a sizable number of
nonofficials "recommended" by statutory bodies and
certain class interests. According to the rules
framed and published by the Madras Government in
April 1893, seven seats in the local council were
to be filled by this process of recommendation by
local bodies, mercantile interests, and the Madras
University. The remaining seats were to be occupied by nominees of the government, who were to be
selected "in such a manner as shall secure a fair
representation of the different classes of the
community."122

The Muslims were assured of a seat, as were
the landed aristocracy, but these arrangements did
not satisfy the Muslims. On the one hand, those
Muslims who had consistently opposed the introduction of the elective system for fear of Hindu domination felt aggrieved that any change along these
lines should have been contemplated. To them, the
system of recommendation was only a covert form of
election which would allow Hindus already dominating local bodies in the metropolis and *mofussil* to
return their own representatives to the legislature.
Moreover, the British decision to reform the legislatures was regarded in Muslim circles as a concession to Congress agitation. The Muslims were
aggrieved that their loyalty had not been rewarded:
they still had only one seat in the Madras legislature, and, even here, they had to be content with
allowing the government the sole right of choosing
the Muslim member unfettered by the wishes of the
community.123

It was at this juncture, in June 1893, that
the House of Commons passed a snap resolution calling upon the Indian authorities to implement the
Congress demand for simultaneous civil service examinations. The Congress leaders were jubilant, and
they organized countrywide meetings to demonstrate
the nation's "entire satisfaction at the verdict of
the House of Commons, and press earnestly for

immediate practical application" of the resolution.[124] In Madras, a mass meeting was convened by
the Madras Standing Congress Committee in August
1893, and the gathering resolved that simultaneous
examinations were an absolute necessity "not only
to satisfy the legitimate aspirations of the people
of India, but also to ensure the adequate fulfil-
ment of the promises contained in the Proclamation
of 1858." A memorial to Parliament was adopted,
welcoming its resolution and urging its immediate
implementation.[125]

To Muslim leaders in South India, already critical of British intentions, the Commons' resolution was yet another example of British retreat in
the face of Congress clamor. For many years, Muslim leaders in Madras had declared their opposition
to simultaneous examinations on the grounds that it
would lead to the transfer of the highest executive
positions in the country from the hands of the British, the "neutral class," to the Hindus. Not surprisingly, the Muslim press reacted angrily to the
Commons' resolution. The *Jarida-i-Rozgar*, an Urdu
weekly, argued that the implementation of this
resolution would only strengthen the position which
the *bhadralok* of Bengal and the Brahmins of South
India already enjoyed in certain levels of the
administration. It claimed that these groups were
"inimically opposed towards the Muhammadans" and
would subject them to "all sorts of trouble and
annoyance."[126] Similar sentiments were also expressed by some Anglo-Indian newspapers. The *Madras
Times*, in an editorial, argued that if the wishes
of the "English Radical" were to be met, Indian
administration would be "almost entirely Hindu."
It went on to remark:[127]

But the onus of opposing 'Native opinion'
would be thrown upon the Musulman instead of
the Englishman, and we doubt not that the former would gladly do what he considered to be
his duty. The most ardent believer in progress
in India cannot seriously argue that the time

is ripe for a very rapid expansion of Hindu
influence in the administration, more especially in the executive branch. It must never be
forgotten that the Hindu has to deal with the
Mahomenadan as well as the Englishman; if he
contrives to get more of his own way with the
latter than is at present given, he may have
to reckon with the former in a fashion that is
now, happily, out of date.

The protest meeting of the Madras Muslims
against the Commons' resolution was held on 26 August 1893. In a memorial adopted at the meeting,
the Muslims described the demand for simultaneous
examinations as embodying "the political aspirations of Hindus only, or, with more exactitude, of
those two sections known as the Bengalis and the
Brahmans." Protesting against any concession to
this "microscopic minority," whose aim was "at
nothing short of a complete extinction ultimately
of the European element in the Civil Service," the
Muslim memorialists urged the Indian authorities to
ignore the Commons' resolution.
     Some speakers at this meeting also voiced the
concern felt in Muslim circles about the radical
English support for the Congress. Mohamed Yasin
was reported as saying:

India was divided into two camps; one consisting of the Moslem moderates who were willing
to leave the progress of the country in the
hands of the rulers, and the other the red-hot
radicals, who claimed the most comprehensive
surrenders, supported by a class of English
cranks, who were justly charged by a facetious
English journal with 'breathless benevolence.'

Yasin claimed that since the advent of the Congress there had been "much wilful misrepresentation"
about Indian affairs, with the *bhadralok* in Bengal
and the Brahmins in South India "arrogating to themselves the power of controlling the destinies of

the country" by maintaining that "the only legitimate opinion was their own opinion." He also
accused the Congress of trying "to delude the world
into the belief that there was no political differences between the Mahomedans and the Hindus, and to
that end stray Mahomedans had been picked up from
the highways and by-ways, and ostensibly paraded on
the Hindu platform." Although Hindus had shown
skill in organization, he asserted that Muslims
would not join them "for the purpose of furthering
political ends by means of agitation."[128]

Even if political agitation remained distasteful to Muslim leaders, there was nevertheless some
rethinking of the kind of overall strategy they
should adopt in countering the Congress. More so
than ever before, with escalating Hindu demands and
an apparent weakening in the resolve of the British
rulers, Muslim leaders came to recognize the importance of inner cohesion. Factional differences
among the Muslims in Madras had robbed their
leaders of the authority to speak for the community
as a whole, and had even enabled the Congress to
pit them against each other. Hence, soon after the
meeting of August 1893, when almost all shades of
Muslim opinion had come together, Muslim leaders in
the metropolis began discussions to find some ways
of resolving their past dissensions. By February
1894 an agreement was reached, and a circular was
issued to launch a new body to embrace all Muslim
factions in the city. This circular carried the
signatures of seven Muslim leaders, among them,
Walji Lalji Sait and Syed Mahomed Nizamuddin, both
of whom were long identified with the Congress and
had served in the Madras Standing Congress Committee. The circular claimed that recent events,
notably, the simultaneous examinations issue, had
revealed the need "to organise some schemes that
will concentrate Muslim opinion." The apathy of
the community as a whole was deplored, but the proposed association was intended to channel Muslim
energies to the political, social, and moral advancement of the community and to arrest the

progressive deterioration in its condition. The circular also gave expression to Muslim dissatisfaction with some aspects of official policy, although it was not the intention of the new association to imitate the methods of the "Indian Radicals."[129] The Central Mahomedan Association, as the new body was called, was formally inaugurated in March 1894.[130]

Almost simultaneously, Muslims in the *mofussil* were showing a similar capacity for unity and organization. Responding to the call of the Mahomedan Educational Conference to organize "educational Anjumans" to further the cause of Muslim education, leaders in the *mofussil* had hastened to form such bodies, which in most instances were the only tangible expression of Muslim concern for their community's problems. By 1894 almost every center of Muslim concentration in the Presidency, including, Dindigul, Vizianagram, Cuddapah, Madura, Trichinopoly, and Salem, could boast of its own educational association. Here was Muslim communal solidarity in its incipient form, finding manifestation largely as a counterpoise to the "Hindu" Congress.

The extent to which the Congress had lost the support of the minority groups in South India was brought into sharp relief when the tenth session met in Madras in December 1894. The local reception committee, hoping to emulate the feat of 1887, exerted all its influence to secure the participation of the various minority groups in South India. The only positive response came from the Indian Christians, with many of their leaders serving in the reception committee.[131] The Eurasian and Anglo-Indian Association declined the invitation, adhering loyally to the decision it had taken in 1891.

The focus of Congress efforts, however, was the Muslims. But the Central Mahomedan Association ended any hopes of Muslim participation when it resolved in October 1894 that all Muslims should "hold rigidly aloof," on the grounds that the Congress was "not conducive to the general political welfare of the country, nor to the special

interests of the Mahomedan community."[132]   Although
eighteen Muslims eventually attended the meeting
from various parts of South India, the important
leaders were conspicuous by their absence. Rangiah
Naidu, Chairman of the Reception Committee, conceded in his welcoming speech to all delegates that
"an important section of our Mahomedan fellow-
countrymen have stood aloof of our movement."[133]

The secession of the Muslims reflected the
problems of the Congress in trying to resolve some
of the contradictions inherent within Indian society. Since 1887, when the annual session of the
Congress was held in Madras, the Hindu politicians
in the city had made an ambitious drive to broaden
the base of the nationalist movement by incorpor-
ating the minority groups in South India. Though
this drive seemed to have made some headway initially, in the long run it only brought to the
surface the underlying antagonisms that existed between the various ethnic and religious groups in
the Presidency. The Hindu politicians, despite
their political sophistication and organizational
skills, were unable to reconcile the conflicting
aspirations which informed the actions of these
minority groups. Hence, even before the nineteenth
century drew to a close, the politics of communal
separatism had begun to obstruct the integrative
role of territorial nationalism in South India.

7. Hindu Revivalism and the Age of Consent Bill Controversy

The search for minority support was not the only problem which the Congress encountered during the early years of its existence. No less troublesome was the problem of reaching accommodation with the protagonists of social reform, who, since the Congress first met in 1885, had become increasingly vocal in demanding the inclusion of social issues on its agenda. Reformers, like B. M. Malabari, the Parsi editor of the *Indian Spectator* of Bombay, and Raghunatha Rao of Madras, often reminded their political counterparts that the Congress, if it aspired to become a truly national assembly, could scarcely deny social reform its due place in its debates. The Congress leadership resisted such arguments by asserting, as Dadabhai Naoroji did in his presidential address to the second Congress in December 1886, that an all-India gathering, such as the Congress, was hardly the forum to discuss the traditions, customs, and prejudices of a country as sharply segmented as India was by differences of creed, caste, and language. "A National Congress," Naoroji declared, "must confine itself to questions in which the entire nation has a direct participation and it must leave the adjustment of social reforms and other class questions to class Congresses."[1] Implicit in Naoroji's argument was the fear

that the Congress had not attained sufficient organizational strength to bear the strains which the
discussion of social issues was bound to create.
M. G. Ranade, whose political instincts convinced
him that this fear was real, was, however, not prepared to accept Naoroji's thesis that social change
could only be attained through sectional and class
organizations. "We are in a sense," Ranade told
his social reform friends in 1888, "as strictly
national socially, as we are politically. Though
the differences are great for purposes of immediate
and practical reform, yet there is a background of
common traditions, common religion, common laws and
institutions and customs and perversions of such
customs, which make it possible to deliberate together in spite of our differences."[2] And it was
Ranade, aided by a few other social reformers, who
brought into existence the National Social Conference in December 1887 to provide a platform to debate reformist issues of an all-India character.

Although the Social Conference was modelled on
the Congress, and it met annually alongside the
Congress, sharing facilities and even delegates,
this was a compromise arrangement between two unequal parties. The Social Conference found itself
in a subordinate relationship to the Congress.
That the Congress leadership accepted this arrangement was doubtless inspired by the desire to relieve itself of charges from friendly and hostile
quarters that it was neglecting social problems.
However, such an arrangement did not always exempt
the Congress from becoming embroiled in social issues. The best-known instance of such involvement
was the controversy that erupted in 1890 over the
Age of Consent Bill. Although the Congress in its
collective capacity successfully resisted pressures
to take a stand on this issue, it was a decision
which failed to satisfy those Congress politicians
who had become deeply involved in the controversy.
In South India, as in many other parts of the country, the Age of Consent Bill provoked a stormy debate in which prominent Congress leaders found

themselves in opposing camps. To grasp the nature
and implications of this controversy, it is important to know something of a new phenomenon which
was making its influence felt in the Presidency at
this juncture, namely, Hindu Revivalism.

HINDU REVIVALISM

For much of the nineteenth century, Hinduism
was on the defensive against a variety of pressures
released by the Western impact. First, there was
the challenge of the Christian missions, who made
no secret of their desire to destroy Hinduism and
its social institutions. Second, there were the
disintegrative features associated with certain
British policies. In their efforts to outlaw practices which they deemed repugnant to decency and
humanity, the British authorities enacted laws
which impinged upon long-established usages associated with Hinduism. A third source of pressure
came from reformist-minded Hindus, mostly those who
were educated in high schools and colleges and who
had imbibed the rationalist teachings of Western
philosophy and science. They were critical of many
aspects of their traditional religious system, and
some called for a thoroughgoing reformation in
order to do away with such notions as pollution and
untouchability, and to minimize the rigors of infant marriage and enforced widowhood. Some educated Hindus, like the Veda Samajists, even contemplated the formation of a theistic Hindu church
where sectarian divisions would be disavowed and
idolatry discarded. Hinduism, attacked from various quarters, found little intellectual succor,
even from its own adherents, during the 1860s and
1870s. Not surprisingly, some observers discerned
"the visible signs" of its waning vitality, reflected in its decaying temples, the ignorant pundits, the corrupt priesthood, and factious temple
committees presiding over the spoliation of their
rich endowments.[3]

However, despite such gloomy portrayals of the
future Hinduism, few ventured to predict its ultimate overthrow. Such expectations had vanished by
the 1850s when Hinduism successfully weathered the
massive assault of the Christian missions. The
British rulers, despite legislation against certain
taboos associated with Hinduism, had achieved surprisingly little in changing the matrix of social
and religious rites of the Hindus. The caste system, with all its harsh inequalities and its offensive concepts about pollution and untouchability,
had shown resilience and even found new modes of
expression through more effective and extended
caste organization, helped no doubt by modern communications. Popular Hinduism, with its interminable family and communal rites, had lost none of
its hold upon the Hindu masses. Indeed, the introduction of rail communications further popularized
Hindu festivities, notably, visits to sacred
shrines in different, and sometimes, remote parts
of the country. Even Western-educated Hindus, despite their intellectual skepticism and radical
outpourings in the press and on the platform,
rarely missed out in these family and communal ceremonies. Be they Brahmins or non-Brahmins, matriculates or graduates, administrators or lawyers,
they continued to adhere faithfully to many of the
time-honored customs, particularly the laws governing commensality and marriage.
     One complaint frequently heard about the
Western-educated Hindus was their lack of enthusiasm or conviction in their religion. It was often
said that they discharged their religious responsibilities without any conception of their origin or
significance. Many ascribed this to the secular
education that they received in state schools. The
obsessive concern of parents to send their children
to such schools, the latter's anxiety to pass the
numerous and exacting examinations, and their eager-
ness to find a vocation and make a success of it
had left them with little time or energy to become
acquainted with their religion. This was true as

much of the Brahmin as non-Brahmin youth, although
in the case of the former they would have learned
by rote some relevant stanzas from the Vedas to be
able to recite them at their daily prayers, though
in many cases the true meaning of what they recited
escaped them.

It was a state of affairs which led to demands
from certain Hindu circles, beginning in the late
1870s, for some kind of religious instruction in
schools. Some argued that, unless this was done,
the government would be turning out a class suf-
fused with religious skepticism, even "downright
atheism," and the consequences would be dangerous
not only to the established social order but also
to the long-term political security of the British
Raj.[4] Some believed that the fault lay with the
Hindu pundits whose failure to provide a meaningful
intellectual exposition of their religion had lost
them the respect of the Western-educated class. It
was asserted that, unless the pundits could generate some kind of intellectual debate, Hinduism
could not conceivably rally the support of its
most intelligent and active adherents.[5] This debate, oddly enough, was initiated during the early
1880s by a foreign agency, the Theosophical Society.

Founded in New York in 1875 by Colonel H. S.
Olcott and Madame H. P. Blavatsky, this Society, in
the words of one of its founders, aimed at three
main objectives: "to promote a feeling of brother-
hood among men, regardless of race, creed, or
colour; to promote the study of Aryan and other
religions, philosophies, and sciences; and to promote experimental research into the hidden laws of
Nature and the latent capabilities of man."[6] In
1879 the Society shifted its headquarters to Bombay,
presumably to pursue its inquiry into the esoteric
teachings of Indian religions. As Olcott explained
in his first major lecture to an Indian audience in
March 1879, a search into the early literatures of
the East, especially of countries like India, Egypt,
Tibet, and Persia, was expected to reveal "the
occult laws of nature," which in turn would provide

some of the answers to the unresolved puzzles of
Western science.[7]

The Theosophical Society, because of its professions and because it was founded by two Wes-
terners of somewhat obscure background, was bound
to attract attention in an India whose own cultural
and literary legacy had long been at a discount and
where interest in the "natural phenomena," about
which Blavatsky had written at length in her *Isis
Unveiled*, had always been deep rooted. Consequently, on their arrival in Bombay, the Theosophist
leaders were flooded with queries, emanating as
much from Indians as Europeans, from friends as
from critics, and from North as from South India.
Many of these genuine queries were answered in
public lectures, social gatherings, and through
the columns of the Society's journal, the *Theosophist*.

Some hostile critics had also to be answered.
One story that gained wide currency was that Olcott
and Blavatsky were Russian spies seeking to subvert
British rule in India. Olcott assured the government in 1879: ". . . our existence threatens no
Government, feeds no political cabal, attacks no
pillar of social order."[8] A request was also made
to the Indian authorities to free the Society from
police surveillance, and this was acceded to in
1880.[9] Olcott also felt constrained to clarify the
Society's association with the natural phenomena.
He claimed that many Indians saw the Society as "a
miracle club" and wished to join it "to get their
fill of wonders." If they were disappointed, they
cast aspersions upon the Society and abused its
founders. Olcott felt compelled to come to the defence of Blavatsky. He felt that her critics had
slandered her most unjustly: "See this great,
generous-hearted soul, filled with love for humanity; longing to throw light into the darkened minds
of those who still believe in miracles, and still
clank the chains of superstition; devoting her life,
sacrificing the sweets of home, and family and ease,
and a high social position, to go about the world

in search of truth, and spreading it so that all
may partake."10

Although miracles and occult science continued
to receive attention, the Theosophist appeal in
India stemmed largely from Olcott's exposition of
the country's great achievements in the past, the
causes of its present plight, and the panacea for
its future regeneration. In his lecture tours to
various parts of the country, and in his orations
at the anniversary meetings of the Society, Olcott
entered into lengthy disquisitions about the grandeur of India's early achievements in religion,
science, and philosophy. He contended that the re-
searches of Sir William Jones had led the way into
the "splendid garden of Sanskrit literature" which
astonished the West with "its glorious flowers of
poesy, its fruits of metaphysics and philosophy,
its crystalline rivulets of science, [and] its mag-
nificent structures of philology." Then, the re-
searches of Max Muller and other Sanskrit scholars
of the contemporary generation had given substance
to the theory that "Aryavarta was the cradle of
European civilization, the Aryans the progenitors
of the Western peoples, and their literature the
source and spring of all Western religions and
philosophies." Olcott believed that with further
intensive research the world would come to know
"the whole truth about Aryan civilization."

Turning from the past to contemporary India,
Olcott found it difficult "to escape a sense of
crushing despair." He asked: "Where are the sages,
the warriors, the giant intellects of yore? Where
the happiness, the independence of spirit, the
self-respecting dignity, that made an Aryan feel
himself fit to rule the world, nay, to meet the
very gods on equal terms?" Instead, Olcott saw
poverty, starvation, and famine. There was disunity: "province is arrayed against province, race
against race, sect against sect, brother against
brother"; the big cities of the past had crumbled;
the hallowed repositories of religion were in ruins;
the Brahmins served in menial professions as clerks

and merchants, while those in temples "repeat their
slokas and sastras in a parrot-like way." The
youth of the country were "turning materialists under the influence of European educators," wholly
ignorant of their grand past heritage.

While drawing this portrait of contemporary
India, Olcott did not extinguish all hopes for regeneration. His panacea for the country's ills was
the dissemination of Aryan science and religion,
especially the Vedas. "An Indian civilization
resting upon the Vedas," Olcott said, "and other
old national works, is like a strong castle built
upon rocks." He stressed that the new edifice must
have "a strictly national character. Whoever is a
true friend of India will make himself recognized
by his desire to nationalise her modern progress;
her enemy is he who advocates the denationalization
of her arts, industries, lines of thought, and
aspirations." He placed high hopes on Western education which he believed would create *"a new class
which is to guide the nation up the hill."* If the
existing political stability continued, and positions of trust in the government were increasingly
thrown open to Indians, Olcott felt that the existing barriers that had kept Indians apart would be
removed:[11]

> Gradually they are realizing that, however dis-
> tant the Punjab may be from Travancore, or
> Cutch from Bengal, the people are yet brothers,
> children of the same mother. When this convic-
> tion shall once possess the whole body of these
> twenty-four crores then will the renascence of
> this nation have indeed arrived.

The activities of the Theosophist leaders had
attracted attention in South India, but actual contact with them was only established in October 1881
when Olcott and Blavatsky visited Tuticorin and
Tinnevelly in the course of their extended tour to
Ceylon. Tinnevelly had the distinction of forming
the first branch of the Theosophical Society in

South India, and it was at the invitation of this branch that the Theosophist leaders visited the district. An enthusiastic reception greeted them on their arrival, with leading Hindu officials and priests forming the welcoming party, while the managers of a Siva temple in Tinnevelly invited them to visit its inner precincts where Olcott lectured to a large audience. Called the "American Pundit," Olcott impressed Hindu listeners with his "deep erudition, extraordinarily instructive and impressive orations, soldiery and venerable appearance, and pleasing deportment."[12]

But, rather predictably, the visitors ran into opposition from the Christian missionaries who distributed leaflets attacking Theosophy and its organizers.[13] Olcott, replying to his critics, asserted that ever since the Society was organized its founders had been pursued by "the bigots of Christian theology." He alleged that it was "these insatiate enemies that have set police spies to track our footsteps throughout India; that have charged us with being adventurers; that have circulated numberless lies about us; that have forged letters we never wrote."

In a speech at Tuticorin, Olcott launched a frontal assault on Western civilization for its materialism, for its addiction to opium and liquor, and for its aggressive instincts which had led to wars and subjugation of weaker nations. Christianity might have an excellent moral code, argued Olcott, but that was not the real test of the quality of a civilization:

> Christendom has as fine a moral code as could be wished for; but she shows her real principles in her Krupp and Armstrong guns and whiskey distilleries, in her opium ships, sophisticated merchandise, prurient amusements, licentiousness and political dishonesty. Christendom we may almost say, is morally rotten and spiritually paralysed.[14]

The visit to Tinnevelly district, lasting only
four days, was too brief for the Theosophists to
make any great impression on the Presidency as a
whole. However, Olcott and Blavatsky decided to
follow up this modest beginning by undertaking in
April 1882 a six-week tour of South India.   In
Madras Olcott reiterated what he had been preaching
in other parts of the country. He appealed to the
"old men and young men of Madras" to cooperate with
the Society in its task of working for the restoration of India's "ancient religion, for the vindication of her ancient glory, for the maintenance of
her greatness in science, in the arts, [and] in
philosophy."[15] This appeal found a response, and
a Madras Branch of the Theosophical Society was
organized, with Reghunatha Rao as President, G.
Muthusamy Chetty and P. Srinivasa Rao, both Judges
of the Court of Small Causes, as Vice-Presidents,
and T. Subba Rao, a Vakil in the High Court, as
Secretary. Later, Olcott and Blavatsky travelled
to Nellore and Guntur, among other places, and
branch bodies were formed there as well. Their
reception, even in such remote places as Guntur,
exceeded their expectations, with large crowds
turning out to give them an enthusiastic welcome.
In Nellore, an address of welcome was presented to
them in which the Theosophist leaders were praised
for their devoted efforts "to regenerate the
Indian natives by reviving their recollection of
the scientific glory of their country which once
in times of yore, shone forth in radiant lustre,
but which, owing to the progress of a well-known
cycle in the destinies of nations, has been practically over-darkened some centuries past."[16]
    It was during this visit that the possibility
of shifting the Society's headquarters to Madras
was discussed with local leaders. As Olcott later
recorded, the Society had been in financial difficulties in Bombay, having to contend with high
rent and other charges,[17] and being obviously unable to raise enough subscriptions to meet them
punctually. Madras was considered as an

alternative as Theosophy was gaining popularity
there. This was reflected in the warm reception
that the founders received during their tour, in
the fact that Madras was outstripping Bombay in the
number of subscribers to the *Theosophist* and the
further evidence that the membership of the Madras
branch was the largest in India of any single
branch.[18] In December 1882, following the first
"representative convention of all Indian Branches"
held in Bombay,[19] the Society moved to Madras where
a commodious building was purchased in Adyar which
was, henceforth, to serve as the nucleus of the
Society's activities in India and beyond.

The shift to Adyar underlined the determination of Olcott and Blavatsky to exploit their popularity by covering the entire Presidency with a
network of Theosophist branches. By January 1883
at least nine centers in South India were known to
have organized local branches. Those in Bellary,
Palghat, Chingleput, Cuddapah, and Madura had done
so at the initiative of local leaders.

Olcott wanted to build on this organization,
and, leaving Blavatsky to run the *Theosophist,* he
embarked on his crusading tours, which, in the
course of the year, took him over seven thousand
miles of Indian territory. No place was too remote
for him, and his itinerary was not affected either
by hot weather or the monsoon. In July-August
1883 he undertook an extensive tour of the Tamil
and Malayalam-speaking areas, visiting Trichinopoly,
Tanjore, Kumbaconam, Mayaveram, Negapatam, Madura,
Srivilliputtur, Tinnevelly, Nagercoil, Trevandram,
Palghat, Coimbatore, and Cuddalore. Almost everywhere, he received a warm reception, lectured on
Theosophy, and performed some of his miraculous
cures.[20] Olcott had no illusions as to the reasons
for his popularity: "I was the friend and defender
of their religion, and had a way of curing the sick
that people called the miraculous." In his view,
it was this tour which started the Hindu revival in
South India when "the backbone of the Indian movement towards Materialism was broken."[21]

Essentially, Theosophy appealed only to the Hindus in South India, especially Brahmins and the higher non-Brahmin castes. Foremost in the work of establishing branches were the members of the professional elite, already prominent in local politics by their participation in municipal affairs and the running of district associations and literary societies. Every branch of the Theosophical Society had a lawyer or a teacher, and the well-known personalities who identified themselves with Theosophy included S. Subramania Iyer, Saminatha Iyer, and Kesava Pillay. Equally important, Theosophy attracted many Hindu officials who had kept aloof from nationalist politics. Almost every branch committee included either a deputy collector, district *munsif*, or *tahsildar*. Much of the financial support for the movement came from the merchant class who had always displayed generosity in supporting cultural and religious activities. Although the names of Hindu priests and pundits are rarely to be found in the list of branch committees, their support for Theosophy was attested by their appearance in parties welcoming the Theosophist leaders and by their invitations to Olcott to deliver his stirring lectures in the precincts of their temples.

Although the appeal of Theosophy among such Hindu groups as priests, pundits, and merchants, was only to be expected, what surprised many observers was the strong support which the movement enlisted from Western-educated Hindus in South India, be they the politically radical younger elements of the professional elite, or their elder counterparts in the administration. Olcott claimed in December 1885, with some justification, that the Society had in its ranks the "flower of Indian people," notably, the Indian intelligentsia, the same class which he labelled some years ago as "the most denationalised."[22] T. Madava Rao, writing in the *Madras Times*, attested to the popularity of the movement amongst the educated segment of the Indian people and went on to claim that the

progress in education had created a demand "for
some form of general religion as would commend itself to the vast and heterogeneous population of
India without a direct or destructive conflict with
existing beliefs. Theosophy is acceptable to the
educated natives on account of its broad national
basis."[23] The *Christian College Magazine,* dissen-
ting from this view, argued that Theosophy had
gained "cheap and temporary success by following
the obscurantist role, and exalting the past at the
expense of the present."[24]

However, by far the most penetrating analysis
into the popularity of the Theosophical Movement
came from the editor of the *Madras Mail.* Writing
soon after Olcott's remarkably successful tour of
South India in July–August 1883, the editor dismissed explanations which attributed the success of
the movement to "the native fondness for tamashas"
or to the thrust and content of Olcott's lectures.
No doubt Olcott's "charming simplicity, a profound
belief in himself and in his work" did help the
cause, but the editor felt that the real answer to
Theosophist success in South India must be sought
elsewhere:[25]

Part of the answer at least is to be found in
the undoubted fact that of late years there
has been a decided revival of national Indian
feeling. In spite of the disintegrating power
of caste, which splits the Hindu peoples into
so many fragments at constant feuds with each
other, a new generation has realised to some
extent the truth that Indians ought to be one.
The old apologetic tone which characterized
the utterances of natives regarding everything
Indian a short time ago, has given place to a
tone of self-assertion, not quite so pleasant
to the ruling class perhaps, but certainly
very much more natural and healthy . . . The
old school Hindu considered it his duty to
take meekly the rebukes of Europeans, and even
to esteem them as precious evil. The new

school has no such amiable weakness. European
scholars have taught them, not certainly to
know their own classics, for that is what few
can boast of, but to believe in them. If once
it should become possible to regard Hindu
literature, science, and religion as ahead of
the times, nothing would be wanting to enable
the Hindu to boast himself not only as the
equal, but as the superior of the European.
The hour brought forth the man, and the man
was Colonel Olcott.

The fact that the Western-educated Hindus,
known for their religious skepticism and disregard
for their inherited cultural traditions, should
have responded to Theosophy in the way they did can
only be explained in terms of their changing attitudes towards British rule in general and Western
cultural impact in particular. Since the beginning
of the nineteenth century, Indians had been on the
defensive politically and culturally, with the
British rulers recasting their political and administrative institutions and imposing their own laws
and standards of social morality, with Christian
missionaries threatening to dismantle the very
bases of the Indian social and religious system and
to reorder it along Western lines, and with English
educationists implanting a system of instruction in
India alien not only in content but also in the
mode and language of teaching. Indians, by and
large, had been passive recipients of this Western
cultural package, although they resisted strongly
whenever overt attempts were made to interfere in
their religious or social usages. One product of
this cultural package was the Western-educated
class, raised in the ethos of its political masters
and sometimes even an instrument in the diffusion
of some aspects of this alien culture in the country at large.
    The Theosophist leaders arrived in India at a
time when the Western-educated Hindus were experiencing the first stirrings of modern political life,

soon to be translated into provincial and all-India organizations and conferences. Although the political models were essentially Western, the politicians who adopted them in India were conscious that their claims for a distinctive Indian identity could not be grounded on borrowed culture, or a culture which they regarded as inferior. National pride required something more, and it was here that the Theosophical Society fulfilled an important role. By discovering, or purporting to discover, the achievements of ancient India in the fields of religion, science, and philosophy, and by extolling the virtues of some of the country's social and cultural traditions, Theosophy breathed a new sense of pride into Hindus and replaced the old myth of India's inferiority with the new myth of superiority. To reinforce this, the Theosophist leaders denounced many aspects of Western civilization, especially the growth of materialism and skepticism. Though such sentiments were by no means novel in India, the fact that they were made by two representatives of the West carried greater conviction. Theosophy had given India's Western-educated class a new sense of self-respect for itself and its country as such. It took to heart Olcott's dictum that "a nation that respects itself can never sink low."[26] Herein lay the reason for the popularity of Theosophy during the eighties.

The relationship between Theosophy and Hindu Revivalism, in the form that it emerged in South India at this time, was a direct and intimate one. In drawing attention to India's hoary past, in demanding that the Vedas and Shastras should form the bedrock on which India's future should be built, and in calling for the instruction of the country's youth in their own scriptures, the Theosophical Society had struck at the very core of the Revivalist program, which was to be widely debated during the coming decades. Equally significant, both Olcott and Blavatsky were anxious to mobilize the widespread enthusiasm that they had roused among the Hindus to undertake certain practical

schemes which they believed would give permanence
to their work.

One such scheme was the starting of Sanskrit
schools. Soon after the Society's headquarters
were shifted to Adyar, Olcott gave a lecture to a
Madras audience in which he complained that the
youth of the country was not being taught "the
first principles of their national religion." As a
remedy, he suggested the starting of special classes, like the Sunday schools of the Christians, to
which Hindu youth could be sent to learn the tenets
of their faith. To facilitate teaching, Olcott
also indicated that a series of catechisms and
readers be compiled, embodying the fundamental principles of Hinduism culled from Sanskrit classics.
The proposals were welcomed, and a committee was
set up under the chairmanship of Gajapati Rao.[27]
By July 1883 the committee had finalized plans for
starting Sanskrit schools in Triplicane, Mylapore,
and Black Town, and the local Theosophists agreed
to send their children to these schools before admitting them into English schools.[28] The idea also
won support in some of the major *mofussil* centres,
notably, Madura, Bellary, Nellore, Vizianagram,
Trichinopoly, and Guntur, where Sanskrit schools
were opened under the auspices of the branch committees of the Theosophical Society.

Far more ambitious, both in conception and
execution, was the Adyar Oriental Library.
Olcott's grand design for a "national Sanskrit movement" in India revolved mainly around an Oriental
library which would attract not only Indian pundits
but also Western orientalists. If the scheme succeeded, Olcott had visions of Adyar becoming "a
second Alexandria, and on these lovely grounds a
new Serapion may arise."[29] The library was intended to be a repository of "the best religious,
moral, practical, and philosophical teachings of
the ancient sages," and he appealed to fellow
Theosophists and patriotic Indians to make gifts of
such works to the library, where he would edit,
translate, and superintend their publication with

the help of learned scholars. At the same time,
this institution would also train pundits, and impart to them a more intimate and deeper understanding of their ancient literature and religion,
which would enable them to command the respect of
the "educated men, especially that of the rising
generation." In December 1886 the Adyar Oriental
Library was formally opened at a ceremony graced
by religious dignitaries from Hinduism, Islam, Buddhism, and Zorastrianism.[30]

The Theosophical Society also inspired Hindu
revivalists to work on their own initiative. A
number of revivalist societies sprang up in South
India to disseminate the tenets of Hinduism, to
purge it of certain impurities accumulated over the
centuries, and to find ways to check inroads by
other faiths, notably, Christianity. One such
society was the Hindu Sabha, founded in 1880 by A.
Sankariah, Dewan-Peishkar of Trichur in Cochin
State. It professed to promote social and religious reforms among the Hindus with "the support of
pundits and priests of social standing," and to
eliminate "dogmas, schisms and practices opposed to
the consolidation of the Hindu Nation."[31] Branches
of the Sabha were established in some *mofussil*
towns, and a monthly journal, called the *Hindu Reformer and Politician,* was started in 1882 to remove misconceptions about the social and religious
institutions of the Hindus.[32] An appeal was made
to all educated Hindus to join, irrespective of
their sectarian or caste background, and within two
years it claimed a membership of 150 "representing
every district, caste and sect and service and
occupation."[33] Its published list of members revealed a high proportion of graduates, many of them
occupying important positions in administrative,
legal, and teaching professions. The Hindu Sabha
had also entered into an alliance with the Theosophical Society, and played an active part in the
welcome that Olcott and Blavatsky received when
they first visited Madras in April 1882.

Working less ostentatiously in the cause of

Hindu Revivalism was Sivasankara Pandiah, a
Gujerati Brahmin, who had taken his B.A. in 1878
and then become a teacher in Pachaiyappa High
School. A scholar of Sanskrit, Tamil, and Telugu,
Pandiah had been influenced by the activities of
the Theosophical Society. As he said some years
later, it was the Society's "strong and rational
advocacy" of India's ancestral faiths which led him
to labor for "the moral and spiritual regeneration"
of the country.[34] He shared the Theosophist dislike of those Hindus who pursued "novelty for
novelty's sake" and regarded "everything new as pro-
ductive of benefits, and everything old as produc-
tive of evils." Pandiah was convinced that there
was much that was good in Indian society and saw no
reason for any servile imitation of the ways of the
West. "We have," he said, "the precious stones of
social and moral truths at our very doors. We have
only to dig them up."[35]

A person of sincerity and singular dedication,
whom Olcott characterized as "an eloquent and intense man,"[36] Pandiah emerged during the eighties
as one of the leading champions of Hindu Revivalism
in South India. He devoted his spare hours to conducting moral and religious classes and compiling
readers explaining the basic tenets of Hinduism.
At times, his straitened pecuniary circumstances
prevented him from publishing some of his works.
Partly to overcome this difficulty, Pandiah launched
in April 1887 the Hindu Tract Society with the help
of some of his close friends. This society pledged
itself to "spread Hinduism and to defend it against
the attacks of its opponents," while at the same
time seeking to promote "the cause of morality and
sound learning" among the Hindus.[37] Over the next
two years, the Hindu Tract Society established
branch bodies in the *mofussil* towns, published and
distributed numerous tracts on Hinduism, and engaged Hindu preachers to tour the districts.[38]

With the growth of revivalist societies in
South India seeking to spread their message through
preachers and tracts, Hinduism began to acquire a

new consciousness of its own strength and a heightened sensitiveness to attacks from any hostile
quarter.

This was clearly revealed in the so-called
"Christian College Disturbance" of April 1888. A
Brahmin student in this leading missionary college
of South India, wishing to convert to Christianity,
had taken shelter in a missionary's house for fear
of "personal violence." His fellow Hindu students,
believing that conversion was contemplated without
his parents' being consulted, urged the College
authorities to postpone baptism. Although the request was conceded, the Hindu students carried
their protest a stage further by criticizing College teachers for their methods of teaching scripture. The College authorities rejected these
complaints, but, when students in one senior class
misbehaved by "uproariously and persistently imped-
ing work," they took disciplinary action by suspending them and imposing a fine.

This sparked off a more widespread "disturbance," with "a riotous throng" swamping the corridors of the College while some students "mobbed"
their professors. At this point, the College
decided on firmer measures and expelled two students believed to be the ringleaders. This led to
a student boycott of classes, with meetings held in
which the College authorities were urged to drop
punitive action and to readmit the expelled
students.[39]   Two Hindu leaders, Ananda Charlu and
Chentsal Rao, met the College principal in an
effort to find a settlement without the students
being subjected to any "harsh conditions." The
Principal seemed to be sympathetic, but the College
Council insisted on an apology as a condition of
readmission, as well as a fine on those students
who had absented themselves during the boycott of
classes. The bulk of the students returned to the
College after fulfilling these conditions, but
some decided to stay away.[40]

This incident and its ramifications can only
be understood against the wider setting of

deteriorating relations between Christianity and
Hinduism in South India. In its version of the disturbance, the Free Church Mission claimed that in
recent years some societies had been waging a campaign against the Christian missions. It alleged
that the students were affected by this campaign,
and an atmosphere of distrust had been created between missionary teachers and students. In the
disturbance of April 1888, the Free Church Mission
claimed the protesting students were "stirred up by
outsiders" into adopting extreme tactics.[41]

    There is a germ of truth in this version, but
it glosses over the fact that the College authorities and teachers, for their part, had also contributed their share in precipitating the incident.
Though teachers in missionary institutions had
always in the past made slighting references to
Hinduism in their scripture classes, they failed to
realize that the immunity that they had long enjoyed from any form of retaliation was coming to an
end, notably, since Theosophy and revivalist groups
began to preach about India's ancestral religion,
science, and philosophy.

    In December 1884 at the annual convention of
Theosophists, Olcott had supported a resolution
calling for the formation in all centers of an
"Aryan League of Honour," restricted to youths between ten and twenty-one, in order to meet "a
strong feeling of love" which college and high
school students had shown for "the cause of Aryan
moral regeneration."[42] This must have come as a
surprise to those who believed that the revelations
of Madam Coulomb, published recently by the
Christian College Magazine to "expose the fraudu-
lent nature of the phenomena" associated with the
founders of Theosophy,[43] would have discredited the
Society in general and Blavatsky in particular.
Apparently, they did not do so as far as college
students in Madras were concerned. In December
1884, when Blavatsky returned to Madras after an
overseas visit, students from various colleges in
the metropolis, including many from the Madras

Christian College, presented her an address in
which they expressed their country's debt to her
and Olcott for undertaking "that gigantic labour of
love--the vivifying on the alters of Aryavarta the
dying flame of religion and spirituality." The students, in this address, also rejected the charges
which some teachers of Christian College had made
against Blavatsky following the revelations that
were published in the College journal.[44]

Thus, it was apparent that many Hindu students
were feeling the currents of Theosophy and revivalist fervor which had already affected their
parents, and it was not surprising that they chose
Christian College as the target to vent their
feelings against missionary attacks on their religion.

One Hindu who felt very strongly about this
entire episode was Sivasankara Pandiah. In a
letter to the *Hindu*, he ascribed the student
trouble in Christian College to "the gross insult
offered to Hinduism by the bigoted Missionary-
Professors." He asserted that the time had
arrived for orthodox Hindus to show their patriotism and zeal for their religion by starting
"National schools and colleges" throughout the
country.[45] He also announced the establishment of
a "Hindu Theological College Fund," designed to
raise money to build a national college in Madras
where secular and religious instruction would be
imparted. Assurances of support had come from
many Hindus, and Pandiah appealed to Hindu rulers,
zamindars, landholders, merchants, and lawyers to
contribute to the fund in order that the proposed
college could be started in the following year.[46]

Pandiah's hopes of realizing his scheme depended largely on the reaction of the influential
Hindu groups in Madras. Much to his disappointment,
Hindu opinion was divided between those who supported him and those who wished to raise Pachaiyappa College from a second to a first-grade college. Pandiah, himself, was not opposed to the
elevation of Pachaiyappa College, but he felt that

this move by itself was inadequate to combat Hindu
dependence on missionary educational institutions.[47]
In May 1888 a public meeting was held in Madras,
attended by, among others, Madava Rao, Raghunatha
Rao, Ananda Charlu, and G. Subramania Iyer, to discuss the rival proposals, and it was then decided
that it would be more expedient to strengthen
Pachaiyappa College rather than embark on a fresh
venture.[48] This was a blow to Pandiah's hopes and,
to aggravate matters, he was forced to resign his
position in Pachaiyappa College following a sharp
exchange of letters between him and William Miller,
Principal of Christian College. John Adam, Principal of Pachaiyappa College, pressed for Pandiah's
resignation on the grounds that he had shown "a
want of inter-collegiate etiquette and courtesy."
Pandiah's resignation in July 1888, according to
one account, caused "quite a sensation in the Hindu
quarters" of Madras.[49]

These setbacks, far from daunting Pandiah,
spurred him on to even more determined efforts to
realize what he claimed was "the dream of my
life."[50] In a series of discourses, he explained,
at length, the necessity of establishing a theological college and called for generous Hindu contributions. His strongest financial backers were
some Hindu merchants in Madras, principally, M.
Balakrishniah Pantalu and T. Gopinath Tawker,
Treasurer and Secretary, respectively, of the Hindu
Theological College Fund. Ramakrishniah Pantalu, a
Theosophist, was a wealthy merchant in Sowcarpet,
while Gopinath Tawker belonged to a long-
established diamond firm in Mint Street, which had
made a large fortune through sales of gems and
stones to the ruling aristocracy and wealthy
Indians and Europeans.[51] Although Pandiah had estimated that about Rs 500,000 would be required to
launch a college, subscriptions had been considerably less. By September 1888, Rs 31,000 had been
raised,[52] and it was decided that this amount was
adequate to start a high school. In January 1889
the Hindu Theosophical High School was formally

opened with a student enrollment of 300 and with
Pandiah as headmaster.[53] At the end of the year, a
spacious building was purchased in the hope of giving "stability and permanence" to the institution.[54] Financial support continued to come, sometimes even in large amounts. In 1891, for example,
the Raja of Ramnad donated Rs 15,000 following his
visit to the institution, and Pandiah even cherished hopes that with more such donations a theological university might be eventually established
which could give diplomas to students specializing
in Hindu theology.[55]

The Hindu Theological High School was only one
expression of the growing influence of Hindu
Revivalism in South India. As this movement gained
in strength, relations with the Christian missionaries progressively worsened. Any onslaught by the
latter on Hinduism, either through student conversions or street preachings at Hindu festivals, provoked an angry response from the Hindu revivalists.
One missionary complained in September 1889 that
Hindus did not appreciate "the spirit of true
toleration." He wrote:

> Hinduism is tolerant in name but not in reality.
> Every week brings fresh evidence of its in-
> tolerant spirit. Every conversion arouses
> latent intolerance, which manifests itself in
> indignation meetings and bitter reproaches upon
> the padres and all who have been connected with
> the conversion.[56]

Another missionary, Rev. J. C. Peattie of the
Free Church Mission, expressed his deep concern
over "the new style warfare" which the Hindu revivalist societies had introduced in South India.
In an appeal to the Western-educated class, he
accused these societies of "rousing prejudice and
ill-feeling in their worst forms, and of inducing
youth to practise all manner of rudeness and
bravado." He welcomed Hindu cooperation, particularly to arrest the deterioration in student

behavior in Madras.[57]

If European missionaries had misgivings about
Hindu Revivalism, Hindu social reformers in Madras
seemed to have regarded it as an ally of their
cause. Some social reformers, notably, of the traditional school, believed that revivalists would
help their cause by propagating the true doctrines
of Hinduism. Raghunatha Rao, for example, saw in
Hindu Revivalism a means to restore the "golden
age" of India when the conduct of the Hindus would
again be determined by the Shastras.[58] A member of
the Theosophical Society, he had established the
Association for the Propagation of True Religion in
1886 to encourage the study of the Shastras.[59] The
Hindu, whose editor and managing proprietor were
active in social reform organizations, saw the
revivalist movement as "the result of a generous
spirit of improvement, a general renaissance, that
is rapidly permeating the whole Hindu nation." The
paper denied that there was intolerance or unreason-
ableness in this movement, and was confident that
it would herald beneficial changes within Hindu
society.[60] How far the social reformers entertained ideas of support for their cause from the
forces of Hindu Revivalism is not clear, but their
patronage of the latter movement yielded small divi-
dends, indeed, when the Age of Consent Bill controversy flared up in 1890.

THE AGE OF CONSENT BILL CONTROVERSY

The appeal for state help to effect social reform, the ultimate weapon in the armory of Indian
reformers, was made in earnest in August 1884 when
Malabari's "Notes" on "Infant Marriage in India"
and "Enforced Widowhood" were published. Malabari
portrayed in graphic terms the evils arising from
these essentially high caste Hindu practices. Much
of what he said about the nature and consequences
of these social evils was well known in India, at
least in reformist circles, but the remedies   that

he suggested had an aspect of novelty, if not of
severity. Although he was not seeking "a legal
ban" against infant marriage, a practice which he
felt contributed largely to the problem of widowhood, Malabari wanted the government to show its
disapproval of the practice by barring married students from colleges after a five-year period of
grace and giving preference to unmarried applicants
in the public service.[61] He also urged a similar
"interposition of authority [of the State] to a
small extent" to break down the restrictions that
caste had imposed on widow remarriage. Priests
were to be deprived of the power of excommunicating
widows seeking remarriage, while protection was to
be extended to widows wishing to liberate themselves from enforced seclusion or other disabilities that Hindu customs inflicted on them.[62]

Reformers in South India, while readily admitting the evils which Malabari complained of,
had reservations about the wisdom of invoking
state intervention to solve social ills.
Raghunatha Rao asserted that in principle "anything connected with Hindu religion should not be
interfered with by the Government." Social reforms,
he felt, should "come from within and not from
without."[63] S. Subramania Iyer, while echoing
these sentiments, warned that legislation would
more "retard than promote progress," a danger which
weighed heavily with many reformers. Chentsal Rao,
for example, argued that social legislation would
lead to "no beneficial results" and, indeed, might
"shake the confidence of the people in the neutrality of Government in religious matters and
create a reaction in favour of the very evils which
it is our wish to repress."[64] Reactions from reformers elsewhere in the country were equally adverse to state intervention, and the Indian
Government had little option but to reject Malabari's plea, though expressing a willingness to
consider legislation against proven social evils
if such legislation had been "asked by a section,
important in influence or number, of the Hindu

community itself."[65]

Although Malabari's proposals failed to gain general support, they were nevertheless useful in eliciting replies from a wide range of reformist and official sympathizers. Some of these replies were an exercise in finding more realistic and feasible remedies to the evils afflicting Hindu society. As expected, much attention was paid to the question of state intervention, and an attempt was made to define those areas within which the state could legitimately and with safety intervene. In the main, reformist thinkers were divided between those who wanted to ban infant marriage and those who favored the raising of the age of consent. In the former camp were Raghunatha Rao and Madava Rao, while in the latter camp was K. T. Telang, a Bombay lawyer, who believed that reform was "most urgently called for in regard to the time of consummation, and not so much in regard to the time of marriage." Presumably anticipating opposition to "external" interference, Telang argued that delaying consummation would be "a reform from within."[66] It was Maxwell Melvill, Judicial Member of the Bombay Government, who in effect suggested that the age of consent could be safely raised to twelve. Replying to Malabari in May 1886, he claimed that infant marriage was "not necessarily a bad institution, or at all events not so bad as to render legislative interference desirable."[67] He drafted a scheme to amend section 375 of the Indian Penal Code, raising the age of consent from ten to twelve.

The formal discussion of this issue did not take place until the third National Social Conference assembled in Bombay in December 1889. Opposition to this idea was expected, as a circular had been distributed from Poona which urged reformers to disavow state intervention and achieve their aims through voluntary methods.[68] At the Conference there was "an animated debate" verging on "apparent disorder" before the resolution welcoming the raising of the age of consent was passed.[67]

Passing resolutions on reformist platforms, however, was hardly considered adequate to convince those sections of public opinion in the country which had doubts about invoking 'legislative intervention by the state to remedy a social evil. In South India reformist leaders decided to explain through the columns of the press and on the platform the need for such legislation and, thereby, to dispel any untoward fears that such action might give rise to in certain quarters.

Two leaders who took an active part in this campaign were Raghunatha Rao and G. Subramania Iyer. Raghunatha Rao had played a part in ensuring that the recent National Social Conference accepted the raising of the age of consent, and on his return to Madras he explained to his local friends why he had changed his mind on the question of state intervention. In a letter to the *Madras Times*, Raghunatha Rao explained that for some years he had been urging the government to appoint a commission to inquire and report on the Hindu laws of marriage, and, thereby, help in the promulgation of a code of Hindu law founded on the Shastras.[70] His wish had not been granted and, therefore, he was prepared to support piecemeal legislation, such as the Age of Consent Bill, provided that it conformed to the Shastras.[71] Raghunatha Rao also published a pamphlet to demonstrate that the Vedas, the "highest authority" of the Hindus, weighed on the side of those urging that the age of consent be raised.[72]

If Raghunatha Rao resorted to the authority of Hindu scriptures to fortify his cause, G. Subramania Iyer appealed with equal conviction to Western rationalist writers, like Spinoza and T. H. Green, to justify state intervention on social issues. As early as June 1889, Subramania Iyer had made a strong plea for reforms in all directions, rather than concentrating on the political front alone. In a speech to the Madura Union, he asserted that there were "radical defects in all our institutions, social, domestic and political. It is not enough that we labour *politically* alone.

Our advancement in politics must commensurate with
our advancement in other directions." He expressed
regret that "the whole educated activity" of the
country was channelled more towards "political
progress than in the line of social or domestic
progress." To rectify this imbalance, he wanted
the cause of social reform to be served by "an organization as large as and as influential as the
Congress," which he believed would generate greater
discussion on such issues as overseas travel,
female education, and inter-caste marriage, and,
thereby, influence public opinion.[73]

G. Subramania Iyer's speech was frankly a challenge to the prevailing assumption among his colleagues in the professional elite that political
reform must have priority over social reform. Ever
since K. T. Telang delivered his widely publicized
speech on this issue in 1886, this view had almost
attained sanctity among Congress politicians.
Subramania Iyer obviously wanted to review the position, and he returned to the theme in a speech he
gave in Madras in January 1890. He argued that, if
the political aspirations of the Congress were to
be ultimately realized, then "social reform must
advance along with political reform, if, indeed, it
is not to precede the latter." Political enfranchisement, he argued, depended upon "the fitness of
the people to exercise that power," and would only
be conceded after "a long process of discipline and
training" when the nation became "more sincere,
more disinterested, more courageous," and had
raised itself to the "intelligence and moral power"
of the European countries. The existing "social
customs and institutions" of India, he believed,
were "entirely opposed to the development of these
great qualities," and he urged reformers to remove
these social and religious obstacles which impeded
the country's regeneration.

In seeking to define the role of the state in
modifying social institutions and usages, G. Subramania Iyer drew freely from the writings of T. H.
Green. He viewed the state as "a moral and

spiritual organism" whose obligations to society were not exhausted by merely providing for the maintenance of law and order:

> The sole end of the State is not merely protection of property, is not merely happiness of people, is not justice (the realisation of law); the State lives for something higher than merely keeping man from mischief. Law and justice are a condition of politics more than their end. The true definition of the proper and direct end of the State is the development of national capacities, the perfecting of national life, and finally, its completion.

Subramania Iyer was far from advocating any *carte blanche* interference by the state in social issues. Interference, he emphasized, must be "timely and cautious," within the bounds of "some precautions," and should never be directed against "the liberty of the individual and the liberty of convenience." Ideally, he would have preferred reforms through the progress of education and by "voluntary agencies," but in the existing Hindu society neither of these methods was effective enough to combat "the tyranny of caste and orthodoxy." Education, he complained, operated with "extreme slowness. You cannot convert an ignorant into an educated nation in a year or two." The voluntary agencies, "excellent as far as they go," could "only go a little way and exert very little influence on the enormous mass of ignorance that blocks the way of reform." Nor was Subramania Iyer convinced that state interference must be opposed when the ruling authority was "alien." Such an argument, he said, had force in a society which was "vigorous and self-working," but not in a society which was like "a sick man requiring external stimulus to keep him up."[74]

As the editor of the *Hindu*, G. Subramania Iyer wielded a powerful weapon which he could use to

bolster his cause. This was precisely what he did
during the long months when the Age of Consent Bill
controversy convulsed the country. The *Hindu's*
editorial and correspondence columns became the
main forum for the frank, and sometimes bitter, debate about the merits and demerits of the proposed
legislation. To a large extent, the editorial
columns reflected the thinking of Subramania Iyer
who produced a stream of editorials justifying legislative intervention, dispelling the fears of
those who had reservations about the motives of the
British rulers, and exhorting the Western-educated
class to throw in its support behind the legislation. The *Swadesamitran*, published in the same
premises as the *Hindu*, conducted a similar campaign
to mobilize support among its Tamil readers.

The extent of the *Hindu's* involvement in the
Age of Consent Bill controversy invited strong
criticism from various quarters in Madras. Some
believed that the paper, as the representative
organ of Indian opinion in South India, should not
assume such a partisan attitude on an issue in
which its readers held widely divergent views.
Others alleged that the editor was "unduly aggressive" in his advocacy of the proposed legislation
and was guilty of using "violent language" against
those who opposed the measure. One correspondent
claimed that the editor, by making "all sorts of
extravagant and extreme demands and impossible expectations," was retarding rather than promoting
India's progress.[75] Another critic of the *Hindu*
alleged in March 1890, with some justification,
that the paper had recently given "a radical twist"
to its discussions on social reform. It was
claimed that "moral and religious radicalism" was
subversive to Hindu social order and pregnant with
dangerous consequences to the country.[76] A rumor
also gained wide currency in October 1890 that
"such native papers as are advocating Legislative
interference with Hindu marriage and other customs,
are experiencing a large falling off in their circulation." The editor of the *Hindu* dismissed this

rumor as without foundation.[77]

The fact that the *Hindu* became a center of fierce controversy during the Age of Consent Bill debate could be largely traced to the widely held belief in Madras that there had been a radical change in its editorial policy ever since the editor decided to remarry his widowed daughter. In 1889 G. Subramania Iyer's daughter of twelve was widowed before consummation, and this placed him in the dilemma of either consigning his daughter to a harsh life of enforced widowhood, or of courting orthodox anger and ostracism by remarrying her. It was a very difficult and painful decision, and, after some months of soul-searching, he decided on the latter course, for, as he told W. S. Caine, M.P., he "could not face the life-long misery of a daughter whom he loved as his own soul, and preferred the risk of ex-communication." The wedding was celebrated at Bombay in December 1889 on the occasion of the fifth Congress gathering there. According to the *Madras Times,* though there was "no organised opposition, there had been visible signs of silent disapprobation on the part of the orthodox, of culpable indifference on the part of educated bigotry."[78] Many of Subramania Iyer's friends and relatives soon deserted him, while according to Caine "no priest will minister his family, no servant will enter his household, no Hindoo who is not a Congress-wallah will openly associate with him or marry into his family." Subramania Iyer found the experience almost unnerving, while his wife was overcome by the stress of ostracism and died in April 1890.[79]

One person who was acutely embarrassed by the *Hindu's* being dragged into a controversy with its readers was Viraraghava Chari, the managing proprietor of the paper, who had played no less an important role than G. Subramania Iyer in making it the leading Indian paper in South India. He shared some of Subramania Iyer's enthusiasm for social reform, and supported the Age of Consent Bill in principle, but he believed that the *Hindu* should

adopt a less partisan stand and show greater respect for the feelings of those who had strong
reservations about legislative action to solve
social problems. In an effort to achieve this, and
to scale down what he felt was the undue emphasis
that the *Hindu* had recently given to social issues,
Viraraghava Chari suggested the idea of "a separate
weekly paper solely devoted to social and moral reforms."[80] The proposal led to the founding of the
Indian Social Reformer in September 1890, but this
did not remove the *Hindu* or its editor from the
center of a controversy which was then reaching a
critical stage.

It was evident at this juncture that opinion
in South India was becoming polarized. The majority of the vernacular newspapers were opposed to
legislative interference in the social usages of
their country.

Also, some prominent leaders were beginning to
express their dissent, though without clearly
articulating their reasons. One of them was Madava
Rao, who had resigned from the Congress in April
1890 following a bitter dispute over the introduction of an elective element in the Indian legislatures. How far this event affected his attitude
on social issues is not clear, but he seems to have
showed little of the enthusiasm that he had in the
past displayed for social reform. He attacked the
editor of the *Hindu* for not representing the views
of "the millions who constitute the great bulk of
the Hindu community,"[81] and some months later
hailed it as "a matter of great congratulation,"
when rumors were current that newspapers advocating
social legislation were experiencing a fall in circulation.[82]

Other Hindu leaders, often known for their
liberal views on social questions, refrained from
any public expression of their views on the question of the Age of Consent Bill, and this, not unnaturally, raised suspicions that these leaders did
not have the courage of their convictions and were
not prepared to be dragged into a controversy in

which they might incur unpopularity.

It was this attitude which exasperated reformers like G. Subramania Iyer. In a speech at the
Triplicane Literary Society in September 1890,
Subramania Iyer accused the intelligent men of
"running away from the responsibility that the present position had created; there was a spirit of
evasion, a spirit of explaining away, excusing
oneself, a running away as it were from the responsibility of the post." He said that this attitude
had caused great pain to him and others who supported legislative action as the most effective
way to cure social evils. Talk of "mass rebellion,"
Subramania Iyer said, was "simple nonsense" and he
urged that pressure be maintained on the government
to effect the proposed change.[83]

Anxious to "show to the world the strength of
the reform party," the supporters of the Age of
Consent Bill in Madras convened a meeting in October 1890 to discuss the issue. An appeal was made
to the "Dravidian social reformers and their
leaders" to attend the meeting, as it was argued
that the issue had become one of "great national
importance."[84] Raghunatha Rao was the main speaker
for the proposed legislation, and he tried to dispel fears that this measure would interfere with
the law or performance of Hindu marriage, or that
it threatened the integrity of Hinduism in any way.
Some sections of the audience did not agree. T. P.
Kothandarama Iyer, a lawyer in the Madras High
Court, questioned the necessity for such legislation. He also alleged that the proposed measure
would place "undue power in the hands of the police,
who might abuse it to the detriment of people at
large." Another lawyer, Sundram Sastri, agreed
contending that there was no necessity for legislation as the evil complained of did not exist in
South India. However, despite spirited opposition,
the meeting endorsed a petition to the Indian
Government welcoming legislation to raise the age
of consent to twelve.[85]

Opponents of the measure did not take long to

plan a counter-demonstration. A preliminary meeting, held in November 1890 at the home of Madava Rao, finalized measures to hold a public meeting of those opposing state intervention in social issues. Attended by some of the "distinguished pleaders, officials and educationists," including Somasundram Chetty, Sundram Sastri, and Kothandarama Iyer, the meeting agreed that it was "not desirable that the Legislature should raise the Age of Consent." A small committee was constituted to convene a "meeting of sympathisers," at which a protest memorial was to be adopted for submission to the Indian Government.[86] The *Madras Times* described this meeting as "the spectacle of a few 'old men' in the city" swimming against the general current of reform and progress in the country.[87] Raghunatha Rao remarked that the participants in the meeting "should be either ignorant of their religion, or be pandering to the prejudices of their co-religionists."[88] This comment brought an immediate retort from Madava Rao, who announced his resignation from the National Social Conference, a gesture reminiscent of his resignation from the Madras Standing Congress Committee in April 1890 after the controversy over the Cross Bill.[89]

The meeting against the Age of Consent Bill took place in early December and was attended by leaders of both factions. With feelings running high, and with both sides having marshalled their supporters to full strength, there were all the signs of a major clash. After a brief speech from the chairman, Somasundram Chetty, Madava Rao rose to move the first resolution, which claimed that the measure was "unnecessary so far as this Presidency, at all events, is concerned." He described the Bill as "a gigantic deception" and "the most preposterous ever heard in old Asia." As the British were "a *just, wise* and *considerate* Government," Madava Rao felt constrained to warn them "against the *covert* designs of a batch of so-called Social Reformers even *microscopically inappreciable.*" "An imperial race," he continued, "should not trust

such *shallow* reformers backed by a few, stray, vin-
dictive outcastes." When he turned his anger on
Raghunatha Rao and Malabari, interruptions started
from the audience, and Raghunatha Rao rose to demand the right of reply.[90] Madava Rao refused to
yield, contending that it was a meeting of those
opposed to the Age of Consent Bill. With the chairman virtually helpless and other speakers trying
to mount the platform, the meeting degenerated into
"one of uncontrollable disorder and rowdyism" and
was adjourned without passing a single resolution.[91]
    Each group blamed the other for the unhappy
spectacle. The organizers of the meeting laid the
blame on the reformers, claiming that they should
not have attended a meeting convened to protest
against the Age of Consent Bill. The reformers, in
reply, asserted that the circular announcing the
meeting invited "the General Public of Madras," and,
as such, their views deserved to be heard as much
as those of their opponents. Neutral observers,
however, were agreed that the real cause of the up-
roar was Madava Rao's frontal attack on the reformers. However, as one discerning observer remarked,
this meeting did not enhance anyone's reputation:[92]

> Consequently, beyond giving an opportunity to
> some zealots of the Hindu Tract Society to
> cry at the top of their voices that the Church
> was in danger and utter disrespectful remarks
> against worthy men . . . beyond furnishing an
> opportunity for Rajah Sir T. Madhava Row to
> dig a grave for the interment of his reputa-
> tion, and beyond supplying an enjoyable half-
> hour of popular excitement to youngsters, the
> meeting did no good to anybody.

    However, the events of the first meeting did
not deter its organizers from holding a second meeting soon afterwards to record their protest against
the Age of Consent Bill. While recognizing "the
evils of early consummation," the meeting resolved
that such instances were too rare in South India to

warrant preventive legislation.[93]   Also, at this
time, Muslims in Madras held a meeting to protest
against the measure.

Amid the strong emotions which this issue had
aroused in Madras, only the Triplicane Literary
Society seemed to have discussed it with any degree
of restraint and to have suggested creative improvements in the proposed law. In a petition to the
Indian Government submitted in November 1890, the
Society welcomed the reasons for the measure and
urged that the age of consent be raised to fourteen.
However, it opposed the scale of punishment prescribed, which was transportation, contending that
such severity might "defeat the very end in view."
It also urged that the courts should not take
notice of such offences except where death or
grievous hurt resulted. In this way, the Society
believed that the dangers of "vexatious arrest and
investigations into delicate family matters" by the
police could be reduced.[94]

The breach caused by the Age of Consent Bill
among the metropolitan leaders was also evident in
the *mofussil*. In the majority of the *mofussil* centers where the issue was discussed at public meetings, notably, Salem, Palghat, Coimbatore, Masulipatam, Tanjore, Mayaveram, and Chingleput, resolutions were passed opposing the Bill. Support for
the Bill only came from Cocanada, where Norton's
speech appeared to have persuaded the audience to
accept the measure, provided that amendments were
made along the lines suggested by the Triplicane
Literary Society.[95]

The Indian press in the Presidency was also
divided on this issue. In the metropolis, the
principal supporters of the Age of Consent Bill
were the trinity of Mount Road publications: the
Hindu, *Swadesamitran*, and *Andhra Prakasika*. In the
mofussil, the measure was welcomed by *Kerala Patrika* and *Kerala Sanchari*, two well-known Malayalam
weeklies of Calicut. The majority of the other
newspapers opposed the Bill, including almost every
Urdu paper in the Presidency.

It was at the height of this agitation that the Congress and National Social Conference assembled at Calcutta in December 1890. The *Hindu*, though in the past opposed to the discussion of social issues in the Congress agenda, advocated the inclusion of the Age of Consent Bill on the grounds that it was a national issue affecting all classes and creeds in the country.[96] W. S. Caine, a British M.P. with influence in Congress circles, "almost passionately appealed to his native friends in Madras" to raise the issue in the Congress as he feared that attempts to ignore it would seriously discredit the organization "in the eyes of all Englishmen" and endanger their demands for political concessions.[97] The Madras deputation was converted but the Subjects Committee, which was responsible for drafting resolutions before they were debated at the open Congress sessions, refused to depart from its past policy of neutrality on social issues.[98]

If the reticence of the Congress was understandable, the attitude of the Social Conference perplexed many reformers in the country. Despite pressure from delegates from Madras, the Conference decided to omit any reference to the Age of Consent Bill for fear of precipitating an open rupture. The editor of the *Hindu*, aghast at this silence "on the burning question of the hour," asserted that the Conference should have recorded its verdict on the issue irrespective of the consequences.[99]

In January 1891 the Bill came up for discussion in the Supreme Legislative Council. Voicing the sentiments of those opposed to the measure was Romesh Chandra Mitter, who warned Council members that the Bill was "likely to cause widespread discontent in the country." The editor of the *Hindu* accused Mitter of becoming "the mouthpiece of the uneducated masses" and criticized the speech as "not quite worthy of him."[100] This sparked off a fresh outburst of protests against the editor of the *Hindu*. P. S. Sivasamy Iyer, a lawyer and a Congress stalwart, protested against the editor's having "used so strong a language and indulged in an attack on one of our most distinguished country-men." V. Krishnaswamy Iyer, a leading member of the Madras Standing Congress Committee, remon-strated strongly against the "objectionable" way in which the *Hindu* dealt with those who disagreed with its views. He reserved his support for the Bill so long as its "obnoxious provisions" remained and the "necessary safeguards" were not incorporated into it.[101]

With the Congress leaders being drawn into angry exchanges over this issue, Hume felt that he ought to intervene to prevent any possible damage to his organization. In a published statement in January 1891, Hume denied that the Congress was op-posed to the measure. Except for Bengal, he claimed that "a major portion of his native friends" supported the Age of Consent Bill.[102] However, in a private letter to the viceroy, Hume urged for certain amendments to the Bill to "throw oil upon the troubled waters" and "sweep away the great mass of those angry and embittered feelings" that the measure had roused in the country. As "a golden bridge for all parties," he advocated Mitter's sug-gestion that puberty rather than an age limit be prescribed as the age of consent, but, subsequently, withdrew this proposal claiming that his "party" would not accept it.[103] Lansdowne refused to com-promise and the Supreme Legislative Council passed an unamended Age of Consent Bill in March 1891.

THE AFTERMATH

Although it is hazardous to try and gauge the strength and direction of popular opinion on issues of this kind, contemporary observers were in little doubt that public opinion in South India was largely opposed to this legislation. The *Christian College Magazine* remarked at the height of the controversy that many prominent Indians had openly expressed their misgivings about the Age of Consent Bill,

while many more "who do not care to make their
opinions public, entertain the feeling that legislation is inadvisable."[104] This impression is confirmed by the reading of the contemporary press,
especially the vernacular press, and the speeches
made at meetings to discuss the issue in the various parts of the Presidency.

Although many of the ardent supporters of the
measure conceded that popular opinion was against
them, what they found intolerable were some of the
tactics which their opponents had adopted to frus-
trate the proposed legislation. In February 1891
the editor of the *Hindu* urged the Indian Government
to pass the Bill quickly to put an end to the
"nauseating discussion" of its opponents. He
agreed with the editor of the *Indian Mirror* that
early legislation would close "the columns of newspapers from spreading moral leprosy in the land."
He also accused the Western-educated class of
"successfully playing on the credulity of the
masses" and ignoring the fact that agitation should
be strictly constitutional.[105]

This controversy was significant in dispelling
one popularly held myth, namely, that the Western-
educated class were allies in the cause of social
reform. The *Hindu* asserted that this class, far
from taking an enlightened view of the issue and
guiding public opinion, had only shown its "stolid
conservatism and mischievous spirit of false
patriotism."[106] Many prominent figures in the
Presidency, notably, Madava Rao, Somasundram Chetty,
Vijiaraghava Chari, and Saminatha Iyer, had come
out in total opposition to the Age of Consent Bill.
Another group of leaders, including, S. Subramania
Iyer, Chentsal Rao, Muthusamy Iyer, Seshia Sastri,
Bhashyam Iyengar, and Krishnaswamy Iyer, had expressed strong reservations about the punitive provisions of the Bill and tended to cast doubts upon
the efficacy of solving social problems through
legislation. Then again, a number of others, like
Ananda Charlu, Rangiah Naidu, and Balaji Rao, had
chosen to remain silent rather than declaring their

stand. Such deep cleavages, and the fact that the
debate over the Bill was conducted with considerable bitterness, were bound to have far-reaching
implications for the Presidency as a whole.

For social reform, the immediate consequence
of this controversy was the rupture in the alliance
between the traditional and rationalist wing of the
movement. This alliance had existed since the
early 1880s, with the leadership vested in the
hands of the traditional wing. However, during the
Age of Consent Bill debate, the rationalist wing
came to play the more active role, led by such
leaders as G. Subramania Iyer, K. Subba Rao, sub-
editor of the *Hindu*, K. Natarajan, managing proprietor of the *Indian Social Reformer*, and A. Subba
Rao, lecturer in the Madras Presidency College. It
was these activists who started the *Indian Social
Reformer* in September 1890 in order to generate support for the proposed legislation. They also became critical of the methods pursued by the traditional wing, questioning in particular the latter's
reliance on the Shastras as the guideline for reform. The editor of the *Hindu*, for example, asserted in March 1891 that what was important was
"moderate but steady reform" guided by "the suggestions of science and reason" and "without looking
to Shastras or any writings of ancient personages
for authority or sanction."[107] In February 1892
discussions began among members of the Hindu Marriage Association of Madras to define afresh "the
fundamental principles of the Association," but no
common ground was found whereby the two wings of
the body could continue their former partnership.[108]

The inevitable rupture came when Raghunatha
Rao refused to partake in a symbolic dinner given
on the occasion of a widow remarriage in August
1892. The rationalist wing rebuked him for not discharging his duty as the president of the Hindu
Marriage Association. Raghunatha Rao, stung by
growing criticisms of his leadership, challenged
those reformers opposed to the Shastras to form
their own organization.[109] The challenge was

accepted, and in November 1892 the rationalist wing
launched the Madras Hindu Social Reform Association.

The emergence of this Association symbolized a
more radical break with Hindu tradition on the part
of the reformers. Its declared objectives were the
promotion of female education, reform of domestic
and marriage habits, and the "Amalgamation of
Castes." Social usages, like infant marriage,
nautch-going, and untouchability, were fearlessly
denounced. Nor did these reformers inhibit themselves in the choice of methods to achieve their
goals. Members of the Association were required under its constitution to educate women in their
household, defer marriage of daughters until after
the age of ten, partake in inter-caste dining and
attend parties for remarried couples. Both the
press and the platform were to be used to popularize reform, while state intervention was to be
sought to remove proven social ills.[110] Unlike
earlier bodies, the Madras Hindu Social Reform Association demanded more than a mere "verbal and intellectual assent" to its program, and, indeed, began
to draw a distinction between the so-called "thinking reformer" and the "courage-of-conviction
reformer." The former was often the object of ridicule, accused of wanting "moral courage, self-
confidence" and leading "a double life."[111]

Opposition to the Madras Hindu Social Reform
Association came from both the traditional reformers and Hindu revivalists. S. Subramania Iyer,
who belonged to the former group, claimed in 1894
that the activities of the Association were "retarding rather than advancing the progress of our
cause." He urged the "ardent reformers" to avoid
"narrow dogmatism" and to seek social changes
"gradually, cautiously and in a reasonable and
truly patriotic spirit." In a pointed reference to
the methods pursued by the radical reformers,
Subramania Iyer cautioned that "no one has a right
to demand from another that amount of self-sacri-
fice, which is consistent with his thoughts and
ideas."[112] M. Ranga Chari, a professor at

Trevandram College, was even more critical of the
methods of the radical group. He charged the editors of the *Indian Social Reformer* with displaying
"a kind of radical restlessness and destructive
ire" in their writings and even "the faint touch of
innocent malice."[113] A similar charge was also
made by Raghunatha Rao. He contended that the term
reform had become a cover for "almost all irreli-
gious and vicious acts."[114] The breach between the
traditional and rationalist wing remained unhealed
throughout the 1890s. In 1894, when the National
Social Conference was held in Madras, Ranade urged
both sides "to make up the quarrel."[115] Though
they did cooperate during the Conference, the split
remained.

However, the mantle of opposing the radical
reformers was increasingly assumed by revivalist
groups. The latter's counterblast against the reformers was directed at the "denationalising" tendency of the reformist program and the "revolutionary" methods that were employed to achieve social
change. The reformers were "atheistical, irrever-
ent and materialistic," and "too fond of western
dress and manners and despise too much their own
nationality."[116] In some revivalist circles, it
was even claimed that the reformist censure of the
Hindu social system and religious traditions was
"unpatriotic" and wounding to the "national self-
respect" of the Hindus.

The Hindu revivalists found a ready ally in
the Theosophical Society. Since 1893, when Annie
Besant arrived in Madras to join Olcott, the Theosophical movement had found a fresh impetus and had
begun to recapture some of the popularity that it
had enjoyed in South India during the preceding
decade. In this revival, Besant played a crucial
role. Possessing considerable personal charm, she
stirred her Indian audiences by the eloquence of
her lectures and by her knowledge of Hindu philosophy, religion, and science. Like Olcott before
her, Besant considered materialism the greatest
threat to India, and she regarded her Indian

sojourn as a mission to redeem Hindus, especially
the younger generation, from the pitfalls of materialism. She urged her Hindu friends to follow
"the Indian simplicity of material life instead of
the costly and more luxurious Western habits" and
to preserve their "various national costumes,"
their close family ties, and the four-fold caste
system. At the same time, she proclaimed the superiority of Hinduism over other world religions,
contending that it was "the source of all great
religions and philosophies." In an interview for
an English newspaper, the *Daily Chronicle*, Besant
was quoted as saying: "I regard Hindooism as the
most ancient of all religions, and as containing
more fully than any other the spiritual truths
named Theosophy in modern times. Theosophy is the
ancient Brahma Vidya of India."[117]

Such sentiments, expressed in her numerous
lectures in various parts of the country, warmed
the hearts of Hindu revivalists, for, as one of
them remarked, the Theosophist leaders had "brought
back to us Hindus the vital spark of self-respect
which we were about to lose."[118] Her critics, however, complained that she was seeking popularity by
"her outrageous flattery of Indians and of everything connected with India" and by her attacks on
Western materialism and what she termed "dogmatic
Christianity."[119] The Hindu social reformers, for
their part, lamented that Besant strengthened the
"spiritual pride" of the Hindus "with a bigotry
and plausibility of reasoning unknown to the
Orthodox."[120]

It would be wrong, however, to regard the reformers and revivalists as forces of innovation and
reaction in South India. Indeed, it would be
truer to say that these opposing groups were essentially forces of change offering alternative models
for achieving social modernization within the Hindu
community. If the reformers sought to inspire
change along rationalist lines and in the light of
Western social experience, the revivalists wanted
to find largely Indian prescriptions to regenerate

their society. That the latter were committed to
change was attested by their decision to organize
the Madras Hindu Association in 1904. In defining
their objectives, the leaders of this body pledged
to promote "Hindu social and religious advancement
on national lines in harmony with the spirit of
Hindu Civilisation." The major planks of the reformist platform were incorporated into their program,
including female education, encouragement of adult
marriages, foreign travel, and the uplift of the
depressed classes.[121]

The contest between the reformers and revivalists found its echo in the equally stormy argument that was to divide the Congress into contending political camps during the first decade of the
twentieth century. In the past, the ideology of
the Congress had been largely inspired by Western
political experience. Hume and his Indian allies,
who were behind its formation, were convinced of
their ability to work towards the ideal of parliamentary self-government for India through gradual
and orderly stages, and they were fortified in this
ideal by the support that they received from the
liberal section of public opinion in Britain and by
the attainment of self-rule by such British colonies as Canada, Australia, and New Zealand. In formulating their program and in conducting their
political work, these Congress leaders imitated
British political style. Equally, in stressing
secularism, fundamental liberties, and democratic
institutions, they also showed their attachment to
the values and norms of Western liberalism.

This so-called "Moderate" style of politics
came to be questioned during the 1890s not only in
terms of its effectiveness in securing India's
national regeneration but also in terms of its rele-
vance to the country's societal needs and problems.
The stress on fundamental liberties, democratic
institutions, and secularism, was challenged on the
grounds that these were alien importations, unsuited to the requirements and capacity of the
Indian people. Mrs. Besant, in a lecture attended

by several Congress delegates in Madras in December 1894, claimed that India was becoming "a strange compound of conflicting ideas, of an ancient nation ruled politically by a foreign power; and in her there is the double idea--one the old idea, of duty, and the other the idea of democracy transported to Indian soil, not in the certainty that the soil is suited to the exotic plant." Arguing that radical European concepts, such as the "rights of man," were being introduced into India without any awareness of possible consequences for the country, Besant urged that Indian politicians, in formulating their political ideology, ought to provide "a basis of philosophy of conduct, or else the conduct will be erratic and unsatisfactory."[122]

A more forthright critic of the Congress was K. Sundararaman, a college professor who had attended its inaugural meeting at Bombay in 1885. In an essay, "The National Movement in India," published in 1903, Sundararaman claimed that there were "two alternative courses" open to Indians seeking to regenerate their country:

> One is to take up the ideas and aims of European civilisation and try to work them up as best we can into the framework, the marrow, and bone, of our own civilisation; the other is to study our own civilisation and its place in the order of the world in the light of past experience and to base our collective life and new organisation on the results afforded by an intelligent comprehension of the capabilities of the national genius.

He labelled the advocates of these two schools of thought the "party of the West" and the "party of the East." In his view, the former represented the "revolutionary ideal," because it aimed at destroying "the traditional social organisation and the dominant ideals of life in India." Such methods, Sundararaman contended, were not new in India, for he regarded Buddhism, Jainism, and Islam

as earlier attempts to overthrow by revolution
India's national life and habits. The advent of
British rule, he claimed, had released new revolutionary currents into the country, notably,
Christianity, Western rationalism, and "the socia-
listic dogma of the natural equality of all men in
every respect." He admitted that these influences
had an appeal among the Western-educated class,
some of whom had organized the Congress and were
seeking to mold India along Western patterns.
While he expressed broad sympathy for the Congress
ideal of progressive advance in the country's
material and moral condition under British supremacy, Sundararaman was clearly skeptical of its
ability ever to build up "a National State" in
India in the Western sense. Hence, he criticized
those Congress leaders who, misled by their idealism, were seeking to undermine the country's
social organization and its ancient spiritual
values. He charged that these Congress leaders,
despite their annual demonstrations, passing of
resolutions and producing of reports, had made
neither great sacrifices nor undergone any real
sufferings to evoke popular sympathy in India or to
win the respect of the British rulers. He reminded
the Congress supporters

> . . . that speeches and resolutions do not
> form social forces. It is the power of faith
> that can touch human hearts, and faith comes
> only to those who undergo great sacrifices
> and sufferings in what they conceive to be a
> great aim of human life and endeavour. The
> Congress politicians and speakers have assu-
> redly made no great sacrifices or undergone
> such sufferings as to touch human hearts in
> India with the power of faith or to communi-
> cate that magic power to human hearts else-
> where.

Sundararaman claimed that the Congress, after
seventeen years of existence, had little to show in

terms of actual political gains. He felt that all
the important concessions which India had gained
were "a voluntary gift of the British people,"
rather than the product of Congress exertions or
sacrifice. Moreover, he deplored the Congress tendency to ask for favors from the rulers. "Political privilege," he declared, "cannot fittingly be
bestowed as alms, but must be earned and claimed as
the legitimate due of civic merit in the subject."[123]

Disillusionment with the ideology and tactics
of the Congress was accompanied by growing complaints about the decline in the vigor of the Party
as a political force in South India. In December
1891 the editor of the *Hindu* lamented that the
"first enthusiasm for the Congress has apparently
cooled down, and we seldom hear now of meetings,
pamphlets and so forth to popularise the Congress
programme or to enlist the sympathy of the masses
to advance the work."[124] This impression was confirmed by Ananda Charlu, a member of the Madras
Standing Congress Committee, who claimed in 1893
that politics in South India had suffered "a re-
lapse into its old traditions of insular apathy,"
and some were led to believe that "the energy of
1887 was but a spasmodic outburst, which (as is
natural) was followed by a re-action, with its
attendant evil of immobility and diminished and
diminishing warmth."[125]

If this claim of waning enthusiasm for the
Congress was true, then it must partly account for
the difficulties which the Congress leadership in
South India faced in raising adequate funds to
meet its commitments. The financial outlay of the
Congress had been substantially enhanced since the
formation of the British Committee in London in
July 1889. Congress leaders in Madras had hoped
to share the burden with the district subcommittees
in the *mofussil*, but "spasmodic efforts" on the
part of the latter in raising funds had interrupted
the annual remittance to London, at times causing
political embarrassment. In 1891 the Madras

Standing Congress Committee recommended the appointment of professional agents in every district to
"popularise the Congress cause as well as to facilitate the collection of funds from each District."
While urging the district subcommittees to meet
their allotment punctually, the Madras leaders
warned that failure to do so would result in the
possible expulsion of the offending districts from
the movement.[126] This threat did not seem to have
any significant effect, for, throughout the 1890s,
complaints were heard about dilatoriness on the
part of the Congress leaders in South India in meeting their annual contributions to the British
Committee.

Although the prevailing political mood of the
professional elite during the 1890s was one of
general despondency, which found expression in its
impatience over organizational weaknesses and lack
of progress in securing desired, political concessions, there were, nevertheless, moments when this
elite group was able to make a more realistic ap-
praisal of its achievements after a decade of organized political agitation. Undoubtedly, the
emergence of the Congress was the single most important political event of the nineteenth century. In
the eyes of the professional elite, the advent of
the Congress had led to "a marked awakening throughout the country" and had transformed the Indian
people from "a condition of political serfdom to a
condition of political energy."[127] In South India,
it was claimed that the Congress had provided an
elaborate organization, capable of kindling political activity even in the remote centers of the
Presidency. Viraraghava Chari, Joint Secretary of
the Madras Standing Congress Committee, asserted in
1890 that had "it not been for the Congress, Madras
[Presidency] would have been nowhere. It had been
greatly helping the people of Madras. Before that
time Madras was called benighted. Now we have,
throughout the Presidency, Standing Congress Committees to help the Central Committee at Madras."[128]
Equally important, the coming of the Congress

was believed to have stimulated "the growth of enlightened patriotism" in the country and helped to
remove some of the barriers created by caste,
language, and creed. In a valedictory address to
Hume during his farewell visit to Madras in December 1893, the Madras Standing Congress Committee
testified to the new spirit of unity which the
Congress had evoked among the various communities:
"The Hindu and Mahomedan, the Parsee and the Sikh
have been taught to acknowledge the elementary
axiom that one common thread of humanity runs
through all the composite fabrics of colour, caste,
and creed. Organization has effected union. . . ."[129]
        Even if some of the minority groups dis-
puted this claim, the professional elite remained
unshaken in its belief that the spread of Western
education, among other agencies, would eventually
persuade the minority groups to accept the credentials of the Congress to speak for India as a whole.
        Finally, the professional elite recognized the
importance of the Congress as an instrument in extracting concessions from the rulers. The leaders
of this elite group had accepted Hume's thesis that
the British rulers needed a loyal opposition in
India which would not only provide an outlet to the
political ferment in the country but would also
play the creative role of formulating a rational
political program capable of being implemented
without fear of causing any major disruption--
either to the established administrative patterns
or to the existing balance of political forces in
the country. Here, the Congress leadership had
cause to be moderately satisfied with its early
achievements, notably, in getting the age limit of
entry into the Covenanted Civil Service raised to
twenty-three in 1888 and in obtaining a larger and
more democratic Indian representation in the country's legislatures four years later. The latter
concession was regarded as most important and was
hailed by the Madras Congress leadership as "the
first instalment of political freedom" for the
Indian people.[130]

Undoubtedly, a genuine pride in its past achievements came to sustain the professional elite in its belief that similar exertions in the future would result in the gradual transfer of administrative and political power to Indian hands and, ultimately, secure self-rule for India. It was this vision of self-governing India, still a distant ideal as the nineteenth century drew to a close, which moved the editor of the *Hindu* to observe on 3 December 1893:

> The change that has come over the people during the eight short years since the foundation of the Congress is marvellous, and the new sense of power that strengthens their hearts and the success that has so far crowned their efforts will sustain them in the further exertions to develop into maturity the tender plant of political freedom.

Conclusion

Nationalism is the most powerful of the political emotions to stir the peoples of Asia and Africa during the past century. Like other modern ideological movements, nationalism is European in origin and was borne to the non-Western world primarily on the wave of European imperial expansion. What was remarkable about this new phenomenon was the way in which the subject peoples of the third world fashioned this alien ideology into a formidable weapon to eject the European intruders from their shores. Nationalism, in short, acted as the solvent of Western colonialism in Asia and Africa.

It is important for analytical purposes to make a distinction between nationalism and the traditional resistance movements. Although some writers portray the latter as a form of nationalist activity,[1] the burgeoning literature on the subject points to the fact that these two movements were really dichotomous. Except for their shared desire to end alien rule, they had little in common. These two phenomena had a different vision of the kind of state they wished to establish; they drew their leaders from different social milieus; and they employed different ideological and organizational weapons.

Studies on colonial nationalisms in the third world have revealed that they were fostered by an almost identical set of circumstances. These circumstances have been largely traced to the Western impact. Among other things, European intrusion into Asia and Africa created the framework of modern states, initially, by carving up much of these two continents into separate territorial entities with fixed and defensible frontiers, and, then, by imposing upon these entities common economic, educational, and communication systems. Peoples who lived within such defined colonial territories found themselves subjected to the same laws and methods of administration. They came to share common grievances and aspirations. A sense of common destiny became manifest, which then expressed itself in movements towards unity and the search after the political kingdom. Nationalism is a shorthand to describe this interplay of sentiment and action.

One striking characteristic of nationalism in the third world was that it was almost always conceived by an elite raised in the Western intellectual tradition. In India, the connection between Western education and the rise of nationalism has long been noted by scholars. The fact that the British rulers introduced a fairly uniform system of higher education in the country, with English as the medium of instruction, led many historians to perceive in the products of this training a new homogeneous class capable of forging countrywide links in order to promote common goals. McCully, writing in 1940, asserts that "higher education provided an element of unity, a synthetic force which transcended linguistic and regional differences and drew its beneficiaries together into a fairly homogeneous grouping on the basis of a common culture." He goes on to argue that this Western-educated class, despite "the shortcomings of its hybrid culture," was imbued with European political doctrines, including nationalism, and was capable of propagating these doctrines through novel forms of organization borrowed from the West. The founding of the Congress is seen as the handiwork of this class.[2]

Recent scholars of Indian nationalism have introduced certain refinements to the above analysis.
Anil Seal, in his study of the emergence of Indian
nationalism, claims that the movement "was not formed through the promptings of any class demand or
as the consequence of any sharp changes in the
structure of the economy." While ascribing nationalism to Western education, Seal argues that education's uneven spread in the country affected
political mobilization more conspicuously than any
other factor. According to Seal, Western education
only made headway in the three coastal presidencies
and, even there, only among certain groups who resorted to it in order to conserve or improve their
group status. In his calculations of the political
arithmetic of India during the 1870s and 1880s,
Seal discovers that those who had taken advantage
of the new learning were the *bhadralok* of Bengal,
the Mahratta Brahmins and Parsis of Bombay Presidency, and the Tamil and Telugu Brahmins of Madras
Presidency. Outside of these groups and presidencies, Western education had made little advance.
Given this uneven spread of education, and given
the intense preexisting rivalries between groups
within each region, he reasons that "there was
little possibility of unity between the graduates
and their societies." In the Madras Presidency,
for example, Seal claims that rivalries between
Brahmins, who had "as yet no serious competitors in
the advance towards western education," and the
rest of society were so sharp that there was neither solidarity nor sympathy between them. If collaboration between graduates and their societies
was impossible, Seal nonetheless discerns one
level--"and this was the level of all-India"--at
which the educated elites of Bengal, Bombay, and
Madras could work together. "In so doing," he suggests, "their main purpose may well have been to
strengthen their position inside their local societies." To put it differently, the Western-
educated, as they moved into modern, secular politics, "remained riddled with allegiances to caste

or community, and what from a distance appear as
their political strivings were often, on closer examination, their efforts to conserve or improve the
position of their prescriptive group." In other
words, nationalism was a device of the castes educated in the Western mode to service their own
interests. Self-gain was rationalized with reference to the nation.[3]

Two qualifications can be made in relation to
Seal's generalizations on the origins of Indian
nationalism. First, it is important to recognize
that the circumstances conducive to political mobilization are not found exclusively in the realm of
education. Just as important are the economic
transformations brought about by the Western impact.
In this study, it was seen that the growth of a
market society consequent to the establishment of
the British Raj had created opportunities for a
Hindu commercial elite to rise to prominence in
Madras. Acquisitive, enterprising, and endowed
with entrepreneurial skills, this elite took advantage of the openings provided by expanding international and domestic trade to amass wealth and
acquire status and influence. It was this elite
which first experimented with the Western forms of
protest and organization in South India, initially,
by galvanizing the Hindu population in the southern
metropolis to resist Christian missionary pressures
to overthrow the official policy of religious
neutrality and, subsequently, by founding the
Madras Native Association to enlist the support of
sympathetic groups in Britain on behalf of political and economic reforms in the Presidency.

The other qualification which ought to be made
to Seal's generalizations relates to the need to
make some kind of a distinction between the educated who became administrators under the Raj and
those who joined the independent professions. In
South India, the first generation of the Western-
educated who had studied at the Madras High School
had become mainly administrators and achieved mobility and prestige in the service of the colonial

regime. Their exemplary habits of industry, integrity, and loyalty won them recognition and rewards from their European superiors. Not surprisingly, this administrative elite favored close and enduring partnership between India and England, even if this partnership was of an unequal kind. Hence, when the younger and more numerous elements in the independent professions emerged during the 1880s to vigorously espouse the cause of nationalism, the administrative elite voiced its misgivings about the aims and methods of such a movement. In its eyes, nationalism sought to drive a wedge between the rulers and the ruled, thereby endangering the stability and ordered progress which India was making under British tutelage. To some extent, its reservations about nationalism were rooted in its generational conflict with the professional elite.

The three elites that have been delineated in this study are examples of the transformations that have attended the intrusion of the West in South India. It is extremely doubtful if Indian nationalism would have emerged in the form that it did without these Western-inspired transformations, notably, through the growth of a market economy, the introduction of modern secular education, and the spread of urbanization and communication networks. The effect of such changes was to provide avenues for individual mobility, whether in business, small-scale industry, the bureaucracy, or the independent professions. Those who successfully exploited these opportunities came to form new elites. Admittedly, they were drawn almost exclusively from certain segments of Indian society, but it should be emphasized that they were open elites, with individual achievement the hallmark of their status.

Another characteristic of these elites should also be noted: they were essentially urban groups whose values, and even life styles to an extent, were modified by the influence of their environment. Urbanization was one important feature in the transformation which colonial rule effected in nineteenth

century India. Towns had grown up to meet the
needs of administration, trade, and communications.
Some of these towns, like Madura, were ancient
dynastic capitals while others, like Madras, were
almost entirely colonial creations. Whether old or
new, these urban centers became magnets, attracting
people from the surrounding countryside in search
of work, education, or release from the constraints
of the traditional social system. Equally, these
centers provided the arena for new and exciting
forms of interaction and association among people
of diverse social and economic backgrounds.
Hodgkin's point about the role of new towns in
Africa applies with equal force to the towns of
colonial India:[4]

> By providing opportunities for a greater de-
> gree of specialisation, towns enable men (and
> women) to acquire new skills and powers. By
> mixing men from a variety of social back-
> grounds they make possible the discovery of
> new points of contact and interest. Around
> these interests there develops a network of
> new associations, through which for the first
> time men come to think of their problems as
> social rather than personal; as capable of
> solution by human action rather than part of
> the natural order.

If urban centers became focal points where new
forms of social relationships could be explored and
developed, the initiative and direction behind much
of this activity came from the new elites which the
Western impact had brought into existence. These
elites not only assumed positions of secular leadership in their society but also formulated programs
which offered challenges to the policies and
actions of the colonial rulers.
It was the professional elite which displayed
a strong sense of attachment to the ideals of
Indian nationalism. This can be briefly explained.
The professional elite represented the third

generation since British power was established in
South India. Its cohesion stemmed from its common
social origins, its shared educational background,
and its association with one or another of the independent professions which became important during
the nineteenth century. Ambitious and resourceful,
this elite sought outlets for its talents in local
bodies, statutory boards, educational institutions,
and cultural and literary societies. At the same
time, it pressed for changes in the colonial administration, calling for greater Indian participation
in the executive and legislative organs of government. Doubtless, self-interest dictated this demand, for the desired changes would not only
strengthen the elite's role in government but would
also enhance its political stature in South India.
In a more indirect way, it could also be argued
that the castes from which the elite was recruited
would predictably augment their influence in
society.

      However, having said this, it ought not to be
inferred that the nationalist demands of this elite
sprang from any conscious effort to conserve or
improve the position of the prescriptive groups
from which it was drawn. Such a view fails to take
into account the psychological and political urges
that prompted the elite to espouse the cause of
nationalism. The decision of the professional
elite to link Madras Presidency with the mainstream
of all-India nationalism stemmed primarily from a
deeply-felt conviction that the peoples of India
should not remain permanently chained to a position
of political subordination to an alien regime.
Such a situation was deemed to be offensive to
notions of racial pride and self-respect, as well
as detrimental to the material advancement of the
country as a whole. The professional elite, secure
in its belief that it had the intellectual and
political resources to provide creative leadership,
argued forcibly for changes in the colonial administrative system to ensure that the subject peoples
be more closely associated in the affairs of

government. Such changes were also regarded to be
fully consistent with past British pledges to equip
Indians in the difficult and challenging task of
self-government.

Two factors acted as catalysts in persuading
the professional elite to enter the threshold of
nationalist politics during the 1880s. First, the
elite was antagonized by the unpopular policies and
actions of the Madras administration under the
governorship of Grant Duff. A capricious proconsul,
Grant Duff gave free rein to his official subordinates to exercise discretionary authority over
sensitive communal and economic issues. The effect
of such actions was to cause a breach between the
local administration and the articulate sections of
public opinion in the Presidency. The second
factor which precipitated matters was the European
opposition to the Ilbert Bill. The political ex-
plosion that erupted over this issue aggravated
racial tensions in the country. Indian politicians
became resentful of the fact that the small European minority was not only seeking to influence
official policies in its favor but was also hoping
to legitimize the myth of white supremacy in the
eyes of the British Indian government. Although
racial passions did not reach dangerous proportions,
largely on account of Ripon's immense popularity
with the Indians, the political situation in the
country had undergone an almost qualitative change.
The birth of the Congress in the wake of the Ilbert
Bill episode was but one expression of this changed
political climate.

The nationalist movement which emerged in
South India with the advent of the Congress bore
characteristics not untypical of similar movements
in colonial Asia and Africa. There was a marked
bitterness about racial prejudices and inequalities;
a certain antipathy towards the European; a pas-
sionate attachment to the ideal of national honor
and well-being; and an unquestioned assumption that
the educated elements should provide leadership to
the movement. However, it should not be assumed

that the nationalists deliberately fostered anti-
European sentiment or that there was a conscious
rejection of everything European. Far from it.
The Congress, after all, owed its birth largely to
the efforts of an European. Equally, Congress
leaders went out of their way to acknowledge their
debt to British rule and pledged to model their
political institutions on the image of the West.

Nationalism in South India found its earliest
supporters among those elements mobilized under
the Western impact. This, however, imposed a major
disability upon the way that nationalism developed
during the late nineteenth century. Since the
mobilized groups came exclusively from certain,
upper Hindu castes, it was not surprising that
nationalism came to be identified with these
castes. Other groups in South India, especially
Muslims, Eurasians, and Harijans, regarded the
Congress as the creation of the higher Hindu castes
seeking political power within the colonial situation. Doubtless, there were preexisting rivalries between these groups, stemming from ethnic,
religious, and social factors, which made collaboration between them difficult. However, what gave
these rivalries a new dimension was the uneven
nature of the Western impact. The upper Hindu
castes had generally taken advantage of the opportunities provided by British rule and had maintained, if not improved, their position in the
educational, administrative, and economic life of
South India.

On the other hand, the Muslims, Eurasians, and
Harijans were slower to respond, and there was
little overall improvement in their status after
almost a century of British rule. Initially, some
of these groups blamed the British rulers for their
depressed condition. Later, about the time when
nationalism dawned in the country, these backward
groups began to direct their hostility against the
upper Hindu castes, especially the Brahmins. In
their eyes, the Congress was an attempt on the part
of the dominant higher castes to strengthen further

their position in society, notably, by gaining
easier access to the legislative and executive
branches of government. Given such suspicions,
there was little prospect of the nationalists enlisting the cooperation of the backward groups. In
other words, the discontinuities that developed under the British Raj posed major obstacles in the
path of the Congress leaders in South India.

The problems of the nationalists were aggravated by the dual strategy which the backward
groups employed in their efforts at group uplift.
First, backward groups emphasized the importance of
group unity as a prerequisite for self-improvement.
In South India, appeals for group unity were invariably accompanied by the starting of associations,
educational institutions, newspapers, scholarships,
and other schemes catering to the interests of the
group. Such efforts inevitably strengthened group
exclusiveness. Second, it became common practice
among groups which had organized in self-defense to
demand favored treatment for themselves from the
government. The government was urged to accord
special educational facilities for each group, re-
serve places in the administration, and provide
separate representation in the legislature. Implicit in this strategy was the belief that the
British rulers were in the most efficacious position to help the backward groups in their desire
for equality with the advanced groups. It was a
strategy which did not augur well for the nationalist movement.

The attitude of the Muslims demonstrated the
difficulties which the nationalists encountered in
wooing groups which were slow to respond to the
Western impact. Congress leaders in South India
attached considerable significance to the Muslim
community for, as the largest minority in the subcontinent, its reactions would be crucial in deter-
mining the national character of the organization.
Congress approaches to the Muslims soon brought to
the forefront the underlying tensions between them
and the Hindus. No doubt, it can be argued that

these tensions were long standing and were the outcome of sharp doctrinal differences and bitter
memories of past conflicts. However, what made collaboration between these two groups difficult during the nationalist era was as much their uneven
rate of development under the British Raj as it was
their historic differences. While the Muslims had
lost their empire and gradually had sunk to a position of political obscurity and poverty, the Hindus
had registered significant gains and come to occupy
a prominent place in the intellectual, professional,
administrative, and economic life of the subcontinent. It is little wonder that the Muslims became
resentful of their more successful rivals over whom
they had once ruled. In this frame of mind, the
Muslims were hardly prepared to enter into any kind
of a collaboration with the Hindus in the pursuit
of nationalist goals.

    The Muslim attitude towards the Congress,
though dramatized by the importance that the
nationalists attached to this community, was in no
way unique. Other, similarly placed groups in South
India adopted an almost identical posture towards
the Congress. The Eurasians, after a brief period
of cooperation with the nationalists, withdrew from
the Congress, convinced that their interests would
be better served by relying upon the goodwill of
their colonial rulers. The Harijans, without doubt
the most depressed community in South India, also
evinced similar hostility towards the Congress.
This group had shown early signs of political
awakening during the 1890s when its leaders in
Madras began to formulate ideas for the advancement
of the group. The strategy that was devised was
broadly similar to that pursued by the other backward groups. The Harijans founded their own associations, schools, and newspapers; and they appealed to the government to initiate ameliorative
measures on behalf of the community. Some Harijan
leaders also called for the destruction of the
caste system, claiming that it was largely responsible for their degraded condition. Criticisms

were levelled against the higher castes, not only
for their past misdeeds but also for their continued efforts to maintain their privileged status
in society. The Congress came to be depicted as an
instrument of the higher castes, especially Brahmins, to perpetuate their domination over the lower
castes.[5] It was this identification of the Congress with the higher Hindu castes which largely
obstructed Harijan participation in the nationalist
movement.

It must be noted that the backward groups in
South India had by and large acted in isolation in
their efforts to attain equality with the more advanced groups. Each group entered the political
arena at different times when it became conscious
of its depressed status. As more groups became
awakened in this way, it was inevitable that an element of competition came to inform their actions,
especially as each group pressed its own demands on
the government. How far such competition was perceived by the leaders of these groups to be detrimental to their long-term interests is not clear.
In any case, during the second decade of the twentieth century, some non-Brahmin groups decided to
band together in a concerted bid to overthrow the
dominance of the Brahmins in the administrative and
political life of South India. The formation of
the South Indian Liberal Federation in 1916 inaugurated an era of sharpening conflict between the
nationalists and certain sectional interests seeking group uplift by capturing executive and legislative power at the provincial level.[6]

These facts bring into focus some of the disabilities under which nationalism functioned in
South India. However, it should not be assumed
that these disabilities were in any sense peculiar
to India; similar contradictions have, in varying
degrees, characterized nationalist movements
throughout Asia and Africa. Today, when the nationalist struggles in the third world have been more
or less successfully concluded, the problem of resolving these contradictions remains. In other

words, the disabilities under which the nationalists labored during the colonial era have now come
to haunt the leaders of free Asia and Africa. The
extent to which these social tensions are overcome
will determine whether the political map of the
third world will require any drastic revision in
the years to come.

APPENDIX

Appendix

Officeholders of the Madras Mahajana Sabha, 1886–1887

Name	Year of Birth	District of Birth	Caste or Communal Affiliation
1. P. Rangiah Naidu	1828	Madras	non-Brahmin
2. S. Subramania Iyer	1842	Madura	Brahmin
3. P. Somasundram Chetty	1824	Madras	non-Brahmin
4. P. Savalay Ramaswamy Mudaliar	1840	Pondicherry	non-Brahmin
5. R. Balaji Rao	1842	Tanjore	Brahmin
6. A. Sabapathy Mudaliar	1838	Bellary	non-Brahmin
7. C. Ramachandra Rao	1845	Tanjore	Brahmin
8. M. Jagga Rao Pillay	?	?	Indian Christian
9. P. Kotaswamy Devar	?	Madura	non-Brahmin
10. S. Pulney Andy	1831	?	Indian Christian
11. P. Gurumurti Iyer	?	?	Brahmin
12. G. Subramania Iyer	1855	Tanjore	Brahmin
13. C. Sankaran Nair	1857	Malabar	non-Brahmin
14. Salem Ramaswamy Mudaliar	1852	Salem	non-Brahmin
15. Gulam Dastagir Saheb	?	?	Muslim
16. P. S. Subramania Iyer	1864	Tanjore	Brahmin
17. P. Subramania Iyer	?	?	Brahmin
18. P. V. Krishnaswamy Chetty	?	?	non-Brahmin

Educational and/or Professional Qualification (with year of graduation)	Occupation	Honorary or Elective Posts Held in Statutory and Public Bodies
Proficient's certificate (1851) Pleader's Test (1856)	Vakil, Madras High Court	Chingleput District Board Member; Municipal Commissioner, Madras
B.L.(1868)	Vakil, Madras High Court	Municipal Commissioner, Madura; Member of Madras Legislative Council
---	Merchant, Madras	Municipal Commissioner, Madras; Trustee, Pachaiyappa Charities
---	Dubash, Arbuthnot & Co., Madras	Sheriff of Madras, Municipal Commissioner, Madras
B.L.(1869)	Vakil, Madras High Court	Municipal Commissioner, Madras; Fellow, Madras University
---	Merchant and industrialist, Bellary	Municipal Commissioner, Bellary
B.L.(1870)	Vakil, Madras High Court	---
B.A.(1866); B.L.(1870)	Vakil, Madras High Court	---
---	Landlord	Committee Member, Madura People's Association
M.D.(?)	Medical Practitioner, Madras	---
B.A.(1872); B.L.(1874)	Vakil, Madras High Court	---
B.A.(1877)	Journalist, Madras	Committee Member, Triplicane Literary Society
B.A.(1875); B.L.(1879)	Vakil, Madras High Court	Member, Malabar Land Tenure Commission
B.A.(1871); M.A.(1873); B.L.(1875)	Vakil, Madras High Court	Secretary, Madras Native Association; Municipal Commissioner, Madras
---	Merchant, Madras	---
B.A.(1882); B.L.(1884)	Vakil, Madras High Court	Committee Member, Mylapore Athenaeum
---	Articled clerk, Madras	---
B.A.(1867); B.L.(1872)	Vakil, Madras High Court	---

Appendix (con't)

Officeholders of the Madras Mahajana Sabha, 1886–1887

Name	Year of Birth	District of Birth	Caste or Communal Affiliation
19. P. Ananda Charlu	1843	North Arcot	Brahmin
20. M. Viraraghava Chari	1857	Chingleput	Brahmin
21. C. V. Sundram Sastri	1848	North Arcot	Brahmin
22. K. P. Sarkara Menon	?	Malabar	non-Brahmin
23. K. Subba Rao	?	Tanjore	Brahmin
24. P. Thengaroya Chetty	1852	?	non-Brahmin
25. T. Nemberumal Chetty	?	?	non-Brahmin
26. G. Mahadeva Chetty	?	?	non-Brahmin
27. P. Ethirajulu Naidu	?	?	non-Brahmin
28. T. V. Seshagiri Iyer	1860	?	Brahmin
29. T. Chellapa Naicker	?	?	non-Brahmin
30. K. Naraina Rao	?	?	Brahmin
31. Abboi Naidu	?	?	non-Brahmin
32. C. Singavavelu Mudaliar	?	?	non-Brahmin
33. A. Balakrishna Mudaliar	?	?	non-Brahmin
34. A. Danakoti Mudaliar	?	?	non-Brahmin
35. R. Balakrishna Chetty	?	?	non-Brahmin
36. C. Bthirajulu Naidu	?	?	non-Brahmin

Sources: Indian Mirror, 20 October 1886; V. L. Sastri, ed., Encyclopaedia of the Madras Presidency and the adjacent states (Madras, 1921); Administration report of the Madras Municipality, 1878–86; University of Madras, Calendar for 1893–94, I; Asylum Press Almanac & Compendium of Intelligence, 1868, 1875, 1880 and 1886.

Educational and/or Professional Qualification (with year of graduation)	Occupation	Honorary or Elective Posts Held in Statutory and Public Bodies
B.L.(1869)	Vakil, Madras High Court	Vice-President, Triplicane Literary Society; Municipal Commissioner, Madras
B.A.(1877)	Journalist, Madras	Committee Member, Triplicane Literary Society
B.A.(1869); B.L.(1872)	Vakil, Madras High Court	Municipal Commissioner, Madras
B.A.(1878); B.L.(1881)	Vakil, Madras High Court	---
B.A.(1888)	Journalist, Madras	---
B.A.(?)	Merchant, Madras	Municipal Commissioner, Madras
B.A.(1879)	Building contractor, Madras	---
---	Merchant, Madras	---
---	Dubash, Madras	Municipal Commissioner, Madras
B.A.(1881); B.L.(1885)	Vakil, Madras High Court	Committee Member, Triplicane Literary Society
---	Retired district munsif	---
B.A.(1881); B.L.(1884)	Vakil, Madras High Court	---
---	Merchant, Madras	---
---	Merchant, Madras	Municipal Commissioner, Madras; Trustee of Pachaiyappa Charities
---	Merchant, Madras	---
---	Landlord, Madras	Municipal Commissioner, Madras; Board member, Monegar Choultry
---	Merchant, Madras	Municipal Commissioner, Madras
---	Merchant, Madras	Municipal Commissioner, Madras; Board member, Monegar Choultry

NOTES, BIBLIOGRAPHY, INDEX

Notes to the Chapters

Introduction
Pages 1-7

1. M. N. Vasantha Devi, "Some Aspects of the Agricultural Geography of South India," *Indian Geographical Journal*, XXXIX:1-2 (1964):4.
2. Much of the data on the physical environment of South India is gleaned from O. H. K. Spate and A. T. A. Learmonth, *India and Pakistan*, 3rd ed. (London, 1967), pp. 642-785; and M. N. Vasantha Devi, "Some Aspects of Agricultural Geography," pp. 1-41, 59-122.
3. The above data on Kerala is mainly drawn from the following studies: G. Woodcock, *Kerala. A Portrait of the Malabar Coast* (London, 1967); K. M. Panikkar, *Malabar and the Dutch* (Bombay, 1931); and M. J. Webb, "The Coast Plains of Kerala," *Indian Geographical Journal*, XXXVI:1 (1961): 1-27.
4. For further discussion of Tamil history and regional traits see J. Filliozat, "Tamil and Sanskrit in South India," *Tamil Culture*, IV:4 (1965):286-300; K. A. N. Sastri, *The Culture and History of the Tamils* (Calcutta, 1964); and N. Subramanian, *Sangam Polity* (London, 1966).
5. The relationship between physical environment and economic activity is discussed in O. H. K. Spate and A. T. A. Learmonth, *India*, pp. 739-85; and Vasantha Devi, "Some Aspects of Agricultural Geography," pp. 59-122.
6. For details of the early history of Andhra see K. Gopalachari, *Early History of the Andhra Country* (Madras, 1941); A. B. Mukerji, "Succession of Cultural Landscapes in Telengana Reddi Villages," *Indian Geographical Journal*, XXXIX:1-2 (1964):47-56; and M. S. Sarma, *History of the Reddi Kingdoms* (Waltair, 1948).
7. S. S. Harrison, *India. The Most Dangerous Decades* (Princeton, 1960), p. 27.
8. C. Drekmeier, *Kingship and Community in Early India* (Stanford, 1962), p. 117.
9. For a discussion of the impact of the devotional movement in South India see V. Raghavan, "Methods of Popular Religious Instruction in South India," in *Traditional India: Structure and Change*, ed. M. Singer (Philadelphia, 1959), pp. 130-38.
10. A. L. Basham, *The Wonder That Was India* (London, 1954), pp. 327-32.
11. For studies on these Saivite sects see S. C. Nandimath, *A Handbook of Virasaivism* (Dharwar, 1942); V. Paranjoti, *Saiva Siddhanta* (London, 1954); and G. Subramania Pillai, *Introduction & History of Saiva Siddhanta* (Annamalainagar, 1948).

12. R. Temple, *Men and Events of my Time* (London, 1882), pp. 459-60.
13. Ravinder Kumar, *Western India in the Nineteenth Century* (London, 1968), p. 44.
14. R. E. Frykenberg, "Traditional Processes of Power in South India: An Historical Analysis of Local Influence," *Indian Economic and Social History Review*, 1:2 (1963):123-26.
15. A. Beteille, *Caste, Class, and Power* (Berkeley, 1965), pp. 61-72; and T. Venkasami Rao, *A Manual of the Tanjore District* (Madras, 1883), pp. 164-71.
16. For a perceptive analysis of this elite group see J. P. Mencher, "Namboodiri Brahmins: An Analysis of a Traditional Elite in Kerala," *Journal of Asian and African Studies*, I (1966):183-96.
17. J. A. Dubois, *Hindu Manners, Customs and Ceremonies*, translated and edited by H. K. Beauchamp, 3rd ed. (Oxford, 1959), pp. 289-95.
18. For a graphic description of conditions in the interior Andhra districts on the eve of British rule see W. Hamilton, *A Geographical, Statistical, and Historical Description of Hindostan, and the Adjacent Countries* (London, 1820), pp. 326-30.
19. T. H. Beaglehole, *Thomas Munro & the Development of Administrative Policy in Madras 1792-1818* (Cambridge, 1966), pp. 55-63.
20. S. Srinivasa Raghavaiyangar, *Memorandum on the Progress of the Madras Presidency during the last forty years of British Administration* (Madras, 1892), p. 74.
21. *MEP*, Vol. 280, September 1875, No. 15, Logan to Carmichael, 30 August 1875.
22. Beaglehole, *Thomas Munro*, pp. 7-10 and 128-31.
23. A. J. Arbuthnot (ed.), *Major-General Sir Thomas Munro*, I (London, 1881), p. 95.
24. For a fuller discussion of the traditional agrarian structure of South India see Dharma Kumar, *Land and Caste in South India* (Cambridge, 1965), pp. 14-33.
25. The origins of these disturbances are discussed in W. Logan, *Malabar*, I (Madras, 1883), pp. 537-99.
26. Beaglehole, *Thomas Munro*, pp. 111-17.
27. R. E. Frykenberg, *Guntur District 1788-1848* (Oxford, 1965), pp. 97-98.
28. A. J. Arbuthnot (ed.), *Major-General Sir Thomas Munro*, II, pp. 9-10.
29. C. S. Srinivasachari, "Village Organization in South India at the Advent of British Rule," in *D. R. Bhandarkar Volume*, ed. B. C. Law (Calcutta, 1940), pp. 36-38; and Beaglehole, *Thomas Munro*, pp. 111-17.
30. *PPHC*, XVIII (1859):143, W. Elliot to GOM, 20 November 1854.
31. H. Ricketts. *Report of the Commissioners for the Revision of Civil Salaries and Establishments throughout India*, I (Calcutta, 1858), pp. 333-34.
32. Frykenberg, *Guntur District*, pp. 71 and 83-84.
33. The extent to which British revenue policy had encouraged official corruption in South India during the first half of the nineteenth century is ably discussed in a semiofficial account by J. D. Bourdillon, *Remarks on the Ryotwari System of Land Revenue, as it exists in the Presidency of Madras* (Madras, 1853).
34. For a general discussion of the socio-economic impact of Europe on the nonwestern world, see W. Woodruff, *Impact of Western Man. A study of Europe's role in the World's Economy 1750-1960* (New York, 1967).

Chapter 1

1. For a contemporary description of Madras and its suburbs see *A Gazetteer of Southern India* (Madras, 1855), pp. 182-88.
2. H. D. Love, *Vestiges of Old Madras 1640-1800*, II (London, 1913), pp. 44-45.
3. M. J. Seth, *Armenians in India* (Calcutta, 1937), pp. 579-81.
4. _____, *Madras, the Birthplace of Armenian Journalism* (Calcutta, 1937), pp. 1-2.
5. *Madras Almanac and Compendium of Intelligence* (1812), p. 248. For an excellent study of an European agency house in this period see H. Brown, *Parry's of Madras* (Madras, 1954).
6. H. B. Lamb, "The Indian Merchant," *Traditional India: Structure and Change*, ed. M. Singer, pp. 25-34.
7. C. S. Srinivasachari, *History of the City of Madras* (Madras, 1939), pp. 51-52.
8. _____, "Pachaiyappa. His Life, Times and Charities," *Pachaiyappa's College Madras. Centenary Commemoration Book 1842-1942* (Madras, 1942), pp. 7-33.
9. *Asiatic Journal*, October 1834 quoted in *Madras Male Asylum Herald*, 7 March 1835.
10. A. J. Arbuthnot, *Major-General Sir Thomas Munro*, II, pp. 216-17.
11. *Madras Almanac & Compendium of Intelligence for 1851*, pp. 338-39.
12. Love, *Vestiges of Old Madras*, II, p. 503.
13. Srinivasachari, "Pachaiyappa. His Life, Times and Charities," pp. 14-17.
14. K. Ingham, *Reformers in India 1793-1833* (Cambridge, 1956), p. 1.
15. F. Penny, *The Church in Madras*, III (London, 1922), pp. 277-78.
16. E. Hoole, *Madras, Mysore, and the South of India*, 2nd edition (London, 1844), pp. 377 and 408-10.
17. R. Caldwell, *The Tinnevelly Shanars* (London, 1850), p. 69.
18. *PPHC*, XL (1849), 621:437.
19. J. W. Kaye, *Christianity in India* (London, 1859), p. 389.
20. *Church Missionary Record*, IV (1833):76.
21. *PPHC*, XLIII (1837), 357:1-5.
22. *Ibid.*, XLIII (1857-58), 79:1-6.
23. *Church Missionary Record*, XIII (1842), 251.
24. *Madras Native Herald*, August 1861, p. 60.
25. *The Dawn in the East* (Edinburgh, 1854), p. iv.
26. K. Venkataswami Naidu, "History of Pachaiyappa's College 1842-1942," *Pachaiyappa College Madras. Centenary Commemoration Book*, pp. 64-65.
27. J. B. Norton, *The Educational Speeches of the Hon'ble John Bruce Norton, B.A.* (Madras, 1866), p. 4.
28. G. Norton, *Native Education in India* (Madras, 1848), p. 27.
29. For the full text of these lectures see G. Norton, *Rudimentals; being a series of discourses* (Madras, 1841).
30. *Madras Male Asylum Herald*, 26 November 1834.
31. G. Norton, *Native Education in India*, pp. 31-34.
32. *Athenaeum*, 5 October 1844.
33. *Madras New Almanac for 1852*, p. 494.
34. C. Paramaswaran Pillai, *Representative Men of Southern India* (Madras, 1896), pp. 145-50.
35. Speech of G. N. Gajapati Rao at Lakshmanarasu Chetty memorial meeting, *Athenaeum and Daily News*, 18 September 1868.
36. J. L. Wyatt (ed.), *Reminiscences of Bishop Caldwell* (Madras, 1894), p.56.

37. *PPHL*, XXX (1852-53), 41; Evidence of Cameron, 203-4.
38. *Madras Native Herald*, 1845, pp. 204-19.
39. Caldwell, *Tinnevelly Shanars*, p. 110.
40. G. U. Pope, *Mission of Sawyerpooram*, Pt. V (London, 1849), pp. 8-9.
41. *Church Missionary Record*, XVII (1846):39-41.
42. *Madras Christian Instructor and Missionary Record*, IV (1846):637-42.
43. *Ibid.*, III (1845):475-76.
44. *Proceedings at the public meeting of the Hindu Community* . . . (Madras, 1846), pp. 1-16.
45. *Tweeddale Collection*, MSS. Eur., F.96, No.6, Tweeddale to Hobhouse, 26 October 1846.
46. *Native Herald*, 1843, p. 98.
47. *Spectator*, 18 May 1844.
48. Cited in *Spectator*, 15 October 1846.
49. Cited in *Athenaeum*, 21 January 1851.
50. *Spectator*, 19 March 1846.
51. *Ibid.*, 1 March 1852.
52. *Madras Almanac & Compendium of Intelligence* (1852), pp. 338-39.
53. *MRP*, Range 282, Vol.43, Torture Commission to GOM, 27 November 1854.
54. *Spectator*, 16 and 19 July 1852.
55. *Petition to the Imperial Parliament from the members of the Madras Native Association* . . . 10 December 1852 (Madras, 1852).
56. *Spectator*, 24 January 1853.
57. *Madras Times*, 30 January 1864.
58. *Spectator*, 29 December 1856.
59. *Ibid.*, 1 August 1853.
60. *Indian Mirror*, 1 August 1863.
61. *Athenaeum*, 22 April 1854.
62. *Hansard*, CXXXV, pp. 59-66.
63. *Report of the Commissioners for the investigation of alleged cases of torture in the Madras Presidency* (Madras, 1855), pp. 4-5 and 45.
64. W. Holloway, *Notes on Madras Judicial Administration* (Madras, 1853), pp. 59-60.
65. *Athenaeum*, 22 April 1854.
66. *Wood Collection*, MSS. Eur. F.78, No.32, Pottinger to Wood, 23 December 1853.
67. *Athenaeum*, 13 July 1854.
68. *Ibid.*, 23 February 1856.
69. *Fifth petition to the Imperial Parliament from the members of the Madras Native Association*, 26 January 1856 (Madras, 1856).
70. *PPHC*, XXIX (1857), 117:90-93.
71. *Memorial to the Right Honorable Lord Stanley* . . . *on the subject of government interference in religious matters* (Madras, 1859), pp. 3-32.
72. *MPP*, Range 249, Vol.69, Minute by Trevelyan, 28 June 1859.
73. *Athenaeum*, 17 April 1860.
74. *Ibid.*, 1 May 1860.
75. *Athenaeum and Statesman*, 5 April 1862.
76. *Madras Times*, 25 July 1862.
77. For a brief discussion of the possible factors which led to the dissolution of the MNA see my article, "The Madras Native Association: A study of an early Indian political organization," *Indian Economic and Social History Review*, IV:3 (1967):251-52.

Chapter 2

1. *Opening of the Madras University, on the 14th April 1841* (Madras, 1841), pp. 1 and 20.
2. Cited in S. Satthianadhan, *History of Education in the Madras Presidency* (Madras, 1894), p. 14.
3. *Opening of the Madras University,* Appendix 1, Minute of Elphinstone, 12 December 1839.
4. *Ibid.,* pp. 2-4.
5. *ARGMU* (1842), 8-9.
6. *ARGMU* (1851-52), 8.
7. *Opening of the Madras University,* pp. 9-10.
8. T. Madava Rao, *Three Addresses* (Madras, 1884), p. 17.
9. B. V. Kamesvara Aiyar, *Sir A. Sashiah Sastri, K.C.S.I. An Indian Statesman. A Biographical Sketch* (Madras, 1902), pp. 16-17.
10. *ARGMU* (1844), Appendix C.
11. *Ibid.,* 5-10.
12. *RPIMP* (1854-55), Appendix A, No.IX.
13. Norton, *Native Education in India,* p. 44.
14. *ARGMU* (1845), 17.
15. *PPHL,* III (1852-53), 20; Evidence of G. Norton, 96-104 and 110-11.
16. *ARGMU* (1851-52), 6.
17. J. A. Richey, *Selections from Educational Records,* Pt. II, 1840-1859 (Calcutta, 1922), p. 197.
18. *ARGMU* (1845), 8-9.
19. *RPIMP* (1854-55), Appendix A, No.IX.
20. *Elphinstone Papers,* MSS. Eur. F.78, No.5G, Norton to Elphinstone, 16 March 1840.
21. *ARGMU* (1842), 6-9.
22. *Ibid.,* pp. 17-18.
23. Richey, *Selections,* p. 180.
24. G. Paramaswaran Pillai, *Representative Men of Southern India* (Madras, 1896), pp. 73-79.
25. _____, *Representative Indians* (London, 1897), pp. 116-17.
26. Kamesvara Aiyar, *Sir A. Sashiah Sastri,* pp. 30-31.
27. C. Karunakara Menon, *A Critical Essay on Sir A. Seshia Sastri, K.C.S.I.* (Madras, 1903), pp. 38-54.
28. *ARGMU* (1850-51), 51.
29. *Wood Collection,* MSS. Eur. F.78, Letter Book IV, Wood to Dalhousie, 24 December 1853.
30. *PPHC,* XL (1854-55), 435: Minute by Harris, 19 April 1855.
31. *Wood Collection,* MSS. Eur. F.78, No.21, Harris to Wood, 14 March 1855.
32. *MRP,* Range 282, Vol.68, No.88, Minute of Consultations, 24 December 1857.
33. *MPP,* Range 249, Vol.68, No.48, G.O. 22 January 1859.
34. *MRP,* Range 287, Vol.72, No.47, J. L. Lushington to J. D. Bourdillon, 4 April 1859.
35. *Madras New Almanac* (1864), pp. 110-110a.
36. Kamesvara Aiyar, *Sastri,* pp. 122-23.
37. M. P. Duraiswamy Aiyar, *Memories of Sir Tiruvarur Muthusami Ayyar* (Tanjore, n.d.), pp. 67-68.
38. *MRP,* Range 282, Vol.73, No.68, Taylor to Bourdillon, 16 June 1859.
39. *Ibid.,* Range 282, Vol.74, No.55, Enclosure B.
40. Kamesvara Aiyar, *Sastri,* pp. 127-30.

41. *Wood Collection*, Eur. MSS. F.78, No.59, Trevelyan to Wood, 22 January 1860; *MRP*, Range 282, Vol.73, No.65, Minute by Trevelyan, 14 June 1859.
42. J. B. Norton, *The Educational Speeches*, pp. 29 and 83.
43. Paramswaran Pillai, *Representative Indians*, pp. 120-22.
44. *Ibid.*, pp. 149-50.
45. M. P. Duraiswamy Aiyar, *Memories of Sir Tiruvarur Muthusami Ayyar*, pp. 57-88.
46. C. P. Ramaswami Aiyar, *Biographical Vistas. Sketches of some Eminent Indians* (London, 1968), p. 13.
47. Kamesvara Aiyar, *Sastri*, p. 154.
48. V. Nagamiah, *Raja Sir T. Madava Rao*, Part I (Tanjore, 1915), p. 63.
49. Madava Rao, "An Essay on Native Education," *ARGMU* (1845-46), 34-47.
50. *Madras Times*, 1 March 1864.
51. *Athenaeum and Daily News*, 27 February 1864.
52. *Ibid.*, 17 May 1864 and 14 November 1865.
53. Letter of P. M. Murugasem Mudali to the editor, *Athenaeum and Daily News*, 29 September 1865.
54. Letter to the editor, *Madras Times*, 13 July 1865.
55. D. Narasiah, *Letters on Hindu Marriages* (Madras, 1867), p. 11.
56. *Athenaeum and Daily News*, 4 and 9 October 1865; *Madras Times*, 6 October 1865.
57. M. Carpenter, *Six Months in India*, I (London, 1868), p. 149.
58. *Athenaeum and Daily News*, 11 January 1867.
59. *Ibid.*, 7 March 1868.
60. *Ibid.*, 29 June 1867.
61. Letter of Sesha Iyengar to the editor, *Athenaeum and Daily News*, 19 May 1873.
62. *Athenaeum and Daily News*, 7 October 1873.
63. *Ibid.*, 3 June 1874.
64. Letter from "A Hindu" to the editor, *Athenaeum and Daily News*, 12 June 1874.
65. Letter to the editor, *Madras Times*, 12 November 1878.
66. J. Gurunadhan, *Viresalingam. The founder of Telugu Public Life* (Rajahmundry, 1911), pp. 24-42 and 93-101.
67. R. Raghunatha Rao, *A Lecture on the Marriage of the Hindoos* (Indore, 1887), pp. 2-5.
68. *Madras Standard*, 27 October 1885.
69. Raghunatha Rao, *A Lecture on the Marriage of the Hindoos*, pp. 5-7.
70. *Madras Times*, 11 February 1885.
71. Raghunatha Rao, *A Lecture on the Marriage of the Hindoos*, pp. 8-9.
72. *Madras Times*, 7 January 1885.
73. *Ibid.*, 25 February 1882.
74. *Ibid.*, 6 July 1883.
75. *Ibid.*, 9 March 1883.
76. *Ibid.*, 11 June 1883.
77. *Ibid.*, 9 September 1884.
78. *Ibid.*, 5 January 1885.
79. *Ibid.*, 28 January 1885.
80. *Indian Mirror*, 26 December 1888.
81. *Hindu*, 2 May 1884.
82. Duraiswamy Aiyar, *Memories of Sir Tiruvarur Muthuswami Ayyar*, pp. 216-17.
83. S. C. Srinivasa Charier, *Political Opinions of Raja Sir T. Madava Rao, K.C.S.I.* (Madras, 1890), p. 10.
84. Cited in Kamesvara Aiyar, *Sastri*, pp. 257-58.

85. Paramaswaran Pillai, *Representative Indians*, p. 127.
86. *The Cosmopolitan Club. Madras. Platinum Jubilee Souvenir 1873-1954* (Madras, 1954), pp. 21-25.
87. *Hindu*, 11 May 1887.
88. Cited in Kamesvara Aiyar, *Sastri*, p. 254.
89. W. S. Blunt, *India under Ripon. A Private Diary* (London, 1909), pp. 38-39.
90. R. Ragunatha Rao, *A Letter Addressed to the Right Honorable Sir Charles Trevelyan, K.C.B., on the 1st June 1860* (Madras, 1890), p. 1.
91. _____, *A Memorandum on Famines in India* (Indore, 1878), pp. 1-10.
92. Blunt, *India Under Ripon*, pp. 38-39.
93. *Hindu*, 16 November 1883; *Madras Times*, 17 December 1883.
94. *Madras Standard*, 17 December 1883.
95. *Madras Times*, 1 February 1884.
96. T. Madava Rao, *Three Addresses* (Madras, 1884), pp. 1 and 30.
97. *Ibid.*, pp. 9-10 and 30-31.
98. *Indian Mirror*, 24 February 1885.
99. Nagamiah, *Raja Sir T. Madava Rao*, p. 103.
100. *RINC* (1887), 68.
101. *Indian Mirror*, 18 January 1889.
102. *Hindu*, 4 November 1889.
103. *Madras Times*, 5 March 1890.
104. *Madras Standard* cited in *Hindu*, 14 April 1890.
105. *Madras Times*, 21 March 1890.
106. *Ibid.*, 19 March 1890.

Chapter 3

1. J. B. Norton, *The Educational Speeches*, pp. 94-98.
2. McCully, *English Education*, p. 161.
3. Syed Mahmood, *History of English Education in India* (Aligarh, 1895), pp. 87-90.
4. A. M. Monteith, "Note on the state of education in India during 1865-66," *Selections from the Records of the Government of India, Home Department*, No.LIV (Madras, 1867), p. 14.
5. Satthianadhan, *History of Education*, p. 79.
6. *RPIMP* (1887-88), 48-49.
7. *Education Commission. Report by the Madras Provincial Committee* (Calcutta, 1884), pp. 18-19.
8. *RPIMP* (1885-86), 103-04.
9. McCully, *English Education*, p. 160.
10. *RPIMP* (1865-66), cli.
11. *Ibid.* (1875-76), 120.
12. *Education Commission. Report by the Madras Provincial Committee*, p.151.
13. H. Naraina Rao, "The Intellectual Progress of the Kanarese People under British Rule," *Madras Christian College Magazine*, XIII:3 (1895):162-63.
14. Thurston, *Castes and Tribes*, V, pp. 156-60.
15. *Education Commission. Report by the Madras Provincial Committee*, evidence of C. M. Barrow, p. 104.
16. T. Venkasami Row, *A Manual of the District of Tanjore, in the Madras Presidency* (Madras, 1883), pp. 247-49.
17. *Hindu*, 16 May 1891.
18. Speech of S. Ranga Chariar, *Athenaeum*, 26 August 1864.

19. Cited in H. L. Singh, *Problems and Policies of the British in India 1885-1898* (London, 1963), p. 26.
20. *Report of the PSC, 1886-87*, pp. 11 and 27.
21. *RPIMP* (1858-59), Appendix F.
22. B. B. Misra, *The Administrative History of India 1834-1947* (Bombay, 1970), p. 212.
23. *Proceedings of the PSC*, V, pp. 47-48.
24. *Appendices to the Report of the PSC, 1886-87* (Calcutta, 1888), pp.397-99.
25. *Ibid.*, pp. 312-19.
26. *Report of the PSC 1886-87*, pp. 422-27.
27. *Hindu*, 19 February 1892.
28. *Ibid.*
29. *Proceedings of the PSC*, V, Sec.2, p. 48.
30. *Proceedings of the Sub-Committee. PSC. Registration Department* (Bombay, 1887), pp. 30-33.
31. *Madras Census Report* (1871):1, p. 196.
32. *MEP*, Vol.3045, No.386, G.O. 27 July 1887.
33. *MPP*, Vol.5041, No.273, Chief Secretary, GOM, to Chief Secretary, GOI, 22 February 1896.
34. Venkasami Row, *A Manual*, p. 170.
35. Lady Mary Hobart (ed.), *Essays and Miscellaneous Writings of Vere Henry, Lord Hobart*, I (London, 1885), p. 163.
36. *RPIMP* (1878-79), 177.
37. *The Speeches and Writings of Sir T. Muthuswamy Aiyar* (Madras, 1895), p. 77.
38. *Madras Times*, 30 March 1878.
39. Cited in *Hindu*, 7 March 1890.
40. *Ibid.*, 8 August 1892.
41. K. Subba Rao, *Revived Memories* (Madras, 1933), p. 43.
42. *Report of the Indian Educational Commission* (Calcutta, 1883), pp. 589 and 625.
43. C. M. Barrow (ed.), *Madras Educational Calendar and Directory for 1890-91* (Madras, 1890), pp. 103-05 and 128-32.
44. *RPIMP* (1890-91), 44 and 107-08.
45. G. Gopal Menon, "History of Commercial Education in South India," *Bhashoddharraka Sri V. Venkateswara Sastrulu Commemoration Volume* (Madras, 1941), p. 20.
46. *Indian Magazine*, No.181 (January 1886):32-33.
47. *Papers relating to Technical Education in India 1886-1904* (Calcutta, 1906), pp. 86-87.
48. *Ibid.*, pp. 90-91.
49. *Education Commission. Report by the Madras Provincial Committee*, pp. 115-16.
50. *RPIMP* (1894-95), 94-95.
51. *Indian News*, 16 January 1852.
52. *RPIMP* (1885-86), 17.
53. *Hindu*, 7 November 1897.
54. Speech by Eardley Norton, *Hindu*, 23 July 1889.
55. A. D. Campbell, *A New Abridged Edition of the Code of Regulations . . . of the Madras Territories*, II (Madras, n.d.), pp. 269 and 321-22.
56. *FSG Gazette*, 10 May 1884; *Madras Mail*, 26 May 1893.
57. *Pioneer*, cited in *Hindu*, 5 September 1893.
58. A[nanda] C[harlu], *The Madras Bar and how to improve it* (Madras, 1883), pp. 23-24.

59. V. C. Gopalaratnam, *A Century Completed. (A History of the Madras High Court) 1862-1962* (Madras, n.d.), pp. 125-26.
60. *Madras Census Report* (1881), 141.
61. *Madras Law Journal*, X (1900):322.
62. *The Speeches and Writings of Sir.T. Muthusawmy Aiyar*, p. 30.
63. *Advocates' Association, Madras. Golden Jubilee Souvenir, 1939* (Madras, n.d.), pp. i-iii.
64. *Madras Law Journal*, VII (1897):93-95.
65. *Hindu*, 16 November 1899.
66. *Education Commission. Report by the Madras Provincial Committee*, p. 81.
67. *Hindu*, 13 July 1889.
68. *Madras Census Report*, XIII (1891):346.
69. *Hindu*, 19 February 1892.
70. J. Adam, "The Duties of Indian Citizens," *Madras Review*, I:1 (1895): 27-29.
71. V. S. Srinivasa Sastri, "The Schoolmaster's Test," *Educational Review* (February-March 1896):73-74 and 123.
72. *Educational Review* (December 1895):561-62.
73. *Hindu*, 23 September 1901.
74. K. Ingham, *Reformers*, pp. 96-111.
75. *Madras Male Asylum Herald*, 13 January 1836.
76. *Supplement to Madras Male Asylum Herald*, 15 April 1833.
77. *Madras Herald*, 20 October 1841.
78. K. P. Viswanatha Aiyar, "A History of Journalism in Madras," *The Madras Tercentenary Commemoration Volume* (Madras, 1939), pp. 451-57.
79. *MNNR* (February 1877).
80. *Hindu*, 22 September 1903.
81. *MPP*, Vol.3971, No.232, Vernacular Newspapers published in the Madras Presidency in 1890.
82. *Hindu*, 22 September 1903.
83. *Ibid.*, 21 September 1903.
84. Subba Rao, *Revived Memories*, pp. 83-84.
85. *Hindu*, 7 December 1897.
86. *Madras Census Report* (1881), 140.

Chapter 4

1. C. Karunakara Menon, *A Critical Essay on Sir A. Seshia Sastri* (Madras, 1903), p. 29.
2. *Madras Times*, 15 July 1878.
3. *Madras Mail*, 5 July and 9 August 1878.
4. *Athenaeum and Daily News*, 8 July 1878.
5. *Madras Mail*, 21 August 1878.
6. *Ibid.*, 5 August 1878.
7. *Ibid.*, 5 September 1878.
8. *Indian Mirror*, 25 March 1883.
9. G. Subramania Iyer, "Salary for Native Officials," *Madras Times*, 22 August 1878.
10. _____, "A Word for Brahmans" and "Corrupt Native Officials," *Madras Mail*, 29 August 1878.
11. *Review of the Madras Famine, 1876-1878* (Madras, 1881), p. 43.
12. M. Viraraghava Chari, "'The Hindu.' Its Origin and History," *The Hindu Golden Jubilee 1878-1928* (Madras, 1936), pp. 2-3.

13. *Madras Times*, 19 March 1877.
14. *Ibid.*, 23 March 1878.
15. Cited in *Madras Times*, 20 April 1877.
16. Viraraghava Chari, "'The Hindu.' Its Origin and History," p. 3.
17. G. M. Sundram Pillai, *Sri G. Subramania Iyer* (Tamil) (Madras, 1907), pp. 1-9; C. L. Parekh, *Eminent Indians on Indian Politics* (Bombay, 1892), pp. 429-30.
18. *G. Subramania Iyer. His Life and Career* (Madras, 1909), pp. 12-14.
19. Viraraghava Chari, "'The Hindu.' Its Origin and History," p. 4.
20. *G. Subramania Iyer. His Life and Career*, p. 30.
21. *India*, 6 March 1891.
22. Viraraghava Chari, "'The Hindu.' Its Origin and History," pp. 4-5.
23. Subba Rao, *Revived Memories*, pp. 82-83.
24. Viraraghava Chari, "'The Hindu.' Its Origin and History," pp. 7-11.
25. *Hindu*, 17 March 1881.
26. V. L. Sastri (ed.), *Encyclopaedia of the Madras Presidency and the Adjacent States* (Madras, 1921), p. 557.
27. Cited in *G. Subramania Iyer. His Life and Career*, p. 31.
28. Subba Rao, *Revived Memories*, pp. 157-58 and 169-70.
29. *Ibid.*, pp. 153-54.
30. *MPP*, Vol.2818, No.2753, C. D. Macleane to GOM, 2 December 1886.
31. Address of welcome to Grant Duff from Triplicane Literary Society, *Madras Times*, 8 November 1881.
32. *Hindu*, 10 November 1881.
33. *Madras Times*, 8 November 1881.
34. C. Benson, *A Statistical Atlas of the Madras Presidency* (Madras, 1895), p. 211.
35. C. S. Crole, *The Chingleput Manual* (Madras, 1878), p. 67.
36. *Madras Times*, 25 July 1881.
37. *Madras Mail*, 23 November 1881.
38. *Ibid.*
39. *Ibid.*, 8 December 1881.
40. *Ibid.*, 25 January 1882.
41. Cited in *Madras Mail*, 21 February 1882.
42. *Madras Mail*, 28 February 1882.
43. *Madras Standard*, 8 March 1882.
44. *Madras Mail*, 1 July 1882.
45. *JPP*, Vol.196, No.349, Minute by Under-Secretary of State for India, 26 February 1887.
46. For a fuller discussion of the origins of the riots, see my article "The Salem Riots, 1882. Judiciary versus Executive in the Mediation of a Communal Dispute," *Modern Asian Studies*, III:3 (1969):193-208.
47. *MJP*, Vol.1967, August 1882, No.1050-A, G.O. 21 August 1882.
48. *Madras Times*, 16 October 1882.
49. *RAMP* (1882-83), 19.
50. *JPP*, Vol.94, No.466, Macleane to Madras Government, 26 January 1883.
51. *MJP*, Vol.2161, January 1883, No.266, Macleane to Madras Government, 24 January 1883.
52. *Ibid.*, No.1423-A, Madras Government to Secretary of State, 30 May 1883.
53. *Hindu*, 25 January 1883.
54. *Ibid.*, 1 May 1883.
55. *Athenaeum and Daily News*, 29 February 1884.
56. *Madras Times*, 22 March 1884.
57. *Ibid.*, 6 May 1884.

58. *Madras Mail*, 16 July 1884.
59. D. Brandeis, *Suggestions regarding Forest Administration in the Madras Presidency* (Madras, 1883), pp. 1-2.
60. Blunt, *India Under Ripon*, p. 241.
61. *RAMP* (1880-81), 41-42.
62. See particularly the addresses presented by Bellary and Cuddalore, reproduced in full in *Madras Mail*, 2 February and 16 February 1884.
63. *MLP*, Vol.1777, No.95, September 1882, A Bill for the regulation and enforcement of Kudimaramat.
64. *Ibid.*, No.173, October 1883, Memorial of MNA to Madras Government, 29 September 1883.
65. *Ripon Papers*, Ripon to Grant Duff, 28 February 1884.
66. *Madras Mail*, 18 March 1884.
67. *Madras Times*, 23 January 1884.
68. *Madras Mail*, 3 January 1884.
69. *Hindu*, 19 July 1883.
70. Cited in *Madras Mail*, 19 March 1884.
71. *Ripon Papers*, Ripon to Hughes, 8 December 1882.
72. *Ibid.*, Ripon to Kimberley, 10 July 1883.
73. *Dufferin Collection*, Reel 501, Grant Duff to Dufferin, 3 January 1885.
74. *Ripon Papers*, Ripon to Foster, 9 May 1883.
75. *Proceedings of the MNA on the resolution of the GOI on local self-government* (Madras, 1883), Appendix A.
76. *Madras Times*, 7 December 1882.
77. *Hindu Reformer and Politician*, May 1882, p. 188.
78 *Proceedings of the MNA on the resolution of the GOI on local self-government*, pp. 1-26.
79. *Athenaeum and Daily News*, 24 August 1882.
80. *Ibid.*, 24 August 1882.
81. *Hindu*, 3 May 1883.
82. *Ibid.*, 19 January 1881.
83. *Ibid.*, 26 April 1883.
84. *Ibid.*
85. *Hindu Reformer and Politician*, June 1883, p. 678.
86. *Hindu*, 31 May 1883.
87. *Madras Standard*, 21 May 1883.
88. For the origins of this measure, see S. Gopal, *The Viceroyalty of Lord Ripon 1880-1884* (Oxford, 1953), Chapter IX.
89. *Hindu*, 5 April 1883.
90. C. Dobbin, "The Ilbert Bill: A Study of Anglo-Indian Opinion in India, 1883," *Historical Studies. Australia and New Zealand*, XII, No.45 (1965): 98-99.
91. *Hindu*, 19 July 1883.
92. *Ibid.*, 28 June 1883.
93. *Ibid.*, 5 October 1883.
94. *Ibid.*, 5 December 1883.
95. *Ibid.*, 28 January 1884.
96. *Ilbert Collection*, MSS. Eur. D.594, No.18, Telang to Ilbert, 24 December 1883.
97. *Ibid.*, No.16, Telang to Ilbert, 3 January 1884.
98. *Madras Times*, 7 January 1884.
99. *Madras Mail*, 22 January 1884.
100. *Madras Times*, 30 January 1884.
101. *Northbrook Collection*, MSS. Eur. C.144, No.6, Grant Duff to Northbrook, 10 March 1884.

102. Cited in *Voice of India,* 15 February 1884.
103. *Madras Times,* 31 January 1884.

Chapter 5

1. *Madras Times,* 25 July 1862.
2. *Madras Standard,* 9 February 1872 quoted in *Native Opinion,* 18 February 1872.
3. S. N. Banerjea, *A Nation in Making* (London, 1925), p. 50.
4. *Madras Times,* 23 March 1878.
5. *Ibid.,* 31 July 1877.
6. Cited in *Madras Times,* 20 April 1877.
7. *Madras Times,* 7 August 1878.
8. *Statesman,* cited in *Madras Times,* 5 October 1878.
9. C. P. Ramaswami Aiyar, *Biographical Vistas,* pp. 130-31.
10. *Hindu,* 23 March 1894.
11. *Madras Standard,* 20 May 1881.
12. *Madras Mail,* 13 December 1881.
13. *Ibid.,* 20 December 1881.
14. *Proceedings of the MNA on the resolution of GOI on local self-government,* pp. 1-26.
15. *Education Commission. Report by the Madras Provincial Committee,* pp. 290-93.
16. *Hindu,* 14 November 1883.
17. Blunt, *India Under Ripon,* p. 410.
18. *Athenaeum,* 12 August 1868.
19. *RPIMP* (1885-86), XII-XIV.
20. *Athenaeum and Daily News,* 4 November 1879.
21. *Madras Times,* 8 November 1881.
22. *Ibid.,* 7 December 1882.
23. J. Murdoch, *India's Needs: Material, Political, Social, Moral, and Religious* (Madras, 1886), p. 114.
24. *Hindu,* 19 May 1881.
25. *Madras Standard,* 21 May 1883.
26. *Hindu,* 14 November 1883.
27. *Ibid.,* 17 December 1883.
28. *Ibid.,* 14 November 1883.
29. *Ibid.,* 23 January 1884.
30. *Ibid.,* 26 April 1883.
31. *Ibid.,* 15 February 1884.
32. *Madras Mail,* 19 February 1884.
33. *Madras Standard,* 19 March 1884.
34. *Madras Mail,* 20 May 1884.
35. *Proceedings of the (First) Conference of Native Gentlemen, held at Pacheappa's Hall under the auspices of the Madras Mahajana Sabha in January 1885* (Madras, 1885), pp. 1-2.
36. M. Williams, *Modern India,* p. 155.
37. P. Somasundram Chetty, *Memoirs* (Madras, 1889), pp. 1-10.
38. *Hindu,* 9 May 1898; *Madras Mail,* 10 May 1898.
39. *Madras Times,* 1 September 1885.
40. *Ibid.,* 4 March 1886.
41. Raja Ram Rao, *Sir S. Subramania Aiyar. A Biographical Sketch* (Trichinopoly, 1914), pp. 11-17.

42. *Proceedings of the (First) Conference of Native Gentlemen*, p. 1.
43. *The Madras Mahajana Sabha. Annual Report for 1885-86* (Madras, 1886), pp. 64-84.
44. Of the 796 members, 602 were *mofussil* members. cf. *The Madras Mahajana Sabha. Annual Report for 1885-86*, pp. 64-84.
45. *Proceedings of the (First) Conference of Native Gentlemen*, p. 1.
46. *Hindu*, 20 August 1888.
47. For a list of the Corresponding Members, see *The Madras Mahajana Sabha. Annual Report for 1885-86*.
48. *Hindu*, 10 May 1893.
49. *Ibid.*, 14 December 1887.
50. *Ibid.*, 13 October 1885.
51. *Athenaeum and Daily News*, 22 December 1884.
52. *Ibid.*
53. *Proceedings of the (First) Conference of Native Gentlemen*, pp. I-III and VII.
54. *Ibid.*, pp. III-IV.
55. For text of this paper, see *Proceedings of the (First) Conference of Native Gentlemen*, pp. 1-19.
56. *Ibid.*, pp. VII-IX.
57. *Madras Times*, 3 January 1885.
58. *Voice of India*, 31 July 1884.
59. *Madras Standard*, 15 October 1884.
60. *Report of the PSC 1886-87*, p. 26.
61. *IHP (Public)*, Vol.2505, May 1885, No.29, Memorial of the Madras Mahajana Sabha to GOI, 3 February 1885.
62. *Ibid.*, No.30, GOI to GOM, 5 May 1885.
63. *The Madras Mahajana Sabha. Annual Report for 1885-86*, pp. 11-16.
64. *Hindu*, 15 October 1885.
65. *Ibid.*, 1 September 1885.
66. *Ibid.*, 15 October 1885.
67. *Proceedings of the Second Conference of Native Gentlemen held at Pacheappa's Hall under the auspices of the Madras Mahajana Sabha in December 1885* (Madras, 1886), pp. 6-8 and 90.
68. *Ibid.*, pp. 1-3.
69. *Hindu*, 7 January 1886.
70. *IHP (Public)*, Vol.2703, November 1886, No.79 Memorial of the Madras Mahajana Sabha to Secretary of State, 23 December 1885.
71. *Madras Standard*, 25 December 1885.
72. *Madras Mail*, 24 December 1885.
73. *Ibid.*, 26 December 1885.
74. *Proceedings of the Second Conference of Native Gentlemen*, pp. 25-27 and 90-101.
75. *Madras Mail*, 26 December 1885.

Chapter 6

1. *Athenaeum*, 11 April 1854.
2. N. S. Bose, *The Indian Awakening and Bengal* (Calcutta, 1960), p. 108.
3. P. S. Basu, *Life and Works of Brahmanda Keshar*, 2nd edition (Calcutta, 1940), pp. 119-22.
4. *Madras Times*, 5 and 6 September 1881.

5. *Madras Standard*, 9 January 1878.
6. For a fuller account of the agitation against these measures, see J. C. Bagal, *History of the Indian Association, 1876-1951* (Calcutta, 1953), pp. 17-41.
7. *Madras Mail*, 3 June 1879.
8. *Madras Times*, 5 May 1880.
9. *Hindu*, 19 May 1881.
10. *Ibid.*, 18 January 1883.
11. *Ibid.*, 12 July 1883.
12. *Ibid.*
13. *Ibid.*, 2 August 1883.
14. *Ibid.*
15. *Ibid.*, 21 November 1883.
16. *Ibid.*, 26 December 1883.
17. Seal, *The Emergence of Indian Nationalism* (Cambridge, 1968), p. 271.
18. Letter of A. O. Hume, *Hindu*, 19 April 1883.
19. Cited in *Indian Mirror*, 22 April 1883.
20. Shettjee Sahibjee, *Open Letters to Public Persons on Public Questions* (Calcutta, 1884), pp. 54-58.
21. *Ripon Papers*, Add. MSS.43616, Hume to Ripon, 30 December 1882.
22. *Hindu*, 19 April 1883.
23. *Ripon Papers*, Add. MSS.43616, Hume to Ripon, 7 May 1883.
24. *Indian Mirror*, 17 September 1884.
25. *Hindu*, 31 October 1884.
26. *Ibid.*, 19 November 1884.
27. M. Townsend, *Asia and Europe* (London, 1901), p. 108.
28. *Hindu*, 22 December 1884.
29. *Madras Standard*, 23 January 1885.
30. *Hindu*, 26 December 1884.
31. *Ibid.*, 16 March 1888.
32. P. Ananda Charlu, "The Indian National Congress: A Suggestive Retrospect," *Hindustan Review and Kayastha Samachar*, VII:1-2 (1903):1-7.
33. Letter to the *Hindu*, 9 June 1905.
34. *Dufferin Collection*, Reel 528, No.173, Dufferin to Reay, 17 May 1885.
35. *Hindu*, 12 November 1885.
36. *Ibid.*, 10 October 1885.
37. *Madras Standard*, 27 January 1886.
38. *Hindu*, 5 December 1885.
39. *The Madras Mahajana Sabha. Annual Report for 1885-86*, p. 6.
40. *RINC* (1885), 10-11.
41. *Indian Mirror*, 5 January 1886.
42. *Tribune*, 16 January 1886. (I am indebted to Dr. S. R. Mehrotra for this quotation.)
43. *Hindu*, 29 December 1885.
44. *Indian Daily News*, cited in *Indian Mirror*, 7 January 1886.
45. *RINC* (1886), 1.
46. *Supplement to Madras Times*, 1 December 1886.
47. *Hindu*, 21 December 1887.
48. *Ibid.*, 2 September 1887.
49. *Madras Mail*, 17 May 1881.
50 *Ibid.*, 1 August 1884.
51. *Athenaeum and Daily News*, 12 September 1883.
52. *Hindu*, 8 October 1885.
53. *Madras Standard*, 8 September 1886.

54. *Madras Times*, 25 August 1886.
55. *PPHC*, LII (1960) 219: Minute by Trevelyan, 4 June 1859, 49-50.
56. Hafiz Sudrool Islam, *Remarks on India* (Madras, 1874), pp. 14-15.
57. Lady Mary Hobart (ed.), *Essays*, pp. 272-279.
58. R. M. Macdonald, "Mahomedan Education in the Madras Presidency," *Journal of the National Indian Association* (1881):500-05.
59. *Education Commission. Report by the Madras Provincial Committee*, p. 59.
60. *MEP*, Vol.278, October 1872, No.25, Resolution of GOM, 7 October 1872.
61. Lady Mary Hobart (ed.), *Essays*, pp. 275-76.
62. *Proceedings of the PSC*, V, Sec.II, Evidence of Mohidin Sheriff, Ahmad Mohidin and Safdar Hussein, pp. 110-12 and 313-14.
63. *RPIMP* (1885-86), 6-7.
64. S. Pulney Andy, *A Collection of Papers connected with the Movement of the National Church of India* (Madras, 1893), pp. 17-18 and 29-36.
65. *Ibid.*, pp. 13-15 and 91-93.
66. S. Satthianandhan, *Missionary Work in India* (Madras, 1893), pp. 31-33.
67. Pulney Andy, *A Collection*, p. 40.
68. *Ibid.*, p. 11.
69. *Madras Standard*, 30 April 1888.
70. *Madras Times*, 29 March 1889.
71. Pulney Andy, *A Collection*, p. 11.
72. *Athenaeum and Daily News*, 27 December 1862.
73. *Ibid.*, 8 October 1879.
74. *Ripon Papers*, Add. MSS.43588, Memorial of D. S. White to Secretary of State, 7 June 1883.
75. *Athenaeum and Daily News*, 8 October 1882.
76. *Madras Standard*, 5 September 1883.
77. *Athenaeum and Daily News*, 11 October 1883.
78. *Hindu*, 2 March 1887.
79. *Ibid.*, 21 December 1887.
80. *RINC* (1887), 10.
81. Cited in *Hindu*, 26 January 1887.
82. *RINC* (1887), Appendix I.
83. *Christian College Magazine* (1884), 383.
84. *Hindu*, 29 August 1887.
85. *Proceedings of the PSC*, V, Sec.2, Evidence of Ahmad Mohidin, pp. 112-15.
86. *Muslim Herald*, cited in *Voice of India* (1887), 16-17.
87. *Ibid.* (1887), 552-53.
88. *Ibid.* (1888), 60.
89. *RINC* (1887), Appendix I.
90. Cited in *Indian Mirror*, 28 October 1887.
91. Cited in *Hindu*, 29 April 1887.
92. *Masani Collection*, Hume to Naoroji, 12 December 1887.
93. *Madras Mail*, 9 December 1887.
94. *Tyabji Papers*, Congress circular no.6, Appendix A, Hume's letter, n.d.
95. *Hindu*, 21 December 1887.
96. *Indian Mirror*, 18 October 1887.
97. For biographical details see *Eardley Norton's Speeches and Writings*, No. I (1935), pp. 1-42.
98. *Hindu*, 30 April 1884.
99. *Madras Standard*, 17 April 1885.
100. Lecture by Norton to Chintadripettah Literary Society, *Hindu*, 29 September 1885.
101. *Indian Mirror*, 14 January 1888.

102. *MNNR*, Fortnight-ending 31 January 1888 and 15 February 1888, pp. 2 and 38.
103. Cited in *Voice of India* (1888), 176.
104. *Madras Standard*, 27 January 1888.
105. *Ibid.*, 2 April 1888.
106. *Madras Times*, 4 and 9 May 1888.
107. *Hindu*, 1 and 13 June 1888.
108. *Ibid.*, 4 July 1889.
109. *Madras Standard*, 18 May 1888.
110. *Indian Mirror*, 21 January 1888.
111. A. O. Hume, *A Speech on the Indian National Congress* (London, n.d.), p. 8.
112. *Hindu*, 25 December 1889.
113. Hume, *A Speech*, p. 9.
114. *Madras Times*, 27 December 1888.
115. *Madras Mail*, 4 March 1889.
116. *Ibid.*, 24 October 1889.
117. *Ibid.*, 15 December 1890.
118. *Ibid.*, 8 October 1891.
119. Cited in *Madras Times*, 21 September 1891.
120. *Hindu*, 18 June 1891.
121. *Ibid.*, 16 December 1893.
122. *IHP (Public)*, Vol.4108, October 1892, No.157, GOM to GOI, 3 September 1892.
123. Letter of "A Muslim" to *Hindu*, 29 June 1893.
124. *Madras Times*, 11 August 1893.
125. *Ibid.*, 2 August 1893.
126. *MNNR*, Fortnight-ending 15 July 1893, p. 165.
127. *Madras Times*, 10 August 1893.
128. *Ibid.*, 27 August 1893.
129. *Ibid.*, 26 February 1894.
130. *Ibid.*, 9 March 1894.
131. *Hindu*, 25 August 1894.
132. *Ibid.*, 31 October 1894.
133. *RINC* (1894), 14.

Chapter 7

1. *RINC* (1886), 54.
2. Cited in Heimsath, *Indian Nationalism*, p. 190.
3. *Madras Census*, I (1871), 107.
4. "Moral Education for Hindus" by "A Brahmin," *Madras Times*, 22 November 1878.
5. *Athenaeum and Daily News*, 22 August 1876.
6. H. S. Olcott, *Theosophy. Religion and Occult Science* (London, 1885), p. 40.
7. *Ibid.*, pp. 60-62.
8. *Ibid.*, p. 56.
9. *Supplement to Theosophist*, July 1883.
10. Olcott, *Theosophy*, pp. 190-92.
11. This is an abridgement of a lecture which Olcott delivered at Amritsar in October 1880 entitled "India: Past, Present, and Future." For the full text, see Olcott, *Theosophy*, pp. 257-83.
12. Secretary, Tinnevelly Branch of Theosophical Society, to editor, *Madras Mail*, cited in *Supplement to Theosophist* (December 1881), p. 47.

13. *Madras Times*, 17 November 1881.
14. Olcott, *Theosophy*, pp. 284-300.
15. *Ibid.*, pp. 110-13.
16. *Supplement to Theosophist*, June 1882, p. 3.
17. H. S. Olcott, *Old Diary Leaves*, Second Series, 1878-1883 (London, 1900), pp. 392-93.
18. *Theosophist* (1882), 263.
19. Olcott, *Old Diary Leaves*, Second Series, p. 391.
20. *Supplement to Theosophist*, September 1883, pp. 1-3.
21. Olcott, *Old Diary Leaves*, Second Series, pp. 454-55 and 461.
22. *Supplement to Theosophist*, January 1886, p. xxxiv.
23. "Native Thinker," *Madras Times*, 3 January 1884.
24. *Christian College Magazine* (February 1884):506.
25. Cited in *Supplement to Theosophist*, October 1883, pp. 11-12.
26. *Ibid.*, January 1886.
27. *Ibid.*, February 1883, p. 1.
28. *Ibid.*, August 1883, pp. 3-4.
29. *Ibid.*, January 1886, pp. xxxvii-xxxviii.
30. H. S. Olcott, *Old Diary Leaves*, Third Series, 1883-1887 (London, 1904), pp. 387-95.
31. *Hindu Reformer and Politician* (1882), 121-22.
32. *Ibid.*, pp. 1-2.
33. *Ibid.*, p. 294.
34. *Madras Times*, 30 December 1890.
35. *Hindu Excelsior Magazine* (1885):194-97.
36. Olcott, *Old Diary Leaves*, Third Series, p. 380.
37. R. Sivasankara Pandiya, *The Duties of the Natives of India to their Rulers and their Country* (Madras, 1888), pp. 16-17.
38. *Madras Times*, 18 March 1890.
39. *Christian College Magazine* (1888):872-75; *Hindu*, 18 May 1889.
40. *Hindu*, 7 May 1888.
41. *Ibid.*, 18 May 1889.
42. *Supplement to Theosophist*, February 1885, p. 2.
43. *Christian College Magazine*, September, 1884.
44. *Supplement to Theosophist*, March 1885, p. 1.
45. Pandiah to editor, *Hindu*, 7 May 1888.
46. S. Pandiya, *The Duties of the Natives*, pp. 15-16.
47. *Indian Mirror*, 19 May 1888.
48. *Hindu*, 16 May 1888.
49. *Indian Mirror*, 9 September 1888.
50. *Hindu*, 7 May 1888.
51. For a brief description of this firm, see S. Playne (Compiler), *South India. Its History, People, Commerce, and Industrial Resources* (London, 1914-1915), p. 708.
52. *Indian Mirror*, 19 September 1888.
53. *Madras Times*, 17 January 1889.
54. *Ibid.*, 28 July 1890.
55. *Ibid.*, 13 October 1891.
56. K. Gulliford, "Religious Toleration," *Christian College Magazine* (1889): 483-85.
57. *Christian College Magazine* (1889):219-20.
58. *Madras Times*, 31 December 1888.
59. *Madras Standard*, 16 April 1886.
60. *Hindu*, 21 May 1888.

61. *GOI. Home Department. Selections from the Records*, No.ccxxiii, Papers relating to Infant Marriage and Enforced Widowhood in India, pp. 3-4.
62. *Ibid.*, pp. 5-7.
63. *Madras Times*, 11 March 1885.
64. *MPP*, Vol.2595, September 1885, S. Subramania Iyer to GOM, 5 January 1885; Chentsal Rao to GOM, 15 January 1885.
65. *GOI. Home Department. Selections from the Records*, No.ccxxiii, Resolution of GOI, 8 October 1886, p. 2.
66. Heimsath, *Indian Nationalism*, p. 161.
67. *Indian Spectator*, 25 July 1886.
68. *Hindu*, 9 December 1889.
69. *Ibid.*, 20 January 1890.
70. Raghunatha Rao to editor, *Madras Times*, 10 January 1890.
71. *Ibid.*, 27 September 1890.
72. R. Raghunatha Rao, *The Hindu Shastrick Aspect of the Question of the Age of Consent* (Madras, 1891), pp. 1-6.
73. *Hindu*, 26 June 1889.
74. *Madras Times*, 1 February 1890.
75. Letter from "A Brahmin," *Hindu*, 21 October 1890.
76. *Ibid.*, 7 March 1890.
77. *Ibid.*, 25 October 1890.
78. *Madras Times*, 28 April 1890.
79. W. S. Caine in *Manchester Examiner*, cited in *Hindu*, 6 February 1891.
80. K. Subba Rao, *Revived Memories*, pp. 217-19.
81. *Hindu*, 24 February 1890.
82. *Ibid.*, 25 October 1890.
83. *Madras Times*, 30 September 1890.
84. Raghunatha Rao to the editor, *Hindu*, 11 October 1890.
85. *Madras Times*, 15 and 16 October 1890.
86. *Ibid.*, 18 November 1890.
87. *Ibid.*, 19 November 1890.
88. *Ibid.*, 26 November 1890.
89. *Ibid.*, 27 November 1890.
90. *Hindu*, 8 December 1890.
91. *Madras Times*, 8 December 1890.
92. *Ibid.*
93. *Ibid.*, 19 December 1890.
94. *Hindu*, 24 November 1890.
95. *Ibid.*, 5 March 1891.
96. *Ibid.*, 29 December 1890.
97. *Ibid.*, 27 January 1891.
98. *Ibid.*, 6 March 1891.
99. *Ibid.*, 7 January 1891.
100. *Ibid.*, 21 January 1891.
101. *Ibid.*, 19 January 1891.
102. *Ibid.*, 24 January 1891.
103. *Lansdowne Papers*, Hume to Lansdowne, 12 and 14 February 1891.
104. *Christian College Magazine* (1891):540.
105. *Hindu*, 28 February 1891.
106. *Ibid.*, 21 May 1891.
107. *Ibid.*, 26 March 1891.
108. *Ibid.*, 1 March 1892.
109. *Ibid.*, 30 August 1892.
110. *Ibid.*, 20 December 1892.

111. *Ibid.*, 27 November 1893.
112. C. Y. Chintamani (ed.), *Indian Social Reform*, Part III (Madras, 1901), pp. 169–75.
113. *Hindu*, 17 December 1892.
114. *Madras Mail*, 30 May 1901.
115. K. Subba Rao, *Revived Memories*, p. 241.
116. *Hindu*, 4 June 1896.
117. Cited in *Madras Times*, 4 May 1894.
118. Speech of T. Sadasiva Iyer, *Hindu*, 4 June 1896.
119. S. Sathianadhan, *Theosophy* (Madras, 1893), pp. 8–15.
120. K. Srinivasa Rao, *Papers on Social Reform* (Madras, 1906), p. 70.
121. N. Subbarau Pantalu (ed.), *Hindu Social Progress* (Madras, 1904), Appendix B.
122. *Madras Times*, 31 December 1894.
123. K. Sundararaman, *Four Political Essays* (Madras, 1903), pp. 146–85.
124. *Hindu*, 1 December 1891.
125. *Ibid.*, 25 November 1893.
126. Report of the Madras Standing Congress Committee, 1890–91, *Hindu*, 4 July 1891.
127. *Madras Times*, 4 December 1893.
128. *RNIC* (1890):66.
129. *Madras Times*, 4 December 1893.
130. *Ibid.*

Conclusion

1. See for example J. S. Coleman, *Nigeria. Background to Nationalism* (Berkeley, 1963), pp. 169–70.
2. McCully, *English Education*, pp. 391–96.
3. Seal, *Emergence of Indian Nationalism*, pp. 22–24, 110–13, and 341–42.
4. T. Hodgkin, *Nationalism in Colonial Africa* (New York, seventh impression, 1965), p. 63.
5. *MNNR*, Fortnight-ending 15 October 1894, p. 367.
6. For a discussion of this subject see E. F. Irschick, *Politics and Social Conflict in South India* (Bombay, 1969).

Bibliography

Proceedings of Political Organizations and Public Meetings

Madras Native Association
Petition to the Imperial Parliament from the members of the MNA, 10 December 1852 (Madras, 1852).
Supplementary petition to the Imperial Parliament from the members of the MNA, 21 May 1853 (Madras, 1853).
Fourth petition to the Imperial Parliament from the members of the MNA, 7 April 1855 (Madras, 1855).
Fifth petition to the Imperial Parliament from the members of the MNA, 26 January 1856 (Madras, 1856).
Sixth petition to the Imperial Parliament from the members of the MNA, 26 January 1857 (Madras, 1857).
Memorial to the Right Honorable Lord Stanley, Secretary of State for India: from the members of the MNA and others (Madras, 1859).
Letter to the Right Honorable Sir Charles Wood, K.C.B. Principal Secretary of State for India, from the Committee of the MNA, 10 September 1859 (Madras, 1859).
Report of the Proceedings at the presentation of an address to John Bruce Norton, Esq. Agent to the Ranees of Tanjore, by the MNA (Madras, 1860).
Proceedings of the MNA on the resolution of the Government of India on Local Self-Government (Madras, 1883).

Madras Mahajana Sabha
Proceedings of the [First] Conference of Native Gentlemen, held at Pacheappa's Hall under the auspices of the Madras Mahajana Sabha in January 1885 (Madras, 1885).
Proceedings of the Second Conference of Native Gentlemen held at Pacheappa's Hall under the auspices of the Madras Mahajana Sabha in December 1885 (Madras, 1886).
The Madras Mahajana Sabha. Annual Report for 1885-86 (Madras, 1886).

Miscellaneous
Proceedings of the public meeting of the Hindu community, 7 October 1846 (Madras, 1846).
The memorial of Hindu inhabitants of Madras Presidency to the Court of Directors, 12 May 1847 (Madras, n.d.).

Proceedings of the Madras Branch of the British Indian Association, and of the Deccan Association (London, 1852).

Minutes of proceedings of the second Annual General Meeting of the Bombay Association (Bombay, 1855).

The third Annual Report of the Madras Hindu Reading Room, for 1855 (Madras, 1856).

The sixth Annual Report of the Madras Hindoo Debating Society, from 1856-58 (Madras, 1859).

Proceedings of the Native inhabitants of Madras, 7 May 1860 (Madras, 1860).

Removal of the seat of government of Madras, from Madras to Ootacamund . . . Report of the public meeting at Madras, 3rd July 1884 (Madras, 1884).

Report of the Indian National Congress, 1885-1900 (Annual).

Report of the fourth National Social Conference held in Calcutta on 28 December 1890 (Poona, 1891).

Letter Book of the Madras Congress Reception Committee, September 1894-June 1895.

Proceedings of the Madras Congress Reception Committee, Executive Committee and General Purposes Committee, July 1894-February 1896.

Newspapers and Periodicals

Newspapers
Athenaeum and Daily News (Madras) 1845-85.
Bengalee (Calcutta) 1884-94.
Hindu (Madras) 1881, 1883-85 and 1887-1902.
Indian Mirror (Calcutta) 1861-63 and 1883-89.
Indian Social Reformer (Madras) 1894-98.
Madras Mail (Madras) 1878-1901.
Madras Male Asylum Herald (Madras) 1833-36.
Madras Standard (Madras) 1880-88.
Madras Times (Madras) 1859-95.
Spectator (Madras) 1844-58.
Voice of India (Bombay) 1883-89.

Periodicals
Asylum Press Almanac & Compendium of Intelligence, 1868-90.
Christian College Magazine (Madras) 1883-88 and 1895-1900.
East and West (Bombay) 1901-06.
Educational Review (Madras) 1895-99.
Hindu Excelsior Series (Madras) 1885-86.
Hindu Reformer and Politician (Madras) 1882-83.
Hindustan Review and Kayastha Samachar (Allahabad) 1900-10.
Indian Law Reports, Madras Series (Madras) 1878-83.
Indian Review (Madras) 1900-10.
Journal of the East India Association (London) 1884-94.
Journal of the National Indian Association (after 1887 renamed *Indian Magazine)* (London) 1870-94.
Madras Almanac and Compendium of Intelligence (Madras) 1812, 1824, 1827, 1833, 1836, 1838, 1846-47, 1851-52 and 1859.
Madras Christian Instructor and Missionary Record (Madras) 1843-50.
Madras Journal of Literature and Science (Madras) 1880-90.
Madras Missionary Record (Madras) 1847-52.

Madras Native Herald (Madras) 1841–45.
Madras New Almanac, and General Directory (Madras) 1841, 1844, 1851–54
and 1864.
Madras Review (Madras) 1895–1905.
Missionary Register (London) 1825–33.
Quarterly Journal of the Poona Sarvajanik Sabha (Poona) 1878–90.
Theosophist (Madras) 1883–91.
University of Madras. Annual Calendar (Madras) 1859–95.
University of Madras. Annual Report (Madras) 1841–54.

Unpublished Official and Private Papers

Official
Madras Educational Proceedings, 1870–90.
Madras Judicial Proceedings, 1880–95.
Madras Legislative Proceedings, 1876–95.
Madras Public Proceedings, 1850–59 and 1890–95.
Madras Revenue Proceedings, 1850–65 and 1880–95.
India Home Proceedings (Public) 1884–95.
India Office Judicial and Public Papers, 1880–95.

Private
Cross Collection, India Office Library MSS Eur.E.243.
Denison Papers, India Office Library microfilm.
Dufferin Collection, India Office Library microfilm.
Elgin Collection, India Office Library MSS Eur.F.84.
Elphinstone Papers, India Office Library MSS Eur.F.87.
Ilbert Collection, India Office Library MSS Eur.D.594.
Lansdowne Papers, British Museum I.S.420.
Northbrook Collection, India Office Library MSS Eur.C.144.
Ripon Papers, British Museum Add. MSS and I.S.290.
Tyabji Papers, National Archives of India.
Tweeddale Collection, India Office Library MSS Eur.F.96.
Wood Collection, India Office Library MSS Eur.F.78.

Published Official Papers

Parliamentary Papers
PPHC, VII, 1812 (377), Fifth report of the Select Committee on the affairs
of the East India Company.
PPHC, IX, 1831–32 (735–1), Minutes of evidence taken before the Select
Committee on the affairs of the East India Company.
PPHC, XLIII, 1837 (357), Memorial of the European population of Madras to
the governor of the Presidency.
PPHC, XXXIV, 1845 (216), Copy of the orders of the Government of India for
the establishment of the Council of Education at Bengal and at the other
Presidencies.
PPHC, XL, 1849 (621), Idolatry: copies of communications in relation to
the connection of the Government of British India with idolatry or
Mahomedanism.
PPHL, III, 1852–53 (20), Second report from the Select Committee of the
House of Lords, appointed to inquire into the operation of the Act 3

and 4, Will.4, c.85, for the better government of Her Majesty's Indian
Territories.
PPHC, XXVII, 1852-53 (426), East India: first report from the Select Com-
mittee on Indian Territories, together with minutes of evidence.
PPHC, XXIX, 1852-53 (897), East India: sixth report from the Select Com-
mittee on Indian Territories.
PPHC, XLII, 1857-58 (71), East India: missionaries; idolatry.
PPHC, XLIII, 1857-58 (79), Correspondence respecting the resignation, by
Sir Peregrine Maitland, of the office of Commander-in-Chief of Madras.
PPHC, XXV, 1859 (158), Recent disturbances in Tinnevelly.
PPHC, LII, 1860 (219), Nawab of Carnatic.
PPHC, LII, 1860 (503), Copy of minutes of Sir Charles Trevelyan after
visiting the different forts of the Presidency of Madras.
PPHC, XLII, 1861 (284), Report of the Commission to investigate into the
Vellore Mutiny.
PPHC, XLIII, 1863 (394), Act passed by Governor-General in Council to en-
able the government to divest itself of the management of religious
endowments.
PPHC, LIV, 1890 (c.5950), Copies of, or extracts from, correspondence re-
lating to the numbers and functions of the several Councils in India.

Reports
Administration report of the Madras Municipality, 1878-1886 (Annual).
Appendices to the report of the Public Service Commission 1886-87 (Cal-
cutta, 1888).
Croft, A., *Review of education in India in 1886* (Calcutta, 1888).
Education Commission. Report by the Madras Provincial Committee (Calcutta,
1884).
*Imperial Census of 1881. Operations and results in the Presidency of
Madras*, 1 (Madras, 1883).
Papers relating to technical education in India, 1886-1904 (Calcutta,
1906).
Proceedings of the Public Service Commission, V (Calcutta, 1887).
Raghavaiyangar, S. Srinivasa, *Memorandum on the progress of the Madras
Presidency during the last forty years of British Administration*
(Madras, 1892).
Report on the administration of the Madras Presidency, 1880/1-1895/6
(Annual).
Report on the census of the Madras Presidency 1871, I (Madras, 1874).
Report on the census of India 1891, XIII: *Madras* (Madras, 1893).
*Report of the commissioners for the investigation of alleged cases of
torture in the Madras Presidency* (Madras, 1855).
Report of the committee on local self-government in Madras, 1882 (Madras,
1883).
Report of the Finance Committee, 1886, 1 (Calcutta, 1887).
Report of the Indian Education Commission (Calcutta, 1883).
Report of the Public Service Commission 1886-87 (Calcutta, 1888).
Report on native newspapers in the Madras Presidency, 1876-1900 (Fort-
nightly).
Report on public instruction in the Madras Presidency, 1854/5-1895/6
(Annual).
Review of the Madras Famine 1876-1878 (Madras, 1878).
Ricketts, H., *Report of the commissioners for the revision of civil sala-
ries and establishments throughout India*, I (Calcutta, 1858).

Statement exhibiting the moral and material progress and condition of India during the years 1891-92 (London, n.d.).

Selections from the records of the Government of India
No.LIV, "Note on the state of education in India during 1865-66," by A. M. Monteath (Calcutta, 1867).
No.CCV, "Correspondence on the subject of the education of the Muhammadan community in British India and their employment in the public service generally" (Calcutta, 1886).
No.CCXXIII, "Papers relating to infant marriage and enforced widowhood in India" (Calcutta, 1886).

Selected Books and Articles

Contemporary
Aiyar, Duraiswami. *Memories of Sir T. Muthusamy Ayyar*. Tanjore, n.d.
Aiyar, Kamesvara. *Sir Sashiah Sastri, K.C.S.I., An Indian Statesman*. Madras, 1902.
Baden-Powell, B. H. *The Land-Systems of British India*. III, Oxford, 1892.
Banerjea, S. N. *A Nation in Making*. London, 1925.
Besant, A. *The means of India's regeneration*. Benares, 1895.
_____. *The place of politics in the life of a nation*. Madras, 1895.
Blunt, W. S. *India under Ripon. A private diary*. London, 1909.
Boag, G. T. *The Madras Presidency 1881-1931*. Madras, 1933.
Bourdillon, J. D. *Remarks on the ryotwari system of land revenue as it exists in the Presidency of Madras*. Madras, 1853.
Buckland, C. E. *Dictionary of Indian Biography*. London, 1906.
Caldwell, R. *The Tinnevelly Shanars*. London, 1850.
Carpenter, J. E. *The life and work of Mary Carpenter*. London, 1881.
Chari, M. Viraraghava. "'The Hindu.' Its origin and history." *The Hindu Golden Jubilee 1878-1928*. Madras, 1936.
Charier, S. C. Srinivasa, ed. *Political opinions of Raja Sir T. Madava Row*. Madras, 1890.
_____. *Opinions on social matters of Raja Sir T. Madava Row*. Madras, 1890.
Charlu, P. Ananda. *The sixfold need of Indian politics*. Madras, 1895.
_____. *The Madras bar and how to improve it*. Madras, 1883.
_____. *Letters on Indian politics*. Madras, 1889.
_____. "The Indian National Congress: A suggestive retrospect." *Hindustan Review and Kayastha Samachar*. VII, 1903.
Chetty, P. Somasundram. *Memoirs*. Madras, 1889.
Chintamani, C. Y., ed. *Indian Social Reform*. Madras, 1901.
Collet, S. D., ed. *The Brahmo Samaj. Lectures and tracts. By Keshub Chunder Sen*. London, 1870.
Cotton, H. *India & Home memories*. London, 1911.
Crole, C. S. *The Chingleput Manual*. Madras, 1878.
Digby, W. *India for Indians*. London, 1885.
Gurunadhan, J. *Viresalingam. The founder of Telugu public life*. Rajahmundry, 1911.
Hamilton, W. *A geographical, statistical, and historical description of Hindostan, and the adjacent countries*. London, 1820.
Heyne, Benjamin. *Tracts, historical and statistical, on India*. London,

1814.

Hobart, Mary, ed. *Essays and miscellaneous writings by Vere Henry, Lord Hobart.* II, London, 1885.

Holloway, W. *Notes on Madras judicial administration.* Madras, 1853.

Hume, A. O. *The Old Man's Hope.* Calcutta, 1886.

_____. *A Speech on the Indian National Congress.* London, n.d.

_____ and A. Colvin. *Audi Alteram Partem.* London, n.d.

"Indicus." *A black quinquennium.* London, 1887.

Kaye, J. W. *Christianity in India.* London, 1859.

Kerr, J. *The domestic life, character and customs of the natives of India.* London, 1865.

Lewin, M. *Torture in Madras.* London, 1857.

_____. *The way to lose India.* London, 1857.

Logan, W. *Malabar.* I, Madras, 1887.

Menon, C. Karunakara. *A critical essay on Sir Seshia Sastri, K.C.S.I.* Madras, 1903.

Murdoch, J. *India's needs: material, political, social, moral, and religious.* Madras, 1886.

Nagamiah, V. *Raja Sir T. Madhava Row.* Madras, 1915.

Narasiah, D. *Letters on Hindu marriages.* Madras, 1867.

Norton, Eardley. *The National Congress vindicated.* Lucknow, 1889.

_____. *Two memorable speeches of Eardley Norton.* Lucknow, 1889.

_____. *Speeches and writings.* Nos. 1-2, Madras, 1935.

Norton, George. *Rudimentals.* Madras, 1841.

_____. *Native education in India.* Madras, 1848.

_____. *Proselytism in India.* London, 1859.

Norton, John Bruce. *The administration of justice in Southern India.* Madras, 1853.

_____. *A letter to Robert Lowe.* Madras, 1854.

_____. *The educational speeches of the Hon'ble John Bruce Norton, B.A.* Madras, 1866.

Olcott, H. S. *Theosophy, Religion and occult science.* London, 1885.

_____. *Old diary leaves.* 2nd and 3rd series, London, 1900-04.

Pandiah, S. *The duties of the natives of India to their rulers and their country.* Madras, 1888.

Pantalu, Subbrau, ed. *Hindu social reform.* Madras, 1904.

Parekh, C. L. *Eminent Indians on Indian politics.* Bombay, 1892.

Pharoah. *Gazetteer of Southern India.* Madras, 1855.

Pillai, Paramaswaran. *Representative men of Southern India.* Madras, 1896.

_____. *Representative Indians.* London, 1897.

Pillai, Sundram. *Sri G. Subramania Iyer.* (Tamil), Madras, 1907.

Pope, G. U. *Mission of Sawyerpooram.* Part V, London, 1849.

Ramaswami, C. V. *A digest of different castes of India.* Madras, 1837.

Rao, C. Hayavadana. *The Indian biographical dictionary, 1915.* Madras, n.d.

Rao, T. Madava. *Three addresses.* Madras, 1884.

Rao, N. S. Prasada. *East coast worthies.* Madras, 1901.

Rao, R. Raghunatha. *Hindu law on marriage.* Madras, 1882.

_____. *A review of the progress of knowledge of Hindu law and custom.* Madras, 1885.

_____. *The Hindu shastrick aspect of the question of the age of consent.* Madras, 1891.

Rao, Raja Ram. *Sir Subramania Aiyer. A biographical sketch.*

Trichinopoly, 1914.
Rao, K. Srinivasa. *Papers on social reform.* Madras, 1906.
Rao, K. Subba. *Revived memories.* Madras, 1933.
Rao, T. Venkasami. *A manual of the district of Tanjore.* Madras, 1883.
Sastri, V. L., ed. *Encyclopaedia of the Madras Presidency and the adjacent states.* Madras, 1921.
Satthianadhan, S. *History of education in the Madras Presidency.* Madras, 1894.
_____. *Sketches of Indian Christians.* Madras, 1896.
Sen, Keshub Chandra. *Diary in Madras and Bombay.* Calcutta, 1887.
Stuart, A. J. *A manual of the Tinnevelly district.* Madras, 1879.
Sundararaman, K. *The Hindu ideal and practice of duty.* Madras, 1892.
_____. *Four political essays.* Madras, 1903.
Thurston, E. *Castes and tribes of Southern India.* I-VII, Madras, 1909.
Vadivelu, A. *The aristocracy of Southern India.* II, Madras, 1908.
Vivekananda, Swami. *Swami Vivekananda's Madras Lectures.* Madras, 1897.
Wathen, J. *Journal of a voyage in 1811 and 1812, to Madras and China.* London, 1814.
Wedderburn, W. *Allan Octavian Hume, C.B.* London, 1913.
Wheeler, J. T. *Madras in the olden time.* I-III, Madras, 1861-62.
Williams, M. *Modern India and the Indians.* 2nd ed., London, 1878.
Wyatt, J. L. *Reminiscences of Bishop Caldwell.* Madras, 1894.

Modern
Aiyar, C. P. Ramaswami. *Biographical vistas. Sketches of some eminent Indians.* London, 1968.
Aiyar, K. P. Viswanatha. "A history of journalism in Madras." *The Madras Tercentenary Commemoration Volume.* Madras, 1939.
Arokiaswami, M. *The Kongu country.* Madras, 1956.
Bagal, J. C. *History of the Indian Association, 1876-1951.* Calcutta, 1953.
Barns, M. *The Indian press. A history of the growth of public opinion in India.* London, 1940.
Basham, A. L. *The Wonder that was India.* London, 1954.
Beaglehole, T. H. *Thomas Munro and the development of administrative policy in Madras 1792-1818.* Cambridge, 1966.
Beteille, A. *Caste, class, and power.* Berkeley, 1965.
Bose, N. S. *The Indian awakening and Bengal.* Calcutta, 1960.
Broomfield, J. H. "The regional elites: A theory of modern Indian history." *Indian Economic and Social History Review.* III:3, 1966.
Brown, H. *Parry's of Madras.* Madras, 1954.
Chandrasekhar, S. "Growth of population in Madras City 1639-1961." *Population Review.* VIII:1, 1964.
Chandrasekharan, K. *V. Krishnaswami Aiyar.* (Tamil), Madras, 1944.
_____. *V. Krishnaswami Aiyar.* Masulipatam, 1963.
Cosmopolitan Club, Madras. Platinum Souvenir 1873-1954. Madras, n.d.
Diehl, C. G. *Instrument and purpose: studies on rites and rituals in South India.* Gleerup, 1956.
Dobbin, C. "The Ilbert Bill: A study of Anglo-Indian opinion in India, 1883." *Historical Studies. Australia and New Zealand.* XII:45, 1965.
Dodwell, H. *The nabobs of Madras.* London, 1926.
Farquhar, J. N. *Modern religious movements in India.* London, 1929.
Frykenberg, R. E. "Traditional processes of power in South India: An historical analysis of local influence." *Indian Economic and Social*

History Review. I:2, 1963.

Frykenberg, R. E. "Elite groups in a South Indian district: 1788-1858." *Journal of Asian Studies.* XXIV:2, 1965.

_____. *Guntur district 1788-1848.* Oxford, 1965.

_____. "Elite formation in nineteenth century South India: An interpretive analysis," in *Proceedings of the first international conference seminar of Tamil studies.* I, Kuala Lumpur, 1965.

Ghosh, P. C. *The development of the Indian National Congress 1892-1909.* Calcutta, 1960.

Ghosh, S. "The British Indian Association (1851-1900)." *Bengal Past and Present.* LXXVII:2, 1958.

Gopal, S. *The viceroyalty of Lord Ripon, 1880-1884.* Oxford, 1953.

Gopalaratnam, V. C. *A century completed. (A history of the Madras High Court) 1862-1962.* Madras, n.d.

Gough, E. Kathleen. "Changing kinship usages in the setting of political and economic change among the Nayars of Malabar." *Journal of the Royal Anthropological Institute.* LXXXII:L, 1952.

_____. "Caste in a Tanjore village," in *Aspects of Caste in South India, Ceylon and North-West Pakistan.* Ed. E. Leach. Cambridge, 1960.

Grover, B. L. *A documentary study of British policy towards Indian nationalism 1885-1909.* Delhi, 1967.

Hardgrave Jr., R. L. *The Dravidian movement.* Bombay, 1965.

_____. "The breast-cloth controversy: Caste consciousness and social change in Southern Travancore." *Indian Economic and Social History Review.* V:2, 1968.

_____. *The Nadars of Tamilnad.* Bombay, 1969.

Harrison, S. S. *India. The most dangerous decades.* Princeton, 1960.

Heimsath, C. H. *Indian nationalism and Hindu social reform.* Princeton, 1964.

Hodgson, G. H. *Thomas Parry, Free merchant Madras 1768-1824.* Madras, 1938.

Ingham, K. *Reformers in India 1793-1833.* Cambridge, 1956.

Irschick, E. F. *Politics and Social Conflict in South India.* Bombay, 1969.

Kumar, D. *Land and caste in South India.* Cambridge, 1965.

Leonard, J. G. "Politics and social change in South India: A study of the Andhra movement." *Journal of Commonwealth Political Studies.* V:1, 1967.

Love, H. D. *Vestiges of old Madras, 1640-1800.* I-III, London, 1913.

Madras Mahajana Sabha. Diamond Jubilee Souvenir. Madras, 1946.

Mahalingam, T. V. *Administration and social life under Vijayanagar.* Madras, 1940.

_____. *South Indian polity.* Madras, 1965.

Majumdar, B. B. *Indian political associations and reform of legislature (1818-1917).* Calcutta, 1965.

Markandan, K. C. *Madras legislative council. Its constitution and working between 1861 and 1909.* Delhi, 1964.

Mason, P., ed. *India and Ceylon: Unity and diversity.* London, 1967.

Mayer, A. C. *Land and society in Malabar.* Bombay, 1952.

McCully, B. T. *English education and the origins of Indian nationalism.* New York, 1940.

Mencher, J. P. "Kerala and Madras: A comparative study of ecology and social structure." *Ethnology.* V:2, 1966.

_____. "Namboodiri Brahmins: An analysis of a traditional elite in

Kerala." *Journal of Asian and African Studies.* I, 1966.
Menon, K. P. S. *C. Sankaran Nair.* Delhi, 1967.
Miller, E. J. "Caste and territory in Malabar." *American Anthropologist.* LVI:3, 1954.
Misra, B. B. *The Indian Middle Classes.* London, 1961.
Mody, H. P. *Sir Pherozeshah Mehta.* Reprint, Bombay, 1963.
Mukherjee, N. *The ryotwari system in Madras 1792-1827.* Calcutta, 1962.
Nandimath, S. C. *A handbook of Virasaivism.* Dharwar, 1942.
Nair, Sankaran. *Autobiography.* Madras, 1966.
Narasimhan, V. K. *Kasturi Ranga Iyengar.* Delhi, 1963.
Natarajan, S. *History of Indian journalism.* Delhi, 1954.
_____. *A century of social reform in India.* London, 1959.
Panikkar, K. M. *Malabar and the Dutch.* Bombay, 1931.
Parel, A. "Hume, Dufferin and the origins of the Indian National Congress." *Journal of Indian History.* XLII:3, 1964.
Parthasarathy, R. T. *Dawn and achievement of Indian freedom.* Salem, 1953.
Rao, A. V. Ramana. *Economic development of Andhra Pradesh (1766-1957).* Bombay, 1958.
Raju, A. Sarada. *Economic conditions in the Madras Presidency 1800-1850.* Madras, 1941.
Ransom, J. *A short history of the Theosophical Society.* Adyar, n.d.
Ratcliffe, S. K. *Sir William Wedderburn and the Indian reform movement.* London, 1923.
Sarma, M. Somasekhara. *History of the Reddi kingdoms.* Waltair, 1948.
Sastri, K. A. Nilakanta. *Studies in Cola history and administration.* Madras, 1932.
_____. *Development of religion in South India.* Madras, 1963.
Seal, A. *The Emergence of Indian Nationalism.* Cambridge, 1968.
Seth, M. J. *Madras, the birthplace of Armenian Journalism.* Calcutta, 1937.
_____. *Armenians in India.* Calcutta, 1937.
Singer, M., ed. *Traditional India: Structure, and Change.* Philadelphia, 1959.
Singh, H. L. *Problems and policies of the British in India 1885-1898.* London, 1963.
Sitaramayya, B. P. *The history of the Indian National Congress (1885-1935).* Madras, 1935.
South Indian Maharashtrians. Silver jubilee souvenir. Madras, 1937.
Spate, O. H. K. and A. T. A. Learmonth. *India and Pakistan.* 3rd ed., Suffolk, 1967.
Srinivas, M. N. *India's Villages.* Reprinted, Bombay, 1963.
_____. *Social change in modern India.* Berkeley, 1966.
Srinivasachari, C. S. *History of the city of Madras.* Madras, 1939.
_____. *Ananda Ranga Pillai, The "Pepys" of French India.* Madras, 1940.
_____. "Pachaiyappa. His life, times and charities." *Pachaiyappa's College Madras. Centenary Commemoration Book 1842-1942.* Madras, 1942.
Tayyeb, A. *Pakistan. A political geography.* London, 1966.
Thomas, P. J. and B. Natarajan. "Economic depression in the Madras Presidency (1825-54)." *Economic History Review.* VII:2, 1936.
Tinker, H. *The foundations of local self-government in India, Pakistan and Burma.* London, 1954.
Venkatarangaiya, M., ed. *The freedom struggle in Andhra Pradesh.* I, Hyderabad, 1965.

Wasti, Syed Razi. *Lord Minto and the Indian nationalist movement 1905-1910.* Oxford, 1964.

Webb, M. J. "The coast plains of Kerala." *Indian Geographical Journal.* XXXVI:1, 1961.

Index